Frommer's™

P9-AGC-558

Vancouver Island, the Gulf Islands & the San Juan Islands

2nd Edition

by Chris McBeath

Here's what the critics say about Frommer's:

"Amazingly easy to use. Very portable, very complete."
—**BOOKLIST**

"Frommer's Guides have a way of giving you
a real feel for a place."
—**KNIGHT RIDDER NEWSPAPERS**

John Wiley & Sons Canada, Ltd.

Published by:

JOHN WILEY & SONS CANADA, LTD.

6045 Freemont Blvd.
Mississauga, ON L5R 4J3

Library and Archives Canada Cataloguing in Publication
McBeath, Chris, 1953-
    Frommer's Vancouver Island, the Gulf Islands & the San Juan Islands / Chris
McBeath. — 2nd ed.
Includes index.
ISBN 978-0-470-15735-0
    1. Vancouver Island (B.C.)—Guidebooks. 2. Gulf Islands (B.C.)—Guidebooks.
3. San Juan Islands (Wash.)—Guidebooks. I. Title. II. Title: Vancouver Island,
the Gulf Islands & the San Juan Islands.
FC3844.2.M326 2009   917.11'2045   C2008-907364-9

Editor: Gene Shannon
Project Manager: Elizabeth McCurdy
Project Editor: Pauline Ricablanca
Editorial Assistant: Katie Wolsley
Project Coordinator: Lynsey Stanford
Cartographer: Lohnes+Wright
Vice President, Publishing Services: Karen Bryan
Production by Wiley Indianapolis Composition Services

Front cover photo: Ocean kayaking from Rebecca Spit, Quadra Island, British Columbia.
Back cover photo: A totem pole from Vancouver Island, British Columbia.

SPECIAL SALES

For reseller information, including discounts and premium sales, please call our sales department: Tel. 416-646-7992. For press review copies, author interviews, or other publicity information, please contact our marketing department: Tel. 416-646-4584; Fax: 416-236-4448.

Wiley also publishes its books in a variety of electronic formats. Some content that appears in print may not be available in electronic formats.

Manufactured in the United States of America

1 2 3 4 5 RRD 13 12 11 10 09

CONTENTS

8 NORTHERN VANCOUVER ISLAND 174

9 THE GULF ISLANDS 211

10 THE SAN JUAN ISLANDS 241

APPENDIX: FAST FACTS, TOLL-FREE NUMBERS & WEBSITES 264

INDEX 274

LIST OF MAPS

AN INVITATION TO THE READER

In researching this book, we discovered many wonderful places—hotels, restaurants, shops, and more. We're sure you'll find others. Please tell us about them, so we can share the information with your fellow travelers in upcoming editions. If you were disappointed with a recommendation, we'd love to know that, too. Please write to:

Frommer's Vancouver Island, the Gulf Islands & the San Juan Islands, 2nd Edition
John Wiley & Sons Canada, Ltd. • 6045 Freemont Blvd. • Mississauga, ON L5R 4J3

AN ADDITIONAL NOTE

Please be advised that travel information is subject to change at any time—and this is especially true of prices. We therefore suggest that you write or call ahead for confirmation when making your travel plans. The authors, editors, and publisher cannot be held responsible for the experiences of readers while traveling. Your safety is important to us, however, so we encourage you to stay alert and be aware of your surroundings. Keep a close eye on cameras, purses, and wallets, all favorite targets of thieves and pickpockets.

ABOUT THE AUTHOR

A full-time writer who globe-trots and scribes for a living, author Chris McBeath makes her home in these islands of the Pacific Northwest. Because she has worked in so many facets of the tourism industry, she has an insider's eye for what makes a great travel experience. Chris maintains a travel website (www.greatestgetaways.com), and, although she contributes to publications worldwide, this book represents a part of the world that is closest to her heart.

ACKNOWLEDGMENTS

Grateful thanks to Frommer's editor Gene Shannon, project coordinator Pauline Ricablanca, and copy editor Laura Johnston. Thank you also to Holly Lenk at Tourism Victoria, Lana Kingston with Tourism Vancouver Island and the Gulf Islands, and Robin Jacobson on the San Juan Islands. A special hug goes to Bill Vanderford who acted as patient driver and companion on many of the miles traveled to experience, first hand, what you'll find in this book.

Other Great Guides for Your Trip:

Frommer's British Columbia

Frommer's Canada

Frommer's Vancouver & Victoria 2009

FROMMER'S STAR RATINGS, ICONS & ABBREVIATIONS

Every hotel, restaurant, and attraction listing in this guide has been ranked for quality, value, service, amenities, and special features using a star-rating system. In country, state, and regional guides, we also rate towns and regions to help you narrow down your choices and budget your time accordingly. Hotels and restaurants are rated on a scale of zero (recommended) to three stars (exceptional). Attractions, shopping, nightlife, towns, and regions are rated according to the following scale: zero stars (recommended), one star (highly recommended), two stars (very highly recommended), and three stars (must-see).

In addition to the star-rating system, we also use seven feature icons that point you to the great deals, in-the-know advice, and unique experiences that separate travelers from tourists. Throughout the book, look for:

Finds	Special finds—those places only insiders know about
Fun Facts	Fun facts—details that make travelers more informed and their trips more fun
Kids	Best bets for kids, and advice for the whole family
Moments	Special moments—those experiences that memories are made of
Overrated	Places or experiences not worth your time or money
Tips	Insider tips—great ways to save time and money
Value	Great values—where to get the best deals

The following abbreviations are used for credit cards:

AE	American Express	DISC	Discover	V	Visa
DC	Diners Club	MC	MasterCard		

FROMMERS.COM

Now that you have this guidebook to help you plan a great trip, visit our website at www.frommers.com for additional travel information on more than 4,000 destinations. We update features regularly to give you instant access to the most current trip-planning information available. At Frommers.com, you'll find scoops on the best airfares, lodging rates, and car rental bargains. You can even book your travel online through our reliable travel booking partners. Other popular features include:

- Online updates of our most popular guidebooks
- Vacation sweepstakes and contest giveaways
- Newsletters highlighting the hottest travel trends
- Podcasts, interactive maps, and up-to-the-minute events listings
- Opinionated blog entries by Arthur Frommer himself
- Online travel message boards with featured travel discussions

What's New in the Islands

Whoever said, "The more things change, the more they stay the same," could have been describing the San Juan and Gulf islands. Their slower way of life is their very appeal, and while development is certainly heating up, visitors come here for a rural charm that feels, at any rate, as if it belongs to another time. Up until a few years ago, the same could be said of Vancouver Island. Here's where you'll notice the most change since the last edition of *Frommer's Vancouver Island, the Gulf Islands and the San Juan Islands:*

PLANNING YOUR TRIP Although the weakened U.S. dollar means that Canada is no longer the bargain it once was for travelers from south of the border, at least the taxes are slightly lower. The federal Goods and Services Tax (GST) is now 5% rather than 6%. U.S. citizens take note: A driver's license no longer cuts the mustard; you need a passport not only to get into Canada, but to get back into the United States. In lieu of a passport, you can now register for the new Passport Card Program and fast-track passes such as NEXUS and CANPASS.

ACCOMMODATIONS Located within steps of Victoria's Inner Harbour, the **Oswego Hotel,** 877 Oswego St. (© **877/7-OSWEGO** [767-9346]), is the city's first purpose-built boutique hotel and feels like a low-key translation of the hyper W brand. See p. 71 **Villa Marco Polo,** 1524 Shasta Place (© **877/601-1524**), is at the other end of the scale, exploring lavishly themed decor in keeping with the style of its namesake. See p. 76. Just south of Victoria, in the seaside

town of Sidney, the contemporary **Sidney Pier Hotel & Spa,** 9805 Seaport Place, Sidney (© **866/659-9445** or 250/655-9445) overlooks the San Juans and is a great base for exploring the south island. In high season, consider it a quiet alternative to staying in downtown Victoria. See p. 112.

In the mid-island region, **Beach Club Resort,** 181 Beachside Dr. (© **888/760-2008** or 250/947-2101), has opened in Parksville with a spacious mix of studios and suites that showcase custom furnishings and lots of glass, wood, and slate to give it an outdoorsy, West Coast ambiance. See p. 150.

Until recently, traveling north meant foodies headed for gourmet (that is, expensive) destinations and hikers took their boots to a campsite or utilitarian inn. **Coastal Trek Health & Fitness Resort,** 8100 Forbidden Plateau Rd., Courtenay (© **250/897-8735**) now offers a serious and comfortable choice for foodie-oriented hikers. See p. 181. Further north, at Port McNeil, recent upgrades at the **Cluxewe Resort,** 1 Cluxewe Campground Rd. (© **250/949-0378**), now make this a much more comfortable choice for kayakers, families, and wildlife-watchers. See p. 208.

With Ucluelet fast becoming the destination of choice on the western shores, vacation condominiums and lodge resorts are establishing many a foothold. Since 2007 these include **Cabins at Terrace Beach,** 1090 Peninsula Rd. (PO Box 315), Ucluelet (© **866/438-4373** or 250/726-2101), and, more recently, **Black Rock**

Oceanfront Resort, 596 Marine Dr. (☎ 877/762-5011; www.blackrockresort. com). See p. 169 and 161. One of the most intriguing makeovers is at **Cable Cove Inn,** 201 Main St., Tofino (☎ 800/ 663-6449 or 250/725-4236), which now has an Ayurvedic essence. You won't find any '60s style joss sticks scenting the air; what you will find are luxurious Indian silks, ornamental teaks, and North America's first Auycare Spa Centre. See p. 165.

On the smaller islands, things are largely as they were in 2007 save for Friday's Historic Inn, now called **Bird Rock Hotel,** 35 1st St., Friday Harbor (☎ 800/352-2632 or 360/378-5848), which has reinvented itself as a (still quirky) boutique hotel. See p. 250.

DINING Nowhere on the islands has change been more widely felt than in the restaurant business. Generally, that's not surprising; the restaurant business is notorious for change. What is revealing is the number of slow-food and island-aware restaurants that have come onto the scene. Many are headed up by fine-dining chefs who have discovered the largesse of available local foods throughout the year, and the collaboration among them, islandswide, is unexpected. Most of these are in Victoria and Vancouver Island. At **Café Vieux Montreal,** 1314 Government St. (☎ 250/382-7700), all meats are cured in-house; at **Smoken Bones Cookshack,** 101-721 Station St. (☎ 250/391-6328), barbecue pork is done slow and easy, southern style in special barbecue cookers; and the **Stage,** 1307 Gladstone Ave. (☎ 250/388-4222), near the Belfry Theatre, is always abuzz with pre- and post-theatre crowds, and people in between, with diners feasting on an ever-changing range of tapas selections that reflect the season's local fare. See p. 82, 86, and 82. Other worthwhile newbies include **Bon Rouge Bistro & Boulangerie,** 611 Courtney St. (☎ 250/220-8008), a Parisian-style cafe and charcuterie (p. 81); and

Niche Modern Dining, 225 Quebec St. (☎ 250/388-4255), where the items hint to the excellence the chef learned at the famed Pointe Restaurant at the Wickanninish Inn. See p. 79.

Outside of Victoria, you'll find a number of quality local-fare eateries at country inns, vineyards, and farms—**Sea Cider Farm & Ciderhouse,** 2487 Mt. St. Michael Rd., Saanichton (☎ 250/544-4824), is a recent arrival. See p. 112. Most feature West Coast fare—seafood is especially good, and some, such as **Amuse Bistro,** 753 Shawnigan-Mill Bay Rd., Shawnigan Lake (☎ 250/743-3667), turn local produce into a creative mélange of flavor. See p. 128. One newcomer, the **Fox & Hounds,** 247 Milton St. (☎ 250/740-1000), relishes its English heritage. Here, good English food is not an oxymoron; it's really as good as it gets, especially if served up with a traditional pint. See p. 141.

Even on the wild, wet coast, your main-street restaurant is none too shabby. **Sobo,** 311 Neill St. (☎ 250/725-2341), has a new, much larger, location in downtown Tofino, while in Ucluelet, **Ukee Dogs,** 1576 Imperial Lane (☎ 250/726-2103), might be housed in a converted garage, but the home-style cooking—soups, chili, slow-cooked roasts—is superlative. See p. 172 and 173.

ATTRACTIONS Golf has always been a big island attraction, so it's big news that **Bear Mountain Golf Resort,** 1999 Country Club Way, Victoria (☎ 888/533-BEAR [2327] or 250/391-7160), is set to complete its second Nicklaus course. See p. 77. **The Nanaimo District Museum,** 100 Museum Way, Nanaimo (☎ 250/753-1821), has relocated to the new Port of Nanaimo Centre, which opened in 2008 as the anchor for the new conference center and a gaggle of shops and cafes. See p. 135. On Quadra Island, the Kwagiulth Museum has been renamed the **Nuyumbalees Cultural Centre,** 34 WeiWai Rd., Cape Mudge Village (☎ 250/285-3733).

See p. 197. Eco-adventurers will appreciate the opening of a new section of the **Wild Pacific Trail**, near Ucluelet, and the new **North Coast Trail** in Cape Scott Provincial Park at the northernmost reaches of the island. See p. 161 and 207.

SHOPPING The islands are havens for artists and farmers, so there's a proliferation of at-home studios and local markets to enjoy. In Victoria, new galleries and food-oriented shops echo this abundance. To wit, the considerable expansion of **Silk Road Aromatherapy & Tea Company,** 1624 Government St. (© **250/704-2688**), complete with tea tasting bar, and the arrival of **Plenty Epicurean Pantry,** 1034 Fort St. (© **250/380-7654**), a tiny groceteria stacked with an eclectic range of foodstuffs and foodie gift items. See p. 100.

In an effort to promote niche shopping, the city is developing a **Designer District** at the edge of Chinatown where home decor ideas are the name of the day. See p. 96. **Stoneworld Studio,** 450 Manastee Rd. © **250/539-3262**), is one of the most unusual galleries and is a showcase of beautifully carved stones, rocks, and granite compounds that even leaves professional sculptors of marble and clay somewhat in awe. See p. 229.

AFTER DARK Outside of Victoria, nightlife anywhere on the islands is pretty sleepy, and the city scene, such as it is, is doing well not to have diminished in the last few years. **UP After Dark** (537 Herald St.; © **250/380-0005**) is one nifty new night spot, though be aware, it's very laid back and casual. See p. 104.

The Best of Vancouver Island, the Gulf Islands & the San Juan Islands

There's a geological reason, having to do with movement of the various layers of the earth's crust, that explains why these islands on the Northwest coast of the North American continent came into being. But to my mind, it is the words of one island resident that best describe this creation of nature: "When God made this continent, He finished up with Vancouver Island," he explains. "But there was a little material left, so God stood up, and brushed off His hands. The results are jewels in the water that we know today as the San Juans and the Gulf Islands."

However it happened, these islands in the Pacific Northwest are home to some of the most beautiful and pristine wilderness on earth today. An archipelago that stretches along the coastline of both sides of the 49th parallel, the islands number in the hundreds. Some are large enough to sustain small communities as diverse as the islands themselves, while others are no more than seagull perches that disappear at high tide.

Vancouver Island is the largest. Separated from the British Columbia mainland by the Georgia Strait, it offers the best of all worlds. In the south, the city of Victoria has the urban sophistication of a cosmopolitan center, and lies within easy reach of soft adventure activities such as hiking, whale-watching, and cycling. In the north, the countryside grows untamed, opening a door to exhilarating eco-adventures such as mountaineering, spelunking, surfing, and canoeing. This diversity consistently earns Vancouver Island high marks from leading travel publications.

The smaller Gulf Islands and San Juan Islands are equally appealing, and their communities reflect the isolation of their water-bound environments. Each has a different history and ambience, whether it is sleepy Lopez Island or eclectic Galiano Island. It's a sense of magic, though, that is their charm. Island residents prefer to live outside the mainstream: They are writers, artists, and craftspeople, city retirees looking for a sense of community, or specialty producers farming everything from llama and sheep to organic orchards and cottage dairies. They've chosen to live on "island time," an easygoing tempo that bewitches visitors the moment they set foot on the soil. Although visitors are certainly welcome (in summer they swell island populations tenfold), islanders like to keep outside influences at arm's length, lest they change that special way of life too dramatically. Islanders are self-professed stewards of the land, and as such, keepers of the island faith. When writer James Michener wanted to describe his love of islands, he made up a word for it: *nesomania*, from the Greek *neso* (island) and *mania* (extreme enthusiasm). Explore these islands, and you'll discover that nesomaniacs abound—you might even become one yourself!

- **Visiting the Royal British Columbia Museum** (Victoria; ℂ **888/447-7977** or 250/356-7226): This place is so diverse and inspiring that kids may want to stay all afternoon. How often can you say *that* about a museum? See p. 88.

- **Actually enjoying having stick insects navigate their way up your arm at the Victoria Bug Zoo** (Victoria; ℂ **250/384-2847**): The interaction with insects takes the creepy out of crawly. See p. 89.

- **Exploring at Horne Lake Caves Provincial Park** (near Qualicum Beach): Armed with flashlights, helmets, and good shoes, you feel like intrepid adventurers, even though the darkened path has been well scouted. One of the most accessible networks of caverns on the island, the caves can also accommodate extreme spelunkers. See p. 149.

- **Wading through minnows and searching out sand dollars at Rathtrevor Beach Provincial Park** (Parksville): This is one of the most family-friendly parks in British Columbia. The warm, ankle-deep waters seem to go on forever. So does the sand. See p. 147.

- **Exploring the sandstone-sculpted tide pools at Botanical Beach** (Port Renfrew): Discover hundreds of different species of intertidal life, including congregations of sea stars, chitons, anemones, purple sea urchins, barnacles, snails, and mussels. Ridges of shale and quartz jut through the black basalt cliffs, creating some of the most photogenic landscapes on the island. See p. 118.

- **Harnessing up to zip along cables from one Douglas fir to another at Wild Play at the Bungy Zone** (Nanaimo; ℂ **888/668-7874** or 250/714-7874): Zip trips can reach speeds of up to 100kmph (62 mph), and (unlike with bungee jumping) there's no age limit. See p. 136.

- **Playing with sea slugs and urchins at the Ucluelet Mini Aquarium** (Ucluelet; ℂ **604/987-6992**): Students of marine biology share little-known facts and folklore about local underwater wildlife with infectious enthusiasm that will captivate youngsters and charm oldsters! See p. 161.

- **Digging for fossils with the Courtenay & District Museum and Palaeontology Centre** (Courtenay; ℂ **250/334-0686**) along the Puntledge River: It's a dirty business (which kids love), and you get to keep any fossils you find. See p. 179.

2 THE BEST ADVENTURE ACTIVITIES

- **Kayaking through the Broken Group Islands** (Pacific Rim National Park; ℂ **250/726-3500**): It's an oasis of calm waters, seal colonies, and other Pacific Ocean marine life. Better yet, travel there aboard the freighter MV *Lady Rose*. See p. 165.

- **Honing a new outdoor skill at Strathcona Park Lodge** (Strathcona Provincial Park; ℂ **250/286-3122**): Everything from hiking to rappelling is on offer here, for both novice and extremist. See p. 182.

- **Learning to surf on Long Beach:** The waves just keep coming, and whether or not you manage to stand, it's a long and exhilarating ride to shore. See p. 163.

- **Exploring Broughton Inlet's narrow fjordic waterways** aboard the heritage vessel *Columbia III* (Port McNeil; ✆ 888/833-8887 or 250/202-3229): Paddle along two-kayak-wide channels and coves by day; enjoy ship comforts by night. Expect to see whales, eagles, and sea lions just a few paddle-lengths away. See p. 205.

3 THE BEST LEISURE ACTIVITIES

- **Teeing off with kindred spirits at Crown Isle Resort** (Comox/Courtenay; ✆ 888/338-8439 or 250/703-5050) or at Westin **Bear Mountain Resort** (Victoria; ✆ 888/533-2327): Both resorts are deliciously golf-nutty. Bear Mountain has two Jack Nicklaus–designed courses, and Crown Isle is one of more than 20 courses you'll find in the Central Island. See p. 181 and 77.
- **Cruising on the *Aurora Explorer*** (Campbell River; ✆ 250/286-3347): This 12-passenger packet freighter works her way up and down some of the most beautiful coastal inlets in British Columbia. Although cargo is priority, passengers are a lucrative sideline. A casual, offbeat way to travel. See p. 189.
- **Angling for a Tyee in Campbell River:** In fact, angling for anything in these waters is sport-fishing at its best. See p. 188.
- **Scooting around San Juan Island in a Scootcar from Susie's Mopeds** (Friday Harbor; ✆ 800/532-0087 or 360/378-5244): A Scootcar is a hybrid vehicle that shuttles along at a low speed, giving you all the fun of a moped and the cover of a car. See p. 245.
- **Whale-watching on the bluffs at Lime Kiln Point State Park** (San Juan Island; ✆ 360/378-2044): This is the only park in the world dedicated to this purpose. Your chances of spotting orca, minke, or pilot whales are particularly good in late August and early September, during the salmon runs. See p. 249.
- **Storm-Watching** (Tofino/Ucluelet): Pick a spot from anywhere along Vancouver Island's westernmost coast that's open to the fury of the Pacific Ocean and get set for an OMNIMAX-style show. Suffice to say, it puts the movie *The Perfect Storm* into perspective. See chapter 7.
- **Wining (and dining) through the Cowichan Valley:** The wine scene has become as diverse as it is sophisticated. Include a visit to a cidery as a change of pace, and be sure to eat en route. Most menus feature local, organic, artisan foods. See p. 124.
- **Day sailing aboard MV *Uchuck III*** (Gold River; ✆ 250/283-2515): A day trip with this converted minesweeper takes you to some of Vancouver Island's most isolated (and picturesque) communities, from logging camps to water-bound hamlets. It's a great value cruise. Bring your binoculars. See p. 195.

4 THE BEST HIKING TRAILS

- **The boardwalks of the Wild Pacific Trail** (Ucluelet): You can make believe you're in training for the West Coast Trail or a trek to Cape Scott. Great for 8- and 80-year-olds alike, it has all the dramatic views with absolutely none of the true-grit challenges. See p. 161.

- **The West Coast Trail** (Pacific Rim National Park): This trek is one of the world's best to test the mettle of the hardiest and most experienced hiker. Many don't make the grade. But if you do, you'll have bragging rights for years to come. You'll also have some of the most spectacular coastal scenery shots to prove it—just be sure your camera has waterproof protection, and travel with a stack of fully charged batteries. See p. 164.

- **The northernmost tip of Vancouver Island via the Cape Scott Trail:** A West Coast Trail alternative, this trail sees you through marshland, across beaches, and over suspension bridges, with turn-back points to suit your stamina level. The rain always turns this trail into a mucky quagmire. Choose the moderate 3-hour round trip to San Josef Bay or the full 8-hour trek to Cape Scott. There's also a new North Coast Trail that's a part of a larger plan to construct a trail all the way from Cape Scott to Port Hardy. When complete, it will be longer than the famous West Coast Trail. See p. 207.

- **The Juan de Fuca Trail** (Sooke-Port Renfrew): Here's another West Coast Trail alternative with (almost) equally impressive scenic beauty, wildlife viewing, and roaring surf crashing against the coast. Moderate 1-day hikes string together for a multi-day excursion that's a good rehearsal for more grueling expeditions. And all within an hour's drive of civilization. See p. 115.

- **Cathedral Grove** (Coombs-Port Alberni): This ancient stand of Douglas firs grows so close to the heavens, you feel you're in a medieval cathedral. The trails are easy—at the very least, pull into the parking lot to understand why tree-huggers fought so hard to save this area from logging. See p. 154.

- **Galloping Goose Trail** (Victoria–Sooke): A great trail for walking, and better still if you're on wheels—in-line skates or bicycle. The Goose is mostly graded, relatively level, and passes through some of Victoria's most picturesque neighborhoods and urban wilderness—all the way to Sooke. Allow a day if you're wanting to travel the whole Goose. See p. 90.

- **East Sooke Coast Trail** (Sooke): It can be challenging in places (think coastal rainforest to surf-beaten rocks), but this kind of wilderness hiking within a half-hour's drive of a major city is what makes Vancouver Island an eco-adventurer's dream destination. See p. 116.

- **Brookes Point bluff** (South Pender Island): If you're prepared to scramble up a small rock face from Gowland Point, you can walk through waist-high dried grasses, along the edge of the bluff, to Brookes Point. The views are stunning, making it an intimate spot for a romantic picnic. See p. 225.

- **The trail to Iceberg Point** (Lopez Island): Cutting through private property, this trail delivers you to a windy walk along the cliff's edge. Good walking shoes, and perhaps a picnic, are all anyone needs to enjoy the bluffy landscape. See p. 262.

5 THE MOST SCENIC DRIVES

- **Following the shoreline between Sooke and Port Renfrew:** The views are expansive, and the beaches along the way provide an excellent excuse to pull over and stretch your legs. If you can't make it all the way to Botanical Beach Provincial Park (well worth the effort), the restaurant at the **Point No Point**

Resort (℡ 250/646-2020) is, well, a good point to regroup, refresh, and turn around. See chapter 6.

- **Driving the scenic route from Victoria to Swartz Bay:** Hwy. 17A runs along the western shores of the Saanich Peninsula. It's only about 42km (26 miles), but with wineries, U-Pick flower fields, and roadside stands selling produce, eggs, and homemade jams, the 45-minute drive can easily take hours, especially if you "do lunch" en route or spend half a day at Butchart Gardens. See chapter 6.

- **Taking Hwy. 4 across Vancouver Island from Parksville to Tofino:** Bisecting the island east to west is a topographical treasure. You'll pass through forests, rivers, and snow-capped mountains before hitting the wind-swept shores and beaches of the west coast. See chapter 7.

- **Leaving the main highway (Hwy. 19) and following the starfish signs along Hwy. 19A, the Oceanside Route:** Take any exit near Parksville and meander up to Campbell River through seaside communities overlooking the Georgia Strait, past artisan studios, and across lush farmlands. A sage farmer once said that if the cows are lying down, inclement weather is brewing. Keep an eye open, and check the theory out. See chapter 7.

- **Cruising the Coastal Circle Route:** The drive from Victoria to Courtenay, over the Malahat, takes you from urban charm to mountain vistas and then down into a valley of wineries. From Courtenay, take the car ferry across to Powell River for a drive down along coastal rainforest to more ferry connections heading for Horseshoe Bay and Vancouver. See chapter 8.

6 THE BEST WILDLIFE VIEWING

- **Spotting bald eagles at Goldstream Provincial Park** (Victoria): When the salmon run ends, thousands of eagles come to feast on the carcasses. From early December until late February, the park puts on many eagle-oriented programs, including a daily count that has reached as many as 276 sightings in one day. See p. 30.

- **Whale-watching at Robson Bight** (Port McNeil): There are many whale-watching opportunities throughout the islands, including a grey whale migration that passes by the West Coast. But nothing beats the orcas in Robson Bight, a one-of-a-kind ecological whale preserve. See p. 203.

- **Catching up with marmots** (Nanaimo): One of the most endangered species in the world, the marmot is found only on Vancouver Island. Take a hike into the wilds surrounding Nanaimo and you might get lucky and see these highly inquisitive creatures popping up from their underground burrows. See p. 144.

- **Hearing the breeding call of a bull Roosevelt elk** (San Juan River): It's a haunting refrain, heard every fall, as the bull searches out new females to add to his harem. Roosevelt elk are a formidable sight anytime of year, and finding their shed antlers is a fine reward for a hike. This species of elk is found only on Vancouver Island and the Queen Charlotte Islands; herds hang out near Gold River, Jordan River Meadows, and in the Nanaimo Lake region. See p. 193.

7 THE BEST PLACES TO EXPERIENCE FIRST NATIONS CULTURE & HISTORY

- **Quw'utsun' Cultural Centre** (Duncan; ✆ 877/746-8119): Owned and operated by the Cowichan Band, the center shares the band's cultural heritage through live demonstrations, dance, Native food, and the knitting of its famous Cowichan sweater. See p. 124.
- **Eagle Aerie Gallery** (Tofino; ✆ 250/725-3235): Acclaimed artist Roy Vickers owns this stunningly moody and inspiring gallery, primarily a showcase for his own work, as well as a chosen few other artists. See p. 159. Henry Vickers, Roy's brother, is also an acclaimed artist with his Shipyard Gallery in Cowichan Bay. Both brothers are recipients of the Order of British Columbia, among other awards.
- **U'Mista Cultural Centre** (Alert Bay; ✆ 250/974-5403): Even if you're not an aficionado of aboriginal art, a guided tour around the center's collection provides an invaluable perspective on First Nations culture. See p. 203.
- **Eagle Feather Gallery** (Victoria; ✆ 250/388-4330): Although you'll find many small studios scattered throughout Vancouver Island, if you're staying south and you've only time for one stop, this shop carries some of the best jewelry, arts, and crafts. See p. 98.

8 THE BEST SPAS

- **The Ancient Cedars Spa** (The Wickaninnish Inn; ✆ 250/725-3100): This spa offers hot stone massages in a little cedar hut perched on the rocks as the Pacific Ocean crashes below. A very sensual experience. See p. 168.
- **Willow Stream Spa** (The Fairmont Empress; ✆ 250/384-8111): Regardless of what type of service you've booked, this spa throws in time in the steam room and in its mineral pool, so that you can turn a manicure into an afternoon event. See p. 101.
- **The Madrona del Mar Spa** (Galiano Inn; ✆ 250/539-3388): The concept of a healing sanctuary rises to new levels with private glass-and-marble steam rooms, a sea-flotation bath, and new guest rooms that even have a Murphy bed–style massage table for fireside treatments. See p. 231.
- **The Spa at Delta Victoria Ocean Pointe** (✆ 800/575-8882 or 250/360-5858): Prepare yourself for upscale pampering all the way, all the time, with a sauna, pool, and complete fitness facility thrown in for good measure. See p. 101.
- **The Grotto Spa** (Tigh-na-Mara Resort; ✆ 250/248-2072): British Columbia's largest resort spa features a sizeable cave-like mineral pool and two-story waterfall. See p. 151.
- **The Kingfisher Oceanside Spa** (Courtenay; ✆ 800/663-7929 or 250/338-1323): One of the first destination resort spas on the island, this is a great spot for group spa getaways. It offers the only Pacific Mist Hydropath in North America (a kind of "walking hydrotherapy") as well as tidal baths carved out of rock, mineral soaks, and a steam cave. See p. 182.
- **Essence of Life Spa** (Brentwood Bay Lodge; ✆ 888/544-2079 or 250/544-2079): The Couples Massage here is just one more great reason why you won't want to leave this contemporary, and very romantic, sanctuary. See p. 101.

- **Sante Spa** (Bear Mountain; ☏ **888/533-2327** or 250/391-7160): One of the island's top spa destinations, it's that rare breed of MediSpa where licensed

services include medical esthetics. So why not add a little Botox to your facial? See p. 101.

9 THE BEST HOTELS & RESORTS

- **The Fairmont Empress** (Victoria; ☏ **800/441-1414** or 250/384-8111): Like a grand old dowager, this magnificent hotel commands the Victoria Inner Harbour as her fiefdom, and beckons her audience inside. If you're going for broke, stay here; the experience is what North Americans think England is all about. See p. 69.

- **Brentwood Bay Lodge & Spa** (Brentwood Bay; ☏ **888/544-2079**): As British Columbia's only member of Small Luxury Hotels of the World, this contemporary lodge boasts an oceanfront location and a service ratio nearing three staff per one guest room. Expect all the amenities of a five-star-rated resort. See p. 109.

- **Clayoquot Wilderness Resort** (Clayoquot Sound; ☏ **888/333-5405** or 250/725-2688): Accessible only by water, the resort is quite isolated, so you feel as if you're completely one with the wilderness. But it's the luxurious safari-style campsites that steal the show. See p. 166

- **Wickaninnish Inn** (Tofino; ☏ **800/333-4604** or 250/725-3100): With only floor-to-ceiling triple-glazed windows standing between you and the churning Pacific Ocean, this place elevates storm-watching to an art. See p. 168.

- **Rosario Resort** (Orcas Island; ☏ **800/562-8820** or 360/376-2222): Situated on a peninsula, Rosario exudes an air of 1920s grace. Listed on the National Register of Historic Places, the beautifully refurbished resort has something

for everyone: elegant dining, spa services, a children's program, and a see-it-to-believe-it, 1,972-pipe Aeolian organ. Concerts nightly. See p. 257.

- **Sonora Resort** (Sonora Island; ☏ **888/576-6672** or 604/233-0460): Accessible only by air (the resort has its own state-of-the-art helicopter) or by boat, this resort makes getting there half the fun. Fishing is the number-one activity, though visiting the spa, hiking, and going on wildlife excursions are catching up quickly. The private lounge theater is like something made for reclusive movie moguls—and the popcorn's made to order. See p. 191.

- **Poets Cove** (Pender Island; ☏ **888/512-POET** [7638] or 250/629-2100): This resort offers a wide variety of accommodations that beckons families (and boaters) in the summer and romantics at every other time of the year. It's so self-contained, you can eat, sleep, spa, and cocoon—all in one place. See p. 226.

- **Painter's Lodge Holiday & Fishing Resort** (Campbell River; ☏ **800/663-7090** or 250/286-1102): This is *the* place for fishing enthusiasts. These folks also own activity-oriented April Point Lodge & Spa across the channel, and because guest privileges flow from one to the other, it's almost like staying in two resorts for the price of one. See p. 191.

10 THE BEST BED-AND-BREAKFASTS & COUNTRY INNS

- **Abigail's Hotel** (Victoria; ☎ 800/561-6565 or 250/388-5363): This inn is the essence of old-world charm and hospitality in a phenomenal downtown Victoria location. See p. 73.

- **Hastings House** (Ganges, Salt Spring Island; ☎ 800/661-9255 or 250/537-2362): Everything you would want in an English country inn is here, but so much better—Hastings House is a member of the exclusive Relais & Châteaux network. Expect wonderful gardens, inspired guest rooms, and world-renowned cuisine. Catching your own crab dinner is *the* most fun eating experience. See p. 219.

- **Friday Harbor House** (Friday Harbor, San Juan Island; ☎ 360/378-8455): This is a modern, beautifully furnished inn sitting high above busy Friday Harbor. The views are outstanding. At night, the twinkling lights make the inn's restaurant a really romantic spot. See p. 250.

- **Inn at Swifts Bay** (Lopez Island; ☎ 800/375-5285 or 360/468-3636): Pull yourself away from the most sumptuously comfortable beds in the Northwest, and you'll find breakfasts that are more than an eye-opener. They're gastronomic adventures, island-renowned for being the best in the San Juans. See p. 262.

- **Oceanwood Country Inn** (Dinner Bay, Mayne Island; ☎ 250/539-5074): If you're lucky, from the dining room you'll see whales passing up Navy Channel. The inn offers a range of top-quality guest rooms (some more affordable than others), extravagant gardens, and lounges featuring heirloom furniture, antiques, and board games. See p. 236.

- **Woodstone Country Inn** (Galiano Island; ☎ 888/339-2022 or 250/539-2022): Tucked in between rainforest and rambling meadows, this lovely inn epitomizes the country inn. The ambience is one of casual elegance, with fireplaces, fresh flowers, and excellent home-cooked food. See p. 232.

- **Wildwood Manor B&B** (San Juan Island; ☎ 877/298-1144 or 360/378-3447): Staying here is like being an honored house guest. The proprietors' attention to detail is extraordinary, and hospitality is so genuine that you'll feel you've made lifetime friends. See p. 252.

- **Turtleback Farm Inn** (Orcas Island; ☎ 800/376-4914 or 360/376-4914): Set on a private 32 hectares (79 acres), this working farm has been cited in *1000 Places to See Before You Die,* and I agree with that assessment. The 1800s green clapboard farmhouse has been lovingly restored. The pastoral views lull you into a relaxed state of nirvana. See p. 259.

- **Villa Marco Polo** (Victoria; ☎ 877/601-1524): Lavish in style and hospitality, influences of Venetian traveler Marco Polo exude an exotic touch to this (not inexpensive) manor house. Definitely a place for special occasions. See p. 76.

11 THE BEST CULINARY INNS

- **Sooke Harbour House** (Vancouver Island; ☎ 800/889-9688 or 250/642-3421): Beyond its reputation as a hideaway for Hollywood's beautiful people, this place offers so much more. Many come for the Wine Spectator

Grand Award–winning wine cellar and the food—an epicurean feast of local and organic fare that seems to go on for as long as you can eat. Be prepared to make reservations at the restaurant, sometimes weeks in advance. See p. 120.

- **The Aerie** (Malahat, near Victoria; ✆ **800/518-1933** or 250/743-7115): Located on the Malahat Mountain, this lavish Mediterranean-style mansion has ocean views—and food that will take your breath away. Ingredients pay tribute to the region's diversity, from morels to asparagus to poultry and lamb, and change frequently as if on an edible journey through the seasons. See p. 126.

- **Coopers Cove** (Sooke; ✆ **877/642-5727** or 250/642-5727): *Oprah* has featured the Cove's ex-Olympiad chef Angelo Prosperi-Porta, who teams up with his guests to create mouth-watering interactive dinners. He claims you'll forge a "spiritual connection to the food you eat." However you interpret that, the results taste heaven-sent! See p. 118.

- **Fairburn Farm Culinary Retreat & Guesthouse** (Duncan; ✆ **250/746-4637**): Part farm, part cooking school, and part country inn, Fairburn exemplifies what the Slow Food movement is all about. Chef Mara Jernigan creates a delicious experience that really raises your consciousness about foods of the land. See p. 126.

12 THE BEST RESTAURANTS

- **Blue Crab Bar & Grill** (Victoria; ✆ **250/480-1999**): This restaurant serves the best seafood in Victoria, along with mouth-watering views of the harbor. See p. 78.

- **Smoken Bones Cookshack** (Victoria; ✆ **250/391-6328**): Mouthwatering, finger-lickin'-delicious BBQ ribs and much more, done southern style in both taste and massive servings. See p. 86.

- **Amuse Bistro** (Victoria; ✆ **250/743-3667**): Because the restaurant is in a former home, dining here is like being a member of an exclusive supper club, especially when everything on the menu is geared to amuse your *palate* with an amazing range of locally produced fare such as roasted venison, chanterelles with brandy and veal jus, and heritage carrots. See p. 128.

- **Deep Cove Chalet** (Saanich Inlet, near Victoria; ✆ **250/656-3541**): This place makes the list for its caviar: Beluga, Ocietra, and Sevugra, from Russia, Iran,

and China, which helps make the elegant French menu a standout. The wine reserve of 18,000 bottles is remarkable too. See p. 112.

- **Fox & Hounds** (Nanaimo; ✆ **250/740-1000**): Even the Brits would have to take their hats off to this pub-style drinking establishment. The steak and kidney pie is as good as it gets and the Guinness is just one of many British Isle imports, many of which you won't easily find elsewhere. See p. 141.

- **The Sushi Bar at the Inn at Tough City** (Tofino; ✆ **250/725-2021**): Surrounded by the bounty of the sea, you would think there would be a proliferation of sushi restaurants on the west coast of Vancouver Island. Not so, which is why this tiny cafe at the Inn at Tough City is such a treat. See p. 172.

- **House Piccolo** (Ganges; ✆ **250/537-1844**): The restaurant inside this tiny farmhouse is consistently recognized by the prestigious Chaine des Rôtisseurs, so you know the cuisine is top-notch.

Many dishes have a Scandinavian twist, as in spiced herring or scallop ceviche. The gorgonzola cheese tart with red onion marmalade is an example of Piccolo's creativity. See p. 226.

- **Pointe Restaurant** (Tofino; © 250/725-3100): The eatery's food is as spectacular as its location, perched on a craggy bluff. This is where you come for an amazing multi-course, gourmet, culinary experience—albeit with gourmet prices to match. See p. 171.
- **Shelter Restaurant** (Tofino; © 250/725-3353): This upbeat restaurant gives the Pointe a run for its money, only here you'll save a few dollars. Perhaps that's because there's no view. But with such

fresh and imaginatively blended flavors before you, you probably won't even notice. See p. 171.

- **Duck Soup Inn** (San Juan Island; © 360/378-4878): The eclectic atmosphere of artsy decor and offbeat paraphernalia is second only to the ever-changing menu, which is created on the fly depending on what the garden is producing at any given moment. The results are imaginative pairings such as lamb with sour cherry port, homemade lemon linguini, and lavender-thyme roasted chicken, all served with spiced, herbed, or nutty breads. See p. 253.

Vancouver Island, the Gulf Islands & the San Juan Islands in Depth

It's no advertising hype when you hear that these islands can be all things to all people. Their coastlines are the envy of sailors from all over the world, and their landscapes are lush with the promises of extraordinary soft adventure, mouthwatering organic produce, and a rich cultural history—a mosaic of ancient Indian settlements, Spanish exploration, trappers and traders, opium dens, and pioneers who believed they had found their Eden.

Magazines such as Conde Nast's *Traveler* and *Travel & Leisure* consistently rank Victoria, and Vancouver Island, among the world's finest visitor destinations. And little wonder. They offer activities at both ends of the spectrum. The island's home-grown, organic food scene is phenomenal, giving rise to a terrific selection of restaurants and inns (especially in Victoria), so you can literally graze your way from point A to point B. Or, you can simply pitch a tent in the rainforest and hike, spelunk, and sea kayak in and around protected inlets, craggy shores, and windswept beaches.

Although tourism is the largest sector of the local economy—it's virtually the only industry on the Gulf and San Juan islands—the tourism scene is only just now hitting its stride. Oceanfront lodges and snazzy boutique hotels are certainly upping the ante in terms of the visitor experience, and they are juxtaposed against a laid-back pastoral charm—sheep dotting the hillsides, cottage wineries, and picturesque communities—that's usually hard to find in such close proximity to sophisticated centers like Seattle and Vancouver. Even Victoria, which is unabashedly touristy with its ornamental architecture, abundant gardens, and horse-drawn carriages, maintains its "Victorianness" in an absolutely authentic way.

1 THE ISLANDS TODAY

While farmers, fishermen, and seafarers were the settlers of these islands, in the 1970s they were joined by hippies, draft dodgers, and those seeking alternative lifestyles to urban living. As demographics began to change, traditional occupations became less profitable; and as more and more artists, writers, and retirees escaped to the islands, the economic profile, now largely dependent on tourism, began to shift.

Regardless, most residents still choose to live here on island time, and tend to resent any progress or development that might counter their rural tranquility. But affluent professionals, retired executives, dot.com millionaires, and others seeking to put their money into vacation properties. Rest assured, the islands are terrific places to visit and seldom will a visitor come across some of the beneath-the-surface controversial issues of island living.

For example, because many new homes are built to comfort-driven specs with spa-like bathrooms, dishwashers, and hot tubs, water usage is a huge issue. City migrants aren't always connected to the islands' conservation efforts and, while their awareness may stretch to the installation of things like low-flush toilets, such token efforts are often negated when a home has multiple bathrooms. Furthermore, although every property has its own well, few homeowners realize that individual wells actually share the same underground aqueduct, so when water spews up mud and silt early on in the summer, it quickly puts a strain on neighborly relations.

Economic sustainability is another issue that divides the old and new. Construction might benefit the local economy in the short term, but the long-term implications are proving to be a different reality. Because homes are purchased as vacation properties, owners are rarely resident and as such, do not participate in community-sustaining activities such as volunteering for the local fire department or helping run the library. And, as buying sprees push the price of real estate upwards, it becomes less affordable for people to live and work on the islands. Consequently, there's an underlying "them versus us" mentality, though locals may not be eager to let you know that. Islanders need the dollars vacation-home owners bring, and the construction industry, in particular, is more than willing to take their money. They'll juggle one project with another, and yet another, until completion deadlines come and go, resulting in some new property owners shipping in entire crews from the mainland just to get the job done on time and on budget. Much to the further chagrin of islanders, of course.

Vancouver Island is quite distinct from its smaller cousins. With a broader population base and a diverse economy of its own, this island is in the throes of change and exceptional growth. Tourism is taking off into the stratosphere. Like the rest of British Columbia, there are still many wilderness areas flying below the radar, but the flood of adventurous spirits is dragging them into the mainstream. You need look no farther than the quota system now in place for the West Coast Trail. Families, retirees, and wealthy Albertans are the main thrust of the island's population growth, first in Victoria and then, driven by affordability, in communities such as Nanaimo, Port Alberni, and Parksville. They are discovering a kinder place to live than hard-edged Toronto or cliquey Vancouver.

If Vancouver Island is becoming the trendy place to live, Victoria has become chic. No longer is the city filled solely with pensioners and civil servants. That said, this is the provincial capital, and British Columbia politics have a time-honored tradition of being anything but dull.

In spite of the many sandal-clad people you'll meet on the islands, and the left-wing discourse of many citizens, British Columbia is surprisingly fond of right-wing parties. Only 14 years of the last 50 have favored left-leaning governments from the New Democratic Party, likely due in part to three scandalous Premier resignations. Although the "Liberal Party" is currently in government, it is in fact mostly made up of right-wingers who migrated to the party when their own went defunct a few years back.

The result? The lawns of the legislature host frequent rallies against poverty, homelessness, and forest clear-cuts, or groups supporting the legalization of marijuana or a woman's right to choose such things as an abortion or gay marriage. Aboriginal rights, particularly land claims, are a long-standing issue that usually draws a crowd. But remember, this is Canada where "niceties" prevail so even though you now have the inside track on issues, most protests are polite, well mannered affairs where encounters in civil disobedience are handled with decorum and a handshake! Besides, isn't it this confluence of diversity—in its people, creative make-up, and geography—that makes this part of the world so richly appealing?

2 LOOKING BACK AT ISLAND HISTORY

The histories of these Pacific Northwest islands are inextricably linked. Geographically, the islands are part of the same archipelago that runs up the western-most coast of the continent, tucked against mainland British Columbia and the north shore of Washington State's Olympic Peninsula. Only climate and formal boundaries have evolved to take on particular characteristics that now set them apart, whether they are the mists that cling to the northerly Queen Charlottes, or the American-British story that textures much of San Juan Island.

THE EARLY YEARS

If you were on a boat and oblivious to any bureaucratic boundaries, you would be traveling in and around islands in much the same way as their earliest inhabitants. Native Americans (referred to as First Nations in Canada) such as the Coast Salish, Samish, and Lummi peoples, led a semi-nomadic life here, harvesting the abundant supplies of salmon, growing crops in the protected landscapes, and sourcing supplies of wild berries. Throughout the islands, the Native influence is still evident. Middens of oyster shells, charcoal, and fish bone mark the site of many a summer camp, petroglyphs can be seen on rockfaces, and burial sites are still being discovered.

Archaeologists date these early inhabitants to as far back as 9,000 years ago; by the time European contact was made in the mid–18th century, these peoples had developed a sophisticated social system with elaborate rituals, art, and spiritual beliefs that represented a way of life in harmony with their natural, wild surroundings.

The farther north you travel, the more evidence remains, especially in places such as Duncan, Alert Bay, and the Queen Charlottes. Here, ancient Haida totem poles sink under the weight of heavy moss, their history returning to the earth just as the Haida pit houses have already done. Little attempt is being made to restore them, since the Haida consider their slow, natural demise to be a part of the life cycle. *Aho* (and so it is).

EUROPEAN EXPLORATION

Although the Golden Hind is rumored to have visited the region during Sir Francis Drake's circumnavigation of the world in the 16th century, serious exploration didn't commence until some 200 years later. The Spanish, who had long been present in Mexico and Central America, started to spread their territorial claims north.

The Spanish frigate *Santiago* was the first to venture up the coast, in 1774, traveling as far as the Queen Charlottes. Although none of her crew set foot on shore (this was to happen on a return trip with the *Sonora,* the following year), they traded goods with the Haida peoples there, ship to canoe. Storms forced the ship to take shelter in the protected waters of Nootka Sound, which 16 years later would become a focal point in history. Trading with members of the Nuu-chah-nulth and Nootka peoples, the Spanish left behind four silver spoons, which in 1790 Spain would cite as evidence that they had reached the region before the arrival of Captain James Cook in 1778.

During the late 1700s, European exploration of the area was particularly frenetic. By then, it involved a competitive quest to find the Northwest Passage as

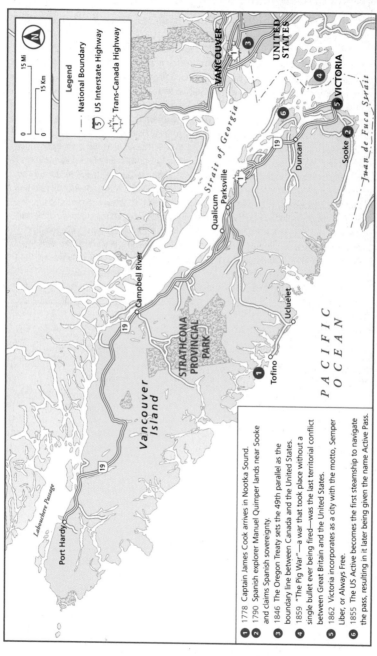

1 1778 Captain James Cook arrives in Nootka Sound.

2 1790 Spanish explorer Manuel Quimper lands near Sooke and claims Spanish sovereignty.

3 1846 The Oregon Treaty sets the 49th parallel as the boundary line between Canada and the United States.

4 1859 "The Pig War"—a war that took place without a single bullet ever being fired—was the last territorial conflict between Great Britain and the United States.

5 1862 Victoria incorporates as a city with the motto, Semper Liber, or Always Free.

6 1855 The US Active becomes the first steamship to navigate the pass, resulting in it later being given the name Active Pass.

(Fun Facts) Name That Island

The San Juan Islands were given the name by the Spanish explorer Francisco de Eliza, who charted the islands in 1791.

The Gulf Islands were named in 1792 for Captain Vancouver's belief that they were located in a gulf, and although he was later proven wrong, the name stuck.

Vancouver Island was originally called Quadra and Vancouver's island, in recognition of the joint explorations of Captain Vancouver and Captain Bodega y Quadra.

When he returned to the region in 1794, Captain Cook was the first to circumnavigate Vancouver Island, thus proving it to be an island.

In 1846, the Oregon Treaty established the 49th parallel as the boundary between Canada and the United States. Although both sides agreed Vancouver Island would remain British, jurisdiction was vague regarding the San Juans. Tensions exploded when an American farmer, Lyman Cutler, shot a British-owned pig that was overly partial to his potato patch (settlers had to row 15 miles across the Strait of Juan de Fuca to the Olympic Peninsula to get seed for crops, so pork rustling was no small matter). Troops were readied, British war ships gathered, and conflict seemed imminent. The Kaiser of Germany eventually arbitrated that the Americans had a stronger claim to the islands. The Pig War is the only war to occur without a shot ever being fired, and was the last territorial conflict between the United States and Great Britain.

much as claiming sovereignty. They were turbulent times: Spain had sided with France against Britain in the fight for American independence; the French Revolution was in full throttle; and the Russians were growing their fur trading interests through the Clayoquot and Queen Charlottes. Consequently, claims to Nootka Sound were never far from mind, especially for long-standing rivals Spain and Britain.

With relations between the two nations as tense as ever, Britain dispatched Captain George Vancouver to represent British interests. In 1792, he traveled up from the Gulf Islands, charting the region en route while his Spanish counterparts, Galiano and Valdes, were doing the same. It wasn't long before the three parties were sharing information, and their work formed the basis of a series of Nootka Conventions which, eventually, led to the negotiation of a mutual withdrawal from the region.

Collaboration was also expediently practical: The British ships were large and quick, so they covered more territory, while the small, Spanish ships could maneuver narrow inlets and shallow waters. But still, the prevailing distrust caused each to double check the other's work and often, a topographical feature that was named by one was then renamed by the other. When American explorer Charles Wilkes arrived some time later (1841), he added to the confusion. Armed with only British maps, he revised most of the Spanish names to bear patriotically American names, mostly for heroes of the War of 1812. By 1847, map names were such a muddle that the British Admiralty reorganized and created official charts of the region—keeping most of the British and Spanish names, and removing most of Wilkes's save for a few such as Chauncey, Shaw, Decatur, Lawrence, and Percival.

Victoria History: A Snapshot

Victoria has been charming visitors since Kipling's time, and although just 137km (85 miles) northwest of Seattle, in so many ways it's another world. Few cities offer such diverse eco-adventures alongside such a lively and colorful history.

- **1790** On June 30, the native people of Albert Head (now part of Sooke) discover Spanish explorer Manuel Quimper on their beach, claiming the land in the name of the king of Spain.
- **1842** James Douglas, Chief Factor, The Hudson's Bay Fur Trading Company, selects Victoria as the site for the company's new depot.
- **1843** Douglas decides to build a fort at the Inner Harbour, and it is eventually named Fort Victoria (now Bastion Square).
- **1846** On June 15, the Oregon Treaty sets the boundary line with the United States as the 49th parallel.
- **1849** The British government grants Vancouver Island to the Hudson's Bay Company for 7 shillings a year, stipulating that it must establish settlements of colonists on the island within 5 years.
- **1850** Richard Blanshard becomes Vancouver Island's first governor.
- **1858** The mainland's gold rush turns Victoria into an important community, funneling some 25,000 miners and their supplies to the gold camps—giving rise to Market Square and Victoria's tiny, bustling Chinatown, one of North America's oldest.
- **1862** Victoria incorporates as a city; the first gas lights go up over the front doors of the saloons; and in September, the Tynemouth, a "bride ship" from England, arrives carrying 61 "well-built, pretty-looking young women, ages varying from 14 to an uncertain figure; a few are young widows who have seen better days" *(Victoria Press)*.
- **1871** British Columbia enters Confederation; Victoria is named the provincial capital; and in December, Emily Carr is born at Carr House at the northeast corner of Government and Simcoe streets.
- **1882** The Hudson's Bay Company gifts Beacon Hill Park to the City of Victoria.
- **1895** Fort Rodd Hill is established as a military outpost, where gun batteries are built to protect the Royal Navy base on Esquimalt Harbour from the Americans.
- **1898** The Provincial Legislature Buildings are completed.
- **1908** The Canadian Pacific Railway completes the Empress Hotel.
- **1910** William Gibson becomes the first person in Canada to design, build, and fly his own aircraft when he takes to the air at Mount Tolmie.
- **1914** World War I breaks out. The Patricia Bay Airport is constructed as a training site for the Allied forces. Today it operates as Victoria International Airport.
- **1918** The Dominion Astrophysical Observatory on Little Saanich Mountain showcases the largest telescope in the world at that time.
- **1932** The first Sidney to Anacortes ferry, the *City of Angels*, makes its inaugural run.
- **1962** The Trans-Canada Highway finishes at Victoria, establishing Mile 0.
- **1986** Victoria experiences the longest period of rainfall of any Canadian city: 33 consecutive days.
- **1994** Victoria hosts the XV Commonwealth Games.

COMMERCIAL EXPANSION

The gold rushes of 1858 (Fraser River), 1862 (the Cariboo), and 1898 (the Yukon), really put the Pacific Northwest on the map. Hopeful pioneers started to settle the larger islands, and still today there is many an old orchard and early homestead that bear testimony to these once-thriving communities. Because of its location, midway between Victoria and the mainland, Miners Bay on Mayne Island became a resting point before crossing the Strait of Georgia. It was the commercial hub for all of the islands and for years afterwards, the postmasters from Galiano and Pender islands had to row to Mayne Island to collect the mail.

Meanwhile, American blacks, Germans, Scandinavians, and Portuguese established produce farms on the San Juans and Salt Spring; the Japanese came with their salteries; and the Hawaiians, working for the Hudson's Bay Company, also settled here—St. Paul's Catholic Church in Fulford Harbour on Salt Spring was built largely with Hawaiian labor. In the Queen Charlottes, whaling stations employed Indians and hundreds of Chinese who migrated here after the completion of Canada's trans-Canada railroad in 1869. Whaling continued through to the 1930s, leaving behind both commercial remnants as well as beachcombing treasures of whale teeth and bone.

As with so much of Canada, the most significant settlement in this region was the Hudson Bay community in Victoria on Vancouver Island. First established in 1843, it became an important center for trading furs and as a supply center for the thousands of prospectors en route to the mainland's gold. Intent on securing an empire where "the sun never set", Victorian Britain coveted this westernmost outpost of the Americas and its new Dominion of Canada, and set out to carve its likeness out of the coastal wilderness. Today, that British influence permeates a palpable charm throughout the peninsula; although, like so many of these island destinations, it is enjoying a far quieter pace than its rough and tumble beginnings.

3 THE LAY OF THE LAND

Although many of the 700 or so islands in the archipelago disappear at high tide, there are still about 400 or so to explore. Some are no more than a raised tuft of land; others are wildlife sanctuaries or privately owned paradises.

The largest, Vancouver Island, seems to capture the essence of all its smaller counterparts. Stretching 520km (323 miles) southeast to northwest, and with an average width of 100km (62 miles), it covers an area comparable to countries such as the Netherlands or Taiwan, yet the population is under one million. Greater Victoria, the largest community, has approximately 350,000; the second largest city is Nanaimo, with a population nearing 85,000. Down its spine, mountains divide the island into two distinct areas, and the result is a glorious mix of urban sophistication; busy fishing; market and logging towns; and most especially, a coast and wilderness as rugged as they were so long ago.

Vancouver Island, the Gulf Islands, and the San Juan Islands are actually the remaining mountain tops of a receding continent much older than the American mainland. Consequently, islands are generally quite hilly, with some flat areas and fertile valleys in between featuring plenty of old-growth forests. Look for cedar; Douglas fir; hemlock; spruce; yew; and most especially, madrona (also known as arbutus), which cling to the cliffs at precarious 45-degree angles. Coastlines are a mix of reef-studded bays and sandy and rock-strewn beaches, which make for great clambering adventures and tidal pools.

Because of the protective shadowing of the nearby American and Canadian mountain ranges, the islands get less rainfall than Vancouver or Seattle. The Gulf Islands, in particular, can get less than 30 inches of rain a year, so water shortages are not uncommon in summer, and even though temperatures don't reach sizzling heights, fire-hazard signs move quickly from no-risk green to high-alert red in the space of a few days.

CONSERVATION

The San Juans together comprise San Juan County, one of the smallest counties in Washington State. The county seat is at Friday Harbor, the islands' largest and only incorporated town; despite their size, the San Juans boast over 15 parks and nature preserves and almost as many national sites. In total, the county claims to have approximately 27% of its land area protected.

The Gulf Islands, on the other hand, are partially governed by The Islands Trust, a government-related bureaucracy which has a unique legislated mandate for protecting and preserving the islands, primarily through land use planning and regulation. Protected areas in the Islands Trust Area now constitute over 15% of the area's land base—more than 987 hectares (2,439 acres). On some islands, landowners can even register a conservation covenant and benefit from reduced property taxes. One of the Trust's most recent and significant accomplishments is likely to set a precedent for the province. Working with the Hul'qumi'num Treaty Group, the Trust has helped negotiate a one-of-a-kind agreement to protect aboriginal "sacred" or "spiritual" places in addition to and apart from archaeological sites that already receive protection. Such an agreement could have prevented the destruction of such First Nations treasures as the spirit caves at Bear Mountain Resort on Vancouver Island.

Since the population is predicted to increase by 35% over the next decade, it will become more and more difficult to maintain such unspoiled environs. Already, ecosystems and special habitats are threatened, with water usage being the most obvious problem.

NATURAL RESOURCES

Wherever you are on the islands, you're likely to come across designated national wildlife refuges, and just as likely to notice the number of bird species—more than 250 of them! Situated on the Pacific Flyway, a major bird migration route, you have the opportunity to see bald eagles, hawks, ospreys, woodpeckers, and hummingbirds, as well as shorebirds such as blue herons, oystercatchers, snow geese, and trumpeter swans. These inland waters also are one of the richest marine environments in the world. In addition to harbor seals, stellar sea lions, Dall porpoises, and sea otters, there are resident and transient whale pods that can be seen year-round.

Exploring or exploiting the islands' natural attributes is a double-edged sword for tourism. Sea kayaking, spelunking, wilderness hikes, and wildlife safaris depend on maintaining the islands' fragile ecosystem which, to date, is showing remarkable resilience. The endangered marmot (unique to Vancouver Island) is making a comeback, as are the Roosevelt deer. Offshore, the story is less optimistic. The rich fishing grounds up around the Queen Charlottes are showing strain; runs are down, and fish farms breeding Atlantic salmon in Pacific salmon waters are a contentious issue. Sea lice are an epidemic.

Logging, too, continues to be a debatable hot button. The smaller islands (Galiano being a prime example) have managed to reclaim much of their territory from timber companies, but on northern Vancouver Island and in the back waters near Clayoquot Sound (a UNESCO protected biosphere), logging is still a mainstay of the economy and a rich resource for the province. Although current logging practices include a comprehensive re-plantation program, there remains an innate distrust between tree-hugger and logging company which, every so often, spawns a protest or two when virgin timber comes under threat.

4 THE ISLANDS IN POPULAR CULTURE: BOOKS, FILM, TV & MUSIC

Detour down the most unlikely country lane, and you're liable to find a barn transformed into a potter's studio, or a garden shed converted into a painting place. And once you've visited the islands, you'll start to recognize just how many books and movies use their diverse landscapes as backdrops.

If there is one title that epitomizes the juxtapositions you'll find in this part of the world, it's a book *Fishing with John,* an unusual West Coast love story of a sophisticated New York journalist who gives it all up to marry an impassioned and greatly talented coastal fisherman with a particular distaste for pretension. Although true, the story reads like fiction, and established its author, Edith Iglauer, as one of BC's most popular writers. It was later made into a movie: *Navigating the Heart,* starring Jaclyn Smith and Tim Matheson.

Vancouver Island resident John Hodgins has a battery of books to his name, many of which are set on and around the island, from *Innocent Cities* (based in Victoria) to others that take place in the lush green forests, pulp mills, and seas. *Spit Delaney's Island* is a compelling collection of short fiction and a good introduction to the author's ability to mingle history, personal experience, and imagination. His other island-based, award-winning titles include *Resurrection of Joseph Byrne* (Governor General's Award for Fiction); *Invention of the World* (Gibson's First Novel Award); and *Honorary Patron* (Commonwealth Regional Prize).

If reading's your love, then check out local authors Brian Payton and Joanna Streetly (both have a penchant for the west coast of the island), Bill Gaston, and poet Don McKay, whose book *Deactivated West 100* follows the landscapes of a deactivated logging road (hence the title) in what has been described as a "geopoetic" exploration.

In terms of non-fiction books, there are several resource titles that will broaden your experience of the islands, depending on your interests. *Whales of the West Coast* (Harbour Publishing) by David A. E. Spalding, answers every question you ever had about whales and dolphins of the West Coast, including their natural history, aboriginal and commercial whaling practices, current conservation issues, and a month-by-month list of when and where whales regularly appear. When you're on the San Juan Islands, you'll find many titles about the famous "Pig War," and they all do a good job chronicling those events. *Magic Islands: A Treasure-Trove of San Juan Islands Lore* (Orcas Publishing Company), by David Richardson, and *San Juan: The Powder-Keg Island: The Settler's Own Stories* (Beach Combers), by Jo Bailey-Cummings and Al Cummings, offers the flavor of cultural and anecdotal history of the islands' earliest settlers and their families. One of the most inspired coffee-table books is *Enchanted Isles: The Southern Gulf Islands* by David A. E. Spalding (author), Kevin Oke (photographer)—it's packed with history, information, and stunning photography.

Famous Islanders

The islands have a remarkable collection of celebrities, past and present, who either grew up here or have decided to make this their home.

Robert Bateman, painter: lives on Salt Spring Island
Rick Hansen, wheelchair athlete: born in Port Alberni
Pamela Anderson, actor: born in Ladysmith
Randy Bachman, musician: lives on Salt Spring Island
Diana Krall, jazz musician: born in Nanaimo
Kim Cattrall, actor: raised in the Comox Valley
Alex Shapiro, singer/composer: lives in the San Juan Islands
Warren Miller, filmmaker and ski/snowboard legend: lives on Orcas Island

In terms of movies, *Double Jeopardy* (Tommy Lee Jones and Ashley Judd) manages to incorporate many of the islands' attributes—stunning scenery from ocean-front homes, misty coastlines, and passenger ferry "chases"—while other films use the area more generically. A sampling of movies filmed here include *Insomnia* (Robin Williams, Al Pacino); *Clan of the Cave Bear* (Darryl Hannah); *Cats & Dogs* (Jeff Goldblum, Elizabeth Perkins); *Lake Placid* (Bill Pullman, Bridget Fonda); *Little Women* (Winona Ryder, Gabriel Byrne, Kirsten Dunst); *The Scarlett Letter* (Demi Moore, Gary Oldman, Robert Duvall); *X2* & *X-Men: The Last Stand* (Patrick Stewart, Ian McKellen, Halle Berry); and *The 13th Warrior* (Antonio Banderas).

5 EATING AND DRINKING IN THE ISLANDS

The 100-mile diet—a philosophy of eating based on only consuming what originates within that radius—originated in Vancouver, so it is little wonder that the West Coast has taken to the concept with almost obsessive ownership. And this becomes all the more evident once you set foot on any of the islands, which by their very nature have always tried to practice self sufficiency. Put the two dynamics together, and you have an agri-tourism scene that, in the last 5 years in particular, seems to be taking the region by storm. Local food is not just a fad, it is part of a 130-country-strong Slow Food movement, and Vancouver Island is one of its epicenters.

Vancouver Island has set the pace, largely because it has the climate, resources, and population base to sustain an agricultural economy made up of an enviable wine scene (including meaderies and artisan distilleries), and fresh produce farms that run the gamut from raising alpaca llamas for handmade cloth to venison and bison for smoked meats, hand-crafted cheeses, and more. Add to this the natural bounty of the land—rainforests filled with chanterelle mushrooms, beaches awash with healthful seaweed, and oceans abundant with salmon, halibut, oysters, and crab—and you quickly realize why islanders have adapted the 100-mile diet to an all-islands enclave (a diet inclusive of all growers and food producers on Vancouver Island and the Gulf Islands). In fact, Seattle and Vancouver are so close, and the exchange of goods between island and mainland so great, that it's estimated that if ever Vancouver Island was left to its own devices, it would have only a 3-day food supply for islanders even though it has the resources to be agriculturally independent.

Enter the Island Chefs Collaborative (ICC), a group of like-minded Vancouver Island chefs who shared the vision to create a sustainable food and agricultural system on Vancouver Island and the Gulf Islands. When they visited farms and producers, chefs were amazed at what was available, and in turn, local farmers were often surprised by what chefs wanted to cook with. The result? Competing chefs readily share knowledge and sources with one another, and farmers have become both niche-market savvy and creative. The partnership often sits down with seed catalogues together to choose what should be grown for the following year, and it is the reason why more and more menus are able to include items such as prosciutto from locally-raised pigs, heirloom tomato varieties, and exotic chards. In fact, since establishing itself in 1999, the ICC movement has done much to make food from local farmers, fishers, and foragers an integral part of the islands' experience. It even sponsors a new food celebration: Defending our Backyard Local Food Festival at Fort Rodd Hill and Fisgard Lighthouse in May, a combination tasting and education

event to raise awareness about on-island food sources and how they make their journey to the table. There's everything from oyster shucking and slurping to spit roasting a pig, alongside wine tasting and interesting specialty products. A helpful guide to the island's food culture is Rosemary Neering's book *Eating Up Vancouver Island;* while a few years old now, it's still a relevant (and humorous) resource describing the islands' more established farms, wineries, craft breweries, and seafood markets.

The San Juan and Gulf islands may not be as lushly diverse as Vancouver Island, but they still pride themselves on colorful farmers' markets and a buy-direct mentality that supports local fishermen, cheese makers, vineyards, and farms producing organic herbs and edible flowers, greens, meats, and other culinary delights. Heritage and organic fruit orchards dot the countryside on all the islands (tours and visits are often available), and local producers are the primary source for most island restaurants. In the San Juans, many suppliers and restaurants participate in an Islands Certified Local program (the longest transport time between any of the islands is only 1 hour, so food is certainly fresh). Look for the ICL emblem in restaurant windows. Check out **Farm Products Guides** for Lopez, Orcas, and San Juan, which describe those farms and orchards open to the public. Downloadable guides are available on the WSU Cooperative Extension/San Juan County website: www.sanjuan.wsu.edu/agriculture.

Planning Your Trip to Vancouver Island, the Gulf Islands & the San Juan Islands

The islands of the Pacific Northwest are captivating, and their charm certainly invites impromptu getaway visits. Advance planning, however, will save you time, money, and worry, and is what this chapter is all about. It covers the necessary nuts and bolts to help you plan a successful trip, after which you can turn to the "Fast Facts, Toll-Free Numbers & Websites" appendix on p. 264 for more on-the-ground resources in Victoria and on the respective islands.

1 VISITOR INFORMATION

A great source for information on British Columbia is **Tourism British Columbia,** P.O. Box 9830, Parliament Building, Victoria, BC V8V 1X4, or P.O. Box 9830 Stn. Prov. Government, Victoria, BC V8W 9W5 (② **800/HELLOBC** [435-5622]; www.hellobc.com). Be prepared for lots of glossy magazines to whet your appetite.

For Vancouver Island specifics, contact the **Tourism Association of Vancouver Island,** 501-65 Front St., Nanaimo, BC V9R 5H9 (② **250/754-3500;** www. vancouverisland.travel). Another useful

website is **www.vancouverisland.com**. There is a central reservations service for hotels and B&Bs in the Gulf Islands. Call ② **866/539-3089.** You can also check out **www.gulfislandsguide.com** for general information. For the San Juan Islands, contact **San Juan Islands Visitor Information Services,** P.O. Box 1330, Friday Harbor, San Juan Island, WA 98250 (② **888/468-3701** or 360/378-9551; www.visitsanjuans.com). All these resources also provide excellent destination-specific maps, and many have lively travel blogs.

2 ENTRY REQUIREMENTS

PASSPORTS
ENTERING CANADA All visitors to and from Canada, including U.S. citizens, must carry a passport or proof of citizenship and residence. U.S. **residents** would be also well advised to carry arrival-through-departure records, proof of

sufficient funds for a temporary stay, and evidence of return transportation.

Frequent U.S. travelers may want to consider The Passport Card, a pre-authorized pass issued by the Department of Homeland Security that can be used in lieu of a passport for car/ferry travel between the U.S. and Canada, Mexico, Bermuda, and the Caribbean. Note, however, that while it represents a less expensive and more portable alternative to the traditional passport book, and has the same period of validity, it cannot be used for air travel.

Citizens of most European countries, former British colonies, and certain other countries (Israel, Korea, and Japan, for example) do not need visas, but they must carry passports. Entry visas for citizens of more than 130 countries must be applied for and received from the Canadian embassy in your home country. For further information, check with the **Canadian Consulate** in the city nearest you or contact the Canadian government's **800-Canada information line** (© **800/ OCANADA** [622-6232]), which will link you to numerous government services and programs. Entry requirements to Canada are also on the Citizenship and Immigration website visitors' services page at www. cic.gc.ca/english/index.asp.

ENTERING THE UNITED STATES

All visitors to the United States should carry passports along with arrival and departure information, proof of sufficient funds for a temporary stay, evidence of return transportation, and in many instances student or visitor visas. Canadian citizens, too, now require a valid passport to enter or re-enter the United States. Since border security has become more stringent, a driver's license or other photo ID is no longer sufficient.

The U.S. State Department has a **Visa Waiver Program (VWP)** allowing citizens of the following countries to enter the United States without a visa for stays of up to 90 days: Andorra, Australia, Austria, Belgium, Brunei, Denmark, Finland, France, Germany, Iceland, Ireland, Italy, Japan, Liechtenstein, Luxembourg, Monaco, the Netherlands, New Zealand, Norway, Portugal, San Marino, Singapore, Slovenia, Spain, Sweden, Switzerland, and the

United Kingdom. (**Note:** This list was accurate at press time; for the most up-to-date list of countries in the VWP, consult www. travel.state.gov/visa). Canadian citizens may enter the United States without visas; they will need to show passports (if traveling by air) and proof of residence, however. **Note:** Any passport issued on or after October 26, 2006, by a VWP country must be an **e-Passport** for VWP travelers to be eligible to enter the U.S. without a visa. Citizens of these nations also need to present a round-trip air or cruise ticket upon arrival. E-Passports contain computer chips capable of storing biometric information, such as the required digital photograph of the holder. (You can identify an e-Passport by the symbol on the bottom center cover of your passport.) If your passport doesn't have this feature, you can still travel without a visa if it is a valid passport issued before October 26, 2005, and includes a machine-readable zone, or between October 26, 2005, and October 25, 2006, and includes a digital photograph. For more information, go to **www.travel.state.gov/visa**.

Citizens of all other countries must have (1) a valid passport that expires at least 6 months later than the scheduled end of their visit to the U.S., and (2) a tourist visa, which may be obtained without charge from any U.S. consulate.

As of January 2004, many international visitors traveling on visas to the United States will be photographed and fingerprinted on arrival at Customs in airports and on cruise ships in a program created by the Department of Homeland Security called **US-VISIT**. Exempt from the extra scrutiny are visitors entering by land or those (mostly in Europe; see p. 270) that don't require a visa for short-term visits. For more information, go to the Homeland Security website at **www.dhs.gov/ dhspublic**.

For specifics on how to get a visa, go to **"Visas"** in the **"Fast Facts"** appendix (p. 270).

Cut to the Front of the Airport Security Line as a Registered Traveler

In 2003, the **Transportation Security Administration** (**TSA;** www.tsa.gov) approved a pilot program to help ease the time spent in line for airport security screenings when flying out of the United States. In exchange for information and a fee, persons can be pre-screened as registered travelers, granting them a front-of-the-line position when they fly. The program is run through private firms—the largest and most well-known is Steven Brill's **Clear** (www.flyclear.com), and it works like this: Travelers complete an online application providing specific points of personal information including name, addresses for the previous 5 years, birth date, social security number, driver's license number, and a valid credit card (you're not charged the **C$99 fee** until your application is approved). Print out the completed form and take it, along with proper ID, with you to an "enrollment station" (these can be found in over 20 participating airports and in a growing number of American Express offices around the country, for example). It's at this point where it gets seemingly sci-fi. At the enrollment station, a Clear representative will record your biometrics necessary for clearance; in this case, your fingerprints and your irises will be digitally recorded.

Once your application has been screened against no-fly lists, outstanding warrants, and other security measures, you'll be issued a clear plastic card that holds a chip containing your information. Each time you fly through participating airports (and the numbers are steadily growing), go to the Clear Pass station located next to the standard TSA screening line. Here you'll insert your card into a slot and place your finger on a scanner to read your print—when the information matches up, you're cleared to cut to the front of the security line. You'll still have to follow all the procedures of the day like removing your shoes and walking through the x-ray machine, but Clear promises to cut 30 minutes off your wait time at the airport.

If you're driving across the border, obtaining a **NEXUS** pass is another way to beat the line-ups (www.getnexus.com). NEXUS is a partnership program between the Canadian Border Services Agency (CBSA) and U.S. Customs & Border Protection that pre-clears low-risk, pre-approved travelers between the two countries. The cost is C$50, and you can register on-line. Check out www.getnexus.com. Canadian travelers only can check out **CANPASS** for flight travel. The latter is very similar to the U.S. Clear Pass, and can be obtained via the CBSA at www.cbsa.gc.ca.

Traveling with Children

United States and Canada border officials pay particular attention to minors, especially if they are traveling solo or with a single adult. Any person age 18 and under must carry a letter from a parent or guardian granting him or her permission to travel across the border, plus proof of identity. If parents are divorced, the non-traveling parent must write a similar letter granting permission for the child to accompany the ex-spouse.

PLANNING YOUR TRIP

3

ENTRY REQUIREMENTS

MEDICAL REQUIREMENTS

Unless you're arriving from an area known to be experiencing an epidemic (particularly cholera or yellow fever), inoculations or vaccinations are not required for entry into the United States or Canada. If you have a medical condition that requires **syringe-administered medications,** carry a valid signed prescription from your physician—the Federal Aviation Administration (FAA) no longer allows airline passengers to pack syringes in their carry-on baggage without documented proof of medical need. If you have a disease that requires treatment with **narcotics,** you should also carry documented proof with you—smuggling narcotics aboard a plane is a serious offense that carries severe penalties in both the U.S. and Canada. For **HIV-positive visitors,** requirements for entering either country are somewhat vague and change frequently. According to the latest publication of *HIV and Immigrants: A Manual for AIDS Service Providers,* the Immigration and Naturalization Service (INS) doesn't require a medical exam for entry into the United States, but INS officials may stop individuals if they look sick or if they are carrying AIDS/HIV medicine.

CUSTOMS
What You Can Bring into Canada

Canada Customs is fairly liberal except when it comes to firearms, plants, and meats. These are subject to rigorous inspection; without *precisely* the right paperwork, they won't make it across the border. Pepper sprays are also a big no. For a clear summary of Canadian rules, request the booklet "I Declare," issued by the Canada Border Services Agency (*©* **800/461-9999** in Canada, or 204/983-3500; www.cbsa.gc.ca). Canada allows its citizens a C$750 exemption per 7-day absence, and you're allowed to bring back duty-free one carton of cigarettes, one can of tobacco, 1.5L (40 imperial oz.) of liquor, and 50 cigars. There is also a smaller 48-hour exemption (you can claim C$400 total) as well as a 24-hour exemption of C$50. You must be over 19 to purchase tobacco products and alcoholic beverages, and purchases have to accompany you in your checked or hand luggage.

What You Can Bring into the U.S.

Every visitor more than 21 years of age may bring in, free of duty, the following: (1) 1 liter of wine or hard liquor; (2) 200 cigarettes, 100 cigars (but not from Cuba), or 3 pounds of smoking tobacco; and (3) US$100 worth of gifts. These exemptions are offered to travelers who spend at least 72 hours in the United States and who have not claimed them within the preceding 6 months. It is forbidden to bring into the country almost any meat products (including canned, fresh, and dried meat products such as **bouillon** soup mixes, and so on). Generally, condiments including vinegars, oils, and spices; coffee; tea; and some cheeses and baked goods are permitted. Avoid rice products, as rice can often harbor insects. Bringing fruits and vegetables is not advised, though not prohibited. Customs will allow produce depending on where you got it and where you're going after you arrive in the U.S. Foreign tourists may carry in or out up to $10,000 in U.S. or foreign currency with no formalities; larger sums must be declared to U.S. Customs on entering or leaving, which includes filing form CM 4790. For details regarding U.S. Customs and Border Protection, consult your nearest U.S. embassy or consulate, or **U.S. Customs** (www.cbp.gov).

What You Can Take Home

U.S. Citizens: For specifics on what you can bring back and the corresponding fees, download the invaluable free pamphlet "Know Before You Go" available online at **www.cbp.gov.** (Click "Travel," and then click "Know Before You Go! Online Brochure") Or contact the **U.S. Customs & Border Protection (CBP),** 1300 Pennsylvania Ave., NW, Washington, DC 20229 (𝒞 **877/287-8667**) and request the pamphlet.

Canadian Citizens: For a clear summary of Canadian rules, write for the booklet "I Declare," issued by the Canada Border Services Agency (𝒞 **800/461-9999** in Canada, or 204/983-3500; www.cbsa-asfc.gc.ca).

U.K. Citizens: For information, contact **HM Customs & Excise** at 𝒞 **0845/010-9000** (from outside the U.K., 020/8929-0152), or consult their website at **www.hmce.gov.uk.**

Australian Citizens: A helpful brochure available from Australian consulates or Customs offices is *Know Before You Go.* For more information, call the **Australian Customs Service** at 𝒞 **1300/363-263,** or log on to **www.customs.gov.au.**

New Zealand Citizens: Most questions are answered in a free pamphlet available at New Zealand consulates and Customs offices: *New Zealand Customs Guide for Travellers, Notice no. 4.* For more information, contact **New Zealand Customs,** The Customhouse, 17–21 Whitmore St., Box 2218, Wellington (𝒞 **04/473-6099** or 0800/428-786; **www.customs.govt.nz**).

3 WHEN TO GO

CLIMATE

There's a reason for the lush, green landscape, bountiful flowers, and rich agricultural fields in the Pacific Northwest. It's called rain. So, while you're enjoying the milder temperatures, always tote an umbrella.

In **March,** Victoria boasts the first spring blooms in Canada, parading its daffodils on television newscasts across a country still bound in much chillier climes. It's also a signal for travelers to hit the road. Although weather can still be a little unsettled, the deals on accommodations and uncrowded restaurants are worth the effort of carrying an umbrella. By **May,** cherry blossoms and tulips dot the islands, leading the way to a summer that enjoys at least 16 hours of daylight per day, temperatures that push the mercury to around 77°F/25°C, and a monthly rainfall that averages barely 2.5cm (1 in.). This is

high season, when the islands seem on perpetual parade. **September or October** is a golden time to visit. The days are still long, there's warmth in the air, and the leaves turn to hues of yellow, gold, and red. With the kids back in school, attractions aren't as jam-packed; getaway packages offer great savings. The winter season, from **November to February,** sees more rain than snow, which, if it falls at all, dissolves into the atmosphere within hours. But snow does settle in the mountains and on Vancouver Island's northernmost reaches, making skiing and snowboarding popular pastimes. Along the westernmost coast of Vancouver Island, **winter storms** from the open Pacific Ocean are so dramatic that savvy marketers have successfully created a new high season specifically geared to storm watchers. Yet, for all the rain, gray days are still outnumbered by beautiful, crisp weather, especially in the San Juans.

Vancouver Island's Average Temperature & Precipitation

	Jan	Feb	Mar	Apr	May	June	July	Aug	Sept	Oct	Nov	Dec
Temp. (°F)	39°	41°	45°	46°	52°	61°	66°	66°	63°	45°	45°	41°
Temp. (°C)	4°	5°	7°	8°	11°	16°	19°	19°	17°	7°	7°	5°
Precip. (in./cm)	3.6/ 92	2.6/ 67	1.7/ 42	1.5/ 38	0.9/ 24	0.7/ 19	0.6/ 14	0.8/ 20	1.3/ 32	2.3/ 59	3.6/ 92	3.9/ 99

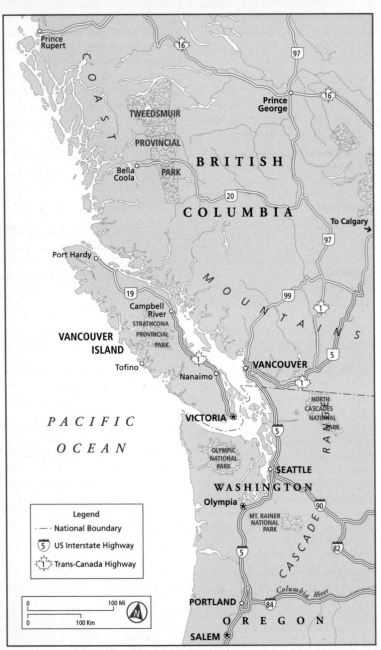

Prince
Rupert

16

97

TWEEDSMUIR

Prince
George

16

PROVINCIAL

B R I T I S H

Bella
Coola

PARK

20

C O L U M B I A

To Calgary

97

Port Hardy

M
O
U
N
T
A
I
N
S

99

1

19

Campbell
River

5

STRATHCONA
PROVINCIAL
PARK

**VANCOUVER
ISLAND**

VANCOUVER

1

Tofino

Nanaimo

NORTH
CASCADES
NATIONAL
PARK

VICTORIA ✸

R
A
N
G
E

5

P A C I F I C

OLYMPIC
NATIONAL
PARK

O C E A N

SEATTLE

W A S H I N G T O N

Olympia ✸

90

MT. RAINER
NATIONAL
PARK

C
A
S
C
A
D
E

82

5

Legend

- - - National Boundary

5 US Interstate Highway

1 Trans-Canada Highway

Columbia River

PORTLAND

84

0   100 Mi

O R E G O N

0   100 Km

SALEM ✸

Note: Temperature may vary among different parts of Vancouver Island by as much as 4° or 5°C; precipitation varies as well. For example, you can expect the northern regions to be the coolest and the Cowichan Valley to be the warmest. Also, the west coast usually gets more precipitation than the east coast. The above chart can be used as a general gauge for conditions on the Gulf and San Juan islands, as well. For island-specific readings, contact the local chambers of commerce or visitor information centers.

VANCOUVER ISLAND, THE GULF ISLANDS & THE SAN JUAN ISLANDS CALENDAR OF EVENTS

Island events tend to be community oriented and not as finessed as you would find in big city centers. Weather dictates that most activities take place in the summer months except for those celebrating wildlife migrations. Victoria and Nanaimo stage the most special events, though you're likely to find small festivities such as outdoor summer concerts and fall agricultural fairs on any one of the Gulf and San Juan islands as well as in Vancouver Island's rural communities. The San Juan Islands Visitors Information Center (© **360/378-6822;** www.visitsanjuans.com) or Vancouver Island Tourism, which also covers the Gulf Islands (© **250/754-3500;** www.vancouverisland.travel), can provide further details. For an exhaustive list of events beyond those listed here, check http://events.frommers.com, where you'll find a searchable, up-to-the-minute roster of what's happening in cities and communities all over the world.

DECEMBER/JANUARY

Annual Bald Eagle Count, Goldstream Provincial Park, Vancouver Island. When the salmon swim up Goldstream Provincial Park's spawning streams, more than 300 bald eagles take up residence with an eye to a month-long feast. Call © **250/478-9414** for exact dates and events.

FEBRUARY

Chinese New Year, Victoria, Vancouver Island. This is when the Chinese traditionally pay their debts and forgive old grievances to start the new lunar year with a clean slate. The Chinese community rings it in with firecrackers, dancing dragon parades, and other festivities. Late January or early February.

Trumpeter Swan Festival, Comox Valley, Vancouver Island. A week-long festival celebrating these magnificent white birds that gather in the Comox Valley. Call the **Tourism Association of Vancouver Island** (© **250/754-3500**) for exact dates.

MARCH

Pacific Rim Whale Festival, Pacific Rim National Park Region, Vancouver Island. Every spring, mid-March through early April, more than 20,000 grey whales migrate past Vancouver Island's west coast, attracting visitors from all over the world. It's a colorful celebration featuring live crab races, storytelling, parades, art shows, guided whale-spotting hikes, and whale-watching excursions in zippy Zodiacs. For information, call Tourism Ucluelet © **250/726-4641** or Tourism Tofino © **250/725-3414.**

APRIL

Brant Wildlife Festival, Parksville/Qualicum Beach, Vancouver Island. A birder's nirvana, this 3-day celebration focuses on the annual black brant migration through the area from Mexico to Alaska (20,000 birds). The event includes guided walks through old-growth forest and saltwater and freshwater marshes, goose-viewing stations, a birding competition, art, photography, and carving exhibitions, as well as numerous children's activities. For exact dates, call ℂ **866/288-7878.**

Victoria Hot Jazz Jubilee, Sidney, Vancouver Island. A small, three-day seaside festival that attracts traditional jazz, swing, bebop, fusion, Dixie, and blues musicians from all over North America. It offers top music with a parochial charm. Call ℂ **250/882-JAZZ** [5299] for performance venues and schedules.

Victoria Harbour Floating Boat Show, Victoria, Vancouver Island. If boating is your thing, this floating show takes up most of the harbor with more than 150 new and pre-owned boats on display, as well as numerous marine-related products from electronics and diving gear to dinghies. Call ℂ **250/416-0097** for details.

May

Swiftsure Weekend, Victoria and Vancouver Island. More than 200 vessels navigate the unpredictable coastal waters in this, the oldest and largest offshore overnight sailing race in the Pacific Northwest. In 2003, it celebrated its 60th anniversary. It is as exciting to watch as it is to participate. Call the **Royal Victoria Yacht Club** (ℂ 250/592-2441) for information.

Artists' Studios Open House, San Juan Island. An island-wide open house featuring weavers, potters, and other craftspeople. Call ℂ **360/378-5594** for information. Last weekend in May.

International Children's Festival, Victoria, Vancouver Island. Scheduled in tandem with Vancouver's acclaimed children's festival, this event is able to attract some of the world's finest performers in arts and culture through circus, dance, drama, acrobatics, storytelling, and puppetry. Call the festival offices for details ℂ **250/590-KIDS** [5437]. Mid-month.

June

Boat Festival, Cowichan Bay, Vancouver Island. Classic boats, a boat-building house for children, Dragon Boat races, folk singers, and dancing are some of the fun activities of this festival. The Fast-and-Furious Boat Building Contest is a highlight: entrants build a boat and race it within 4 hours! Call the Cowichan Bay Maritime Centre for exact dates (ℂ **250/746-4955**).

Multicultural Festival, Nanaimo, Vancouver Island. Since its inaugural festival in 2005, Nanaimo has earned the title of Cultural Capital of Canada, and this event is the official celebration of the city's international mosaic. It starts with Aboriginal Day and ends on Canada Day, July 1, in between which the downtown core features live entertainment, ethnic foods, information exhibits, a children's area, contests, and prizes. ℂ **250/754-8141.**

July

Nanaimo Marine Festival, Nanaimo, Vancouver Island. Lots of activities take place around the harbor, culminating in the famous Bathtub Race between the city of Nanaimo and Kitsilano Beach, in Vancouver. Yes, it's exactly what it sounds like—racers scrunched up in racer-designed bathtub look-alikes that may or may not make it across the chop. Contact **Tourism Nanaimo** (ℂ **800/663-7337**) or the **Loyal Nanaimo Bathtub Society** (ℂ 250/753-7223) for information.

Rodeo Days & KiteFest, Coombs & Parksville, Vancouver Island. Bull riding, steer wrestling, roping, and traditional barn dancing make up this western-style family event. Call ℂ **250/248-1009** for details. The dates always coincide with a community Kite Festival in nearby Parksville where kite flying and championship flight rallies create quite a sky-spectacle. Call ℂ **250/248-6300.**

Lavender Festival, Salt Spring Island. Set amidst rolling hills of lavender, atop Sacred Mountain, this festival features all manner of lavender-related arts, from cheesecake to ice creams and hand-crafted soap, scented wands, and oils. Artists set up shop, too, as do Morris Dancers. Call ✆ **250/654-2315** for dates and details. Early July.

Festival of Murals, Chemainus, Vancouver Island. Chemainus is known worldwide for its ever-changing murals. During the festival, visitors have the opportunity to see local and international artists "decorate" the sides of buildings, walls, and more with new murals— pictorials that have included turn-of-the-20th-century farming scenes, wildlife, aboriginal profiles, and whimsical townspeople characters. From mid-July to mid-August.

AUGUST

BC Open Sandcastle Competition, Parksville, Vancouver Island. Between late July and most of August, the wide, sandy beaches are transformed with imagination and creativity. This event attracts more than 40,000 people. Call ✆ **250/951-2678** for exact dates and information.

Filberg Festival, Comox, Vancouver Island. Widely considered one of the finest arts festivals in BC, this outdoor art exhibition presents the work of more than 150 artisans from throughout British Columbia, including entertainment. For ticket information call ✆ **866/898-8499** or 250/338-2430. Early August.

Victoria Dragon Boat Festival, Victoria, Vancouver Island. Traditional dragon boat races take place in the Inner Harbour, where 120 local and international teams compete. For details, call Tourism Victoria, at ✆ **250/953-2033.** Mid-August.

Symphony Splash, Victoria, Vancouver Island. It only lasts 1 day, but this free event draws a crowd of 40,000 people to hear the Victoria Symphony play from a barge moored in the middle of Victoria's picturesque Inner Harbour. Traditionally, Tchaikovsky's 1812 Overture closes the concert, accompanied by fireworks. Call ✆ **250/385-9771** for details. Early August.

Summertime Blues Festival, Nanaimo & Coombs, Vancouver Island. Usually scheduled one after the other, these bluegrass and blues festivals feature Canada's best artists who play at various venues along Nanaimo's harborfront and in Coombs. Old-time fiddlers (only some of them are quite pint size in years and stature) are always headliners. Call Tourism Vancouver Island ✆ **250/754-3500** for dates and specific locations.

Art in the Park, Orcas Island. Held at Moran Sate Park, this annual event brings together displays by local artists and traditional craftspeople that are normally scattered throughout the San Juan Islands. For information, call ✆ **360/376-2273.**

SEPTEMBER

Saanich Fall Fair, Saanichton, Vancouver Island. The oldest agricultural fair in Western Canada showcases livestock, sheep shearing, show jumping, crafts, produce, home baking, and more. Lots of candy floss and old-style country fun, including a fiddle competition. Call ✆ **250/652-2033** for information. Early September.

Classic Boat Festival, Victoria, Vancouver Island. For boat lovers, this is a showcase of maritime heritage, when as many as 140 classically restored boats moor in the Inner Harbour and vie for prizes such as the Best Restored Sail award and the Best Restored Power award. Call ✆ **250/385-7766** for information.

The Great Canadian Beer Festival, Victoria, Vancouver Island. Held at the Royal Athletic Park, this outdoor event draws some of British Columbia's best microbreweries in a sampling extravaganza of beers from across Western Canada. Call Tourism Victoria for information (© **250/383-2332**). Second week in September.

Harvest of Music, Qualicum Beach, Vancouver Island. Musicians from all over the world playing everything from Gypsy jazz to Japanese taiko drumming gather in 9 days of performances and workshops. Call © **250/752-6133** for information.

Fall Fair, Salt Spring Island. Originated in 1896, this fair is less sophisticated than the one at Saanich, and epitomizes island living as no other. Competition for the biggest dahlias and tastiest pies is hot and heavy; the gymkhana is a hybrid of sheepdog trials and a pony obstacle course; the exotic range of poultry on show is worth the price of admission; and listening to local musicians while sitting on bales of hay is a throwback to yesteryear. Call © **250/537-5252.**

Cowichan Wine & Culinary Festival, Cowichan Valley, Vancouver Island. As the fastest growing wine region in Canada, the range of fruit-filled wines, cider, and mead you'll find in these islands is matched only by the variety of artisan cheeses, fresh produce, seafood, and herbs. This 3-day annual festival started in 2005 and is already among the top events for food and wine aficionados. Call Tourism Cowichan for details (© **250/746-1099**). Last weekend in September.

OCTOBER

Royal Victorian Marathon, Victoria, Vancouver Island. This annual race attracts runners from around the world. The air is fresh, and the temperature is usually just cool enough to keep the runners moving along a course that's not too strenuous. A good trainer for the Boston Marathon course, for which it is a qualifier. 2009 represents the run's 30th annual celebration. Call © **250/658-4520** for information. Canadian Thanksgiving weekend (second weekend in October).

Savor the San Juans, Lopez, Orcas and San Juan islands. 2009 marks the second year of a month-long medley of culinary and cultural events, such as specialty winemaker dinners, cooking classes, art gallery events, theater performances, and presentations. For information, call © **360/378-6822** or visit www.visitsanjuans.com.

NOVEMBER

Oyster Festival, Tofino, Vancouver Island. It seems that every chef in the region gets into the act of shucking, slurping, sampling, and pulling together all manner of culinary delights alongside exceptional regional wines and music. During the festival, some 4,000 oysters are consumed. Call Tourism Tofino for details © **250/725-3414.**

DECEMBER

First Night, Nanaimo, Vancouver Island. Unfortunately, most cities found that despite a no-alcohol policy, First Night celebrations encouraged rowdy crowds, and so they shelved them all together. Nanaimo, however, has modified the concept to create a small family-style gathering at Beban Park with performing arts, fireworks, food stalls, and more. Activities vary each year. Call © **250/756-5200** for details. December 31.

GETTING THERE
By Plane

Western United States is linked with Canada, Europe, and Asia by frequent nonstop flights. Seattle's **Seatac International Airport** (© 206/433-5388; www.portseattle. org; SEA) and **Vancouver International Airport** (© 604/207-7077; www.yvr.ca; YVR) are major hubs; regional airlines connect to Victoria (YYJ), Bellingham (BLJ), and smaller centers throughout the islands. Major carriers include: **Air Canada** (© 888/247-2262; www.aircanada. ca), **WestJet** (© 800/538-5696 or 888/ 937-8538; www.westjet.com), **American Airlines** (© 800/443-7300; www.aa. com), **Continental** (© 800/231-0856; www.continentalairlines.com), **Delta Airlines** (© 800/221-1212; www.delta.com), **Northwest Airlines** (© 800/447-4747; www.nwa.com), and **United Airlines** (© 800/241-6522; www.united.com).

Air Canada and **Horizon Air** (© 800/ 547-9308; www.horizonair.com or www. alaskaair.com), Alaska Airlines' connector, offer direct connections from several U.S. and Canadian cities such as Washington, D.C., Anchorage, San Francisco, and Calgary, to Vancouver, Victoria, and Seattle.

Commercial air carriers between the Seattle area and the San Juan Islands include: **Island Air** (charter only) (© 360/ 378-2376; www.sanjuan-islandair.com), **Kenmore Air** (seaplanes) (© 800/543-9595; www.kenmoreair.com), **Northwest Seaplanes** (© 800/690-0086; www.nw seaplanes.com), and **San Juan Airlines** (© 800/874-4434; www.sanjuanairlines. com).

On the Canada side, regional commuter airlines, including floatplanes and helicopters that fly between Vancouver Harbour on the mainland and Victoria's Inner Harbour, also serve the Gulf Islands.

They include: **Air Canada Jazz** (a subsidiary of Air Canada) (© 888/247-2262; www.flyjazz.ca), **Harbour Air Sea Planes** (© 800/665-0212 or 604/274-1277; www.harbour-air.com), **Helijet Airways** (© 800/665-4354; www.helijet.com), **Kenmore Air** (© 800/543-9595; www. kenmoreair.com), **Pacific Coastal Airlines** (© 800/663-2872 outside Vancouver or 604/273-8666 in Vancouver; www. pacific-coastal.com), and **West Coast Air** (float planes) (© 800/347-2222; www. westcoastair.com).

Overseas visitors can take advantage of the APEX (Advance Purchase Excursion) reductions offered by all major Canadian, U.S., and European carriers. In addition, some large U.S. airlines offer transatlantic or transpacific passengers special discount tickets under the name **Visit USA,** which allows mostly one-way travel from one U.S. destination to another at very low prices. Unavailable in the U.S., these discount tickets must be purchased abroad in conjunction with your international fare. This system is the easiest, fastest, cheapest way to see the country.

Arriving at the Airport

Immigration and Customs Clearance Visitors arriving by air, no matter what the port of entry, should cultivate patience and resignation before setting foot on U.S. soil. Since the terrorist attacks of September 11, 2001, getting through immigration control can take as long as 2 hours on some days, especially on summer weekends, so be sure to carry this guidebook or something else to read.

People traveling by air from Canada, Bermuda, and certain countries in the Caribbean can sometimes clear Customs and Immigration at the point of departure, which is much quicker.

Visitors traveling into Canada may experience the same time-consuming wait depending on your point of entry.

By Car

If you're visiting from abroad and plan to rent a car in the United States or Canada, keep in mind that foreign driver's licenses are usually recognized in both countries; but you should get an international one if your home license is not in English. Both the major centers of Victoria and Seattle have a wide selection of rental agencies (and vehicles). Once on the Gulf or San Juan islands, however, the choice of vehicles is much more limited.

Check out **Breezenet.com,** which offers domestic car-rental discounts with some of the most competitive rates around. Also worth visiting are Orbitz.com, Hotwire.com, Travelocity.com, and Priceline.com, all of which offer competitive online car-rental rates. For additional car rental agencies, see the "Fast Facts, Toll-Free Numbers & Websites," appendix, p. 264.

By Train

International visitors (excluding those from Canada) can buy a **USA Rail Pass,** good for 15 or 30 days of unlimited travel on Amtrak (© **800/USA-RAIL** [872-7245]; www.amtrak.com). The pass is available through many overseas travel agents. Current prices for a 15-day pass are US$389 off-peak, US$499 peak; a 30-day pass costs US$469 off-peak, US$599 peak. With a foreign passport, you can also buy passes at some Amtrak offices in the United States, including locations in San Francisco, Los Angeles, Chicago, New York, Miami, Boston, and Washington, D.C. Reservations are generally required and should be made for each part of your trip as early as possible. If a stopover to the islands is in your overall touring plans, such a pass is a good option. Because **Amtrak** services, and Canada's VIA Rail services across Canada, end in Vancouver, travel to Victoria and Vancouver Island requires connecting to either ferry or plane transportation. **VIA Rail** (© **800/561-8630;** www.viarail.com) connects Vancouver to the rest of Canada. **Amtrak** (© **800/872-7245;** www.amtrak.com) offers a daily service (a combination of train and coach) between Seattle and Vancouver. Schedules for both VIA Rail and Amtrak are posted at **Pacific Central Station,** 1150 Station St. (at the corner of Main St. and Terminal Ave.), Vancouver, and at King Street Station, 303 South Jackson St., Seattle.

GETTING AROUND

If you're planning to stay in Victoria, you can consider leaving your car parked. Public transit is good, and when you tire of walking around this very walkable city,

---

Travel in the Age of Bankruptcy

Airlines go bankrupt, so protect yourself by **buying your tickets with a credit card.** The Fair Credit Billing Act guarantees that you can get your money back from the credit card company if a travel supplier goes under (and if you request the refund within 60 days of the bankruptcy). **Travel insurance** can also help, but make sure it covers against "carrier default" for your specific travel provider. And be aware that if a U.S. airline goes bust mid-trip, a 2001 federal law requires other carriers to take you to your destination (albeit on a space-available basis) for a fee of no more than US$25, provided you rebook within 60 days of the cancellation.

> **Tips** **Prepare to Be Fingerprinted**
>
> Starting in January 2004, many international visitors (including Canadians) traveling into the United States may be photographed and fingerprinted at U.S. Customs through a new program created by the Department of Homeland Security called **US-VISIT.** Non–U.S. citizens arriving at U.S. airports and on cruise ships must undergo an instant background check as part of the U.S. government's ongoing efforts to deter terrorism by verifying the identity of incoming and outgoing visitors. Exempt from the extra scrutiny are visitors entering by land or those from 28 countries (mostly in Europe) that don't require a visa for short-term visits. For more information, go to the Homeland Security website at **www.dhs.gov/dhspublic**. At time of publication, these procedures are not practiced when entering Canada.

there are plenty of getting-around options such as mini-ferry rides across the harbor, horse-drawn carriages, and kabuki pedal cabs. Once you're out of the city, or on one of the islands, public transit is far less conducive to seeing the sights. See the "Getting Around" sections in the respective chapters.

By Plane

There are several regional carriers that commute between the major centers of Victoria, Nanaimo, San Juan and other coastal communities and specific resorts (see "Getting To" information above). Some areas have private landing strips, often grass. Upon arrival, however, car travel is still the best way to explore the area, although if you plan to stay put at a specific resort, bike rentals and mopeds are fun options to consider—yes, some of the islands are that small!

By Car

All the islands are a pleasure to explore and best done by car. In Victoria and Nanaimo, you'll find a number of rental car companies, including **Avis** (© 800/879-2847; www.avis.com), **Budget** (© 800/268-8900; www.budget.com), and **Hertz** (© 800/263-0600; www.hertz.com).

ON VANCOUVER ISLAND Although highways are well maintained on Vancouver

Island, getting from point A to point B can take longer than anticipated. Traffic in and around Victoria tends to be heavy and frustratingly slow—perhaps because so many drivers appear to be cautious retirees. Also, many of the region's more interesting attractions are off the highway on roads that twist and turn through picturesque communities. If you have the time, this beats highway asphalt. Gas is sold by the liter, and was averaging around C$0.85 a liter at press time, but can vary considerably. Speeds and distances are posted in kilometers (1 kilometer = 0.6 miles). Logging roads lead to some of the best places on the island, but if you drive on one, remember that logging trucks have absolute right-of-way. Members of the **American Automobile Association (AAA)** can get emergency assistance from the **British Columbia Automobile Association (BCAA)** (© 800/222-4357; www.bcaa.com).

IN VICTORIA This is a walking city, so don a good pair of shoes and park your car. Those few attractions that are not close to the city core are only a short taxi ride away. Victoria also has a comprehensive public transit system (see "Essentials" in chapter 5).

ON THE GULF & SAN JUAN ISLANDS The easiest way to tour these islands is by car, although some communities have rental scooters, mopeds, and bicycles. With that in mind, be aware that driving here takes extra care. Roads are shared with pedestrians taking a leisurely stroll, bikers, and deer that are especially prevalent at dawn and dusk. Rarely is anyone in a rush to get anywhere. (For details, see "Essentials" in chapter 9 or 10 for the specific island.)

By Train

VIA Rail's Malahat (℃ **888/842-7245;** www.viarail.ca) travels between Victoria and Courtenay, winding through the Cowichan River Valley and Goldstream Provincial Park. Travelers on the Horseshoe Bay–Nanaimo ferry board the train in Nanaimo. It departs from Victoria's **VIA Rail Station** (450 Pandora Ave.). The service runs Monday through Saturday, and the trip takes about 4^1/$_2$ hours. One-way fares from Victoria to Courtenay are C$28 adult, with discounts for youth, student, and senior travelers. Seniors should check into "buy one ticket and travel with a companion for free" promotions.

By Bus & Ferry

Bus travel is often the most economical form of public transit for short hops between cities, but it's certainly not an option for everyone.

Greyhound (℃ **800/231-2222;** www.greyhound.com) is the sole nationwide bus line and offers a Discovery Pass in increments of 7-, 15-, 30-, and 60-day passes for unlimited travel and stopovers in the U.S. and Canada. They range from C$329 to C$750. The pass can be purchased online through www.discoverypass.com and must be ordered at least 21 days before your departure.

TO VICTORIA Pacific Coach Lines (℃ **800/661-1725** or 604/662-7575; www.pacificcoach.com) operates bus service between Vancouver and Victoria. The 4-hour trip from the **Vancouver bus terminal** (Pacific Central Station, 1150 Station St.) to the **Victoria Depot** (700 Douglas St.) includes passage on the **Tsawwassen–Swartz Bay ferry.** One-way fares are C$43 for adults, C$29 for BC seniors; return fares are C$84 for adults, C$55 for BC seniors. Discounts are not offered to out-of-province seniors. Fares for children 5 to 11 are half the adult fare. Departures are daily, every 2 hours, between 5:45am and 7:45pm.

The Victoria Express (℃ **800/633-1589** in season, or year round ℃ 360/452-8088 from the U.S. and 250/361-9144 from Canada; www.victoriaexpress.com) operates a seasonal passenger-only ferry service, June through September, between Port Angeles and Victoria. Crossing time is 1 hour. There are two crossings per day. Reservations are available. Fares are US$13 per passenger; children 1 year and under travel for free.

Clipper Vacations (℃ **800/888-2535;** www.victoriaclipper.com) runs a year-round

ⓘ Tips   Distances and Driving Times from Victoria

Victoria to Sidney: 26km (16 miles), approximately ^{1}/$_2$ hour
Victoria to Nanaimo: 111km (69 miles), approximately 1^3/$_4$ hours
Victoria to Port Alberni: 195km (121 miles), approximately 3 hours
Victoria to Campbell River: 264km (164 miles), approximately 4 hours
Victoria to Tofino: 316km (196 miles), approximately 4^3/$_4$ hours
Victoria to Port Hardy: 502km (312 miles), approximately 7 hours

passenger-only service between Seattle and Victoria aboard a high-speed catamaran called the **Victoria Clipper.** From mid-May to mid-September, there are up to three crossings per day. The rest of the year this is reduced to one crossing per day. The trips are approximately 3 hours. One-way fares mid-May through mid-September are US$89; return fares are US$139. From mid-September to mid-May, in the off season, one-way fares are US$83; return fares are US$119. From mid-May to mid-September, there is one daily crossing aboard the Victoria Clipper from Seattle to Friday Harbor, on San Juan Island. Return fares for all passengers are from US$70. Reservations are recommended.

TO THE GULF ISLANDS Travelers should take the **Pacific Coach Lines coach** from Vancouver to Victoria, as mentioned above, but disembark in **Tsawwassen,** where **BC Ferries** (© 888/BCFERRY [223-3779] or 250/386-3431; www.bc ferries.com) sails year-round to the island of your choice. On Vancouver Island, BC Ferries departs from **Swartz Bay,** north of Victoria. Fares and sailing times range from 1 to 3 hours depending on your final island destination. See "Getting There," in chapter 9 for information about schedules and fares to specific islands.

TO THE SAN JUAN ISLANDS From Seattle's **Seatac International Airport** (© 206/433-5388; www.portseattle.org) and from the **Bellingham Airport** (© 360/671-5674), **Airporter Shuttle** (© 800/235-5247; www.airporter.com) and **Skagit County Bus** (© 360/757-4433; www.skat.org) transport passengers to Anacortes, north of Seattle on the Olympic Peninsula, just east of the San Juans. Connections can be made between Bellingham Airport and Vancouver on **Quick Shuttle** (© 800/665-2122; www.quickcoach.com). There is no bus transportation for travelers from Anacortes to the San Juans; you travel either on foot or in your own vehicle. Once there, visitors

traveling on foot have a choice of taxis, car rentals, moped rentals, or bicycle rentals. See chapter 10.

By Car & Ferry

Car travel is the most cost-effective, convenient, and comfortable way to travel around this westernmost part of North America. The inter-provincial highway system connects cities and towns all over the country; in addition to these high-speed, limited-access roadways, there's an extensive network of federal, provincial, and local highways and roads. Some of the national car-rental companies include **Alamo** (© 800/462-5266; www.alamo.com), **Avis** (© 800/230-4898; www.avis.com), **Budget** (© 800/527-0700; www.budget.com), **Dollar** (© 800/800-3665; www.dollar.com), **Hertz** (© 800/654-3131; www.hertz.com), **National** (© 800/227-7368; www.nationalcar.com), and **Thrifty** (© 800/847-4389; www.thrifty.com).

If you plan to rent a car in either the United States or Canada, you probably won't need the services of an additional automobile organization. If you're planning to buy or borrow a car, automobile-association membership is recommended. **AAA** (the American Automobile Association; © 800/222-4357), is the country's largest auto club and supplies its members with maps, insurance, and, most importantly, emergency road service. The cost of joining runs from C$83 to C$120 depending on packaged benefits, but if you're a member of a foreign auto club with reciprocal arrangements, you can enjoy free AAA service.

TO VANCOUVER ISLAND Hopping across the United States/Canadian border by car is easy, with the main crossing located right on the **I-5 at Peace Arch Park,** just north of **Blaine.** Once in Canada, drive to **Tsawwassen** to catch any number of ferries leaving for Vancouver, Nanaimo, and the Gulf Islands.

From the United States, daily ferry services link Port Angeles, Seattle, and Anacortes, Washington, with port facilities near Victoria. These include **Blackball Transport** (© 360/457-4491 in Washington, or 250/386-2202 on Vancouver Island; www.cohoferry.com), which runs a year-round, first-come, first-served car and passenger service aboard the MV *Coho* between Port Angeles and Victoria. One-way fares are US$50 for a standard-size vehicle and driver, US$13 for adult passengers, and US$7 for children. There are four 1¹/₂-hour daily crossings, from June to mid-September. There is one crossing daily from October to January, and two crossings daily from February to May.

Washington State Ferries (© 800/843-3779 in Washington, 888/808-7977 in Canada, or 206/464-6400; www.wsdot.wa.gov/ferries) runs a passenger and car ferry service from Anacortes, through the San Juan Islands, to Sidney, 26km (16 miles) north of Victoria, and returns. There are two crossings daily, and vehicle reservations are strongly recommended in summer. Reservations must be made by 5:30pm the day prior to travel. Year round, one-way fares are US$16 for adults, US$8 for seniors, US$13 for children 6 to 18, and US$54 for a standard-size vehicle and driver. Crossing time is 3 hours.

Alternatively, you can choose to cross the border just north of Blaine, and catch a **BC Ferries** vessel from Tsawwassen on the mainland to Swartz Bay, a 32km (20-mile) drive from Victoria's city center, or to Duke Point Terminal, near Nanaimo. Ferries leave every hour on the hour during the summer season, June through Labor Day, and on the odd hour for the rest of the year. Extra sailings are often added for holiday periods. Reservations are available, but not always necessary if you're traveling outside of the Friday escape/Sunday night return rush hour. One-way fares average C$13 for adults, C$6.50 children 5 to 11, and C$45 for a standard-size vehicle. BC seniors travel free Monday through Thursday, except on holidays. All BC Ferries have a restaurant and/or coffee bar on board, serving a wide range of soups, sandwiches, burger platters, salads, and snack food.

TO THE GULF ISLANDS BC Ferries (© 888/BCFERRY [223-3779] or 250/386-3431; www.bcferries.bc.ca) operates an extensive network of ferries to the Gulf Islands, linking the islands to one another, to the BC mainland, and to Vancouver Island. There are at least two crossings daily, year round, to each of the Gulf Islands, but departure times vary according to your destination. Ferry travel can be expensive if you're taking a vehicle, and long boarding waits are not uncommon. Ticket prices vary seasonally; midweek travel is slightly less than on weekends and holidays. During these peak periods, book at least 3 weeks in advance to avoid disappointment. Reservations can be made by phone or online. One-way fares from Tsawwassen average C$14 per passenger and C$52 for a standard-size vehicle. One-way fares from Swartz Bay average C$9 per passenger, C$32 for a standard-size regular vehicle. Return fares are less, and vary according to which island you are returning from. Return fares from the islands to Swartz Bay are free. Inter-island trips average C$5 per passenger, C$10 for a standard-size vehicle.

TO THE SAN JUAN ISLANDS From mid-May to September, **Clipper Vacations** (© 800/888-2535; www.victoriaclipper.com) runs one crossing daily from Seattle to Friday Harbor, on San Juan Island, aboard the **Victoria Clipper III** passenger-only ferry. Return fares are US$70 per adult. Children 1 to 11 years are free. The ferry departs Seattle at 7:45am, and returns at 7:15pm daily. Crossing time is 2¹/₂ hours. Reservations are recommended. **Washington State Ferries** (© 888/808-7977 or 206/464-6400;

www.wsdot.wa.gov/ferries) provides multiple crossings daily between Anacortes and each of the larger San Juan Islands. No reservations are available. If you're taking a vehicle, you should arrive at least an hour before scheduled sailings, up to 3 hours beforehand at peak travel times on summer and holiday weekends. Some food service and a picnic area are available near the terminal. Check out **www.ferrycam. net** to see live images of the ferry lanes. From May to mid-October, one-way fares are US$13 for adults, US$7.30 for seniors, US$12 for children 6 to 18, and US$56 for a standard-size vehicle and driver. Fares are lower in the off season. Inter-island travel is US$19 for a standard-size vehicle and driver; passengers and bicycles are free.

5 MONEY & COSTS

The Canadian dollar is stronger than it has been in many years, so you'll often find prices more or less at par between Canada and the United States.

CURRENCY

Canadian denominations are the same as in the United States: C$5, C$10, C$20, C$50, and C$100 (the last two are usually not welcome as payment for small purchases). Bills, however, come in different colors, which is why many Americans call them "Monopoly money"—rather a good-natured insult to Canadian ears. Although the U.S. still has the $1 bill, Canadians have long since replaced their paper dollar with a coin. It is nicknamed a "loonie" for the loon on one side, and the two-toned, two-dollar coin is commonly called a "toonie."

EXCHANGE RATES   In Canada, United States currency is accepted at most tourist-friendly shops and restaurants, but because exchange rates vary, you're better off changing your funds into Canadian currency.

Banks and other financial institutions offer a standard rate of exchange based on the daily world monetary rate. **Hotels** will gladly exchange your notes, but will usually give a slightly lower exchange rate. **Stores and restaurants** can set their own exchange percentages, so these are generally the lowest of all. Your best bet is to withdraw local funds from **bankATMs**—

they often provide the best rate of exchange. Your issuing company will automatically convert the transaction to your currency when you're billed.

In any transaction, always keep the rate of exchange in mind. The prices cited in this guide are given in either Canadian dollars (C$) or U.S. dollars (US$). At press time, the Canadian dollar was worth US$0.80, but because this rate may since changed significantly, it is best to check the most recent exchange rate yourself. *Note:* The "foreign-exchange bureaus" so common in Europe are rare even at airports in the United States and Canada, and nonexistent outside major cities. It's best not to change foreign money (or traveler's checks denominated in a currency other than U.S. dollars) at a small-town bank, or even a branch in a big city.

ATMS

The easiest and best way to get cash away from home is from an ATM (automated teller machine), sometimes referred to as a "cash machine," or a "cashpoint." The **Cirrus** (℃ **800/424-7787;** www.mastercard. com) and **PLUS** (℃ **800/843-7587;** www.visa.com) networks span the globe; look at the back of your bank card to see which network you're on, then call or check online for ATM locations at your destination. Be sure you know your personal identification number (PIN) and daily withdrawal limit before you depart.

Note: Remember that many banks impose a fee every time you use a card at another bank's ATM, and that fee can be higher for international transactions (up to C$5 or more) than for domestic ones (where they're rarely more than C$2). In addition, the bank from which you withdraw cash may charge its own fee. For international withdrawal fees, ask your bank.

Tip: Although ATMs are widespread on Vancouver Island, they are less prevalent on the Gulf and San Juan islands. Some of the Gulf Islands don't even have banks! If you plan to tour the Gulf and San Juan islands, be sure to travel with a **major credit card,** a **direct debit card,** or **traveler's checks,** and, of course, **cash.** Visa and MasterCard are accepted at most locations. Not as many businesses accept American Express.

TRAVELER'S CHECKS

Because most cities and towns have 24-hour ATMs, traveler's checks are not used as much as they once were. However, if you wish to carry larger denominations, banks, bigger stores, and hotels universally accept them. Cashing checks may sometimes incur a small fee, and you may be asked for photo ID to complete the transaction. Be sure checks are denominated in U.S. dollars, as foreign-currency checks are often difficult to exchange. The three traveler's checks that are most widely recognized—and least likely to be denied—are **Visa, American Express,** and **Thomas Cook.** Be sure to record the numbers of the checks, and keep that information in a separate place in case they get lost or stolen. Most businesses are pretty good about taking traveler's checks, but you're better off cashing them in at a bank (in small amounts, of course) and paying in cash. *Remember:* You'll need identification, such as a driver's license or passport, to change a traveler's check.

CREDIT CARDS

Credit cards are another safe way to carry money. They also provide a convenient record of all your expenses, and they generally offer relatively good exchange rates. You can withdraw cash advances from your credit cards at banks or ATMs, provided you know your PIN. Keep in mind that you'll pay interest from the moment of your withdrawal, even if you pay your monthly bills on time. Also, note that many banks now assess a 1% to 3% "transaction fee" on **all** charges you incur abroad (whether you're using the local currency or your native currency).

Canadian businesses honor the same credit cards as do those in the U.S. Visa and MasterCard are the most common, though American Express is also normally accepted in hotels and restaurants catering to tourists. Discover and Diner's Club cards are accepted less frequently.

6 HEALTH

STAYING HEALTHY

Victoria and most of the major towns in the region have hospitals, but some of the Gulf and San Juan islands only operate clinics. These are well equipped for most medical needs, but for life-threatening emergencies airlift services are used. More often than not, medical issues you'll encounter in this area are related to ailments such as allergies to bee stings, horsefly bites, and mosquitoes; sprained ankles and broken limbs from underestimating some of the hikes (and wearing improper footwear), and sunburns. Forewarned is forearmed—travel with appropriate repellents and gear that befits your itinerary.

WHAT TO DO IF YOU GET SICK AWAY FROM HOME

If you suffer from a chronic illness, consult your doctor before your departure. Pack **prescription medications** in your carry-on luggage, and carry them in their original containers, with pharmacy labels—otherwise they won't make it through airport security. Carry the generic name of prescription medicines, in case a local pharmacist is unfamiliar with the brand name. If you need the services of a hospital, these can be found in most of the major cities and towns. On the Gulf and San Juan islands, however, there are only medical clinics—walk-in appointments accepted. For life-threatening situations, airlift services are used.

Be aware, you may have to pay all medical costs up front and be reimbursed later. See "Medical Insurance," under "Insurance," in the "Fast Facts" appendix.

We list **additional emergency numbers** in the "Fast Facts" appendix, p. 264.

7 SAFETY

STAYING SAFE

Because these islands are more laid-back than many other travel destinations, they have a stronger sense of community that is safe and genuinely friendly. This is especially true of the Gulf and San Juan islands. That said, you should still use your common sense and discretion. Avoid hitchhiking; stow things in the trunk of your car, out of sight; hold on to your pocketbook when in a crowd; and keep expensive cameras or electronic equipment bagged up or covered when not in use. Vancouver Island, too, is regarded as pretty safe, including for women solo travelers, though you might find Victoria busy enough to attract pickpockets and petty thieves. Further north, however, the population thins, and some roads are fairly remote. Be sure that your gas tank is full, and take along water and a snack, because if you get into trouble help may take a few hours to arrive. For these reasons, travel with a companion or group. The northerly communities tend to be more conservative, too, so while gay and lesbian travelers are unlikely to experience discrimination, an overly affectionate display between couples may draw unwanted attention and derogatory comments.

8 SPECIALIZED TRAVEL RESOURCES

TRAVELERS WITH DISABILITIES

Most disabilities shouldn't stop anyone from traveling in the U.S. and Canada. Indeed, the law on both sides of the border requires that most public places comply with disability-friendly regulations. Almost all public establishments (including hotels, restaurants, museums, etc., but not including certain National Historic Landmarks) and at least some modes of public transportation provide accessible entrances and other facilities for those with disabilities. However, the nature of certain buildings and small-town layouts makes their compliance inconsistent, especially in the Gulf Islands and the San Juans. Except in towns like Ganges (on Salt Spring Island) and Friday Harbor (on San Juan Island), most streets are like country lanes. The charm or historical ambience of a building often means that access routes are difficult, which doesn't make for easy maneuverability. The **"British Columbia Accommodations**

Guide" details accessibility options at lodgings throughout Western Canada. Contact **Tourism British Columbia,** P.O. Box 9820, Station Prov. Govt., 1803 Douglas St., Victoria, BC VAW 9W5 (✆ **800/ HELLOBC** [435-5622]; www.hellobc. com). For accessibility advice in the San Juans, contact the San Juan Islands Visitor Information Services, P.O. Box 1330, Friday Harbor, San Juan Island, WA 98250 (✆ **888/468-3701** or 360/378-9551; www.visitsanjuans.com).

Many travel agencies offer customized tours and itineraries for travelers with disabilities. Among them are **Flying Wheels Travel** (✆ **507/451-5005;** www.flying wheelstravel.com); **Access-Able Travel Source** (✆ **303/232-2979;** www.access-able.com); and **Accessible Journeys** (✆ **800/846-4537** or 610/521-0339; www.disabilitytravel.com). **Avis Rent a Car** has an "Avis Access" program that offers such services as a dedicated 24-hour toll-free number (✆ **888/879-4273**) for customers with special travel needs; special car features such as swivel seats, spinner knobs, and hand controls; and accessible bus service.

Organizations that offer assistance to travelers with disabilities include **MossRehab** (✆ **215/663-6000** or 456-9900; www.mossresourcenet.org); the **American Foundation for the Blind** (AFB; ✆ **800/ 232-5463;** www.afb.org); and **SATH** (Society for Accessible Travel & Hospitality; ✆ **212/447-7284;** www.sath.org). **AirAmbulanceCard.com** is now partnered with SATH and allows you to preselect top-notch hospitals in case of an emergency.

The community website **iCan** (www. icanonline.net/channels/travel) has destination guides and several regular columns on accessible travel. Also check out the quarterly magazine *Emerging Horizons* (www.emerginghorizons.com), and *Open World* magazine, published by SATH. For more on organizations that offer resources

to travelers with disabilities, go to www. frommers.com/planning.

GAY & LESBIAN TRAVELERS

The larger cities in Western Canada are gay-tolerant, with a number of gay bars, gay-owned businesses, and after-hours clubs. In fact, same-sex union celebrations are one of Canada's hottest tourism products. In Victoria, Gay Pride stages an annual parade in early July, where transvestites and others really strut their stuff. The gay lifestyle is widely accepted throughout the islands, on either side of the border, although in some of the small, northernmost communities on Vancouver Island, discretion is advised. Public displays of affection will not be appreciated. Log into the chat channel at **www.gay victoria.ca** for updates on events and resources around the region.

The International Gay and Lesbian Travel Association (IGLTA) (✆ **800/448-8550** or 954/776-2626; www.iglta.org) is the trade association for the gay and lesbian travel industry and offers an online directory of gay- and lesbian-friendly travel businesses; go to their website and click "Members."

Many agencies offer tours and travel itineraries specifically for gay and lesbian travelers. Among them are **Above and Beyond Tours** (✆ **800/397-2681;** www. abovebeyondtours.com); **Now, Voyager** (✆ **800/255-6951;** www.nowvoyager. com); and **Olivia Cruises & Resorts** (✆ **800/631-6277;** www.olivia.com).

For more gay and lesbian travel resources visit www.frommers.com/planning.

SENIOR TRAVEL

Travelers 65 years of age and over often qualify for discounts at hotels and attractions, so don't be shy about asking. Just be sure to always carry some kind of ID—such as a driver's license—that shows your date of birth. In Victoria and Nanaimo,

PLANNING YOUR TRIP

3

SPECIALIZED TRAVEL RESOURCES

Frommers.com: The Complete Travel Resource

Planning a trip or just returned? Head to **Frommers.com,** voted Best Travel Site by *PC Magazine*. We think you'll find our site indispensable before, during, and after your travels—with expert advice and tips; independent reviews of hotels, restaurants, attractions, and preferred shopping and nightlife venues; vacation giveaways; and an online booking tool. We publish the complete contents of over 135 travel guides in our **Destinations** section, covering over 4,000 places worldwide. Each weekday, we publish original articles that report on **Deals and News** via our free **Frommers.com Newsletters.** What's more, **Arthur Frommer** himself blogs 5 days a week, with cutting opinions about the state of travel in the modern world. We're betting you'll find our **Events** listings an invaluable resource; it's an up-to-the-minute roster of what's happening in cities everywhere—including concerts, festivals, lectures, and more. We've also added weekly **podcasts, interactive maps,** and hundreds of new images across the site. Finally, don't forget to visit our **Message Boards,** where you can join in conversations with thousands of fellow Frommer's travelers and post your trip report once you return.

seniors receive **discounts on public transit.** Passes for persons over 65 (with proof of age) may be purchased at shops in Victoria that display a FareDealer sign (7-Eleven stores are a good bet, as are most newsstands). To locate a FareDealer vendor, contact **BC Transit,** 520 Gorge Rd., Victoria, BC V8W 2P3 (© **250/382-6161;** www.bctransit.com).

Members of AARP (601 E. St. NW, Washington, DC 20049 (© **800/424-3410** or 202/434-2277; www.aarp.org), can get discounts on hotels, airfares, and car rentals. Anyone over 50 can join; members receive a wide range of benefits including a monthly newsletter. The Canadian equivalent can be reached at www.carp.ca.

Many reliable agencies and organizations target the 50-plus market. **Elderhostel** (© **877/426-8056;** www.elderhostel.org) arranges study programs for those aged 55 and over. **ElderTreks** (© **800/741-7956;** www.eldertreks.com) offers small-group tours to off-the-beaten-path or adventure-travel locations, restricted to travelers 50 and older. **INTRAV/Only the Best Travel** (© **888/224-5685;** www.onlythebesttravel.com) is a high-end tour operator that caters to the mature, discerning traveler (not specifically seniors), with trips around the world that include guided safaris, polar expeditions, private-jet adventures, and small-boat cruises down jungle rivers.

Recommended publications offering travel resources and discounts for seniors include: the quarterly magazine *Travel 50 & Beyond* (www.travel50andbeyond.com); *Travel Unlimited: Uncommon Adventures for the Mature Traveler* (Avalon); *101 Tips for Mature Travelers,* available from Grand Circle Travel (© **800/221-2610** or 617/350-7500; www.gct.com); and *Unbelievably Good Deals and Great Adventures That You Absolutely Can't Get Unless You're Over 50* (McGraw-Hill), by Joann Rattner Heilman.

For more information and resources on travel for seniors, see www.frommers.com/planning.

FAMILY TRAVEL

Victoria is one of the most child-friendly, cosmopolitan cities on Vancouver Island, offering a great selection of family activities to enjoy. **Tourism Victoria** (812 Wharf St.; © **250/953-2033;** www.tourismvictoria. com) publishes a good guide for parents, called "Things to Do with Kids." Check out www.kidfriendly.org, too. It's a great site for child-friendly things to do in British Columbia, places to stay, and other ideas.

To locate accommodations, restaurants, and attractions that are particularly kid-friendly, refer to the "Kids" icon throughout this guide.

For a list of more family-friendly travel resources, visit www.frommers.com/planning.

WOMEN TRAVELERS

British Columbia and the entire Pacific Northwest are safe, polite, and a great place for female travelers. As with any destination, common sense should dissuade you from hitchhiking, or walking alone late at night in a city. Otherwise, traveling should be a delight. If you're heading off the beaten track and into the wilds, hike or camp with a friend. A number of Canadian outfitters offer women-only adventure tours.

Check out the award-winning website **Journeywoman** (www.journeywoman. com), a "real life" women's travel-information network where you can sign up for a free e-mail newsletter and get advice on everything from etiquette and dress to safety; or the travel guide *Safety and Security for Women Who Travel* by Sheila Swan and Peter Laufer (Travelers' Tales, Inc.), offering common-sense tips on safe travel.

For general travel resources for women, go to www.frommers.com/planning.

STUDENT TRAVEL

Check out the **International Student Travel Confederation (ISTC)** (www.istc.org) website for comprehensive travel-services information and details on how to get an **International Student Identity Card (ISIC),** which qualifies students for substantial savings on rail passes, plane tickets, entrance fees, and more. It also provides students with basic health and life insurance and a 24-hour helpline. The card is valid for a maximum of 18 months. You can apply for the card online or in person at **STA Travel** (© **800/781-4040** in North America; 132 782 in Australia; 871/2 300 040 in the U.K.; www.sta travel.com), the biggest student travel agency in the world; check out the website to locate STA Travel offices worldwide. If you're no longer a student but are still under 26, you can get an **International Youth Travel Card (IYTC)** from the same people, which entitles you to some discounts.

Travel CUTS (© **800/592-2887;** www.travelcuts.com) offers similar services for both Canadians and U.S. residents. **Council Travel Service** (© **800/226-8624;** www.counciltravel.com), which operates in Canada through **Travel Cuts,** is the biggest student travel agency operation in the world. It is a great resource for travel deals, as well as basic health and life insurance. It also has a **24-hour helpline.** Here's where to obtain a **student ID card** that will be your key to discounts on plane tickets, rail passes, and more. In Canada, you can find a Travel Cuts office at most university campuses across the country. They also have offices in Victoria, at 1312 Douglas St. (© **250/995-8556**) and Vancouver, at 567 Seymour St. (© **604/659-2830**). You can call them toll-free at © **800/667-2887,** or go online to **www.travel cuts.com**.

Irish students may prefer to turn to **USIT** (© **01/602-1904;** www.usit.ie), an Ireland-based specialist in student, youth, and independent travel.

TRAVELING WITH PETS

More and more hotels are becoming pet friendly, though usually at a surcharge of between C$20 and C$50 per night. The local tourism associations can provide you a list of pet-pleasing places; www.petscan-stay.com is another resource. Note that dogs, cats, and most other pets can travel with their owners between the United States and Canada provided you have proof of rabies vaccinations within the past 36 months. In Canada, contact the **Canadian Food Inspection Agency,** 59 Camelot Dr., Ottawa, ON K1A DY9

(*©* **800/OCANADA** [622-6232] or 613/ 225-2342; www.inspection.gc.ca). In the U.S., contact Centers for Disease Control & Prevention, Mail Stop C-14, 1600 Clifton Rd., Atlanta, GA 30333 (*©* **877/394-8747;** www.cdc.gov/ncidod/dq/animal/index.htm

For more resources about traveling with pets, go to www.frommers.com/planning.

9 SUSTAINABLE TOURISM

Sustainable tourism is conscientious travel. It means being careful with the environments you explore and respecting the communities you visit. Two overlapping components of sustainable travel are **ecotourism** and **ethical tourism.** The **International Ecotourism Society** (TIES) defines ecotourism as responsible travel to natural areas that conserves the environment and improves the well-being of local people. TIES suggests that ecotourists follow these principles:

- Minimize environmental impact.
- Build environmental and cultural awareness and respect.
- Provide positive experiences for both visitors and hosts.
- Provide direct financial benefits for conservation and for local people.
- Raise sensitivity to host countries' political, environmental, and social climates.
- Support international human rights and labor agreements.

You can find some eco-friendly travel tips and statistics, as well as touring companies and associations—listed by destination under "Travel Choice"—at the **TIES** website, www.ecotourism.org. Also check out **Ecotravel.com,** which lets you search for sustainable touring companies in

several categories (water-based, land-based, spiritually oriented, and so on).

While much of the focus of eco-tourism is about reducing impacts on the natural environment, ethical tourism concentrates on ways to preserve and enhance local economies and communities, regardless of location. You can embrace ethical tourism by staying at a locally owned hotel or shopping at a store that employs local workers and sells locally produced goods.

Responsible Travel (www.responsible travel.com) is a great source of sustainable travel ideas; the site is run by a spokesperson for ethical tourism in the travel industry. **Sustainable Travel International** (www. sustainabletravelinternational.org) promotes ethical tourism practices and manages an extensive directory of sustainable properties and tour operators around the world.

In the U.K., **Tourism Concern** (www. tourismconcern.org.uk) works to reduce social and environmental problems connected to tourism. The **Association of Independent Tour Operators (AITO)** (www.aito.co.uk) is a group of specialist operators leading the field in making holidays sustainable.

Volunteer travel has become increasingly popular among those who want to

It's Easy Being Green

The sustainable ethos is part of everyday life in this part of the world. Recycling practices have long been the norm, and pity the poor passerby who is seen to litter. LEED buildings (Leadership in Energy and Environmental Design) are front and center in every new development, and in terms of tourism, sustainability has become a product unto itself. Here are a few simple ways you can help conserve fuel and energy when you travel:

- Each time you take a flight or drive a car, greenhouse gases release into the atmosphere. You can help neutralize this danger to the planet through "carbon offsetting"—paying someone to invest your money in programs that reduce your greenhouse gas emissions by the same amount you've added. Before buying carbon offset credits, just make sure that you're using a reputable company, one with a proven program that invests in renewable energy. Reliable carbon offset companies include **Carbonfund** (www.carbonfund.org), **Terra-Pass** (www.terrapass.org), and **Carbon Neutral** (www.carbonneutral.org).

- Whenever possible, choose nonstop flights; they generally require less fuel than indirect flights that stop and take off again. Try to fly during the day—some scientists estimate that nighttime flights are twice as harmful to the environment. And pack light—each 15 pounds of luggage on a 5,000-mile flight adds up to 50 pounds of carbon dioxide emitted.

- Where you stay during your travels can have a major environmental impact. To determine the green credentials of a property, ask about trash disposal and recycling, water conservation, and energy use; also question if sustainable materials were used in the construction of the property. The website **www.greenhotels.com** recommends green-rated member hotels around the world that fulfill the company's stringent environmental requirements. Also consult **www.environmentallyfriendlyhotels.com** for more green accommodations ratings.

- At hotels, request that your sheets and towels not be changed daily. (Many hotels already have programs like this in place.) Turn off the lights and air-conditioner (or heater) when you leave your room.

- Use public transport where possible—trains, buses, and even taxis are more energy-efficient forms of transport than driving. Even better is to walk or cycle; you'll produce zero emissions and stay fit and healthy on your travels.

- If renting a car is necessary, ask the rental agent for a hybrid, or rent the most fuel-efficient car available. You'll use less gas and save money at the tank.

- Eat at locally owned and operated restaurants that use produce grown in the area. This contributes to the local economy and cuts down on greenhouse gas emissions by supporting restaurants where the food is not flown or trucked in across long distances. Visit **Sustain Lane** (www.sustainlane.org) to find sustainable eating and drinking choices around the U.S.; also check out **www.eatwellguide.org** for tips on eating sustainably in the U.S. and Canada.

venture beyond the standard group-tour experience to learn languages, interact with locals, and make a positive difference while on vacation. Volunteer travel usually doesn't require special skills—just a willingness to work hard—and programs vary in length from a few days to a number of weeks. Some programs provide free housing and food, but many require volunteers to pay for travel expenses, which can add up quickly.

For general info on volunteer travel, visit **www.volunteerabroad.org** and **www.idealist.org**. Before you commit to a volunteer program, it's important to make sure any money you're giving is truly going back to the local community, and that the work you'll be doing will be a good fit for you. **Volunteer International** (www.volunteerinternational.org) has a helpful list of questions to ask to determine the intentions and the nature of a volunteer program.

Animal-Rights Issues

Western Canada, specifically British Columbia, is the birthplace of consciousness-raising organizations such as Greenpeace, Westcoast Wilderness Society, and the David Suzuki Foundation. Residents throughout these islands are activists when it comes to saving whales and adopting orphaned sea lions and other wildlife. For example, when an anomalous pelican got swept off its migratory course a few years ago and landed on the chilly shores of the Pacific Northwest, legions of supporters raised funds to charter a special passage aboard an international carrier, returning it to Southern California before it froze to death.

For information on animal-friendly issues throughout the world, visit **Tread Lightly** (www.treadlightly.org). For information about the ethics of getting up close and personal with whales, visit the **Whale and Dolphin Conservation Society** (www.wdcs-na.org).

---

10 STAYING CONNECTED

TELEPHONES

Although the Canadian and U.S. phone systems are the same, the systems are run by private companies, so rates, especially for long-distance service and operator-assisted calls, can vary widely. Generally, hotel surcharges on long-distance and local calls are astronomical, so you're usually better off using a public pay telephone, which you'll find clearly marked in most public buildings and private establishments as well as on the street. Most public phones accept prepaid phone cards, sold at drugstores and convenience stores. Many public phones also accept American Express, MasterCard, and Visa credit cards. Numbers are made up of the 3-digit area code and the 7-digit local number.

On Vancouver Island and the Gulf Islands, this prefix is 250. For the San Juan Islands, the area code is 360. The long-distance prefix is 1. For directory assistance within Canada, dial © **411;** in the U.S., dial **1 + area code + 555-1212.**

CELLPHONES

The three letters that define much of the world's wireless capabilities are GSM (Global System for Mobiles), a big, seamless network that makes for easy cross-border cellphone use throughout Europe and dozens of other countries worldwide. In the U.S., T-Mobile, and AT&T Wireless use this quasi-universal system; in Canada, Microcell and some Rogers customers are GSM. If your cellphone is on a GSM system, and you have a world-capable multiband phone such as many Sony Ericsson, Motorola, or Samsung models, you can make and receive calls across civilized areas around much of the globe. Just call your wireless operator and ask for "international roaming" to be activated on your account. None of the islands mentioned in this book offer any cellphone rental services. *Note:* Other than in the major centers, cellphone signals may vary in strength in different areas of all these islands, ranging from nonexistent to mediocre.

Buying a phone can be economically attractive, as many nations have cheap prepaid phone systems. Once you arrive at your destination, stop by a local cellphone shop and get the cheapest package; you'll probably pay less than C$100 for a phone and a starter calling card. Local calls may be as low as 10¢ per minute, and in many countries incoming calls are free. Outlets include **Future Shop** (102-805 Cloverdale Ave., Victoria; ✆ 250/380-9338) and **Best Buy** (1710 Douglas St., Victoria; ✆ 250/386-5096).

Wilderness adventurers might consider renting a **satellite phone** ("satphone"). It's different from a cellphone in that it connects to satellites and works where there's no cellular signal or ground-based tower. You can rent satellite phones from Road-Post (www.roadpost.com). InTouch USA (www.intouchusa.com) offers a wider range of satphones but at higher rates. Per-minute call charges can be even cheaper than roaming charges with a regular cellphone, but the phone itself is more expensive.

VOICE-OVER INTERNET PROTOCOL (VOIP)

If you have Web access while traveling, consider a broadband-based telephone service (in technical terms, **Voice over Internet Protocol,** or **VoIP**) such as Skype (www.skype.com) or Vonage (www.vonage.com), which allow you to make free international calls from your laptop or in a

cybercafe. Neither service requires the people you're calling to also have that service (though there are fees if they do not). Check the websites for details.

INTERNET & E-MAIL
With Your Own Computer

More and more hotels, cafes, and retailers are signing on as Wi-Fi (wireless fidelity) "hotspots." Mac owners have their own networking technology: Apple AirPort. **T-Mobile Hotspot** (www.t-mobile.com/hotspot) serves up wireless connections at more than 1,000 Starbucks coffee shops nationwide. **Boingo** (www.boingo.com) and **Wayport** (www.wayport.com) have set up networks in airports and high-class hotel lobbies. IPass providers (see below) also give you access to a few hundred wireless hotel lobby setups. To locate other hotspots that provide **free wireless networks** in cities around the world, go to **www.personaltelco.net/index.cgi/Wireless Communities**.

For dial-up access, most business-class hotels throughout the world offer dataports for laptop modems, and a few thousand hotels in the U.S. and Europe now offer free high-speed Internet access. In addition, major Internet Service Providers (ISPs) have **local access numbers** around the world, allowing you to go online by placing a local call. The **iPass** network also has dial-up numbers around the world. You'll have to sign up with an iPass provider, who will then tell you how to set up your computer for your destination(s). For a list of iPass providers, go to www.ipass.com and click "Individuals Buy Now." One solid provider is **i2roam** (✆ 866/811-6209 or 920/235-0475; www.i2roam.com).

In Victoria, the larger hotels are likely to have Wi-Fi and bedroom dataports as well. This cannot be said for inns on the San Juan or Gulf islands. While services have now arrived in this part of the world, reception is sporadic and/or slow.

Wherever you go, bring a **connection kit** of the right power and phone adapters, a spare phone cord, and a spare ethernet network cable—or find out whether your hotel supplies them to guests.

Without Your Own Computer

Most major airports have **Internet kiosks** that provide basic Web access for a per-minute fee that's usually higher than cybercafe prices. Check out copy shops like **Kinko's** (FedEx Kinkos), which offers computer stations with fully loaded software (as well as Wi-Fi).

In Victoria, most hotels have wireless access either in the lobby or lounge. Don't expect to come across very many, if any, cybercafes. So, if living "wired" is essential, call ahead to check. To find public Wi-Fi hotspots, go to www.jiwire.com; for help locating cybercafes and other establishments where you can go for Internet access, check **www.cybercaptive.com**, **www.net cafeguide.com**, and **www.cybercafe.com**. Aside from formal cybercafes, most **youth hostels** and **public libraries** have Internet access. Avoid **hotel business centers** unless you're willing to pay exorbitant rates. Please see "Internet Access" in the **"Fast Facts"** appendix (p. 267).

---

11 TIPS ON ACCOMMODATIONS

Between the large hotels in Victoria, and the picturesque B&Bs and inns in the rest of the region, there really is something for everyone in terms of charm, character, and comfort. Other than in Victoria, you won't come across major chains. The inns and B&Bs on the islands have a special appeal because they're far from cookie-cutter guesthouses. Be aware, however, that accommodations tend to get a little more basic the farther north you travel. In Canada, a big deal is made about the term "Canada Select," which refers to a provincial rating program. If a place is part of the program, then you know to expect a level of cleanliness and service that won't disappoint. Hence, most don't advertise their rating until it reaches in excess of 2—the top being "we've got absolutely everything" 5 stars. That includes having a paved driveway, which some rural destinations have forgone for the sake of ambience, costing themselves half a star in the process.

SAVING ON YOUR HOTEL ROOM

The **rack rate** is the maximum rate that a hotel charges for a room. Hardly anybody pays this price, however, except in high season or on holidays. To lower the cost of your room:

- **Ask about special rates or other discounts.** You may qualify for corporate, student, military, senior, frequent flyer, trade union, or other discounts.
- **Dial direct.** When booking a room in a chain hotel, you'll often get a better deal by calling the individual hotel's reservation desk rather than the chain's main number.
- **Book online.** Many hotels offer Internet-only discounts, or supply rooms to Priceline, Hotwire, or Expedia at rates much lower than the ones you can get through the hotel itself.
- **Remember the law of supply and demand.** Resort hotels are most crowded and therefore most expensive

on weekends, so discounts are usually available for midweek stays. Business hotels in downtown locations are busiest during the week, so you can expect big discounts over the weekend. Many hotels have high-season and low-season prices, and booking even 1 day after high season ends can mean big discounts.

- **Look into group or long-stay discounts.** If you come as part of a large group, you should be able to negotiate a bargain rate. Likewise, if you're planning a long stay (at least 5 days), you might qualify for a discount. As a general rule, expect 1 night free after a 7-night stay.

- **Avoid excess charges and hidden costs.** When you book a room, ask whether the hotel charges for parking. Use your own cellphone, pay phones, or prepaid phone cards instead of dialing direct from hotel phones, which usually have exorbitant rates. And don't be tempted by the room's minibar offerings. Finally, ask about local taxes and service charges, which can increase the cost of a room by 15% or more.

- **Book an efficiency.** A room with a kitchenette allows you to shop for groceries and cook your own meals. This is a big money saver, especially for families on long stays.

- **Consider enrolling in hotel "frequent-stay" programs,** which are upping the ante lately to win the loyalty of repeat customers. Frequent guests can now accumulate points or credits to earn free hotel nights, airline miles, in-room amenities, merchandise, tickets to concerts and events, discounts on sporting facilities—and even credit toward stock in the participating hotel, in the case of the Jameson Inn hotel group. Perks are awarded not only by many chain hotels and motels (Hilton HHonors, Marriott Rewards, Wyndham ByRequest, to name a few), but individual inns and B&Bs. Many chain hotels partner with other hotel chains, car-rental firms, airlines, and credit card companies to give consumers additional incentive to do repeat business.

- **Check with the local island tourism offices for a lead.** Some island homes, usually the more modest ones, aren't advertised too far off-island. Once you're on one of the smaller islands, you're likely to come across cards posted on the bulletin board at the local hardware store advertising short-term and long-term lets.

For tips on surfing for hotel deals online, visit www.frommers.com/planning.

Suggested Itineraries

The coastal islands of the Pacific Northwest are almost as diverse as they are numerous, so explorations can be virtually custom-created according to mood and preference. City lovers can hover around Victoria; urban escapees will likely enjoy touring the San Juan and Gulf islands; while outdoor devotees should head for Vancouver Island's westernmost coast or to its most northern regions. The best thing about this part of the world, though, is that you can mix and match activities to get a little of everything.

1 THE REGIONS IN BRIEF

As the largest of all the islands along the Pacific Northwest coast, **Vancouver Island** offers both urban sophistication and wilderness adventure; it can be as cosmopolitan or extreme as you want.

Victoria, the provincial capital of British Columbia, lies on the southern tip of Vancouver Island, not far from the international boundary. In fact, the U.S. border scoops below the 49th parallel, keeping the island—in its entirety—in Canada. With an ambience that's more English than England ever was, Victoria's beautifully preserved turn-of-the-20th-century buildings dominate its harbor. The city's picturesque charm draws visitors in droves, especially in summer. Shopping, dining, and urban attractions, such as the **Royal BC Museum,** make the city a first-class family destination. From Victoria, there are a number of pleasant day and half-day trips around the southern part of Vancouver Island, including to the famed **Butchart Gardens.** It is also an ideal starting point for exploring farther afield.

As you travel north, the rest of Vancouver Island ranges from rural to wild, and nowhere is this better seen than in the central part of the island. Holiday resorts line the east coast overlooking the protected Georgia Strait, while the open Pacific Ocean pounds against Canada's wildest and most westerly coast. This is where to find the unpredictable **West Coast Trail,** the awe-inspiring **Pacific Rim National Park,** and some of the untouched wilderness areas of **Clayoquot Sound.** Much of the island is home to dozens of First Nations Canadian bands; throughout your travels there'll be opportunities to shop for Native arts and to experience the many different cultures.

At **Port Hardy,** Vancouver Island's most remote and northerly community, you can board a BC Ferries vessel and take a 15-hour trip through the famed **Inside Passage** to Prince Rupert, a port town on the mainland just shy of the Alaska Panhandle. A cruise aboard BC Ferries doesn't compare with the luxurious cruise ships that ply these waters, but you'll save yourself thousands of dollars and still travel through the same spectacular scenery.

The **Gulf Islands** and the **San Juan Islands** are actually a part of the same archipelago, yet, surprisingly, each group of islands has its individual appeal. While all are rural in character, each one offers a slightly different experience. For example, Galiano and Gabiola islands feel as if they're still hanging out in the '60s; Saturna Island is like a rainforest retreat; and in summer, Hornby and Denman islands are a bit like holiday camps, as holiday-makers and day-trippers throng to these sun-drenched havens. The two most sophisticated islands are San Juan—it has a "real" town with a decent range of services save for big box stores—and Salt Spring Island, which is by far the most arts-oriented of all the islands (although Orcas Island gives it a run for its money).

That said, all the islands are very rural. Many of the smaller ones are limited in the number of services they can provide (i.e., don't expect bank machines, let alone banks). The one thing they do share is a milder climate than the rest of BC or Washington State, in large part because they are protected by the coastal mountains, which means more sunshine and less rain than even Vancouver Island.

2 THE SAN JUAN SHUFFLE

Whether you arrive by ferry from Sidney or Anacortes, this short getaway feels like a world away, which is, of course, the islands' main attraction. This itinerary is for a low-key, modestly paced, get-away-from-it-all vacation. Island hopping gives you a real feel for the Pacific Northwest—chances are you'll see whales en route, and it is certainly the only way to appreciate the bucolic diversity of each island, whether it's history-laden San Juan Island, the evolving gentrification of Orcas Island, or the wilder isolation of the smaller isles. If you head for San Juan Island from Anacortes, you can work your way back through the other islands with free inter-island ferry trips. Traveling to/from Sidney on Vancouver Island means you can spend extra days in and around Victoria.

Day ❶: San Juan Island

After stopping off at **Friday Harbor** (p. 246) to see the sights and shops, take the perimeter road south to **American Camp** (p. 247). It's a long stretch of road (watch out for cyclists) with expansive views. On your return, take a slight detour to the **Pelindaba Lavender Farm** (p. 250) before heading along the westerly coast road to **English Camp** (p. 248). Farther along the road, you'll come to the new **Westcott Bay Sculpture Park** (p. 249). From there you can either walk or drive down to **Roche Harbor** (p. 248)—a good stop for the evening.

Day ❷: Orcas Island

Hop onto an early morning inter-island ferry and 35 minutes later you'll arrive at Orcas Island. Local traffic tends to head straight up the main road to Eastsound, but as visitors, choose to make the pictur-esque, winding drive west to **Deer Harbor** (p. 256) to get a sense of how pretty parts of this island can be. Then head north to **Eastsound** (p. 254), where you can browse specialty shops and enjoy lunch. Exploring the eastern arm of Orcas Island, including **Moran State Park** and **Olga Artworks** (p. 256), will take the better part of your afternoon.

Day ❸: Shaw Island/Lopez Island

Shaw Island (p. 259) is a pleasant morning detour en route to Lopez Island, although you'll need to coordinate your day carefully around sailing times. Once on Lopez, there's little left to do but kick back and relax. Enjoy the bucolic atmo-sphere and go on rambles along the bluff at **Iceberg Point** (p. 262) and around **Spencer Spit State Park** (p. 260).

Day ❹: Return Options

Take the return ferry to Anacortes, or plan to sail to Sidney to continue your adven-ture on Vancouver Island.

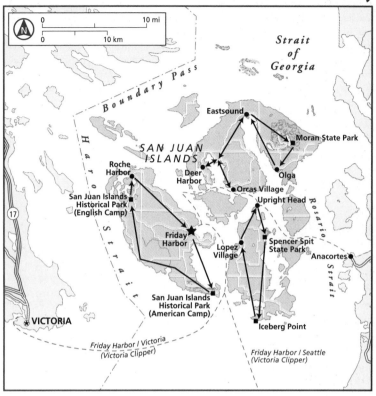

3 GULF ISLANDS GETAWAY IN 1 WEEK

Island hopping around the Southern Gulf Islands will treat you to scenery that's breathtakingly beautiful: dense rainforest, wild shorelines, pretty coves, and pastoral landscapes. Every island has a distinct charm. Just be sure to bring along a book or crossword puzzle to help wile away the inevitable hours you may have to linger waiting for your ferry to come in! Ferry connections aren't always back to back, and ferries can run later than scheduled. This itinerary assumes you're starting from Vancouver. Reverse it for Victoria departures.

Day ❶: Galiano

Although Galiano is the closest island from Vancouver, it's a laid-back community that's worked hard to maintain its rural roots. The road that runs the length of the island's long, skinny shape takes you from a cluster of buildings near the ferry terminal, past pretty coves and marinas, and up to densely packed forests. There are wonderful walks in and around **Galiano Bluffs Park** and **Montague Provincial Park.** Head north to experience the island's "wild" side in and around **Dionisio Point Provincial Park.** Kayaking out of **Montague Harbour** (p. 228) is another great way to fully appreciate the gentleness of this island.

Day ❷: Mayne Island

The small village area around **Miners Bay** (p. 234) boasts a bakery, a few worthwhile eateries and country inns, and sandy beaches. Of all the islands, this one is where you'll find the most accessible history: visit the tiny church, **St. Mary Magdalene** (p. 234); **Active Pass Lighthouse** (p. 234); **Mayne Island Museum**, which is housed in a historic jail; and the **Agricultural Hall** (p. 234), where you can still see island amateur thespians strut their stuff across the stage. The much newer Community Centre is quickly gaining status as *the* gathering spot for local dances, Saturday-night bingo, and second-run movies, for those seeking true local flavor.

Day ❸: The Penders

The marinas and coves here make the Penders a favorite destination for sailors, and with a permanent population base of approximately 2,000, these hilly islands have lots for you to see and do. **Beaumont Marine Provincial Park** (p. 225) is one of the prettiest destinations for hiking. It's also ideal for a picnic—be sure to pick up a bottle of wine from **Morning Bay Vineyard** (p. 224). If you're interested in **kayaking** (p. 224), it's especially easy to reach neighboring Saturna and Mayne islands from here. **Poets Cove** (p. 226) is one of the best destination resorts in the Gulf Islands archipelago.

Day ❹: Saturna

You can tour around Saturna in less than a day; but staying longer means you have time to really appreciate the remote tranquility of this rainforested island. **East Point Regional Park** (p. 239) is a beautiful spot to picnic; en route, be sure to pick up some wine at the **Saturna Island Vineyards** (p. 238).

Days ❺ & ❻: Salt Spring

As the largest and most commercial of all the Southern Gulf Islands, Salt Spring's proximity to Victoria makes it a popular weekend escape. Although developers are catching the wave of recreational property seekers, they haven't yet affected the pastoral and artsy charm of Salt Spring. The **shops, galleries,** and **pubs** in Ganges (p. 216) alone will take at least a half-day to explore (longer if it's **market day** [p. 216]). Take the second day to tour the island's art studios, galleries, farms, and parks (**Ruckle Provincial Park** being the prettiest).

Day ❼: Victoria/the Inner Harbour

Park the car and enjoy the more refined atmosphere of Victoria's Inner Harbour. Here's where you'll find the **Provincial Legislature** (p. 88) and the ivy-clad **Fairmont Empress** (p. 69), both landmark buildings that, not surprisingly, conjure up the era of the city's Victorian namesake. Fun attractions, particularly if you're traveling with children, include **Miniature World** (p. 87), **Pacific Undersea Gardens** (p. 87), and the terrific-at-any-age **Royal BC Museum** (p. 88). When your feet have had enough, hop into a **horse-drawn carriage** (p. 93) for a trip through **Beacon Hill Park** (p. 90), or simply take a **Kabuki Cab** to **Fisherman's Wharf** (p. 91) for a meal of chips and just-caught fish, served in newspaper with salt and traditional malt vinegar.

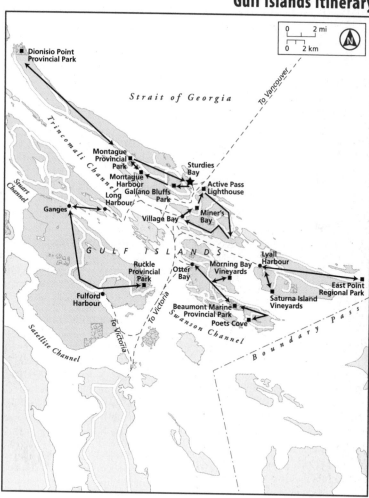

4 THE WILD WEST COAST IN 1 WEEK

To follow this itinerary, you'll need a car; it's the only way to experience the full diversity of what Vancouver Island has to offer. Your trip starts in Victoria with the option to stay in the urban center or venture into the surrounding countryside. Think of it as a teaser of what's to come on the wild west coast, where nature still has the upper hand. The changes in countryside during the drive from Victoria to Tofino, over mountains, through orchards, by seashores, and past fast-moving rivers, are mesmerizing.

Day ❶: Victoria

If you've already enjoyed Victoria's main attractions (described in day 7 of the previous itinerary), explore some of those attractions outside of the Inner Harbour, such as **Craigdarroch Castle** (p. 86), and **Butchart Gardens** (p. 108). If you've been to Victoria before, try going farther afield: Count eagles at **Goldstream Provincial Park** (p. 115), cycle the **Galloping Goose Trail** (p. 90), or make a day trip of hiking and tide-pool exploring along the **Juan de Fuca Trail** (p. 115) to **Botanical Beach** (p. 118). The latter two suggestions are great family excursions.

Day ❷: Cowichan Valley/Duncan

The drive north from Victoria takes you over the vista-filled Malahat before descending into the Cowichan Valley, one of Canada's fastest growing agri-tourism regions. Take your time exploring the back roads and you'll be rewarded with a range of small, quality **wineries** (p. 124), orchards, specialty farms, and dairies. You get a good impression of the island's Native culture in Duncan with its host of totem poles. Nearby Cowichan is home of the must-see **Quw'utsun Cultural Centre** (p. 124), which illustrates the story of the Cowichan people, the original inhabitants of the valley.

Days ❸ & ❹: Tofino/Long Beach

From Duncan, continue north to Parksville and the junction with Hwy. 4, the start of the beautiful, windy, and mountainous drive west. Allow 3 hours to cross the island—longer if you stretch your legs in kitschy **Coombs** (p. 153) or **Cathedral Grove** (p. 154), through which you'll pass. Rain or shine, Tofino and the Long Beach section of the **Pacific Rim National Park**

(p. 164) make the journey worthwhile. Hiking through these rainforests is stunning. Many trails are easy walks; some are strenuous hikes. Whale-watching, surfing, and wildlife-viewing are first rate; and sea-kayaking around the usually calm waters of **Clayoquot Sound** (p. 160) is easy and rewarding.

Day ❺: Ucluelet/Broken Group Island

Located within a 20-minute drive south of Tofino, Ucluelet is less touristy, some might even say a little rougher. It is home base to the impressive **Wild Pacific Trail** (p. 161) with easy-to-navigate **boardwalks** through forested terrain and solidly packed pathways that follow the coast. Ucluelet is nearest to the **Broken Group Islands** (p. 164), and you'll find several boat charters and kayaking outfitters in the marina that run tours across the Pacific Ocean swells directly into this oasis of exceptionally calm waters.

Day ❻: Qualicum/Parksville

Surrounded by six major **golf courses** (p. 148), all within a few minutes' drive of one another, this is tee-off central. For those not fond of the links, there's **Rathtrevor Beach** (p. 147), where you can beachcomb for sand dollars, or take time out to relax in British Columbia's largest spa at **Tigh-Na-Mara Resort** (p. 151).

Day ❼: Return to Victoria

The drive back to Victoria is a chance to catch some of the attractions you missed on the way up. And if the week's adventuring has worked up an appetite, book a table at **The Aerie** (p. 128) atop the Malahat. Savor the immaculately prepared food and your memories of your week exploring Vancouver Island's wild west coast.

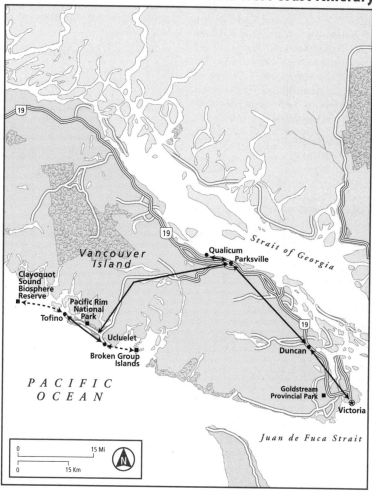

5 AN ADVENTURE TRAVEL WEEK

If you start your itinerary in Nanaimo, all sorts of extreme (and soft) adventure options present themselves beyond what you find in Victoria's environs. This adventure itinerary is geared to take in the best eco-activity in the different regions while showcasing the wild side of Vancouver Island.

Day ❶: Spelunking and Rappelling

From Nanaimo, take Hwy. 19 north to Parksville and Qualicum Beach, keeping your eyes open for the turnoff to **Horne Lake Caves Provincial Park** (p. 149). Pitch your tent here or in nearby Englishman's River and take the afternoon to explore the fossil-filled caverns at **Horne Lake Caves** (p. 149). Tours range from family excursions to extreme adventures.

Day ❷: Hiking and Mountaineering

Continue north and just before Campbell River, take the turnoff to **Strathcona Provincial Park.** Strathcona was British Columbia's first provincial park and it includes Elkhorn Mountain, Golden Hinde, and trail access to Mount Washington (p. 179). Whether you're a neophyte or an experienced adventurer, you'll find plenty of challenges, from rock climbing to wilderness hikes through meadow-filled mountain back-country.

Day ❸: Fishing

Campbell River is nicknamed the Salmon Capital of the World and is where eco-activist and fishing expert Roderick Haig Brown cast his rod. Fishing diehards may want to go for the great Tyee—a Chinook salmon in excess of 14 kilograms (31 lb.) (p. 187) or follow in Haig Brown's footsteps to fly-fish the fast-moving waters of Campbell River.

Day ❹: Sea-Kayaking in Whale Waters

The road north leads up **Telegraph Cove** (p. 201), one of the remaining communities built on stilts over the water. Spend the afternoon sea-kayaking near **Robson Bight** (p. 203), a unique ecological reserve for whales; sightings are almost guaranteed.

Days ❺ & ❻: Extreme Hiking

Cape Scott Provincial Park (p. 208) lies at the end of the road, literally. Its extreme wilderness takes you from relatively easy trails through always damp rainforest to much harder muddy bogs, craggy shorelines, and naturally wild beaches. You need to be self-sufficient to make it through to the very tip of Vancouver Island, and have a plan to keep at least one pair of socks dry.

Day ❼: Return to Nanaimo

Allow 6 hours for the drive back from Cape Scott to Nanaimo; the distance is approximately 450km (280 miles).

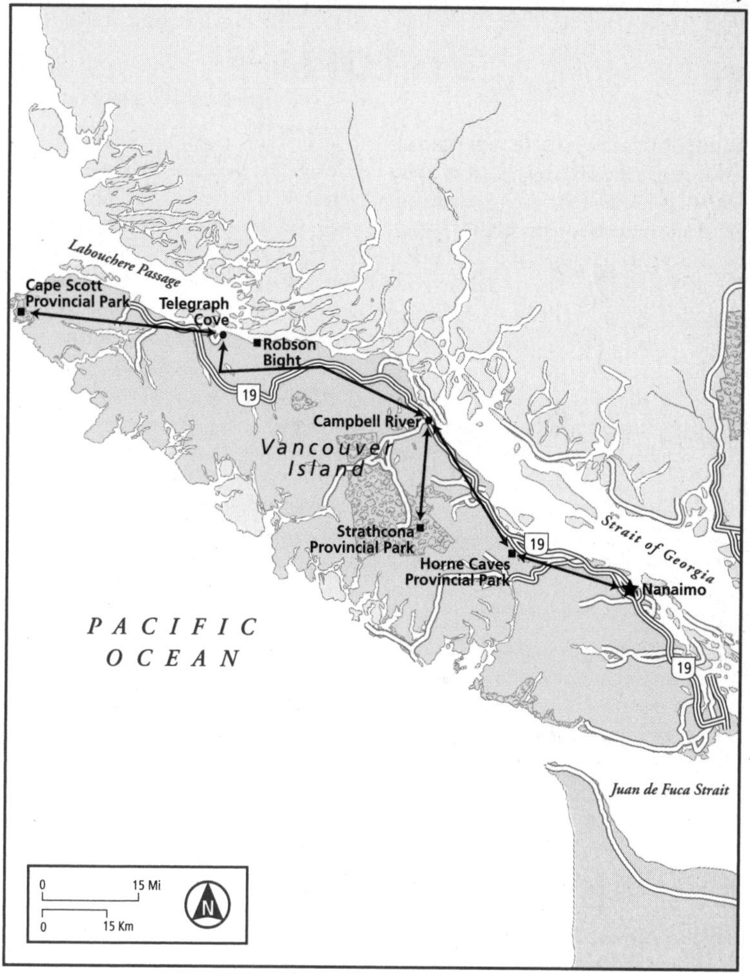
Labouchere Passage
Cape Scott Provincial Park
Telegraph Cove
Robson Bight
19
Campbell River
Vancouver Island
Strathcona Provincial Park
Horne Caves Provincial Park
Strait of Georgia
Nanaimo
PACIFIC OCEAN
Juan de Fuca Strait
0
15 Mi
0
15 Km
N

Victoria

Whoever said Victoria was for the newly wed and nearly dead needs to take a second look. Although it certainly has its fair share of the blue-rinse brigade, Victoria is a romantic place, and in the past decade has evolved into a thriving city. Described by painter Emily Carr as "more English than England," Victoria's charm is moving beyond its quaint facade. Sure, there are still plenty of double-decker buses, heritage brick buildings covered with clambering vines, English-style taverns, and ever-blooming gardens, but there's also a definite zip in the air as the city's staid and sedentary pleasures give way to hipper places to shop and dine and more active pursuits to enjoy. In fact, Victoria is now nicknamed the "recreational capital" of British Columbia, and its range of activities reads like an exhaustive shopping list: year-round golf, whale-watching, fishing, cycling, and much more. Victoria is located around one of Canada's prettiest harbors, and the water is always busy with seaplanes, ships, and kayaks. Accommodations are first-class, many attractions are worthy of a repeat visit, shopping is varied, and restaurants are cosmopolitan and always busy. The flip side of Victoria's growth, and its balmier climate, is a marked increase in panhandlers. There are government promises to remedy the situation before the 2010 Winter Olympics.

You'll want to spend at least two days here, just to get a taste of what Victoria is becoming. It's also the ideal base from which to explore the rest of Vancouver Island. Extending more than 450km (280 miles) from Victoria to the northwest tip of Cape Scott, the island offers some of the most dramatic stretches of coastal wilderness in the Pacific Northwest. (See chapters 6, 7, and 8 for coverage of the rest of Vancouver Island.)

1 ESSENTIALS

GETTING THERE

BY PLANE Most visitors arrive via a connecting flight from either **Vancouver International Airport** (© 604/207-7077; www.yvr.ca), or **Seatac International Airport** in Seattle (© 206/433-5388; www.portseattle.org). Airlines flying into the rapidly expanding **Victoria International Airport** (© 250/953-7500; www.victoriaairport.com) include **Air Canada** (© 888/247-2262; www.aircanada.ca), **Horizon Air** (© 800/547-9308; www.alaskaair.com), and **WestJet** (© 888/937-8538; www.westjet.com). The Victoria International Airport is near the BC Ferries terminal in Sidney, 26km (16 miles) north of Victoria off Hwy. 17. Hwy. 17 heads south to Victoria, becoming Douglas Street as you enter downtown.

Airport bus service, operated by **AKAL Airport** (© 877/386-2525 or 250/386-2526; www.victoriaairporter.com or www.victoriaairportshuttle.com), takes about 45 minutes to get into town. Buses leave from the airport daily, every 30 minutes from 4:30am to midnight. The adult fare is C$15 one-way. Dropoffs and pickups are made at most Victoria area hotels. **Yellow Cabs** (© 800/808-6881 or 250/381-2222), and **Blue Bird**

Cabs (© 800/665-7055 or 250/382-4235) make airport runs. It costs about C$50 one way, plus tip.

Several car-rental firms have desks at the Victoria International Airport, including **Avis** (© **800/879-2847** or 250/656-6033; www.avis.com), **Budget** (© **800/668-9833** or 250/953-5300; www.budgetvictoria.com), **Hertz** (© **800/654-3131** or 250/656-2312; www.hertz.com), and **National (Tilden)** (© **800/227-7368** or 250/656-2541; www.nationalcar.com). Car reservations are recommended from June to September and during peak travel times on holiday weekends.

BY TRAIN   **VIA Rail** trains arrive at Victoria's **VIA Rail Station,** 450 Pandora Ave., near the Johnson Street Bridge (© 888/842-7245; www.viarail.com).

BY BUS   The **Victoria Bus Depot** is at 700 Douglas St. (behind the Fairmont Empress Hotel). **Pacific Coach Lines** (© **800/661-1725** within North America or 250/385-4411 in Victoria; www.pacificcoach.com) offers daily service to and from Vancouver, and it includes the ferry trip across the Georgia Strait between Tsawwassen and Sidney. **Greyhound Coach Lines/Island Coach Lines** (© **800/661-8747** or 250/385-4411; www.greyhound.ca) provides daily service up island to Nanaimo, Port Alberni, Campbell River, and Port Hardy.

BY FERRY   **BC Ferries** offers crossings from the mainland to various points on Vancouver Island (© **888/BCFERRY** [223-3779] in BC outside the Victoria dialing area, or 250/386-3431; www.bcferries.com). For more information, see "Getting There" in chapter 3.

VISITOR INFORMATION

The **Tourism Victoria Visitor Information Centre,** 812 Wharf St., Victoria, BC V8W 1T3 (© **250/953-2033;** www.tourismvictoria. com) is an excellent resource for brochures, ideas for itineraries, and maps. Tourism Victoria also operates a **reservations hotline** (© **800/663-3883** or 250/953-2022) for last-minute bookings at hotels, inns, and B&Bs. The center is open September through April daily from 9am to 5pm, May and June daily from 8:30am to 6:30pm, and July and August daily from 9am to 9pm. Bus no. 1, 27, or 28 to Douglas and Courtney streets.

CITY LAYOUT

Victoria was settled around the Inner Harbour in the mid-1800s and grew out from there. Because of the *curvy* shoreline, the grid system of streets doesn't kick in immediately, but there are three main **north–south arteries** that will get you almost anywhere you may want to reach in Victoria.

Government Street leads from the Inner Harbour to downtown (Wharf St. merges with Government St. in front of the hotel); **Douglas Street** runs behind the Fairmont Empress, parallel to Government Street. It is the city's main business thoroughfare as well as the highway north to Nanaimo and beyond. It's also the Trans-Canada, Hwy. 1—Mile Zero is at the corner of Douglas Street and Dallas Road. **Blanshard Street,** which runs parallel to Government and Douglas streets, becomes Hwy. 17, the route to the Saanich Peninsula including the Butchart Gardens and the ferry terminals to Vancouver and the San Juan Islands.

Three major east–west streets of note are **Johnson Street,** in Old Town/Downtown—the Johnson Street Bridge divides the Upper Harbour and the Inner Harbour. **Belleville Street** runs in front of the Parliament Buildings, along the Inner Harbour's southern edge up to Fisherman's Wharf. It then loops around to become **Dallas Road,** which follows the water's edge towards Oak Bay.

When you're looking for an address, be aware that the suite number precedes the building number which generally speaking, go up in increments of 100 per block as you travel north and east. Addresses for all east–west downtown streets (Fort, Yates, Johnson, and so on) start at 500 at Wharf Street. This means all buildings between Wharf and Government streets fall between 500 and 599; the next block, between Government and Douglas streets, are numbers 600 through 699, and so on. Detailed maps of downtown and farther afield are available for free at the Tourism Victoria Visitor Info Centre. Invariably, hotels have maps they will mark up with a highlighter pen, showing you the quickest, easiest, and most interesting routes.

VICTORIA'S NEIGHBORHOODS IN BRIEF

Victoria central is so compact that it's hard to draw definitive lines dividing the three major neighborhoods. Suffice to say that the nearer you are to the water, the more expensive the hotel room, so unless you're absolutely hooked on having a view, save yourself a few dollars by heading a block or two inland.

INNER HARBOR

For most visitors, this is where it's at, and it's what those glossy tourism brochures depict in their Victoria sell. Framed by the Parliament Buildings on one side and the Fairmont Empress on another, the Inner Harbor is where to find cabs, horse-drawn carriage rides, double-decker tour buses, ferries, floatplanes, whale-watching outfitters, and a host of other tourist services. Attractions such as the **BC Royal Museum** and **Undersea Gardens** are here, alongside some of the city's most expensive hotels. There's an easy waterside stroll that takes you around the harbor perimeter; in summer it fills up with artist-vendors selling photographs, Native carvings, and inexpensive jewelry. It's touristy and expensive, but also picturesque.

DOWNTOWN & OLD TOWN

Head away from the water, and within 2 to 3 blocks you're in Victoria's social and commercial centers. Because the two neighborhoods blend together, Victorians usually refer to them together. **Old Town** tends to include Bastion and Market Squares—the areas that grew up around the original Fort Victoria at View and Government streets. **Downtown** tends to include everything east of Wharf Street, and is where you'll find the bulk of the city's shopping, banking, restaurants, bars, and hotels. Staying here may save you a few dollars, but it can be noisy, especially when the pubs and nightclubs let out.

CHINATOWN

The size of this area belies its history. Although only 2 square blocks, Victoria's Chinatown is the oldest in North America. The historic alleyways and buildings make for an intriguing visit, especially **Fan Tan Alley,** Canada's narrowest commercial street. Just over a meter ($3^1/_4$ ft.) wide, this narrow alleyway cuts a divide between brick buildings that once housed gambling joints and opium dens, but has given way to curiosity and souvenir shops.

JAMES BAY, OAK BAY, ROSS BAY, ROCKLAND & BEAR MOUNTAIN

Largely residential, these peaceful and postcard-pretty neighborhoods boast some large turn-of-the-20th-century manor homes and gardens—some are distinctive B&Bs—as well as newer homes. Oak Bay in particular has retained a quintessential, quieter English ambience and offers excellent beaches, golf courses, and tea houses. Although away from Victoria central, the property taxes are hefty enough here to warrant higher-than-expected room rates. Bear Mountain is a still-developing neighborhood that has turned a rural mountain into a resort hamlet much akin to Whistler in style and setting. Its central focus is year-round golf, which is attracting a mix of investment rental-pool condos; golf-keener retirees; and, at the base of the development, young families. All these neighborhoods are easiest to reach by car.

2 GETTING AROUND

BY PUBLIC TRANSPORTATION

The **Victoria Regional Transit System** (BC Transit) (⊘ **250/382-6161;** www.bctransit. com) operates approximately 40 bus routes throughout **Greater Victoria** and the outer suburbs of **Sooke** and **Sidney.** Regular service on the main routes runs Monday to Friday from 6am to midnight. Call for schedules on the weekends. Consult the **"Victoria Rider's Guide"** for schedules and routes, available at the **Tourism Victoria Visitor Information Centre** (see "Visitor Information," above). The guide outlines transit routes for many of the city's neighborhoods, landmarks, and attractions. Popular routes include no. 2 (Oak Bay), no. 11 (Downtown, James Bay, Beacon Hill Park), no. 14 (Craigflower, University of Victoria), no. 23 (Art Gallery of Victoria), no. 61 (Sooke), no. 70 (Sidney, Swartz Bay), and no. 75 (Butchart Gardens). This route includes a pickup at the Sidney ferry terminal and is handy for those arriving from the mainland without a vehicle.

Fares are no longer based on the number of geographic zones a passenger crosses; they are a flat fare to travel from Sidney to Sooke: C$2.25 for adults and C$1.40 for seniors and children to grade 7, but children 5 and under are free. Transfers are good for travel in one direction with no stopovers. A **DayPass,** which costs C$7 for adults, C$5 for seniors and children, is available at the Tourism Victoria Visitor Information Centre, at convenience stores, and at outlets displaying the FareDealer symbol. See chapter 3, "Specialized Travel Resources."

BY CAR

If you must bring your car (exploring downtown is really best done on foot), make sure your hotel has parking. Parking spaces around the city center are at a premium. (Hotels that have parking are included in "Where to Stay.") For out-of-town activities, car-rental agencies include **Avis,** at 1001 Douglas St. (⊘ **800/879-2847** or 250/386-8468; www.avis. com); **Budget,** at 757 Douglas St. (⊘ **800/268-8900** or 250/953-5300; www.budget victoria.com); **Hertz Canada,** at 2634 Douglas St. (⊘ **800/263-0600** or 250/385-4440; www.hertz.com); and **National (Tilden),** at 767 Douglas St. (⊘ **800/387-4747** or 250/386-1213; www.nationalcar.com). Renting a car costs approximately C$60 per day but may be less with various discounts.

BY TAXI

Yellow Cabs (⊘ **800/808-6881** or 250/381-2222) and **Blue Bird Cabs** (⊘ **800/655-7055** or 250/382-2222) are good bets. But do call ahead—very few stop for flag-downs,

VICTORIA

5

GETTING AROUND

GETTING AROUND VICTORIA

5

ACCOMMODATIONS ■
Abigail's Hotel **39**
Admiral Inn **49**
Andersen House B&B **55**
Beaconsfield Inn **40**
Bedford Regency Hotel **17**
Delta Victoria Ocean Pointe
  Resort & Spa **13**
Fairmont Empress **36**
The Gatsby Mansion **48**
Hatterleigh Heritage Inn **53**
Hotel Grand Pacific **46**
Inn at Laurel Point **50**
James Bay Inn **59**
Magnolia Hotel & Spa **32**
Oak Bay Guest House **28**
Ocean Island Backpackers Inn **21**
Oswego Hotel **57**
Prior House B&B Inn **30**
Queen Victoria Hotel **41**
Royal Scott Inn **47**
Spinnaker's Guest House **7**
Swans Hotel **10**
Victoria Marriott Hotel **38**
Villa Marco Polo **26**
Westin at Bear Mountain **4**

ATTRACTIONS ●
Abkhazi Garden **29**
All Fun Recreation Park **2**
Art Gallery of Greater Victoria **24**
Beacon Hill Children's Farm **60**
Centre of the Universe **3**
Craigdarroch Castle **25**
Finnerty Garden **6**
Hatley Park & Museum **1**
Maritime Museum of BC **16**
Miniature World **35**
Pacific Undersea Gardens **44**
Parliament Buildings **43**
Royal British Columbia Museum **42**
Royal London Wax Museum **45**
Victoria Bug Zoo **33**

RESTAURANTS ◆
Azuma Sushi **19**
Baan Thai **22**
Barb's Place **52**
Black Olive **20**
Blue Crab Bar & Grill **51**
Bon Rouge Bistro **34**
Café Brio **23**
Café Vieux Montreal **12**
Camille's **15**
Herald Street Caffe **8**
Il Terrazzo Ristorante **9**
James Bay Restaurant **58**
The Mark **46**
Niche Dining **54**
Pagliacci's **18**
Pescatore's **37**
Rebar **14**
Red Fish-Blue Fish **31**
Restaurant Matisse **11**
Santiago's **56**
Smoken Bones Cookshack **5**
Stage **27**

especially when it's raining. Rides around the downtown area average C$6 to C$8, plus a 10% to 15% tip.

BY FERRY

Once you're downtown, scooting across the harbor in one of the tiny, 12-passenger ferries operated by **Victoria Harbour Ferry** (ⓒ **250/708-0201;** www.victoriaharbourferry. com) is great fun—and expedient—in getting from one part of the city to another. The squat, cartoon-style boats have big wraparound windows that allow everyone a terrific view. Ferry connections to the Fairmont Empress, the Coast Harbourside Hotel, and the Delta Victoria Ocean Pointe Resort run May through October daily every 15 minutes from 9am to 9pm. From November to April, the ferries run only on sunny weekends from 11am to 5pm. When the weather is "iffy," call the ferry office to check whether the ferries are running that day. The cost per hop is C$4 for adults, C$2 for children. See "Organized Tours," later in this chapter, for other ways to enjoy a ferry ride.

(Fast Facts) Victoria

American Express There is no Victoria office. To report lost or stolen traveler's checks, call ⓒ **800/221-7282.**

Business Hours **Banks** in Victoria are open Monday to Thursday from 10am to 3pm, Friday from 10am to 6pm. **Stores** are open Monday to Saturday from 10am to 6pm. Many stores are also open on Sunday in summers. Last call at the city's bars and cocktail lounges is 2am.

Currency Exchange The best rates of exchange are at bank ATMs. Try the **Royal Bank,** 1079 Douglas St. (ⓒ **250/356-4500**), in the heart of downtown. **Calforex Foreign Currency Services** is open 7 days a week, 606 Humboldt St. (ⓒ **250/380-3711**). **Custom House Currency Exchange** (ⓒ **250/389-6007**), is also open daily, and has locations at 815 Wharf St. and the Bay Centre.

Dentists Most major hotels have a dentist on call. You can also visit the **Cresta Dental Centre,** 28–3170 Tillicum Rd., at Burnside Street, in Tillicum Mall. Open Monday to Friday from 8am to 9pm, Saturday from 9am to 5pm, and Sunday from 11am to 5pm. Call ahead for appointment: ⓒ **250/384-7711.**

Doctors Hotels usually have a doctor on call or are able to refer you to one. Clinics include the **Downtown Medical Clinic,** 622 Courtney St. (ⓒ **259/380-2210),** open Monday to Friday 8:30am to 5:30pm; and the **James Bay Treatment Centre,** 100–230 Menzies St., open Monday to Friday from 9am to 6pm, Saturday 10am to 4pm. Call for appointment: ⓒ **250/388-9934.**

Drugstores Pick up your allergy medication or refill your prescription at **Shoppers Drug Mart,** 1222 Douglas St. (ⓒ **250/381-4321**). Open Monday to Friday from 7am to 8pm, Saturday from 9am to 7pm, and Sunday from 9am to 6pm. **Rexall Drug Store,** 649 Fort St. (ⓒ **250/384-1195**), is open Monday to Saturday from 9am to 6pm, and Sunday and holidays from noon to 4pm.

Emergencies Dial ⓒ **911** for police, fire, ambulance, and poison control.

Hospitals Local hospitals include the **Royal Jubilee Hospital,** 1900 Fort St. (© **250/ 370-8000** or 250/370-8212 for emergencies); and **Victoria General Hospital,** 1 Hospital Way (© **250/727-4212** or 250/727-4181 for emergencies).

Hotlines Emergency numbers include **Royal Canadian Mounted Police** (© **250/ 380-6261**), **Crime Stoppers** (© **250/386-8477**), **Emotional Crisis Centre** (© **250/ 386-6323**), **Sexual Assault Centre** (© **250/383-3232**), and **Poison Control Centre** (© **800/567-8911**).

Internet Access Nearly all hotels have either Wi-Fi or high-speed access in a public lounge or in guest bedrooms The greater Victoria Public Library, 735 Broughton St. (© **250/382-7241**), has a dozen terminals and is open Monday, Wednesday, Friday, and Saturday 9am to 6pm, Tuesday and Thursday to 9pm. Or try James Bay Coffee & Books, 143 Menzies St. (© **250/386-4700**); it's just around the corner from the Parliament Buildings.

Newspapers The *Victoria Times-Colonist* comes out daily. The weekly entertainment paper, *Monday* magazine, comes out, curiously, on Thursday, and is widely distributed in grocery stores, information centers, and elsewhere.

Police Dial © **911** for emergencies. For non-emergencies, the **Victoria City Police** can be reached at © **250/995-7654.**

Post Office The main **Canada Post office** is at 714 Yates St. (© **250/953-1352**). The **Oak Bay post office** is at 1625 Fort St. (© **250/595-2552**). There are also postal outlets in **Shoppers Drug Mart** (see "Drugstores," above).

Safety Crime rates are quite low in Victoria, but transients panhandle throughout the downtown and Old Town areas. Lock items in the glove compartment or trunk when you park your car, and avoid dark alleys and uninhabited areas.

Weather For local weather updates, call © **250/363-6717** and follow the prompts. Or check www.theweathernetwork.com.

3 WHERE TO STAY

Victoria has a wide choice of fine accommodations, and all are in, or within walking distance of, the **Inner Harbour** and **downtown core.** These are the pricier neighborhoods, especially those in sight of the water in the height of summer. Generally speaking, the quality of both service and amenities is also high, or at least is priced accordingly. It's always worth asking about special rates and other discounts, and speaking with the hotel directly instead of a central reservations system (in the case of the big chains), since they're more apt to give you a preferred rate. Victoria relies heavily on visitors from the U.S. and does well to keep its tourist product fresh. Because the city's still small by international standards—it has just acquired its first purpose-built boutique hotel—hospitality still feels genuine. Like in many cities, though, parking is an issue, so if you can get free parking, grab it, or you'll find your reasonable room rate suddenly inflated by $10 or even $28 per night. Thankfully, this is a walking destination, so leave your car at home, even if you decide to stay in a neighboring neighborhood. Further afield in Sooke, Brentwood Bay, and on the Malahat, there are some truly spectacular options. (See chapter 6 for where to stay.)

Very Expensive

Delta Victoria Ocean Pointe Resort and Spa ★ Huge rooms, spacious bathrooms, and great bedding are all part of the relatively clutter-free decor, which highlights the gleaming woods and the soft, natural colors throughout. Located on the north side of the Inner Harbour, many of the guest rooms have floor-to-ceiling windows that view the Parliament Buildings and the Fairmont Empress; they're worth the extra dollars since back-of-house rooms look out onto an industrial landscape. And for still a few dollars more, you get Signature perks of breakfast, evening hors d'oeuvres, and turndown service. All rooms come with the usual toiletries, down duvets, and cuddly robes. The European-style spa rivals the Fairmont's Willow Stream for top spa billing, and is a destination in itself. The hotel's fitness facilities are also extensive; the large indoor pool alone is worth a visit. Surrounded by glass, you feel as if you're swimming outdoors. **Lure Seafood Restaurant and Bar** boasts the best dining-room views in the city, and quality dishes. It's an especially romantic spot when night falls, and you can savor the very pretty night lights of the city's harborfront.

45 Songhees Rd., Victoria, BC V9A 6T3. ℂ 800/667-4677 or 250/360-2999. Fax 250/360-1041. www.delta hotels.com. 250 units. Apr to mid-Oct C$169–C$419 double, C$439–C$799 suite; mid-Oct to Mar C$119–C$319 double, C$329–C$629 suite. Extra person C$30. Children 18 and under stay free in parent's room. AE, DC, DISC, MC, V. Valet parking C$15. Pets accepted (C$35). **Amenities:** Restaurant; ozonated indoor swimming pool; 2 night-lit outdoor tennis courts; 1 indoor racquetball and squash court; extensive health club & spa; children's programs; free shuttle to/from downtown; business center; 24-hr. room service; babysitting; laundry service; dry cleaning. *In room:* A/C, TV, dataport, minibar, coffeemaker, hair dryer, iron.

Fairmont Empress ★★ It's an ivy-adorned iconic harborside landmark, and staying here is the quintessential Victoria experience. Although ongoing renovations maintain the old girl's elegance, the Fairmont folks couldn't make many of the 1908-era rooms any larger, so this still means small rooms (billed as "cozy"), narrow corridors, and a disparity of views that might just as easily include the unsightly rooftops of the hotel's working areas as the harbor. If you're slightly claustrophobic, don't even think about these. They're a lot of money for what you get, too. That said, the deluxe guest rooms, studio-, one- and two-bedroom suites, and all of the Fairmont Gold guest rooms are superb: All have extra-large beds and windows that let the light pour in. Fairmont Gold rooms also have extras such as TVs in the bathrooms and CD players, and guests have private check-in, their own concierge, and a private lounge that has an honor bar, complimentary hors d'oeuvres (sometimes enough for a light supper), and breakfast. The Willow Stream Spa is one of the, if not the, city's finest spa retreats, and some of the services are priced accordingly. Dining choices include the Bengal Lounge (its ceiling fans and tall palms are very colonial India), the Empress Dining Room, and Kipling's. The famous afternoon tea is served year-round in the Main Tea Lobby, spilling into surrounding areas as the number of tea drinkers dictates.

721 Government St., Victoria, BC V8W 1W5. ℂ 800/441-1414 or 250/384-8111. Fax 250/381-4334. www.fairmont.com/empress. 477 units. July–Sept C$249–C$800 double, C$429–C$1,509 suite; C$399–C$1,500 Fairmont Gold; Oct–June C$169–C$479 double, C$229–C$1,269 suite, C$219–C$1,269 Fairmont Gold. Packages available. Children 11 and under stay free in parent's room. AE, DC, DISC, MC, V. Underground valet parking C$28. Bus 5. Small pets accepted (C$25). **Amenities:** 2 restaurants (East Indian, Pacific Northwest); bar/lounge; tearoom; large heated indoor pool; health club & spa; concierge; tour desk; car-rental desk; business center; 24-hr. room service; in-room massage; babysitting; laundry service; dry cleaning. *In room:* A/C, TV w/pay movies, Internet, minibar, coffeemaker, hair dryer, safe.

Hotel Grand Pacific ★★   The "grandness" begins as you approach the hotel beneath a canopy of trees—beside ducks paddling in waterfall-fed pools. Located next to the Parliament Buildings, the Grand Pacific sits right on the waterfront. Guest rooms are more spacious and elegantly contemporary than those in the other waterfront hotels, and because of the wide range of accommodations, from standard rooms facing the Olympic Mountains and smallish bathrooms to multi-room harborview suites with fireplaces and lavishly large bathrooms, you might be able to afford top-notch luxury here for less than what's offered elsewhere. Executive suites feature double Jacuzzis, fireplaces, multiple balconies, and wet bars. The hotel has a quality spa; fitness facilities (with a huge ozonated indoor pool) that are the most extensive in the city; and dining options that include The Mark, geared to high-end, romantic encounters (see "Where to Dine," later in this chapter).

463 Belleville St., Victoria, BC V8V 1X3. © **800/663-7550** or 250/386-0450. Fax 250/380-4473. www. hotelgrandpacific.com. 304 units. Mid-May to Sept C$219–C$389 double, from C$199 suite; Oct to mid-May C$159–C$269 double, from C$259 suite; 1-bedroom suites from C$259. Children 17 and under stay free in parent's room. AE, DC, DISC, MC, V. Parking C$12. Bus 30 to Superior and Oswego sts., 27, or 28. **Amenities:** 2 restaurants (all Pacific Northwest); lounge; indoor ozone-filtered lap pool; squash court; athletic club & spa; whirlpool; sauna; steamroom; concierge; secretarial services; 24-hr. room service; babysitting; laundry service; dry cleaning. *In room:* A/C, TV w/pay movies, high-speed Internet, minibar, coffeemaker, hair dryer, iron, safe.

Expensive

Andersen House B&B ★   This small 1891 house, with its high ceilings, stained-glass windows, and ornate Queen Anne–style fireplaces, is filled with furnishings that echo the old British Empire, only to be spiced up with splashes of Art Deco paintings. The combination is very lively. Every room has a private entrance and is unique. The sun-drenched Casablanca Room has French doors and a window seat overlooking the Parliament Buildings; the Captain's Apartment comes with a claw-foot tub and an extra bedroom; and the ground level Garden Studio, the most secluded and least expensive of the three rooms, has the hot tub. Rates include a sumptuous breakfast.

301 Kingston St., Victoria, BC V8V 1V5. © **250/388-4565.** Fax 250/721-3938. www.andersenhouse.com. 3 units. June–Sept C$225–C$255 double; Oct–May C$135–C$195 double. Rates include full breakfast. MC, V. Free off-street parking. Bus 30 to Superior and Oswego sts. Children under 12 not accepted. **Amenities:** Jacuzzi, nonsmoking rooms. *In room:* TV/DVD, Wi-Fi, coffeemaker, hair dryer, iron, CD player.

The Gatsby Mansion   Overlooking the Inner Harbour, just across from where the Seattle–Port Angeles ferry docks, this 100-year-old heritage complex comprises three buildings, each trapped in a time warp, with its antique furniture, Italian stained glass, velvet tapestries, frescoed ceilings, and meandering hallways. The main Gatsby Mansion (ca. 1897) exudes a Queen Anne style, the Judges House (ca. 1877) incorporates Italian-ate architecture, and the Middle House (ca. 1872) was the site's original cottage. Whatever the building, staying here is like staying in a museum, and if you're drawn to the eccentric, this place will appeal. Each guest room has a different configuration, so you might get a square room or one that has a few corner nooks, or even a 1.5m (5-ft.) corridor into a sitting area. Bathrooms are on the small side and functional. All beds feature the comforts of down duvets and fine linens. A gracious high tea is served every afternoon beneath twinkling chandeliers in what were once the front parlor, drawing room, and dining rooms. Breakfast and dinner are served in the same space. *Tip:* If you want space, forgo the harbor view and opt for a room at the back. These folks also own the **Ramada Huntingdon Hotel & Suites** (© **800/663-7557** or 250/381-3456) next door, which is less ornate: Large rooms, pullout beds, and in-room fridges make it a value option for families and folks on a budget.

309 Belleville St., Victoria, BC V8V 1X2. © **800/563-9656** or 250/388-9191. Fax 250/920-5651. www. bellevillepark.com. 20 units. Mid-May to Sept C$169–C$349 double; Oct to mid-May C$129–C$279 double. Rates include full breakfast. Packages available. AE, MC, V. Free parking. Bus 5 to Belleville and Government sts., 27, 28, or 30. **Amenities:** Restaurant (Pacific Northwest); lounge; Wi-Fi. *In room:* TV w/ pay movies, coffeemaker, iron.

Haterleigh Heritage Inn ★   Located only two blocks from the harbor, this turn-of-the-20th-century inn exudes the sophisticated essence of old world Victoria with antique furnishings, European wall coverings, original stained-glass windows, and attentive touches such as sherry and chocolates at night and gourmet breakfasts in the morning. Even the innkeepers are English! Rooms are large, with sitting areas, large windows, and good-sized bathrooms, all of which have soaker tubs. The inn scores high on the romance quotient, especially with the Day Dreams suite on the main floor, dedicated to honeymooners. The Angels Suite on the third floor has two bedrooms; the Victoriana Suite has an original claw-foot soaker tub.

243 Kingston St., Victoria, BC V8V 1V5. © **866/234-2244** or 250/384-9995. Fax 250/384-1935. www. haterleigh.com. 7 units. Mid-May to mid-Sept C$225–C$299 double; mid-Sept to mid-Oct C$195–C$265 double; mid-Oct to mid-May C$175–C$245 double. Rates include full breakfast. Off-season discounts available. MC, V. Free parking. Pets not accepted. Children under 12 not accepted. Bus: 30 to Superior and Montreal sts. **Amenities:** Lounge; Jacuzzi; Wi-Fi. *In room:* Hair dryer, no phone.

Inn at Laurel Point ★   One of the first modern hotels built on the Inner Harbour, the Inn at Laurel Point has undergone a huge makeover, primarily in its public areas, which has updated its original simple Japanese-style design with West Coast–style slate, fresh earth-toned furnishings, and lots of windows facing the waterfront. Japanese visitors love the place. There are two wings, and all guest rooms have balconies with views; the scene, harbor or inland, helps determine the price you'll pay. Try for a room in the south wing. Rooms here are more spacious and have an Asian theme, including shoji-style sliding doors, down duvets, and plenty of Asian art. The Japanese Garden features a large reflecting pond and a waterfall that cascades over a whopping 21,300 kilograms (47,000 lb.) of rock. The most significant change is the new Aura Restaurant, which is earning kudos from local foodies for its regional food and artisan wines. The inn is within easy walking distance of Fisherman's Wharf, the Parliament Buildings, and the Royal BC Museum.

680 Montreal St., Victoria, BC V8V 1Z8. © **800/663-7667** or 250/386-8721. Fax 250/386-9547. www. laurelpoint.com. 200 units: 135 harbor view, 65 suites. June to mid-Oct C$229 double, C$349 suite; mid-Oct to late May C$144 double, C$239 suite. Packages available. Extra person C$25. Children 18 and under stay free in parent's room. AE, DC, MC, V. Parking C$15. Small pets C$75. **Amenities:** Restaurant (Pacific Northwest); small heated pool; access to nearby health club; concierge; activities desk; business center; room service; in-room massage; babysitting; laundry service; dry cleaning; Internet. *In room:* A/C, TV w/pay movies, Internet, coffeemaker, hair dryer, iron, safe.

Oswego Hotel   From the outside, Victoria's first purpose-built hotel looks like a swish apartment complex with appeal to the W-hotel crowd. Offering a mix of studio rooms and one- and two-bedroom suites, units boast enormous windows; chocolate-colored and crisp-white designer furnishings; full kitchens with snazzy slate floors; granite counter tops; and instead of the obligatory coffeemaker, look for a French coffee press. Bath amenities, too, incorporate an extra touch: a laminated menu of different bath recipes, which are delivered as silk sachets filled with special ingredients and, perhaps, a tea light.

Time for Two (C$12) includes dried hibiscus and rose petals; the Detox (C$12) is an Ayurvedic blend of detoxifying herbs. Just as well that once bathed and relaxed, you'll find the queen beds to be comfortable, and extra sofa beds will accommodate partners with insomnia.

877 Oswego St., Victoria, BC V8V 5C1. ℭ **877/7-OSWEGO** [767-9346] or 250/294-7500. Fax 250/294-7509. www.oswegovictoria.com. 80 units. C$199–C$289 studio; C$249–C$349 1-bedroom suite; C$349–C$459 2-bedroom suite. Children 18 and under stay free in parent's room. C$25 extra person. AE, DC, MC, V. Parking C$10. Pets C$25. **Amenities:** Restaurant; lounge; pub; concierge; Internet; Wi-Fi. *In room:* HD satellite TV, Internet, Wi-Fi, kitchen, coffeemaker, hair dryer, iron.

Moderate

James Bay Inn ⟨Value⟩   There aren't many budget rooms around the Inner Harbour, but this is one of them. Granted, the 1907 manor has a faded quality about it, and rooms are on the small side and very simply furnished, but at least you can say you slept in the same house where Emily Carr, one of Canada's most beloved painters, once lived. Guests get a discount at the on-premises restaurant and pub. The real bargain is the renovated heritage cottage next door. The four suites may be small, but they come with full-size kitchens and somewhat better furnishings. High-season rates here are C$241 with two free parking spaces. A third building nearby sleeps eight and runs at C$197 to C$231 per night.

270 Government St., Victoria, BC V8V 2L2. ℭ **800/836-2649** or 250/384-7151. Fax 250/385-2311. www.jamesbayinn.bc.ca. 45 units. July–Oct C$130–C$240 double; Nov–June C$75–C$138 double. Children 16 and under stay free in parent's room. Extra person C$15. AE, MC, V. Free limited parking. Bus: 5 or 30 to Niagara St. Pets not accepted. **Amenities:** Restaurant; bar; tour desk; nonsmoking rooms; Wi-Fi. *In room:* TV, dataport, hair dryer, iron.

Queen Victoria Inn ⟨Finds⟩   This dear old lady has sat on this corner for 40 years, yet seems to fly beneath the radar in most guidebooks and brochures. The Queen does a good trade in tours, but really deserves a second look by those in-the-know. It's unpretentiously comfortable, with a nice restaurant and inviting hotel lobby. Rooms provide all the comforts of home without frills, unless you get into the suites, where Italian marble creeps into the bathroom (as it does along some of the narrow corridors). The marble baths in the Penthouse suites are enormous. The Italian touches are a direct reflection of the inn's Italian family ownership, which in the bedrooms means colorful Mediterranean prints brightening up the walls. All rooms have balconies, and some have kitchens cleverly hidden behind sliding walls; some can be joined to create multi-room suites. If you're going to pay for parking, it's a steal here.

655 Douglas St., Victoria, BC V8V 2P9 ℭ **800/663-7007** or 250/386-1312. Fax 250/386-0687. www.qvhotel.com. 146 units. May to late Sept C$205–C$230 double, C$300–C$650 suite; Oct–Apr C$112–C$125 double, C$165–C$375 suite. Children under 15 stay free in parent's room. Extra person C$25. AE, MC, V. Parking C$4. Pets not accepted. **Amenities:** Restaurant; lounge; indoor pool; fitness center; Jacuzzi; sauna; free shuttle downtown; business center; coin-op laundry; dry cleaning; Internet; Wi-Fi. *In room:* TV, Wi-Fi, kitchen (some, C$20 fee), fridge (on request), coffeemaker, hair dryer, iron.

The Royal Scot Suite Hotel ★ ⟨Value⟩ ⟨Kids⟩   Situated a block from the Inner Harbour, this suite hotel provides excellent value, particularly if you're not hooked on a waterfront view. Converted from an apartment building, the hotel has large guest rooms with lots of cupboard space. Studio suites include a living/dining area and kitchen; one-bedroom suites have separate bedrooms with king-size, queen-size, or twin beds. Kitchens are fully equipped (including microwaves), and living areas come with sofa beds. This

On the Horizon

A planned $20-million marina in Victoria's Inner Harbour, devoted solely to the growing number of mega-yachts that visit, would be the first of its kind in Canada. If all goes smoothly, the 48-berth marina, with a landscaped, floating concrete breakwater, will open in 2009. It will be geared to owners of yachts that are typically between 20 and 42 meters long and worth about $10 million to $15 million. Concerned locals are worried about noise drifting across the water from all those on-board parties, but at time of writing, plans were still sailing along.

is an ideal home base for families; weary parents in need of a few zzz's will love having their offspring scoot off to the children's games room. The indoor pool gets heavy use, as does the video arcade room. Jonathan's restaurant is fully licensed and has a summer patio. There are nine room types ranging from guest rooms to two-bedroom corner suites, so you're bound to find a good fit. Parking is free (a bonus anywhere in Victoria central) and if you didn't bring your car, the Royal Scot operates a complimentary guest shuttle to downtown. Tip: Internet specials can offer up to 40% savings, even in high season.

425 Quebec St., Victoria, BC V8V 1W7. ℂ 800/663-7515 or 250/388-5463. Fax 250/388-5452. www.royal scot.com. 176 units. C$155–C$249 double; C$185–C$419 suite. Weekly, monthly, and off-season discounts available. Children 11 and under stay free in parent's room. AE, DC, MC, V. Free parking. Bus 30. **Amenities:** Restaurant (Pacific Northwest); small heated indoor pool; hydrotherapy pool; access to nearby health club; sauna; game room; concierge; free downtown shuttle; business center; 24-hr. room service; babysitting; laundry service; dry cleaning; Wi-Fi and Internet (fee). *In room:* TV, coffeemaker, hair dryer, iron.

DOWNTOWN & OLD TOWN
Expensive
Abigail's Hotel ★★   Tucked into a quiet residential cul-de-sac, only 3 blocks from downtown Victoria and the Inner Harbour, this European-style Tudor inn is about as romantic as it can get. Guest rooms are superbly decorated with antiques, wood-burning fireplaces, two-person Jacuzzis, fresh-cut flowers, and welcoming treats such as truffles and fruit. The six Coach House suites have extravagant touches such as four-poster beds, custom-made furniture, and Italian marble bathrooms with Jacuzzi tubs. Since the chef has cooked for the Queen, breakfast is fit for royalty—literally—and will be brought to your bedside on request. The small Pearl Spa offers a full range of quality spa services. Abigail's is geared to adults; children are discouraged.

906 McClure St., Victoria, BC V8V 3E7. ℂ 866/347-5054 or 250/388-5363. Fax 250/388-7787. www. abigailshotel.com. 23 units. Mid-May to late June and mid-Sept to mid-Oct C$199–C$339 double; July to mid-Sept C$249–C$240 double; mid-Oct to late Apr C$189–C$299 double. Rates include full breakfast and evening hors d'oeuvres. Spa, honeymoon, and wine tour packages available. AE, MC, V. Free parking. Pets accepted C$25. Bus 1. **Amenities:** Spa; concierge; business center; laundry service; dry cleaning; Wi-Fi. *In room:* Some with TV/DVD, dataport, hair dryer, iron, some with Jacuzzi.

Beaconsfield Inn   Designed by famed local architect Samuel Maclure in 1905, there's a pleasant English feel to this heritage B&B. Edwardian touches include fir paneling, mahogany floors, antique furnishings, and stained-glass windows. Guest rooms are sumptuously decorated and very romantic. Some have fireplaces. The Gatekeeper Suite has

French windows leading onto a flowery patio, and the Garden Suite has a double hot tub. The Emily Carr Suite remains one of the showpiece rooms, with its romantic double hot tub in front of a fireplace, queen-size bed, and separate sitting area. Another suite features a flowery patio and similar double hot tub. As a bonus, the full breakfast served in the sunroom, afternoon tea, and evening sherry in the library are all included in the rate.

998 Humboldt St., Victoria, BC V8V 1Z8. ℂ **888/884-4044** or 250/384-4044. Fax 250/384-4052. www. beaconsfieldinn.com. 9 units. June–Sept C$169–C$299 double; Oct–May C$109–C$250 double. Extra person C$35. Full breakfast, afternoon tea, and sherry hour included. AE, MC, V. Free parking. Bus: 1 or 2 to Humboldt and Quadra sts. Pets not accepted. Children 12 and over accepted. Nonsmoking. **Amenities:** Jacuzzi; access to nearby health club; Wi-Fi. *In room:* Hair dryer, no phone.

The Magnolia Hotel & Spa ★★   This sophisticated boutique hotel appeals to business travelers and international visitors alike. It has a terrific downtown location and lots of finishing touches to make you feel immediately welcome: a huge bowl of apples, a larger arrangement of fresh flowers, and crisp daily newspapers. The hotel's personalized butler service adds to this attentiveness with an array of complimentary amenities, though, sadly, not a real McCoy butler. Guest rooms are bright, with floor-to-ceiling windows, custom-designed furniture, two-poster beds, and oversize desks. Executive Diamond suites have gas fireplaces. Of special note is the **Aveda concept spa** (www. spamagnolia.com), which is professional with special services for men as well as women. The hotel houses a new high-end steak and seafood restaurant.

623 Courtney St., Victoria, BC V8W 1B8. ℂ **877/624-6654** or 250/381-0999. Fax 250/381-0988. www. magnoliahotel.com. 64 units. June to mid-Oct C$229–C$349 double; mid-Oct to May C$159–C$229 double. Rates include continental breakfast. Children 11 and under stay free in parent's room. Extra person C$30. AE, DC, DISC, MC, V. Valet parking C$15. Bus: 5. Small pets accepted (C$60). **Amenities:** Restaurant (Pacific Northwest); pub; access to nearby health club; spa; concierge; limited secretarial services; limited room service; laundry service; dry cleaning; Internet; Wi-Fi. *In room:* A/C, TV w/pay movies, dataport, Wi-Fi, minibar, fridge, coffeemaker, hair dryer, iron.

Victoria Marriott Inner Harbour   Although its modern and urban ambience makes it seemed geared more to the business executive than a casual visitor, the young and enthusiastic staff will give you a warm welcome. In fact, their service has earned this high-rise hotel both the 2006 Outstanding Customer Service Award from Victoria's Chamber of Commerce and international recognition from its parent company in 2007 as Hotel of the Year. Rooms have all the usual Marriott amenities, including a concierge level that offers a pleasant lounge where you can enjoy complimentary hors d'oeuvres in the evening and a continental breakfast. They even have windows that open, which to many folks is a breath of fresh air. The hotel's location is central, and although set behind the Empress, from the upper-floor guest rooms the views stretch to the Olympic Mountain Range in Washington State. Hotel amenities include a cozy bar, full-size indoor pool, a health club, and the **Fire & Water Fish and Chop House,** a fine-dining restaurant featuring high-quality seafood and steaks—the prime rib is especially noteworthy.

728 Humboldt St., Victoria, BC V8W 3Z5. ℂ **877/333-8338** or 250/480-3800. Fax: 250/480-3838. www. victoriamarriott.com. 236 units. C$150–C$250 standard double. AE, DC, MC, V. Valet or self-parking C$15. **Amenities:** Restaurant; lounge; indoor pool; fitness center; hot tub; 24-hr. room service; laundry service; same-day dry cleaning; Internet; Wi-Fi. *In room:* A/C, TV, free Internet, minibar, fridge, coffeemaker, hair dryer, iron, safe.

Moderate & Inexpensive

Admiral Inn Ⓥalue Ⓚids   The harbor views here will more than make up for the small, motel-like rooms and bathrooms. Besides, they are comfortable and immaculately clean and available at rates that attract couples, families, seniors, and others in search of a multimillion-dollar vista without the expense. Larger rooms have fridges, microwaves, pullout sofa beds, and balconies; the suites have full kitchens. The inn is a family-run operation, so service is empathetic and includes extras like free bicycles, free local calls, free Internet access in the lobby, and lots of friendly advice on what to see and do.

257 Belleville St., Victoria, BC V8V 1X1. © 888/823-6472 or ©/fax 250/388-6267. www.admiral.bc.ca. 32 units. May–Sept C$149–C$229double; Oct–Apr C$99–C$159 double. Extra person C$10. Children under 12 stay free in parent's room. Rates include continental breakfast. AE, DC, MC, V. Free parking. Bus: 5 to Belleville and Government sts. **Amenities:** Complimentary bikes; coin-op laundry; dry cleaning; non-smoking rooms; complimentary Internet access. *In room:* A/C, TV, kitchen/kitchenette (in some units), fridge, coffeemaker, hair dryer, iron.

The Bedford Regency (Finds)

Located on the main commercial drag (the entrance gives the impression that you're entering a shopping mall), the Bedford is one of Victoria's oldest hotels. Although tasteful renovations have brought it up to modern standards, the quirky layout of guest rooms reflects its heritage. All are elegantly comfortable with down duvets and quality toiletries. Some are so tiny, however, that the foot of the bed is just inches from the pedestal sink. Some have a fireplace "around the corner" beside a reading chair, while others are quite spacious, with two queen-size beds facing each other because the room is long and narrow. Bathrooms are small and very Art Deco. The 12 Superior rooms have Jacuzzis and fireplaces. Window boxes mask the busy street scene below, which in summer can be a bit noisy until midnight. Belingo 1140 is an Art Deco–styled jazz/martini lounge located on the mezzanine. If you're looking for something more casual, head for the Garrick's Head Pub.

1140 Government St., Victoria, BC V8W 1Y2. © 800/665-6500 or 250/384-6835. Fax 250/386-8930. www.bedfordregency.com. 40 units. May to mid-Sept C$140–C$200 double; mid-Sept to May C$89–C$179 double. AE, MC, V. Parking C$10. Bus: 5 to Douglas and Johnson sts. **Amenities:** Restaurant (Pacific Northwest); pub; martini lounge; laundry; dry cleaning; Internet; Wi-Fi. *In room:* TV, coffeemaker, fridge, Wi-Fi.

Ocean Island Backpackers Inn (Finds)

This quirky, historic, four-level youth hostel cum apartment building attracts all age groups and families. Dorm accommodations sleep four to six people, and are co-ed as well as women-only. If you're a twosome, the rates are reasonable enough that it's worth booking a whole dorm to yourself. Special family rooms are more hotel-like, and have a private bathroom, multiple beds, and a fridge. This is not a place for shrinking violets. The lounges, bar, and dining room are magnets for lively and multilingual conversations with fellow travelers. In addition, Ocean Island operates a 1907 character house in the James Bay area that contains three self-contained, self-catering suites.

791 Pandora Ave., Victoria, BC V8W 1N9. © 888/888-4180, 866/888-4180, or 250/385-1788. Fax: 250/385-1780. www.oceanisland.com. 80 units. C$20–C$27 dorm; C$27–C$77 private room; C$68–C$128 family room. AE, MC, V. **Amenities:** Lounge; communal kitchen; laundry; Wi-Fi; bike lockup. *In room:* No phone.

Spinnaker's Guest House

Located right on the waterfront at the entrance to Victoria Harbour, Spinnakers is best known by locals for its brewpub (see "Where to Dine," below), and although it can get a bit noisy around closing, the guesthouse operation is a terrific alternative to central lodgings, provided you don't mind a 15-minute walk to downtown or a 5-minute ferry ride. The complex includes two superbly renovated around-1880 buildings, the Heritage House and the Garden Suites, which are more like self-contained studio apartments. All rooms feature queen-size beds, soft earth-toned West-Coast style furnishings, in-room Jacuzzis (except for shower-only room no. 4), and some have wood-burning fireplaces. Room no. 9 is one of the nicest and most spacious. It has a vaulted ceiling close to 4.3m (14 ft.) high, a fireplace, a sitting room, a full kitchen, and a south-facing private sun deck.

308 Catherine St., Victoria, BC V9A 3S3. (C) **877/838-2739** or 250/384-2739. Fax: 250/384-3246. www. spinnakers.com. 10 units. July to mid-Oct C$179–C$279 double; mid-Oct to June C$149–C$249 double. Rates include continental breakfast. AE, DC, MC, V. Free parking. Bus: 24 to Catherine St. **Amenities:** Nonsmoking rooms; Wi-Fi. *In room:* TV (some rooms), kitchen (some units), coffeemaker, hair dryer, iron, fireplace (some units), Jacuzzi (some units), Wi-Fi.

Swans Hotel ★★   The charming Swans offers a warm welcome in an intimately comfortable modern-day tavern. But it's more than a bed-and-beer experience. One of Victoria's best-loved heritage restorations, this 1913 warehouse now provides guests with 30 distinctive—and really spacious—suites. Most of the open concept studios and one- and two-bedroom suites are in fact two-story lofts with 3.3m (11-ft.), exposed-beam ceilings and nifty layouts that have many, if not most, of the comforts of home. The studios have king beds, the rest have queen-size. Accommodating up to six adults, they feature fully equipped kitchens, separate living and dining areas, and private patios. If you want to go for the gusto, there's even a three-level, 279-sq.-m (3,000-sq.-ft.) pent-house with its own Roy Henry Vickers totem pole. Speaking of which, the hotel has one of Canada's largest private art collections, but you only get to see what's in the lobby: Many pieces are in guest rooms. They add to the atmosphere nonetheless. Check out the stylized totem pole in the restaurant lobby. The **Wild Saffron Bistro & Wine Bar** is open daily. Other facilities include **Swans Pub** and **Buckerfields' Brewery,** which offers tours by appointment.

506 Pandora Ave., Victoria, BC V8W 1N6. (C) **800/668-7926** or 250/361-3310. Fax 250/361-3491. www. swanshotel.com. 30 suites. Mid-June to Sept C$199 studio, C$289–C$359 suite; Oct to mid-June C$179– C$189 studio, C$219–C$299 suite. Weekly and monthly rates available. Extra person C$30. Up to 2 children 12 and under stay free in parent's room. Rates include continental breakfast. AE, DC, MC, V. Parking C$9. Bus: 23 or 24 to Pandora Ave. Pets not accepted. **Amenities:** Restaurant (Pacific Northwest); wine bar; brewpub; brewery; nightclub; access to nearby health club; secretarial services; limited room service; babysitting; laundry service; dry cleaning. *In room:* TV, Internet, kitchen, fridge, coffeemaker, hair dryer, iron.

VICTORIA NEIGHBORHOODS
Very Expensive
Villa Marco Polo ★★★   Located within a few minutes' walk of Government House, everything about this Italian Renaissance mansion, set amid classical European gardens, is exotic, and true to its well-traveled namesake. First are the gardens, with their ornamental statues, reflection pool, and fountains. Then there are the public lounges, filled with antiques collected from all over the world. Every one has a story—the Chinese cabinet in the lounge, the handmade books in the library, or the Italian crystal chandelier in the for-mal dining room. Each of the four spacious bedrooms is sumptuously decorated to theme, with plush European linens fitted to king-size beds. The Silk Road suite has vaulted ceilings and hand-painted Tuscan murals; the Persian Suite is decorated with Persian fabrics and antiques; the Zanzibar suite has French doors onto a Juliette balcony; and the most eye-catching, the Alexandria Suite, is adorned with carved Turkish wooden shutters. The top of the house has been beautifully converted into a tiny loft spa and yoga/meditation area. Breakfast is a feast for the senses. Freshly baked goods may include buttermilk 10-grain muffins or caramelized pineapple pecan cakes, while entrees run from hot lemon lavender soufflés to baked eggs Florentine with a Persian pepper hollandaise.

1524 Shasta Place, Victoria, BC V8S 1X9. ℂ **877/601-1524** or 250/370-1524. Fax: 250/370-1624. www.
villamarcopolo.com. 4 units. Mid-June to mid-Sept C$280–C$325 double; mid-Sept to mid-Oct and mid-
Apr to mid-June C$230–C$275 double; mid-Oct to mid-Apr C$190–C$235 double. Rates include gourmet
breakfast, afternoon tea, hors d'oeuvres. 2-night minimum in high season. AE, MC, V. Free parking. **Amenities:** Lounge; spa; concierge services; library; conservatory; fully stocked fridge; Internet; Wi-Fi; garden.
In room: TV//CD/DVD player, iPod, hair dryer, iron, fireplace (some).

Expensive

Prior House B&B Inn   Out in the quiet and pretty Rockland neighborhood, this
luxurious B&B was formerly an English governor's manor. Consequently, both the house
and gardens are among the most picturesque in Victoria. Everything here takes you back
to an earlier time: oak-paneled rooms with wood-burning fireplaces, stained-glass windows, hardwood floors, and a blend of antique and replica Edwardian furnishings. Every
guest room is sumptuously comfortable with custom-made goose-down duvets and
bathrooms fashioned in marble and sporting air-jetted tubs for two. Although the Lieutenant Governor's Royal Suite is the inn's pièce de résistance with its 1880 king-size
canopied bed, crystal chandeliers, and spa-style bathroom with gilded walls, the less
ostentatious Windsor Penthouse Suite is just as much of a private sanctuary. The Hobbit
Garden Studios are more simply decorated, but no less appealing, with private patios into
the well-tended garden. Attention to detail is what this inn is all about; you can even
choose to have breakfast served to you in bed.

620 St. Charles St., Victoria, BC V8S 3N7. ℂ **877/924-3300** or 250/592-8847. Fax: 250/592-8223. www.
priorhouse.com. 6 units. Mid-June to mid-Sept C$219–C$299 double; mid-Sept to mid-Oct and May to
mid-June C$189–C$279 double; mid-Oct to Apr C$159–C$229 double. Rates include gourmet breakfast
and afternoon tea. MC, V. Free parking. **Amenities:** Lounge; concierge services; in-room massage; library.
In room: TV/CD/DVD player, hair dryer, fireplace.

Westin Bear Mountain Golf Resort & Spa   Canada's first and only 36-hole Nick-
laus-designed championship golf courses are the focal point of this new master-planned
resort and residential community. The mountain-lodge style resort also includes five restaurants that range from fine dining to a sushi bar (The Cellar has a 12,500-wine bottle collection), Sante Spa, an excellent medical spa with a whole bunch of therapeutic and
pampering treatments, and a state-of-the-art health club. Guest rooms have an earth-toned,
natural decor with spacious sitting areas, fireplaces, bathrooms with slate tile floors, well-
stocked kitchenettes, and either a balcony or terrace overlooking the fairways and Mount
Finlayson. If you're not a golfer, there are plenty of trails to hike and bike. Be aware of an
optional, daily C$15 resort fee that includes amenities such as parking and Wi-Fi access.

1999 Country Club Way, Victoria, BC V9B 6R9. ℂ **888/533-BEAR** [2327] or 250/391-7160. Fax 250/391-
3792. www.bearmountain.ca. 156 units, all nonsmoking. June–Sept C$229–C$459 double; Oct–May
C$159–C$389 double. Extra person C$30. AE, MC, V. Resort fee (C$15) includes parking, high-speed
Internet, Wi-Fi, Fitness Club access, golf bag valet, and storage. **Amenities:** 5 restaurants; lounge; pub;
saltwater pool; 2 golf courses; health club; spa; mountain-bike rentals; Internet; Wi-Fi. *In room:* TV w/mov-
ies, DVD (in suites), high-speed Internet, Wi-Fi, fridge, coffeemaker, hair dryer.

Moderate & Inexpensive

Oak Bay Guest House Ⓥalue   While a nearby resort still undergoes its from-the-
ground-up redevelopment, this is the only place to stay in residential Oak Bay, and it
exudes old England with few of the faux upgrades you find elsewhere. Step inside the
1912 Tudor-style inn and it has the incoherency of a typical older building trying to
make good in the 21st century. Stairs creak, corridors are narrow, and rooms are odd
shapes because each has had an en suite added as plumbing could dictate. But that's the

VICTORIA

5

WHERE TO STAY

charm of the place. And the value. It's clean, comfortable, offers the basics, and is run by a great staff who really make you feel welcome.

1052 Newport Ave., Victoria, BC V8S 5E3. © **800/575-3812** or 250/598-3812. Fax: 250/598-0369. www. oakbayguesthouse.com. 11 units. May to mid-Oct C$109–C$159 double; mid-Oct to Apr C$99–C$139 double. Rates include breakfast. MC, V. Free parking. **Amenities:** TV lounge; coffeemaker; Wi-Fi. *In room:* Hair dryer, iron on request, no phone.

4 WHERE TO DINE

With the second-highest number of restaurants per capita in North America, Victoria offers something for every taste and budget, and refreshingly, you don't always have to pay through the nose to get good quality. In fact, one or two holes-in-the-wall have excellent food. What you will pay for is the restaurant's proximity to a waterfront view. Most of the best restaurants are all within walking distance of downtown hotels, so you don't have to worry about who'll be the designated driver. While tapas and small plates were the hottest trend since sliced bread a couple of years ago; they're quickly being sidelined with charcuterie selections, and at the lavish end of the scale, multi-course tasting menus, always with the option of wine pairings. That's because Vancouver Island is hugely influenced by the 100-mile diet and Slow Food movement, in addition to being geographically blessed with an extraordinary abundance of micro-climates where fresh produce, fisheries, farms, and vineyards thrive. The collaboration between chefs is creating a very sustainable restaurant- and agri-tourism economy, all of which is best showcased in locally inspired menus. Although there's still a tendency for Victorians to eat early (restaurants are packed 7–9pm), many trendier restaurants accept late-night reservations.

INNER HARBOUR & NEARBY

Expensive

Blue Crab Bar & Grill ★★ SEAFOOD   This is the best seafood spot in the city, with killer views of the harbor to boot, so naturally, it's always busy and has a tendency to get noisy. Blue Crab's seafood specials, featured on their signature blackboards, are what keep this restaurant at the top. Dishes are extraordinary inventions, such as blue crab fish pot, grilled salmon with crispy yucca-root spaetzles, or smoked Alaskan black cod poached in coconut milk with a hint of red curry. For a real treat, the platters for two include sampler morsels from several menu items. There's also a good selection of landlubber dishes for those whose tastes run away from the sea. The wine list is excellent, particularly when it comes to acclaimed BC and California wines. It consistently wins awards, as do its chefs, who in 2008 garnered several accolades at Salon Culinaire at Hotelympia in London, England.

In the Coast Hotel, 146 Kingston St. © **250/480-1999.** www.bluecrab.ca. Reservations required. Main courses lunch C$11–C$22; dinner C$28–C$39. AE, DC, MC, V. Daily 6:30am–10pm. Nibbles available until 1am.

The Mark ★★ CONTINENTAL WEST COAST   The Mark has no view, preferring to create an intimate dining experience within the confines of a discreet, wood-paneled room, but it's perfect for memorable and romantic encounters—it seats only 26 diners. The upscale menu matches the high-end wine list with dishes such as long-pepper rubbed ahi tuna with cardamom-scented white bean and endive marmalade, a Matsutake-glazed fallow venison loin, as well as a mouth-watering frangipane gala-apple pie with Tugwell honey cream and vanilla bean gelato. The tasting menus here are a special treat inasmuch as they are often themed to seasonal produce. Take asparagus, for example, worked into a white asparagus and truffled custard, various side dishes, and even candied for desert, served with currant syrup alongside mascarpone mouse and chocolate cannelloni. Six-course tasting menus are C$70; add C$42 for wine pairings. Waiters are well informed on dishes, and the service has gracious finesse (extra butter arrives quietly almost before you realize it's running out), without staff hovering.

In the Clarion Hotel Grand Pacific, 450 Quebec St. ℭ **250/380-4487.** www.themark.ca. Reservations recommended. Entrees C$30–C$48; 6-course tasting menu C$70. AE, DC, DISC, MC, V. Daily 5–9:30pm.

Niche Modern Dining CONTEMPORARY AMERICAN   This charming heritage house has long been a favorite restaurant destination, and recent changes to implement a more contemporary menu give every indication that it will continue to be so. New chef-owner Jason Leizert comes with culinary experience from the elite Pointe Restaurant at the Wickaninnish Inn (see p. 173), so expectations were high from day one. The menu descriptions are beguilingly simple: beef served with shrimp, goat cheese, and beets; or snapper, chorizo, broth, and squid. They give no hint as to the flavorful combinations, spices and craftsmanship inherent in each choice. Only a tasting menu can give you the full range of what this young man can create. Go on a slower night and ask for a tasting menu (C$55) and hope for mussels infused with bear, honey and thyme; saki-soaked rhubarb; and his home-baked olive bread, which on its own is good, but when served with his chickpea, parsnip, and turnip spreads in lieu of butter is good enough to demolish the entire loaf in short order. The only drawback? This man's an artist; some dishes take time, so relax and enjoy the wine pairings.

225 Quebec St. ℭ **250/388-4255.** www.nichedining.com. Reservations recommended. Lunch C$15; dinner C$23; brunch C$12. MC, V. Wed–Sun 11am–2pm; Mon–Sat 5–10pm.

Pescatore's Fish House ★★ SEAFOOD   Consistently ranked among Victoria's best seafood restaurants, this spot's artsy decor, good service, and extensive, seasonal menu create a great dining alternative to the Blue Crab, even though it hasn't got the view. The daily fresh sheet usually features at least ten items, and whether you go for oysters at the raw bar, crab, clams, salmon, or halibut, you won't be disappointed. Be sure to include the 1-1-1 soup taster in your selection: Pescatore's three chowders—the slightly spiced prawn bisque is a standout. Non-fish entrees—pastas, steak, and lamb—are said to be good, but why you would order these at such a great fish place? There's a late-night tapas-style menu offered after 10pm, and weekend live-jazz brunches.

614 Humboldt St. ℭ **250/385-4512.** www.pescatores.com. Reservations recommended. Main courses C$15–C$35. AE, DC, MC, V. Mon–Fri 11:30am–11pm; Sat–Sun 11am–midnight.

Moderate & Inexpensive

Barb's Place FISH & CHIPS   Absolutely no frills here; this floating restaurant at Fisherman's Wharf serves fish and chips at their very tastiest, although it's received such rave reviews that the eatery is on the verge of being overrated. After all, this is only fish and chips, and it's served in newspaper pouches, not on bone china. Get your cod, oysters, or halibut grilled, steamed, or deep-fried any way you like it. Barb serves it all up with hand-hewn chips. Douse your chippies in salt and vinegar, the way they do in England, and enjoy the feast at picnic tables while watching the boats, seagulls, and other harborside activities.

Erie St., Fisherman's Wharf (at the entrance to the Inner Harbour). ℭ **250/384-6515.** www.barbsplace. ca. Reservations not accepted. Main courses C$5.50–C$17. MC, V. Mar–Oct daily 10am–sunset. Closed Nov–Feb.

The James Bay Tea Room & Restaurant BRITISH   Sadly, the menu here has dumped traditional British fare such as home-style bangers and mash and roast beef with Yorkshire pudding for burgers, soups, salads, and even low-carb, Atkins-friendly items. It is, however, still one of the few places that actually serve kippers for breakfast. Then there's high tea, which starts in earnest mid-morning, and represents better value than most. The decor includes Tiffany lampshades, brass knickknacks, and sepia-tinted family portraits. Tables are crowded with locals, and the atmosphere is lively with English-accented chatter. Tarot card readings are offered on Saturday afternoons.

332 Menzies St. (behind the Parliament Buildings). (© 250/382-8282. www.jamesbaytearoomand restaurant.com. Reservations recommended. Breakfast and lunch C$5.50–C$10; high-tea/dinner C$16–C$29. AE, MC, V. Mon–Sat 7am–5pm; Sun 8am–7pm.

Red Fish/Blue Fish ★ FISH & CHIPS   Move over Barb's (above) as the prima donna of take-out fish-eats, enter one of the most innovative concepts around: a 6.1×3m (20×10-ft.) gourmet fish-and-chip cafe out of a re-purposed ship's container, much like the metal freight boxes you see rolling down the highway atop 18-wheelers. This one was used to ship a Hummer and now has a rooftop garden (which also acts as roof insulation), and a conscientious green program that includes composting and recycling potato starch. It also uses only sustainably harvested seafood, some caught by the owners themselves. Here, you get wild Pacific halibut, salmon, or cod coated with a light tempura batter; twice-fried, hand-cut potatoes, some slathered in curry; grill-seared tuna; fish tacones (taco-cones); and mushy edamame, a quirky twist on mushy peas. Because tables are forbidden on the dock, the cafe provides stools for waterside dining, year-round.

1006 Wharf St. (on the pier below). (© 250/298-6877. www.redfish-bluefish.com. Main courses C$5–C$17. MC, V. Daily 11am–6pm.

Santiago's (Finds) LATIN AMERICAN   Although the colorful ornamental lights make the place look like a Mexican fiesta, they also indicate the upbeat personality of this cheery cafe. The menu is a creative mix of tasty dishes from Malaysia, Spain, and South America, so you get tapas dishes alongside items like Pollo Naranja (chicken with oranges) and a mouth-watering spicy paella that brims with mussels, shrimp, sausage, chicken, and artichoke hearts. Meals come with tortilla chips and salsa, sour cream, and guacamole, and the service is friendly and fast.

660 Oswego St. (© 250/388-7376. Reservations not accepted. Main courses C$8–C$16. MC, V. Daily 8am–9pm.

DOWNTOWN & OLD TOWN
Expensive
Black Olive CONTINENTAL   With nearly 30 years in the restaurant biz, owner Paul Psyllakis has created an elegant dining room that exudes a Mediterranean warmth. The menu has a West-Coast base, with olive-oriented undertones, as in the salmon with artichokes and black olive pesto and a savory bread pudding that uses olive bread, leeks, portobello mushrooms, artichokes, and Greek cheese. Grandma's bread pudding never tasted like this! A good selection of non-olive dishes gives the menu broad appeal: There's an excellent roasted vegetable dish in phyllo pastry; Greek-style beef tenderloin medallions, pan-seared with a mushroom and red wine sauce; as well as a fish of the day that you pick from an iced, central display. Usually there's everything from lobster to colossal shrimp to yellow-fin tuna. Paul's extra virgin olive oil is made from his own olives in Crete, Greece.

Bon Rouge Bistro & Boulangerie FRENCH   If the boulangerie (bakery) doesn't tempt you with its first-class croissant, lemon tarts, and traditional baguettes, then the bistro itself will. Housed in a renovated 1920s building, and unlike some of the posh French eateries around town, this place is like one you would find off the Champs Elysees in chic style and authenticity. Traditional items include a tasty coq au vin and light, fluffy crepes stuffed with savory mixes. The daily plate du jour is a good bet, especially the fish-on-Friday number—a bouillabaisse with a vermouth broth base, and the traditional Sunday roast, usually herbed lamb. Sharing the Chateaubriand-Dungeness crab combination is another great choice, though a bit pricey at C$110.

611 Courtney St. © **250/220-8008** (bakery is at 850 Gordon St.). Reservations not accepted. Main courses C$8–C$16. MC, V. Mon–Sat 11am–3pm; daily 5–11pm.

Cafe Brio ★ WEST COAST   This award-winning, bistro-style restaurant serves delicious Tuscan-inspired West-Coast fare, likely because its two chefs, one Canadian and one Italian, blend their styles into the ever-changing menu that's based on whatever fresh organic produce they purchased that day. The result is a creative mix of natural flavors zinging with just the right amount of added spices. In winter, expect substantial items such as venison shank, free-range chicken, and confit of duck. In summer, items are lighter: a charcuterie menu featuring local salami, lomo, pâtés, and terrines, and served with homemade mustards and pickles; and seared scallops topped with crisp potato rösti. Service is top-notch, and the wine list is exceptional, with more than 300 wines by the bottle and 30 by the glass or half-liter. The Brio Family meal (C$40 per person) is served to share, and usually comprises five or six chef-chosen dishes. The early bird table d'hote menu, available only from 5:30 to 6:15pm, is great value at C$29. Paintings by local artists add splashes of color to the ochre walls, and wide-planked wooden floors add decorative warmth.

944 Fort St. © **250/383-0009.** www.cafe-brio.com. Reservations recommended. Main courses C$26–C$45. AE, MC, V. Daily 5:30–10:30pm.

Il Terrazzo Ristorante ★ ITALIAN   Locals have voted this Victoria's best Italian restaurant year in, year out, so if you find your way to its location in an alley between Yates and Johnson streets, it will be worth the effort. The restaurant's three talented chefs create specialties of their homeland that include wood-oven-roasted pizzas, fresh grilled seafood, and a wide variety of homemade pastas, as well as steaks, osso bucco, and other mostly northern-Italian specialties. The pan-roasted local halibut, with blackberries and green peppercorns, is excellent and kept lightly moist with a mild three-cheese sauce. Set in a converted heritage building, its atmosphere is warmly romantic and features a flower-filled heated courtyard, surrounded by brick fireplaces and lit by wrought-iron candelabras. Inside, exposed brick walls, wooden beams, and intimate nooks and crannies are a delight.

555 Johnson St., Waddington Alley (off Johnson St. at Wharf St.). © **250/361-0028.** www.ilterrazzo.com. Reservations recommended. Lunch C$9–C$19; dinner C$15–C$25. AE, MC, V. Mon–Sat 11:30am–3pm (Oct–Apr no lunch Sat); nightly 5–10pm.

Restaurant Matisse ★ CLASSIC FRENCH   Wrought-iron gates give way to an alluring Parisian ambience. Filled with soft lights and a profusion of fresh flowers, this award-winning 40-seat restaurant has been noted for its service, elegance, and quality, and justifiably so. Savor fresh bread, filet bordelaise, slow roasted duck, or a masterful

VICTORIA

5

WHERE TO DINE

Coquilles St. Jacques a la Perigord—a classic scallop dish with black truffle–scented potato topped with Gruyere cheese, baked in a rich mornay sauce, and a feathery-light crème brûlée. Menu items are always fresh and innovative, presenting new recipes and ideas garnered during annual pilgrimages to France. The four-course chef's sampler prix-fixe dinners are C$49; add C$30 for wine pairings.

512 Yates St. (at Wharf St.). ℂ 250/480-0883. www.restaurantmatisse.com. Reservations recommended. Main courses C$24–C$32. AE, MC, V. Wed–Sun 5:30–10pm.

Stage WEST COAST   Best described as a small-plates wine bistro, its location across from the Belfry Theatre in Fernwood means its 50 seats fill up fast pre- and post-shows. The bar is actually made from a salvaged bowling lane, and the wood floors, open kitchen, and exposed brick walls create a cool vibe that gets very noisy with chatter. If you enjoy sharing platefuls of intriguing flavors with friends, Stage is a winner. Selections are themed to charcuterie, vegetarian, fish, meat, and dessert. If you're tasting wines alongside—bottles average C$45, and many are served in 3- to 5-ounce pours—the organic wood-fired breads and cheese trays are phenomenal. Recommendations include the garlic langos; walnut-arugula pesto; grilled zucchini and blue cheese; the chicken curry with grilled corn naan and house chutney, a delicious sweet-sour accompaniment; and the grilled Sooke trout, house guanciale, and vegetable capellini. Stage owners also operate Paprika Bistro, a French-Hungarian restaurant in Oak Bay.

1307 Gladstone Ave. ℂ **250/388-4222.** Reservations recommended. Plates C$12. MC, V. Daily 5pm–midnight, 4:30pm during Belfry matinees.

Moderate & Inexpensive

Azuma Sushi ⓥalue JAPANESE SUSHI   This modern, busy, and bright restaurant has the best-value sushi in town. Rumor has it that at his previous restaurant Azuma's chef developed quite the following for his special rice sauce, the secret of which he has brought with him. The seafood is top quality (not an imitation crab in sight), and the unagi nigiri and spicy tuna sashimi are especially good. The daily two-for-one bento boxes are a real bargain for hungry appetites.

615 Yates St. (between Broad and Government). ℂ **250/382-8768.** Reservations recommended. Main courses C$10–C$20. Daily 11am–10pm.

Baan Thai THAI   Original art from Thailand creates an elegant restaurant where food and spices are taken seriously. The Singha beer and many ingredients are imported directly from Thailand. The menu has a good variety of classic dishes, pad Thais, stir-fries, curries, and burning hot (count the peppers) garlic prawns. The green curry with eggplants, bamboo shoots, and sweet basil leaves in coconut milk is especially good. Most items can be adapted to accommodate vegetarians, and dishes can be made as hot or as mild as you prefer. Portions are on the small side, however, so if you're sharing, order an extra item.

1117 Blanshard St. ℂ **250/383-0050.** www.baanthaivictoria.ca. Main courses C$12–C$18. Mon–Sat 11:30am–10pm; Sun 5–10pm.

Café Vieux Montreal ★★ FRENCH CANADIAN   It's all too easy to miss the entrance that leads into this slightly scruffy bakery and cafe. Don't let looks fool you. Chef-owner Pierre Bourget is a disciple of the Slow Food movement and traded 25 years in fine dining to get back in touch with real food. He apprentices all his own chefs, and makes everything in-house and/or by hand, including smoking the salmon with ice so the fish doesn't get too hard; he also makes breads with no sugar or oil and minimal yeast, and a vinaigrette that takes 2 days to create. The Montreal smoked meat is excellent, as

Best Breakfasts

Two of the best breakfasts in town are **Blue Fox Café,** 919 Fort St. (✆ **250/380-1683**), a small, always jampacked cafe that oozes with mouth-watering smells of down-to-earth but mountain-high pancake stacks, eight varieties of eggs Benny, and homemade granola. Get there early to avoid long lineups. And **Mole,** 554 Pandora Ave. (✆ **250/385-6653**), a hip and happening hangout for artists and other characters who gravitate towards its bohemian atmosphere, its sage-roasted yam omelet, portobello-stuffed avocado and curry tofu scramble. On Friday and Saturday nights only, it keeps the doors open beyond the usual 4pm closing for dinner and musical jam sessions.

are all the sandwiches, but we say go for the Artisan Platter as sampler tastes, and ask to add the smoked portobello salad and the mushroom bruschetta, which virtually melts in your mouth. On the weekends, the cafe often features very good Swiss-cheese fondues as well as French specialties like escargot and duck confit salad.

1314 Government St. ✆ **250/382-7700.** Main courses C$12. MC, V. Mon–Fri 8am–6pm.

Camille's ★ PACIFIC NORTHWEST   The restaurant's owner was one of the founders of the Vancouver Island Farm Co-operative, so, true to form, the ever-changing menu is seasonal and packed with locally sourced ingredients. This might mean tender fiddleheads in spring, and wild salmon and blackberry desserts in the fall. Canadian bison, wild boar, and caribou might also be on the menu—wild game is a specialty, alongside pheasant, quail, and partridge. Everything has an unexpected touch, such as prawn bisque with ginger and lemon, or fennel cakes in a champagne sauce. Camille's is a very romantic spot with cliché, crisp white linens, exposed-brick walls, stained-glass lamps, soft jazz, and candlelight. As with many Victoria restaurants, the five-course tasting menu (C$50) includes a bit of everything; add C$25 for wine pairings. Wine tastings are held on Sunday evenings.

45 Bastion Sq. ✆ **250/381-3433.** www.camillesrestaurant.com. Reservations recommended. Main courses C$26–C$37. AE, MC, V. Daily 5:30–10pm.

Herald Street Caffe ★ PACIFIC NORTHWEST   Consistently great, and sometimes inspired, the food here is combined with an imaginative martini menu, and a wine list offering French and Canadian labels, along with a selection of local reds and whites. Located in a renovated 19th-century warehouse on the far side of Chinatown, it has a casual, lively atmosphere that's geared to the younger crowd. All desserts, breads, pastas, soups—even the jam—are made in-house. Main dishes focus on fresh, local seafood and organic produce. The clams are superb, and the crab cakes have been written up by *Bon Appétit* and *Gourmet* magazines. Portions are large enough that small eaters might want to share. In topping off your meal with exceptionally good service, this restaurant earns its reputation as one of the city's best.

546 Herald St. (in Chinatown). ✆ **250/381-1441.** Reservations required. Main courses C$16–C$39. AE, DC, MC, V. Daily 5–10pm; Sat–Sun brunch 11am–3pm.

Pagliacci's ITALIAN   Opened in 1979 by expatriate New Yorker Howie Siegal, Pagliacci's is not your ordinary Italian restaurant. Named after the Italian word for *clown,* it's elbow-to-elbow most nights, and tables are quite close together. This is not the place for

VICTORIA

5

WHERE TO DINE

(Value) **Bargain Meals**

These tiny and inexpensive Asian eateries aren't much on decor (wear your jeans) but they're big on flavor and small in price. **My Thai Café** (1020 Cook St.; ℂ **250/472-7574**) doesn't offer a huge variety on the menu, but what there is, is excellent home-cooked Thai food. The beef salad is tasty. **Wah Lai Yuen** (560 Fisgard St. [in Chinatown]; ℂ **250/381-5355**) offers an authentic Chinese dining experience. If you can put up with the sometimes-offhand service, the humongous servings make this a real deal. For carnivores, you can't go wrong with **Pig** (749 E. View St.; ℂ **250/381-4677**), a hole-in-the-wall take-out diner that dishes up some of the best pulled-pork and beef-brisket sandwiches in town—basted, seasoned, marinated to tasty perfection, with trimmings such as pickle on a stick.

And for gamblers? Order the C$10 Mahoney at **Floyd's Diner** (866 Yates St.; ℂ **250/382-5114**) and let the kitchen cook up whatever it wants. After eating, flip a coin, and if you win, the meal is free. If you lose, you pay double.

those wanting a private tête-à-tête nor for connoisseurs in search of exquisite Italian cuisine (those folks need to go to Il Tarrazzo; see above). Pagliacci's is just fun. You can mix and match selections from the menu in true *When Harry Mets Sally* style, especially when items have such a quirky Hollywood take that you'll want to experiment: take Popeye's Salad (with spinach, naturally) or the Mae West Veal Medallions as examples. You'll also find more traditional menu items such as veal parmigiana and almost two dozen a la carte freshly made pastas, including wheatless alternatives. And if all this isn't entertainment enough, there's live jazz Sunday through Wednesday. The likes of Diana Krall and Etta James have played Pagliacci's.

1011 Broad St. ℂ **250/386-1662.** Reservations not accepted. Lunch C$7–C$12; dinner C$12–C$25. AE, MC, V. Mon–Thurs 11:30am–11pm; Fri–Sat 11:30am–midnight; Sun 11am–11pm.

rebar Modern Food ★ (Kids) VEGETARIAN   This bright and funky basement restaurant is likely the best vegetarian cafe on the West Coast. The juice bar alone boasts more than 80 varieties of deliciously healthful smoothies, shakes, wheatgrass drinks, and power tonics. The stress-busting Soul Change—a blend of carrot, apple, celery, ginger, and Siberian ginseng—is a winner. The menu is geared (though not exclusively) to vegetarian and vegan diners, featuring international cuisine from Thai curries and pastas to hummus and fresh shrimp quesadillas. The homemade muesli is dynamite, and the Cascadia Bakery produces everything from decadent vegan Belgian chocolate fudge cake to hand-shaped whole-grain specialty breads. The small wine list offers predominately BC wines, and even when it's really busy (which is most of the time), the service remains fast and friendly. rebar is a number-one choice for juices, a top spot for lunch, and good for dinner only if you're still in your jeans and needing something fast and nutritious.

50 Bastion Sq. (downstairs). ℂ **250/361-9223.** www.rebarmodernfood.com. Reservations not accepted. Main courses C$8–C$16. AE, MC, V. Mon–Thurs 8:30am–9pm; Fri–Sat 8:30am–10pm; Sun 8:30am–3:30pm. Reduced hours in winter.

VICTORIA

5

WHERE TO DINE

The Tea Experience

When the Duchess of Bedford (1788–1861) complained about a "sinking feeling" in the late afternoon, she invented afternoon tea to keep her going until dinner. Today, however, tea has come to mean everything from a genteel cup of Earl Grey to a full-blown meal in itself with scones with whipped cream, savory crustless sandwiches, sweet tartlets, and home-baked biscuits. Among the top choices are:

- **The Fairmont Empress** (721 Government St.; © **250/389-2727**) serves its famed epicurean feast in the Tea Lobby and elsewhere as the throngs of tea-takers dictate. It's expensive (C$49–$C60 in high season) and, quite frankly, overrated, although the inflated price does include a keepsake of nicely packaged Empress tea.
- **The Blethering Place Tearoom** (2250 Oak Bay Ave., Oak Bay; © **250/598-1413**) is slightly less pretentious and has the art of tea down pat. Tea menus start at C$20 and are what a quintessential Victorian teahouse is all about.
- **White Heather Tea Room** (1885 Oak Bay Ave.; © **250/595-8020**) is a local favorite just down the road. Small, bright, and exceptionally friendly, the Big Muckle Giant Tea for Two (C$40) is the grand slam of all teas. Smaller options are available.
- **Point Ellice House** (2616 Pleasant St.; © **250/380-6506**) was where Victoria's social elite gathered in early 1900s. Located only a 5-minute ferry ride from the Inner Harbour, it's a place where today you can enjoy tea (summer only) near the water on beautiful lawns. The cost of C$23 includes a half-hour tour of the mansion and gardens.
- Farther afield, taking tea in the elegant **Butchart Gardens Dining Room** (800 Benvenuto Ave.; © **250/652-4422**) is worth the drive, although you can only enjoy the experience if you've also paid for admission to the gardens. A full tea is C$27.
- **Murchie's Tea and Coffee** (1110 Government St.; © **250-383-3112**) offers the best selection of teas in the city, plus good coffee and everything from snacks to full-blown sandwiches and salads (C$5–C$14).
- **Mela's Tearoom** (792 Humboldt St.; © **250/382-8528**) adjoins Winchester Art Gallery, a contemporary showroom specializing in Canadian, American, and European fine art and prints. It's the only place to take tea with Chagall, Picasso, Warhol, and others. With some paintings commanding several thousand dollars, tea is a welcome respite at C$19.
- **Dutch Bakery** (718 Fort St.; © **250/385-1012**) is where to go for a quick pick-me-up and an authentic, one-of-a-kind baked treat and European-style sugared confectionary. This is a fourth-generation Victoria institution that still feels a part of the '50s era. Try the dollar, a sponge roll and marzipan.

VICTORIA

5

WHERE TO DINE

Moderate & Inexpensive

Smoken Bones Cookshack ★★★ (Value) (Finds) SOUTHERN CAJUN-CRE-OLE Chef-owner Ken Hueston is high up in the food chain of the island's Chefs Collaborative. This unpretentious box-like restaurant lies in a small strip mall and positively pulsates with activity every minute it's open. For good reason. The southern BBQ and Cajun-Creole influenced dishes are phenomenal, the result of natural wood smoking techniques that see pork ribs spending hours in the smoker. The restaurant goes through about 20,000 kilograms (44,000 lb.) of pork ribs a month! Because the island would soon be pigless with this kind of ongoing volume, Hueston does buy about 20% of his products from the mainland. But for everything else, for the spicy Gumbo, fresh-baked cornbread, braised collard greens, and butter fried cabbage, it's backyard shopping. A day's special might just include 6 pints of green beans—all the farmer had left. The portions are generous, so it's a real find for families, with lots of opportunity for sharing plates and eat-all-you-can buffets to satiate hearty appetites.

101-721 Station St., Victoria. ℂ **250/391-6328.** www.smokenbones.ca. Reservations recommended. Main courses C$12–C$18. MC, V. Mon–Sat 11:30am–9pm; Sun noon–9pm.

5 EXPLORING VICTORIA

If you're staying anywhere near the downtown core, trade the car for a good pair of walking shoes, because virtually everything in this chapter is doable on foot. Besides, walking is by far the best way to appreciate some of Victoria's diverse architecture: heritage residences, refurbished turn-of-the-century warehouses, and ornamental showpieces. Start with the attractions around the Inner Harbour and fan out from there for a refreshing walk through Beacon Hill Park, or head in the opposite direction for great shopping. The waterfront is also the departing point for most of the city's tours, whether you're off to Butchart Gardens (see chapter 6), or up for whale-watching or a kayaking excursion. Attractions that are out of Victoria Central, such as Craigdarroch Castle, Abkazi Garden, and Hatley Park, are only a 10-minute cab ride away. *Tip:* If you're planning to do a lot of sightseeing, purchase a City Passport (C$23), a pocket-size book packed with visitor information and discounts on attractions of up to 50% at over 30 Victoria attractions.

THE TOP ATTRACTIONS

Art Gallery of Greater Victoria Located near Craigdarroch Castle, the AGGV, as it's often called, exhibits more than 15,000 pieces of art, drawn mainly from Asia, Europe, and North America. Permanent collections include a life-size dollhouse and an authentic Shinto shrine that is part of Canada's most extensive Japanese art collection. Most compelling is the Emily Carr exhibit, which integrates her visual and written work alongside images from the BC provincial archives, together creating an in-depth portrait of this pre-eminent Victoria artist.

1040 Moss St. ℂ **250/384-4101.** www.aggv.bc.ca. Admission C$12 adults, C$10 students and seniors. Daily 10am–5pm (Thurs to 9pm). Bus: 11, 14, or 22.

Craigdarroch Castle ★★ If you've got it, flaunt it. That's what coal baron Robert Dunsmuir (the wealthiest and most influential man in British Columbia back in the 1880s) decided to do. More than a home, this Highland-style castle rises 87 stairs through five floors of Victorian opulence—and there's not an elevator to be had! Children might think it's like something out of Disneyland. The nonprofit society that runs Craigdarroch does so with impressive care; the stained glass, Persian carpets, and intricate woodwork are treasures to behold. Visitors receive a self-guided tour booklet, and volunteers delight in sharing sidebars of Dunsmuir's family history. Head to the top for a fabulous view of Victoria, the Strait of Juan de Fuca, and the Olympic Mountains. Allow about an hour to tour the castle.

1050 Joan Cres. (off Fort St.). ℭ 250/592-5323. www.craigdarrochcastle.com. Admission C$12 adults, C$11 seniors, C$8 students, C$4 children 6–18, free for children 5 and under. Mid-June to after Labor Day daily 9am–7pm; Sept to mid-June daily 10am–4:30pm. Take Fort St. out of downtown, just past Pandora Ave., and turn right on Joan Cres. Bus: 11 or 14.

Maritime Museum of British Columbia   Located in a former Victoria courthouse, this museum celebrates British Columbia's seafaring history in film and exhibits, from whalers and grand ocean liners to military conflict and 20th-century explorers. Highlights include a replica of the HMS *Temeraire,* constructed entirely of beef and chicken bones by French naval prisoners captured during the Napoleonic Wars. Check out the heritage courtroom renovated by Francis Rattenbury, and one of Victoria's most ornate elevators. Plan to stay $1^1/_2$ hours, longer if you have salt in your veins; the museum maintains a registry of heritage vessels and a wealth of information for maritime buffs. The gift shop has an excellent selection of nautical paraphernalia. Kids' programs include a sleepover in this purportedly haunted place!

28 Bastion Sq. ℭ 250/385-4222. www.mmbc.bc.ca. Admission C$10 adults, C$8 seniors and students, C$5 children 6–11, free for children 5 and under, C$20 family pass. Daily 9:30am–4:30pm. Bus: 5 to View St.

Miniature World (Kids)   If you ever wondered what Gulliver felt like in the land of the Lilliputians, this little world reveals all. Children and the young at heart will love the more than 80 miniature displays (many of them in motion) of solar systems, battle scenes, fancy 18th-century dress balls, a three-ring circus, and dozens of scenes from beloved fairy tales. A big favorite is the Great Canadian Railway, one of the world's largest model railways, although close contenders are the world's smallest operational sawmill and two of the world's largest dollhouses. Allow an hour.

649 Humboldt St. ℭ 250/385-9731. www.miniatureworld.com. Admission C$12 adults, C$9 children 12–17, C$7 children 3–11, free for children 2 and under. Mid-June to Labor Day daily 9am–9pm; after Labor Day to mid-June daily 9am–5pm. Bus: 5, 27, 28, 30, or 31.

Pacific Undersea Gardens (Kids)   The stark exterior looks out of place in Victoria's Inner Harbour, but descend the sloping stairway and you're in another world—below the waterline. From a glass-enclosed sunken vessel, you get to experience the harbor's marine life, which swims all around you in natural aquariums. All manner of fish—from brilliant red snapper to stonefish and octopi—swim through the kelp forest. Divers descend every hour to show the audience some of the harder-to-see creatures, like starfish tucked in rocks, wolf eels, and sharks. The observatory also cares for injured and orphaned seals, many of which prefer to stay in the area after their release. Buy a bag of herring in the gift shop and feed them a feast. Plan to stay about an hour, although feeding the seals is so captivating you may want to hang around.

490 Belleville St. ℭ 250/382-5717. www.pacificunderseagardens.com. Admission C$10 adults, C$9 seniors, C$8 children 12–17, C$6 children 5–11, free for children 4 and under. June–Sept daily 9am–8pm; Oct–May daily 10am–5pm. Bus: 5, 27, 28, or 30.

Eminent Victorian: Francis Mawson Rattenbury

As one of Victoria's most famous people, **Francis Mawson Rattenbury** ("Ratz," as he was known) not only left his architectural mark on the city (including the Parliament Buildings and the Empress Hotel), but also was among Victoria's most controversial residents. In 1892, at 25 years of age, he arrived here from England, having won a competition to design the Parliament Buildings. It was an impressive start to an illustrious career, during which he only ever sought the largest commissions and boldest opportunities. These included branches for the Bank of Montreal, the Vancouver Hotel, and provincial courthouses in Nanaimo, Nelson, and Vancouver.

Rattenbury's reputation, however, suffered when, in his mid-50s, he left his wife Florrie and appeared publicly with his mistress, Alma Packenham—a beautiful woman 30 years his junior and already twice married. After divorcing Florrie, Rattenbury married Alma, and in 1930, when they realized they had become social pariahs, they left for England. But the age differences began to tell, and increasingly, Rattenbury took solace in the whiskey bottle.

In 1934, when 17-year-old George Stoner was hired as their chauffeur, Alma quickly seduced the young man and installed him in the spare bedroom as her lover-in-residence. But, driven wild at the prospect of being discovered, Stoner came upon a dozing Rattenbury in the living room and clubbed him to death. Both Alma and Stoner were charged with murder, and after a sensational trial, Alma was acquitted and Stoner sentenced to hang. Alma, however, was unable to face Stoner's execution, and within 4 days she committed suicide by stabbing herself through the heart. Stoner was later released from prison.

Parliament Buildings   By night, this architectural gem is lit by thousands of lights so that it looks more like the Hogwarts School for Wizards than the provincial Parliament Buildings. Designed by then-25-year-old Francis Rattenbury, one of the most sought-after architects of the day, the buildings were constructed between 1893 and 1898 at a cost of nearly C$1 million. The interior is equally mystical, filled with mosaics, marble, woodwork, and stained glass. If the Legislature is sitting, head up to the visitor's gallery. There's not a lot of room there, but it's fun to watch politicians in action. British Columbia is known for its eccentric politics, and Question Period, in the early afternoon, can be particularly entertaining. The "been there, done that" crowd could do this in 20 minutes; guided tours (summer only) last about 40 minutes and leave every half-hour from the central lobby; they include dialogue with interpretive actors along the way.

501 Belleville St. © 250/387-3046. www.victoriabc.ca/victoria/parliamentbuildings.htm. Free admission. Daily 9am–5pm. Bus: 5, 27, 28, or 30.

Royal British Columbia Museum ★★★ (Kids   This museum is one of the best regional museums in the world and is worthy of at least a half-day. The dioramas are so lifelike you'll feel as if you're stepping back in time—whether it's coming face-to-tusk with a wooly mammoth, tracking through a BC forest or to the edge of a glacier, or meandering down the cobblestone streets of a pioneer town. Feel the train rattle the timbers of the old train station each time it passes, or enjoy old Charlie Chaplin movies in the movie theater. Just like an IKEA store, the museum has a route that doesn't bypass a thing, so start at the top in the Modern History Gallery (the showcases have items from the early 1900s through to the power [']80s that highlight the lifestyles of each decade), and work your way down through the second-floor Natural History Gallery and the First Peoples Gallery with its totems, Native longhouses, and artifacts. The museum also has an IMAX theater, showing an ever-changing variety of large-screen movies (☎ **250/953-IMAX** [4629] or 250/953-4629; www.imaxvictoria.com). Thunderbird Park, beside the museum, houses a cedar longhouse, where Native carvers work on new totem poles. *Note:* Admission rates are sometimes higher during special exhibitions.

675 Belleville St. ☎ **250/356-7226.** www.royalbcmuseum.bc.ca. Admission C$15 adults; C$9.50 seniors, students, and children 6–18; free for children 5 and under; C$38 family pass. Museum-IMAX combination and IMAX-only tickets available. Daily 9am–5pm. Bus: 5, 28, or 30.

Royal London Wax Museum (Kids) If you've been to Madame Tussaud's in London, then you'll be disappointed, but for those who have never seen a wax-works exhibition, it can be quite fun. You'll find celebrities, world leaders, and historical figures mixing and mingling in groupings never dreamed of. There's a gaggle of waxy royal figures (Camilla included) along Royalty Row, an Einstein-esque Wizard of Oz in Storybook Land, and a host of significant others past and present. The Chamber of Horrors doesn't exactly scare up a flutter, even in the faint of heart. The average price tag for each figure is C$10,000, depending on how popular it is. U.S. presidents go cheap; Canadian prime ministers are pricey. Plan to spend 1½ hours if you're with kids—they love the place—and half that time if you've done wax museums elsewhere in the world and are just trying to get in out of the rain.

470 Belleville St. ☎ **250/388-4461.** www.waxmuseum.bc.ca. Admission C$12 adults, C$11 seniors, C$8 students, C$5 children 6–12, free for children 5 and under. May–Sept daily 9am–7:30pm; Oct–Apr daily 9am–5pm. Bus: 5, 27, 28, or 30.

Victoria Bug Zoo ★★ (Kids) In the heart of downtown Victoria, enter an amazing world of international insects: walking sticks, praying manti, tarantulas, and scorpions, to name a few. Although all the creepy-crawlies are behind glass, an entomologist (bug scientist) is on hand to answer questions and show you how to handle some of the mul-tilegged creatures, which include a 400-leg millipede that stretches the length of your forearm. Even if you're spider-wary, this is a fascinating place. Kids will want to spend a couple of hours here.

631 Courtney St. ☎ **250/384-2847.** www.bugzoo.bc.ca. Admission C$8 adults, C$7 seniors, C$6 students, C$5 children 3–16, free for children 2 and under. Family pass C$25. Daily 11am–5pm. Any downtown bus.

PARKS & GARDENS

Victoria is famed for its garden landscapes and for its abundance of flowers. Even if there's not a horticultural bone in your body, you really can't help but appreciate the efforts that have earned the city such acclaim. Look overhead and chances are that there'll be an overstuffed hanging basket trailing with colorful blooms. And in most of the residential neighborhoods, private homeowners take special pride in their gardens.

Among the most spectacular examples are **The Gardens at Government House** (1401 Rockland Ave.; ☎ **250/387-2080;** www.ltgov.bc.ca/gardens), the official (and private) residence of British Columbia's Lieutenant Governor. The formal gardens are free to wander from dawn to dusk, and for rose lovers in particular, they're well worth the visit.

Guided tours run May through September (C$35 for groups of five or fewer) and include areas not normally open to the public.

Nearby **Abkhazi Garden** (1964 Fairfield Rd.; ℂ **250/598-8096;** www.conservancy. bc.ca) is a dramatic, half-hectare (1-acre) jewel of a garden created by Prince and Princess Nicholas Abkhazi in the 1940s. Amid the woodland, rocky slopes and rhododendrons is a quaint tearoom and gift shop. The gardens are open April to September, Wednesday through Sunday, 1 to 5pm. Another once-private residence is **Hatley Park & Museum** (2005 Sooke Rd.; ℂ **250/391-2666;** www.hatleygardens.com). This is actually a National Historic Site and boasts one of the few Edwardian estates in Canada, complete with Italian, Rose, and Japanese gardens. There are hundreds of heritage trees, including 250-year-old Douglas firs, an ecologically important salt marsh estuary, and a series of natural springs. Garden and castle tours are offered weekdays, 1 to 4pm. Admission is by donation. Next door, **Royal Roads University** (ℂ **250/391-2511**) also features extensive floral gardens, which are open to the public, free of charge. The University of Victoria, too, has gardens that are free to wander: **Finnerty Gardens** (3800 Finnerty Rd.; ℂ **250/ 721-7606**) contain one of Canada's best collections of rhododendrons, many of which were started from seed from famous plant explorers. There are over 500 different varieties as well as 1,600 trees, shrubs, companion plants, and ornamentals. The gardens cover 2.6 hectares (6½-acres) and are open daily from dawn to dusk. The entrance to the gardens is near the University Chapel, on the southwest edge of the campus. Proceed around the Ring Road to parking lot 6.

If you're staying put around the downtown core, a walk through **Beacon Hill Park** is a must. Originally gifted to the city by the Hudson's Bay Company in 1882, today it stretches from just behind the Royal BC Museum to Dallas Road. Without doubt, it's the top park in Victoria—an oasis of indigenous Garry oaks, floral gardens, windswept heath, ponds, and totem poles. There's also a children's farm (see "Especially for Kids," later in this chapter), aviary, tennis courts, lawn-bowling green, putting green, playgrounds, and picnic areas. En route, be sure to drop by tiny **Thunderbird Park** (at the corner of Bellevue and Douglas streets, beside the Royal BC Museum). It has several totem poles, and in summer, there's an outdoor studio for experienced carvers to create new poles. Adjacent to the park lies **Helmcken House,** the oldest house still on its original site in British Columbia.

OUTDOOR ACTIVITIES

Vancouver Island, and even urban Victoria, is garnering quite a reputation for its range of outdoor activities. Hiking and biking are big pastimes for both residents and visitors, and there is an abundance of whale-watching companies. Victoria is also a good resource for activities farther afield such as scuba diving (Ogden Point Dive Centre, 199 Dallas Rd.; ℂ **888/701-1177** or 250/380-9119; www.divevictoria.com) and birding (Victoria Natural History Society; ℂ **250/592-3381;** www.vicnhs.bc.ca).

BIKING   Cycling is a popular mode of transportation, and bike paths abound here. There's a scenic **Marine Drive bike path** that takes you around the peninsula and over to Oak Bay. The Inner Harbour also has a bike lane alongside the pedestrian pathway. The city's jewel, however, is the 60km (about 37-mile) **Galloping Goose Trail** (ℂ **250/ 478-3344;** www.gallopinggoosetrail.com, for maps and information). This terrific rail-to-trail conversion starts in Victoria at the south end of the Selkirk Trestle, at the foot of Alston Street in Victoria West, and travels the back roads through urban, rural, and semi-wilderness landscapes. There are access points along the entire trail route with many

On the Waterfront

Be sure to visit **Fisherman's Wharf** near the Laurel Point Hotel. It's a delightful 15-minute walk along the waterfront from the Inner Harbour, at the end of which you'll find a picturesque flotilla of working fishing boats, houseboats, yachts, and other sailing vessels. Here's where to buy fish right off the boats—shrimp, halibut, crab, and whatever is the catch of the day. The other waterfront is **the pier** just below Wharf Street on the far side of the sea wall—look for the bubblegum-pink building—where seaplanes, kayak outfitters, and whale watchers stake their base camps. Either wharf is great for people-watching, and locals will wager with you on which wharf offers the best fish and chips.

parking areas. It is named after a gawky and noisy 1920s gasoline-powered passenger car that operated on the abandoned CNR line between Victoria and Sooke.

Great Pacific Adventures, 811 Wharf St. (✆ **877/733-6722** or 250/386-2277; www. greatpacificadventures.com), rents bikes from C$8 per hour or C$35 per day (call ahead in winter), as does **Cycle BC,** with two locations—at 707 Douglas St. for bikes and 950 Wharf St. for scooters and motorcycles (✆ **250/885-2453**; www.cyclebc.ca). Twenty-one-speed bicycles are C$7 per hour; off-road bikes start at C$12 per hour. Honda Scooters are C$16 per hour for a single seater (C$69/day) and C$19 per hour for a double seater (C$79/day); and for the hard-core biker in us all, a Harley Davidson Road King rents for C$58/hour; C$225/day.

CANOEING & KAYAKING   **Ocean River Sports,** 1824 Store St. (✆ **800/909-4233** or 250/381-4233; www.oceanriver.com), on the waterfront, caters to novice and experienced paddlers alike, with rentals, equipment, dry storage camping gear, and a number of guided tours. Beginners should opt for the 2¹/₂-hour "Explorer" around Victoria Harbour (C$125), with kids at half price. More adventuresome kayakers can go for the multi-day adventure to explore the Gulf Islands (C$595, inclusive of tent accommodations on secluded beaches and meals). Rentals are C$25 for 2 hours, C$50 for an 8-hour day. *Tip:* Because of Ocean River's waterfront location, absolute beginners can rent a kayak for a try-out paddle in the harbor's protected waters.

Victoria Kayak Tours (950 Wharf St. ✆ **250/216-5646;** www.victoriakayak.com) does 2¹/₂-hour naturalist tours to Seal Island (C$59) and a 6-hour excursion to the Strait of Juan de Fuca (C$125).

FISHING   Saltwater fishing is very popular here, and guides will show you the current hot spots. **Adam's Fishing Charters** (✆ **250/370-2326;** www.adamsfishingcharters. com) and **Beasleys Fishing Charters** (✆ **866/259-1111** or 250/381-8000; www.beasleys fishingcharters.com) are good starting points. Fishing charters are C$95 an hour, for a minimum of 5 hours. Full-day charters are C$800.

To fish, you need a **saltwater fishing license,** available at Adam's and the Marine Adventure Centre. For nonresidents, a 1-day license costs C$14, a 3-day license C$26, and a 5-day license C$39. Fees are reduced for BC and Canada residents. If you're interested in taking the wheel yourself, **Great Pacific Adventures,** 811 Wharf St. (✆ **877/ 733-6722** or 250/386-2277; www.greatpacificadventures.com) rents watercraft, including 4.9m (16-ft.) powerboats at C$50 an hour.

For fly-fishing, **Robinson's Outdoor Store,** 1307 Broad St. (℃ **888/317-0033** or 250/385-3429; www.robinsonsoutdoors.com), is an excellent resource for information and all outdoor gear, including specialty flies for area waters, rods, reels, and resource books. They also sell **freshwater fishing licenses.** For nonresidents, a 1-day license is C$21, and an 8-day is C$53, with lower fees for BC and Canada residents.

GOLF Victoria has an enviable number of good courses. The fees are reasonable, the scenery is spectacular, and most courses are open year-round. Co-designed by Jack Nicklaus and his son Steve, the Mountain Course, which lies in the foothills of Mount Finlayson atop **Bear Mountain Golf Resort** (1999 Country Club Way; ℃ **888/533-BEAR** [2327] or 250/391-7160; www.bearmountain.com), is a hot favorite, so book well in advance to avoid disappointment. Rates are C$130 Monday through Thursday and C$145 Friday through Sunday. Rates include a GPS-equipped cart. The Nicklaus duo also co-designed the new Valley Course, 9 holes of which opened in 2008 with completion slated for spring 2009. Check into Bear Mountain's website and you can enjoy all 18 holes in a computer-generated demonstration. The **Olympic View Golf Club,** 643 Latoria Rd. (℃ **800/I-GOLFBC** [445-5322] or 250/474-3671; www.golfbc.com), is one of the top 35 golf courses in Canada, with two waterfalls and 12 lakes sharing space with the greens. The 6,414-yard course is par 72, and green fees range from C$40 winter season to C$80 on a summer weekend. The **Cedar Hill Municipal Golf Course,** at 1400 Derby Rd. (℃ **250/475-7151**), is a more modest 18-hole public course located only 3.5km (2 miles) from downtown Victoria. Daytime fees are C$35; twilight, junior, and winter fees are C$25. Tee-off times are first come, first served. The **Cordova Bay Golf Course,** at 5333 Cordova Bay Rd. (℃ **250/658-4444;** www.cordovabaygolf.com), is midway between the Victoria International Airport and downtown Victoria—about a 20-minute drive from either location. It's par 72; expect some tight fairways and 66 sand traps. May to September, daytime green fees Friday to Sunday are C$69, and Monday to Thursday are C$64, when booked 7 days in advance. Tee times within 7 days are for members only. From October to April, green fees range from C$46 weekdays to C$59 weekends (including Fri).

The website www.vancouverisland.com/golf lists golf courses around the island, including Arbutus Ridge at Cobble Hill and Glen Meadows Golf & Country Club in Sidney. If you're tight for time, call the **Last Minute Golf Hotline** at ℃ **604/878-1833** for substantial discounts and short-notice tee times at courses in and around Victoria. Book online at www.lastminutegolfbc.com.

SAILING Sailors have often remarked that the Juan de Fuca Strait is some of the best and prettiest sailing areas in the world. **Blackfish Sailing Adventures** (℃ **250/216-2389;** www.blackfishal.com) leaves Oak Bay Marina for 3-hour and full-day excursions aboard a 35-foot Beneteau "oceanus" sloop. You can participate, learn to crew, or just relax. Binoculars are provided. Blackfish organizes sails around Vancouver Island, which are available to do in legs, or in its entirety. For an even more romantic option, with **Tall Ship Adventures** (℃ **877/788-4263** or 250/885-2311) you can hop aboard the 55-foot-tall ship *Thane.* It's a 1978 vessel modeled after Joshua Slocum's *Spray,* the first vessel to circumnavigate the world single-handedly, in 1895. Departures are from the Inner Harbour; 3-hour trips are C$69 per person.

WHALE-WATCHING Orcas (killer whales), harbor seals, sea lions, porpoises, and gray whales ply these waters year-round, so whale-watching outfitters abound. Competition keeps prices in line—expect to pay about C$95 for a 2- to 3-hour excursion—so the real choice is between riding the waves in a zippy 12-person Zodiac or in a larger, more leisurely craft. Some reputable outfits include **Orca Spirit Adventures** (© **250/383-8411;** www.orcaspirit.com), which departs from the Coast Harbourside Hotel dock; **Seafun Safaris Whale Watching,** 950 Wharf St. (© **877/360-1233** or 250/360-1200; www.seafun.com); and **Prince of Whales,** 812 Wharf St. (© **888/383-4884** or 250/383-4884; www.princeofwhales.com), which also offers Victoria/Vancouver one-way trips and circle runs with stop-overs at Butchart Gardens and the Gulf Islands.

ORGANIZED TOURS

BUS TOURS   **Grayline of Victoria** (© **800/663-8390** or 250/388-6359; www.grayline.ca) conducts tours of the city and, notably, of **Butchart Gardens.** The 1¹⁄₂-hour **"Grand City tour"** costs C$27 for adults, C$16 for children 2 to 11. In July and August, daily tours depart every 30 minutes from 9:30am to 4:30pm. In spring and fall, tours depart hourly, and in winter there are only three departures a day. Call ahead for exact times. Grayline also offers seasonal tours, such as Ghost Tours and Murder Mysteries, as well as hop on–hop off loop tours aboard colorful trolley buses. The 1-hour loop is C$25 adult; C$13 children 2 to 11, but you can make the loop last all day if you stop off to visit attractions en route. Check the website for details.

FERRY TOURS   Departing from various stops around the Inner Harbour, **Victoria Harbour Ferries** (© **250/708-0201;** www.victoriaharbourferry.com) offers terrific 45- and 55-minute tours of the harbor. See shipyards, wildlife, marinas, fishing boats, and floating homes from the water. Tours cost C$20 for adults, C$18 seniors, and C$10 for children 12 and under. From March 1 to April 30 and for the month of October they operate daily, every 15 minutes from 10am to 5pm. From May 1 to September 30 they run daily from 9am to 9pm. If you want to stop for food or a stroll, you can get a token that's good for reboarding at any time during the same day.

SPECIALTY TOURS   In the mood for something a little different? Climb into one of the bicycle-rickshaws operated by **Kabuki Cabs** (613 Herald St.; © **250/385-4243;** www.kabukicabs.com). They hold up to four people, operate seasonally, and run just like regular taxis; you can flag one down or (usually) find them parked in front of the Fairmont Empress. Rates run about C$1 per minute for a two-person cab, and C$1.75 per minute for a four-person cab. A typical 30-minute tour (you can set your own itinerary) runs about C$30 to C$60.

Tallyho Horse Drawn Tours (© **866/383-5067** or 250/383-5067; www.tallyhotours.com) has conducted horse-drawn carriage and wagon tours in Victoria since 1903. Wagons hold up to 20 strangers and as such, are by far the most affordable of the horse-drawn tours you'll find at C$15 adult, C$12 senior, and C$7 children for a 45-minute

VICTORIA

5

EXPLORING VICTORIA

Ⓜoments   An Overview of the Islands

If time doesn't let you see everything this book has to offer, take a shortcut with a Harbour Seaplane Islands Extravaganza tour—a C$279, 75-minute flight through the Gulf and San Juan islands, and perhaps even a fly over Vancouver Island's wild, most westerly coast (see chapter 7). Add C$50 if you choose to stop over for an hour in Ganges, Salt Spring Island—well worth it if you want to visit the Saturday morning market (see chapter 9).

roll around the city. In summer, tours depart daily, every half-hour from 9am to dusk. By far the most romantic are the turn-of-the-20th-century two-person carriage tours—from a short and sweet 15-minute harbor tour for C\$50 to a 45-minute ride through Beacon Hill Park at C\$130 or a 100-minute Romance tour for C\$240. All Tallyho rides start at the corner of Belleville and Menzies streets (across from the Royal London Wax Museum). Even more picturesque are the new "old" omni-trolley buses that ran around England in the 1920s. These horse-drawn double-decker beauties are operated by **Black Beauty Line Carriage Tours** (© 250/507-0789; www.blackbeautyline.com) at C\$25 adult and C\$13 children 12 and under.

To get a bird's-eye view of Victoria, **Harbour Air Seaplanes** (950 Wharf St.; © 800/665-0212 or 250/384-2215; www.harbour-air.com) provides 30-minute sky-tours of Victoria's panorama for C\$99 as well as a romantic Fly'n'Dine tour that combines a flight to Butchart Gardens, garden admission and dinner, and a limo ride back into town. The cost is C\$299 per person.

You can also take a limousine-only tour with **Heritage Tours and Daimler Limousine Service** (713 Bexhill Rd.; © 250/474-4332) around Victoria; rates start at C\$80 per hour. Stretch limos for 8 to 10 people are also available; hourly rates are C\$90 to C\$100.

WALKING TOURS Victoria is such a great walking city that guided walks proliferate. Sure, there are self-guided walks (maps are available at the Visitor Information Centre), but to get the most out of what you're seeing, nothing beats hearing the history, gossip, and anecdotes that tour guides can offer. **Discover the Past** (© 250/384-6698; www.discoverthepast.com) is the leader of the pack, offering walks conducted by historian and entertaining storyteller John Adams. Ninety-minute tours run year-round from the Visitor Information Centre at Government/Wharf streets and cover eight themes or areas, from ghostly walks in Old Town to historical walks around Chinatown; starting points may vary. Tours run June through September and cost C\$15, cash only.

Walkabout Historical Tours (© 250/592-9255) is the only company that tours the Fairmont Empress. Dressed in turn-of-the-20th-century clothes, guides are exceptionally well informed about this historical hotel (which is said to be haunted). Their knowledge adds a whole new dimension to enjoying high tea there later. The 90-minute, C\$10 tour departs daily at 10am sharp; meet at the Fairmont Empress store located next to the Tea Lobby (on the Belleville St. end of the hotel).

Victoria Bobby Walking Tours (© 250/995-0233; www.walkvictoria.com) offers a variety of walks around the city neighborhoods; they depart from the Visitor Information Centre May through mid-September daily at 11am. Your guide is an English ex-bobby—just look for that distinguishing helmet and bring along C\$15.

Sunday's Best

The **Old Cemetery Society of Victoria**'s (© 250/598-8870; www.oldcem.bc.ca) Sunday-only cemetery tours have become so popular that the group now has a full summer program. Guides take you through Ross Bay Cemetery as well as the Old Burying Ground of Pioneer Square Cemetery (the evening Lantern Tour is quite eerie). Visit the graves and hear Victoria's history through the lives of Emily Carr, Gold Rush prospectors, and others. Meet at 2pm in front of Starbucks, Fairfield Plaza, 1516 Fairfield Rd. Tours are C\$5. No reservations needed.

Travel with Taste (© 250/385-1527; www.travelwithtaste.com) hosts a deliciously
appetizing Urban Culinary Walking Tour around central downtown, during which you
can literally forage your way through hand-crafted chocolates, smoked meats, pâtés, teas,
baked treats, and wine. Four-hour tours cost C$89 per person, operate seasonally, and
begin at 11am near the gates of Chinatown. Advance reservations required.

6 ESPECIALLY FOR KIDS

There's no doubt that Victoria caters well to getaway travelers, whether looking for
romance or simply a quality urban destination. But families with children of all ages also
find much to enjoy here. There are the obvious city attractions such as the touchy-feely,
creepy-crawly **Victoria Bug Zoo** (p. 89) that's bound to be a sure-fire hit; the watery
kingdom of **Pacific Undersea Gardens** (p. 87); the diminutive displays at **Miniature
World** (p. 87); and the **Royal London Wax Museum** (p. 89)—although jaded teenagers
may not think the House of Horrors is macabre enough. Then there's the very unstuffy
Royal BC Museum (p. 88), which really does have something for all ages, especially
when combined with a visit to the **IMAX** theater.

For youngsters, the **Beacon Hill Children's Farm** (Circle Dr., Beacon Hill Park; © 250/
381-2532) is a well-established petting zoo with rabbits, goats, and other barnyard animals, which makes for a great outing, especially when coupled with some kite flying on
Beacon Hill or picnicking at the wading pool and playground nearby.

Outside of the downtown core, remember to check out the **Butterfly Gardens** (p. 108),
Fort Rodd Hill & Fisgard Lighthouse (p. 114), and **Mineral World & Scratch Patch**
(9891 Seaport Place, Sidney; © 250/655-4367; www.scratchpatch.com), an outdoor
garden containing two gold-panning pools, a pond filled with tropical shells, and
mounds of semi-precious gemstones. Admission is free, though if you're stone-digging,
you must buy a collector's bag for C$6 to C$15; anything you find, you can keep. The
Patch is open daily 9am to 6pm, with extended hours to 9pm in July and August.

For more kid-friendly suggestions, take a look at *The Kids' Guide to Victoria,* which
details more than 50 places to go and things to do around Vancouver Island. You can get
this guide by contacting Tourism Victoria (© 250/953-2033; www.tourismvictoria.
com).

All Fun Recreation Park   The park has two go-kart tracks, mini golf, and batting
cages, all priced separately, so it can get expensive. For example, the cost of go-karting is
C$12 per 6-minute session; mini golf is C$6 per adult, C$4.50 per child; and swinging
at 25 baseballs will set you back C$4. Save a few dollars and get a C$20 pass that includes
a go-kart ride, 18 holes of mini golf, and 50 balls in the batting cage.

2207 Millstream Rd. © **250/474-1961.** www.allfun.bc.ca. Mid-June to Labor Day daily 11am–7pm.
Admission C$4–C$20. Observers are C$6, which includes access to an 80-person hot tub and beach vol-
leyball courts.

Centre of the Universe   The larger of the two telescopes trained to the heavens was
once the largest in the world, so you know that the stargazing is good—depending on
the cloud cover. Nighttime vigils for the public are offered somewhat sporadically (especially in winter) as they're scheduled between bookings by professional astronomers. The

daytime 75-minute tour of the aging observatory is still a fun excursion from the downtown core.

5071 West Saanich Rd. (℃) **250/363-8262.** www.cu.hia.nrc.gc.ca. Admission before 7pm C$9 adults, C$8 seniors and students, and C$5 children; 7–11pm C$12 adults, C$10 seniors and students, C$5 children. Tues–Sat 3–11pm.

---

7 SHOPPING

GREAT SHOPPING AREAS

Victoria has dozens of specialty shops that make browsing a real delight. Nearly all are within walking distance of one another. Stores are generally open Monday through Saturday from 10am to 6pm; some are open on Sundays from noon to 5pm.

The first shopping foray for most visitors is to head up the brick-paved **Government Street promenade,** about 5 blocks north from the Inner Harbour. Many of the stores are housed in beautiful heritage buildings, and stepping inside is like stepping back a century. You'll find various specialty shops here, including ones featuring First Nations art. But be warned: Amid the jewels is an excess of souvenir shops, each hip-deep in bottles of maple syrup and Taiwanese knickknacks.

The largest shopping area runs north–south along Douglas Street and east–west along several cross streets, in particular Yates—the focal point of many restaurants and bars, too. It's where to find banks, camera suppliers, music stores, and other outlets. The multi-level **Bay Centre** ((℃) **250/952-5690;** www.thebaycentre.ca) anchors this city core and is where to shop for top-name fashions and mainstream goods. **The Bay** itself is also a popular department store; it got its start over 330 years ago as a series of trading posts across the country and is the oldest corporation in North America. Aside from designer labels and general housewares, you can still buy their famous red-green-and-yellow-striped point blanket, an item that was originally traded for beaver pelts.

Just off Government Street, adjacent to the Bay Centre, are intriguing shopping streets: **Trounce Alley,** Victoria's former red-light district now transformed into chic and hip, complete with authentic 125-year-old gaslights, and nearby **Broad Street,** a small and bustling strip packed with gift shops, galleries, and specialty stores. The area in and around Johnson Street has been dubbed LoJo (short for Lower Johnson) with more owner-operated outlets. Farther north, **Old Town/Market Square** features a fascinating blend of turn-of-the-20th-century buildings housing funky, up-to-date shops. The area is reminiscent of San Francisco's Garibaldi Square, but quainter, with live performances in summer. Nearby, Victoria's **Chinatown** is so tiny you might miss it. Search out **Fan Tan Alley.** It's Canada's thinnest commercial street, just over a meter (3¹⁄₄ ft.) wide at either end, yet crammed with oddball paraphernalia and a maze of doors leading to small courtyards—and even more doors leading to more back alleys, stairs, and living quarters. When the police used to raid gambling clubs, participants could easily escape through the myriad passageways. **Dragon Alley** is another alley weaving through what used to be tenement buildings in the 1880s when 16,000 Chinese lived here, and is now home to a Thai Spa, dog boutique, and sex shop. At the edge of Chinatown, adjacent to City Hall, is an up-and-coming area, which tourism officials are marketing as the city's new **Designer District.** Frankly, it's a bit of a stretch, but if you search, you will find one or two edgy housewares outlets such as *Urban Barn* and *Chintz,* home decor designer studios, and specialty stores like *Miroirs,* which sells mirrors of every ornamental shape, size, and design. If antiquing is your thing, make your way to **Fort Street,** fondly known as Antique Row, on the eastern edge of the downtown core. Items with hefty price tags are right alongside stores selling bric-a-brac, as well as an auction house where an unexpected bargain might be on the chopping block.

THE GOODS A TO Z
Antiques & Collectibles
Renowned for its high-quality British collectibles, Antique Row is a 3-block stretch along Fort Street between Blanshard and Cook streets. Here's where to find some of the finest in estate jewelry, silverware, heritage china, and furniture. In addition to those listed below, check out **Charles Baird,** 1044A Fort St. (✆ **250/384-8809**), for antique furniture; **Britannia & Co.,** 839 Fort St. (✆ **250/480-1954**) for porcelain figurines; and **Romanoff & Co.,** 837–839 Fort St. (✆ **250/480-1543**), for its impressive collection of coins and silverware. For the recreational antiquer looking for a bargain, the **Old Vogue Shop,** 1034 Fort St. (✆ **250/380-7751**), and **Recollections,** 828 Fort St. (✆ **250/385-1902**), are both generalist shops with a hodgepodge of items and styles.

Classic Silverware   A gorgeous shop that specializes in discontinued sterling silver and silver-plated flatware and tea service sets, it also maintains a registry for missing and discontinued china. 826 Fort St. ✆ 250/383-6860.

David Robinson Antiques   Come here for high-quality period furniture, silver, oriental rugs, paintings, and other fine antiques. 1023 Fort St. ✆ 250/384-6425.

Faith Grant's Connoisseur Shop   Housed in an 1862 heritage building, this store has a myriad of rooms filled with high-end household furnishings. 1156 Fort St. ✆ 250/383-0121.

Vanity Fair Antique Mall   With more than 40 dealers of crystal, glassware, furniture, and jewelry all under one roof, this mall offers everything from a mortgage to other more affordable items that might even leave change in your pocket. 1044 Fort St. ✆ 250/380-7274.

Art/Contemporary
Fran Willis Gallery   With its spacious 5m-high (16-ft.) ceilings and high arched windows, Victoria's oldest and largest contemporary gallery is certainly one of the nicest display spaces in the city. Look for established and emerging Western Canadian artists. 1619 Store St. ✆ 250/381-3422. www.franwillis.com.

Jade   Mined along the Coast Range of North America, this jade is renowned for being the brightest, hardest, greenest, and most translucent Nephrite Jade ever found. This gallery opened in 2008 as a showcase for different sculptural pieces as well as jewelry. 911 Government St. ✆ 250/384-5233. www.jademine.com.

The West End Gallery   This open, airy gallery features works by over 100 Canadian artists. Its specialty is original paintings, sculpture, and art glass. 1203 Broad St. ✆ 250/388-0009. www.westendgalleryltd.com.

Winchester Galleries   Offering a diversity of original Canadian art, both historical and contemporary, Winchester Galleries features names that include the Group of Seven, Jack Shadbolt, Mary Pratt, and Toni Onley. The main gallery is in Oak Bay at 2260 Oak Bay Ave. 1010 Broad St. ✆ 250/386-2773. www.winchestergalleriesltd.com.

Alcheringa Gallery   Recognized for its museum-quality (and expensive) aboriginal work from all over the world, this gallery offers many pieces that have a West Coast and Australasia influence. 665 Fort St. 🕐 250/383-8224. www.alcheringa-gallery.com.

Eagle Feather Gallery   This gallery carries one of the finest First Nations collections of authentic jewelry, arts, and crafts, all exclusively created by First Nations artists. A percentage of all profits is donated to First Nations' youth programs. 904 Gordon St. 🕐 250/388-4330. www.eaglefeathergallery.com.

Hills Native Art   One of the most respected stores for established BC First Nations artists, this is the place to find exquisite traditional pieces, such as wooden masks, drums, and talking sticks alongside items for the less serious collector, such as dream catchers and souvenir totem poles. 1008 Government St. 🕐 250/385-3911.

Books

Chapters Downtown   The mothership of all local Chapters bookstores, this location has three floors of book titles, DVDs, and stationery. In addition to the usual bargain tables on the main floor, there are some great deals on kids' books in the basement. 1212 Douglas St. 🕐 250/380-9009.

Chronicles of Crime   Every one of the more than 25,000 new and used book titles is spy-related, criminal, and mysterious. 1067 Fort St. 🕐 250/721-2665.

Munro's   The range of titles within the 1909 former bank building, described as Canada's most magnificent (architecturally speaking) bookstore, is impressive, and the remainder tables are filled with good discounts. 1108 Government St. 🕐 250/382-2464.

Shepherd Books   If you've ever watched the movie *You've Got Mail*, then you'll understand the dilemma of a small, independent bookstore trying to make its way, seemingly on sheer passion for the written word alone. This is one such store, specializing in quality new and second-hand books. Some are rare finds, such as a first edition of *The Little Prince*. 826 Fort St. 🕐 250/383-3981.

Crafts

Cowichan Trading Company   Best known for its authentic Cowichan sweaters and handmade moccasins, this store also sells a slew of junky T-shirts, giftware, and souvenirs. 1328 Government St. 🕐 250/383-0321. www.cowichantrading.com.

Starfish Glass Works   A former bank building now serves as a gallery-cum-workshop. Watch from the mezzanine level as award-winning artists transform molten glass into imaginative works of art. *Note:* Glass is blown during afternoons only, and not at all on Mondays or Tuesdays. 630 Yates St. 🕐 250/388-7827.

Fashion/Women

Although The Bay Centre holds court for many mainstream retailers such as La Senza, Guess?, and Jacob, specialty stores are your better bet for that more memorable purchase.

Edinburgh Tartan Shop   Looking for the *right* custom-fitted kilt in the *right* family plaid? Tartans can also be purchased by the yard and come with a huge collection of kilt pins as well as Highland scarves, brooches, sweaters, and blankets. 909 Government St. 🕐 250/953-7788.

Hughes Clothing   Look for names such as Eileen Fisher (USA), Nougat (London), Xandres (Belgium), and J. Lindeberg (Sweden). 564 Yates St. ℂ 250/381-4405. www.hughes clothing.com.

Not Just Pretty   Shop with a conscience. This sweatshop-free store carries organic, natural-fiber fashions (cotton, wool, and silk) where the production emphasis is on sustaining communities. Items range from T-shirts and skirts to dresses, jackets, cashmere sweaters, scarves, and hats. 1036 Fort St. ℂ 250/414-0414.

She She Bags   The most discriminating of bag fetishists will be satiated here, with all manner of offbeat and jewel-studded bags. Most of the whimsical designs are for the bold at heart, with the occasional classic design thrown in for good measure. 616 View St. ℂ 250/388-0613. www.she-shebags.com.

Smoking Lily   This tiny, home-based 4-sq.-m (43-sq.-ft.) store—one of the smallest in the world—is like a test-run showcase for new ideas in women's clothing and accessories. Consequently, there's always something new and innovative on hand. 569A Johnson St. ℂ 250/382-5459. www.smokinglily.com.

Fashion/Men

British Importers Men's Wear   This exceptionally stylish showroom features high-end continental imports from Arnold Brant, Canali, Hugo Boss, and others. 1125 Government St. ℂ 250/386-1496. www.britishimporters.com.

Outlooks for Men   Victoria's most fashion-forward menswear store will appeal to the younger demographic. Cutting-edge designer labels include Hugo Boss, Orange Label, Z Zegna, Melting Pot, and Horst. 554 Yates St. ℂ 250/384-2848. www.outlooksformen.ca.

W&J Wilson   The Wilson family has operated this clothing store since 1862. Although the store certainly doesn't carry fashions from that era, they do lean toward sensible casuals for men, largely from England, Scotland, and Ireland. 1221 Government St. ℂ 250/383-7177.

Jewelry

Artina's   Featuring the silver and goldsmithing work of more than 20 Canadian and First Nations artists, most necklaces, rings, pendants, and bracelets have a refreshingly modern take on traditional designs, whether aboriginal motifs or simply a stylized heron. 1002 Government St. ℂ 250/386-7000. www.artinas.com.

Jade Tree   Here's where to find jewelry made from British Columbia jade. Mined in northern Vancouver Island, the jade is crafted and polished for a variety of items including necklaces, bracelets, pendants, and small ornaments. 606 Humboldt St. ℂ 250/388-4326.

The Patch   This is the island's largest purveyor of body jewelry—for your nose, navel, nipple, and ears. Many of the studs, baubles, and rings are quite funky and colorful. 719 Yates St. ℂ 250/384-7070.

Shi Studio   Chinese silk brocades, often using traditional dynastic patterns, is fused into pendants, belt buckles, brooches, cuffs, and earrings. This is a working studio, so it's best to call ahead. 420-620 View St. ℂ 250/995-2714. www.shistudio.com.

Violette Veldor   If you love accessories, check out this store's eclectic mélange of jewelry. Look for terrific designs from local talent and international names such as Alex & Chloe and Sugar Lime. 1223 Government St. ℂ 250/388-7752.

VICTORIA

5

SHOPPING

Market Square   This eclectic little shopping and restaurant complex is made up of former warehouse and shipping offices from the 1800s. Shops here sell everything from used cameras, second-hand books, and gourmet dog-biscuits to teddy bears and condoms. The central courtyard comes into its own in the summer, with live performances and casual patio dining. 560 Johnson St. © 250/386-2441.

Specialty Gifts/Souvenirs

As in all touristy destinations, souvenir stores that sell T-shirts and tacky memorabilia are a dime a dozen in Victoria. For ideas that say "Victoria" in a different way, try these suggestions.

Irish Linen Stores   A fixture in this 1884 Victoria Italianate heritage building since 1917, this store sells fine Irish damask towels, linens, laces, and sweaters. 1019 Government St. © 250/383-6812. www.irishlinenvictoria.com.

Plenty Epicurean Pantry   Shelves and corners are stacked with an eclectic range of foodstuffs from all over the world, as well as plenty of local products from Victoria. The store mantra is organic, fair trade, ethnic, and artisan. 1034 Fort St. © 250/380-7654. www. epicureanpantry.ca.

Rogers' Chocolates   A Victoria institution for more than a hundred years, Rogers' offers exquisite cream-filled specialty chocolates that have been enjoyed by royalty and others. The store is equally delightful, filled with original Tiffany glass, ornamental tilework, and old-fashioned, highly polished wooden counters. Old man Roger (who, ironically, hated milk chocolate) is said to haunt the place. 913 Government St. © 250/384-7021. www.rogerschocolates.com.

Silk Road Aromatherapy & Tea Company   This impressive tea emporium in the heart of Chinatown features loose-leaf and exclusive blended teas, equipage, and even tea-based aromatherapy products. There's a tea-tasting bar offering a host of intriguing flavors, as well as a small basement spa offering green-tea facials and the like. 1624 Government St. © 250/704-2688. www.silkroadtea.com.

Simply the Best   Small in size it may be, but the price tags and range of goods are quite the opposite. Simply the Best boasts more than 10,000 items, many of which sport the world's most exclusive brand names in clothing, housewares, and office and dining accessories. 1008 Broad St. © 250/386-6661.

Sydney Reynolds China   Located in an old bank building, Victoria's oldest china shop was established in 1929 and now offers fine porcelains, hand-painted tea sets, and Victorian dolls. 801 Government St. © 250/383-3931. www.sydneyreynolds.com.

Tuscan Kitchen   The glorious colors of Tuscany will draw you into the store; the hand-painted Italian majolica platters, dishes, and gourmet cookware will have you stay a while; the offer to ship worldwide will seal the deal. 653 View St. © 250/386-8191. www. thetuscankitchen.com.

The Wine Barrel   You'll find the largest selection of BC VQA (Vintner Quality Alliance) wines in the province here. Walls are stacked with more than 300 varieties, including ice wines and limited editions, as well as an enormous selection of wine accessories. 644 Broughton St. © 250/388-0606. www.thewinebarrel.com.

Spas in Victoria

Whether nestled in the rainforest, perched on craggy shores, or presented as urban getaways of serenity, spas are plentiful on Vancouver Island. Some of the best ones are in and around Victoria.

Sapphire Day Spa   Although located in a small space, this spa feels fresh and spacious with its clean and contemporary look. It is the only spa in Victoria offering Ayurvedic treatments (alongside European services). It even has a Swedana herbal cedar steam chest, one of the hallmarks of quality Ayurveda services. 714 View St. © **250/385-6676.** www.sapphiredayspa.com.

The Spa at Delta Victoria   A luxurious, European-style sanctuary, this spa includes a complete fitness facility, pool, and sauna. It's consistently rated one of the city's best spas. Ocean Pointe Resort, 45 Songhees Rd. © **800/575-8882** or 250-360-5858. www.thespaatdeltavictoria.com.

Willow Stream Spa   Chic, expensive, and a true spa oasis, Willow Stream Spa's treatments include time in the sauna, steam room, and Hungarian mineral pool, so you can turn a pedicure into a spa getaway. 721 Government St. © **866/854-7444** or 250-995-4650. www.willowstream.com.

Essence of Life Spa   A 30-minute drive from Victoria, this oceanfront spa and aroma garden pulls out the stops on a wide range of European services, especially the Signature Couples Massage. Brentwood Bay Lodge, 849 Verdier Ave. © **888/544-2079** or 250/544-2079.

Spa Magnolia   Veteran spa-goers know the name Aveda, and this Aveda concept spa does the name proud. It's tucked away on the second floor of the hotel, almost as if it's trying to keep itself a secret. A recent expansion, though, is making the spa one of the heavier hitters in town. Magnolia Hotel, 623 Courtney St. © **877/624-6654** or 250/381-0999. www.spamagnolia.com.

Le Spa Sereine   Located in a three-level character building, this independent, urban day spa is a local favorite. Hair, nail, and busy beauty services are separated from the relaxing stuff so the scents of (toxic) hair colors don't ruin the aromas of massage oils. 1144 Government St. © **866/388-4419.**

Sante Spa   Run by Institue de Sante, the premier MediSpa folks in Canada, this is one of the few places where traditional spa treatments are offered alongside medical esthetics such as Botox, laser hair removal, and microdermabrasion. The location atop a mountain is pretty spectacular too. At time of writing, this spa had just changed ownership (watch for a new name) though sources assure the concept will remain. Bear Mountain, 1999 Country Club Way. © **888/533-2327** or 250/391-7160. www.bearmountain.ca.

VICTORIA

5

SHOPPING

8 VICTORIA AFTER DARK

As vibrant as Victoria is by day, once the hour hand passes 10pm, city activity just seems to fade into the darkness. Granted, the pubs and the Yates Street area remain pretty busy, especially on weekends, but all in all, when the theatres, concert venues, and movie houses close up shop, so does downtown.

Monday magazine (**www.mondaymag.com**) covers everything going on in town, from nightclubs and the performing arts to films and poetry readings. You name it, *Monday's* got it. You can also call the **Community Arts Council of Greater Victoria's** events hotline, at © 250/381-ARTS [2787]. Tickets and schedules are also available at the **Tourism Victoria Travel Visitor Information Centre,** 812 Wharf St. (© **250/953-2033**).

THE PERFORMING ARTS

Although Victoria is a primary tourist destination, visitors aren't the mainstay of the city's performing arts. Consequently, there's still a community feel to the audiences and venues, many of which are shared among the professional groups.

VENUES The **Royal Theatre,** 805 Broughton St. (© **250/361-0800**), dates from the early 1900s. Renovated in the 1970s, it hosts concerts (including the Victoria Symphony), dance recitals, and touring plays, as well as performances by Pacific Opera Victoria. The **McPherson Playhouse,** 3 Centennial Sq. (© **250/361-0800**), was built in 1914 as the first Pantages Vaudeville Theatre. It hosts smaller stage plays and performances by the Victoria Operatic Society. The Royal and the McPherson share a box office at the **McPherson Playhouse** (© **888/717-6121** or 250/386-6121; www.rmts.bc.ca). Box-office hours are Monday to Saturday from 9:30am to 5:30pm, and on performance days for the 2 hours prior to showtime. Take bus no. 6 to Pandora and Government streets.

CLASSICAL MUSIC The **Victoria Symphony Orchestra,** 846 Broughton St. (© **250/ 385-6515;** www.victoriasymphony.bc.ca), kicks off its season in August with **Symphony Splash,** a free concert performed on a barge in the Inner Harbour. The regular season begins in September and runs through May at the Royal Theatre or the University Farquhar Auditorium. Tickets average C$60 for adults depending on the series, with discounts for seniors and students.

DANCE Dance recitals and full-scale performances by local and international dance troupes such as **Danceworks** and the **Scottish Dance Society** are scheduled throughout the year. To find out who's performing while you're in town, call **Tourism Victoria** (© **250/953-2033**) or the **Community Arts Council of Greater Victoria** (© **250/381-ARTS** [2787] or 250/381-2787; 1001 Douglas St.).

OPERA The **Pacific Opera Victoria,** 1316B Government St. (© **250/385-0222;** box office © **250/382-1641;** www.pov.bc.ca), presents productions during the months of October, February, and April. Tickets are available at the McPherson Playhouse and Pacific Opera box offices (© **250/386-6121**). The **Victoria Operatic Society,** 798 Fairview Rd. (© **250/381-1021;** www.vos.bc.ca), stages old-time musicals and other popular fare year-round at the McPherson Playhouse. They may not be to the standard of Carnegie Hall, but they make for a good evening out.

THEATER The nationally acclaimed **Belfry Theatre Society,** 1291 Gladstone St. (© **250/385-6815;** www.belfry.bc.ca; bus no. 22 to Fernwood St.), stages contemporary productions in an intimate church-turned-playhouse space. Works are generally of

Canadian origin and are often interspersed with visiting productions, such as *The Syringa Tree*. The **Intrepid Theatre Company,** 301-1205 Broad St. (© 250/383-2663; www. intrepidtheatre.com), runs two theater festivals annually. In late April and early May it's the **Uno Festival of Solo Performance,** a unique event of strictly one-person performances with tickets at C$18 adult, C$16 senior and student. Multi-show passes are also offered. From late August to early September, Intrepid stages the **Victoria Fringe Festival** (© 250/383-2691 box office), an amazingly eclectic selection of alternative theater. More than 50 performances from all over the world are staged in six venues around the city, including the Victoria Conservatory of Music, St. Andrew's School, and the Downtown Community Activities Centre. Compared to mainstream theater, festival tickets are cheap (the artists set their own prices to a maximum of C$12), performances are about an hour, and content is unpredictable. **Theatre Inconnu** (© 250/360-0234; www. islandnet.com/~tinconnu) is Victoria's longest surviving alternative theater company, with more than 20 seasons under its belt. It produces Victoria's annual **Shakespearean Festival,** which takes place in the historic St. Ann's Academy, at 835 Humboldt St., in July and August. Ticket prices (C$15) reflect the groups' semi-professional status, but don't be deterred: Plays are of an exceptionally high caliber. Every year, Theatre Inconnu also stages a two-man adaptation of Charles Dickens's *A Christmas Carol.* The **Langham Court Theatre,** 805 Langham Court (© 250/384-2142; www.langhamcourttheatre. bc.ca), performs works produced by the **Victoria Theatre Guild,** a local amateur society dedicated to presenting a wide range of dramatic and comedic works that are surprisingly good for average theatre-goers. New York critics, however, may disagree. Tickets are a bargain at C$18. Take bus no. 14 or 11 from downtown to Fort and Moss streets.

THE BAR SCENE

There are few places outside of England that do pubs as well as Victoria does, even though some of them lean toward lounge status. Here are the best drinking places; pick according to your mood. Some, like The Bengal Lounge, are classy and elegant; others, like the Sticky Wicket, are as you would find in the old country. Most are hybrids.

The Bengal Lounge ★ This lounge salutes Queen Victoria's role as the Empress of India with a colonial elegance that includes huge leather coaches, oversize palms, ceiling fans, and a lengthy cocktail list. It's the chic place to go, especially for the live jazz on Friday and Saturday nights. This is where to try BC's only handcrafted gin, the product of Winchester Cellars in Saanich. Fairmont Empress Hotel, 721 Government St. © 250/384-8111.

Big Bad Johns Without doubt, this is the rowdiest spot in town. Despite a decor that includes an ever-increasing collection of bras hanging from the ceiling, and a floor inches deep in discarded peanut shells, it's a clean-cut place where half the fun is letting it all hang out. Strathcona Hotel, 919 Douglas St. © 250/383-7137.

Darcy's Wharf Street Pub This large, bright, waterfront watering hole is where you'll find the lively younger crowd enjoying fine brews and pool tables. Live bands play occasionally on the weekends. 1127 Wharf St. © 250/380-1322.

The Reef Strictly speaking, The Reef is a restaurant, though as the evening progresses its upbeat Caribbean tone gives it the feel of a reggae hangout with a mix of martinis, rum punches, and DJ and live music. 533 Yates St. © 250/388-5375.

The Sticky Wicket Reminiscent of a turn-of-the-20th-century Irish pub, this is as close as you can get to a traditional pub (including its pub grub). Most of its stained glass

Suds Up

Victorians take their locally brewed hops seriously, so naturally brewpubs hold a special status in the hearts and taste buds of many a self-professed beer lover. Top spots to sip these artisan brews include:

Harbour Canoe Club   Be prepared for a crowd here; it's always busy, especially with the after-work crowd, many of whom will stay on for dinner. The atmospheric heritage brick-and-beam building has an on-site micro-brewery that produces some excellent brews; the six-small-glass taster option is the best deal in town at C$11 a fleet. 450 Swift St. ✆ **250/361-1940.**

Spinnakers Brewpub ★   It all started here. The original brewpub in town remains one of the best. Though the view across Victoria Harbour almost makes it reason enough to come here, its brewed-on-premises ales, lagers, and stouts are the big draw. There's even an on-site bakery selling beer breads. The pub fare is good too. 308 Catherine St. ✆ **250/386-2739.**

Swans Butterfield Brewpub   If there's a live band scheduled for the weekend, the place gets very busy and noisy. It occupies the ground floor of a heritage warehouse, above which is one of Victoria's most unique inns (see "Where to Stay," earlier in this chapter). The decor features the original brickwork and beams, and it's a showcase for an ever-changing display of First Nations art. The signature British-style ales and German and Canadian beers are brewed on site. 506 Pandora Ave. ✆ **250/361-3310.**

---

windows, dark wood interior furnishings, and long teak bar were shipped over from Ireland. Less Irish is the Strath's resident meandering magician who does sleight of hand tricks at your table, picking up tips along the way. Thankfully, it feels like another world to Big Bad John's in the basement and the volleyball sands of the rooftop patio. Strathcona Hotel, 919 Douglas St. ✆ 250/383-7137.

Suze Lounge & Restaurant   One of *the* places for martinis and Sinatra-flavored schmoozing. Aim for a seat at the 7.6m (25-ft.) mahogany bar. 515 Yates St. ✆ 250/383-2829.

UP After Dark   By day, the Union Pacific is a coffee house in Dragon Alley, Chinatown. By night, it becomes a bohemian spot to chill over a great selection of wines, nibble tasty morsels off a charcuterie plate, and listen to live music, usually on Wednesday nights. 537 Herald St. ✆ 250/380-0005.

THE CLUB SCENE
Dance Clubs & Live Music

New venues come and go with regularity (at time of writing the Strathcona was set to open a new upscale grill and late night lounge), so what's listed below are the tried-and-trues—those clubs that have found a winning formula. Most places are open Monday through Saturday until 2am and Sunday until midnight. Drinks are from C$4 to C$9; some clubs have covers (usually weekends only) ranging from C$3 to C$7.

Hermann's Jazz Club   Although not chic, for 25 years Hermann's has consistently delivered Victoria's best live jazz and Dixieland. Martinis are named after famous musicians such as Duke Ellington and Ella Fitzgerald. The club's usually open Wednesday

Feeling Lucky?

The Great Canadian Casino (1708 Old Island Hwy.; ✆ **250/391-0311;** www.
gcgaming.com) can't compete with the high-stakes tables in Las Vegas; it's the
sort of outing you could take your grandmother to. Games include blackjack,
roulette, sic bo, red dog, and Caribbean stud poker. The casino operates a complimentary shuttle service from downtown Victoria.

---

through Sunday (call ahead to check) and if you play jazz and bring your instrument,
there'll likely be an opportunity to jam. 753 View St. ✆ **250/388-9166.**

The Lucky Bar   This is probably one of Victoria's hottest nightspots. It doesn't get into
gear until after 9pm. Hence, drinks in the long, darkly lit lounge are a natural follow-
through to an earlier meal at Luciano's next door, or you can go just for the martinis and
music, which is a mix of DJ-spun and live bands. 517 Yates St. ✆ **250/382-5825.**

The Red Jacket   There are two rooms, one for boozing and schmoozing, the other for
dancing. Either way, you'll want to dress to impress and express. The DJs spin mainly
Top 40, retro, hip-hop, funk, and R&B. Friday is ladies night, and Saturday fills up
quickly, so get there early. 751 View St. ✆ **250/384-2582.**

GAY & LESBIAN BARS

The gay scene is so small in Victoria that most gay-friendly bars have relaxed any gays-
only policies in order to keep their doors open. Most gays entertain at home, and have
established a by-invitation network to these behind-private-door gatherings. One
resource that might put you in contact with some of the private parties held in people's
homes is www.gayvictoria.ca.

   Hush (1325 Government St.; ✆ 250/385-0566; www.hushnightclub.ca) is one of
the few clubs that has stayed the course, although the crowd is becoming increasingly
straight. Loud music (often live) and electronics pack the place on weekends. With
techno, progressive, drum-'n'-bass, and trance, the experience is more like a rave. Hush
is open Wednesday to Sunday. **Prism Lounge** (642 Johnson St.; ✆ **250/388-0505;**
www.prismlounge.com) is Victoria's only true gay and lesbian nightclub. It has a full
menu and a lounge that's spacious enough to host drag shows. Enjoy a fairly offbeat
selection of techno, disco, and hip-hop music, or pick up a mic and sing a little kara-
oke—there are thick binders full of song titles. Prism is open daily, Monday to Friday
3pm to 2am; and from 1pm on the weekend. There's no cover charge.

Southern Vancouver Island

Exploring the South Island is a relaxing change of pace from visiting downtown Victoria. The entire area can be reached within a day, so itineraries are easy to plan. Or, you can stay in the city and simply make an afternoon of touring the countryside. Places like East Sooke Regional Park, with one of the most accessible and prettiest trails in Canada, Fort Rodd Hill & Fisgard Lighthouse National Historic Site, the picturesque seaside community of Sidney, and the world-famous Butchart Gardens are all within a 30-minute drive from Victoria. All are worthwhile destinations where you can spend a few hours, with or without the kids.

If you're an outdoor enthusiast who really wants to taste the island's wild west coast without traveling too far, the Juan de Fuca Trail delivers rainforest coast, wilderness beaches, and spectacular landscapes. It has earned the reputation of being the easier-to-hike cousin of the famed West Coast Trail. Unlike its arduous relative, the Juan de Fuca can be enjoyed in an afternoon (or multi-day) outing. Botanical Beach lies farther up the coast and is a beachcomber's paradise, with tidal pools and sandstone rock formations to explore.

Goldstream Provincial Park is another terrific outing, offering hikes for all abilities through well-maintained forested trails. One of the more challenging hikes is a direct ascent of Mount Finlayson, while an easier walk leads to an abandoned mine—Goldstream got its name during the 1860s gold rush, and if you arm yourself with a gold pan, the river still yields flecks of gold.

Agri-tourism is one of Vancouver Island's fastest growing movements, and nowhere is this better seen than in the Cowichan Valley, Canada's hottest new food and wine destination. Here's where driving through the back country really pays dividends with farms, orchards, artisan cheese factories, and quality cottage wineries to visit. Little wonder that Slow-Food fans have even dubbed the area the New Provence. The valley deserves a day to do it justice.

If you're staying in Victoria but want to sample its urban wilderness or pastoral beauty, taking in the southern part of Vancouver Island is a great way to do so. When heading north toward Nanaimo, you'll discover some attractions worth building into your itinerary (see "En Route to Nanaimo: The Cowichan Valley," later in this chapter).

1 THE SAANICH PENINSULA

A bustling seaside village, Sidney is filled with scenic parks and gardens, waterfront restaurants, galleries, and more bookstores than any other community on Vancouver Island. It is small-town Canada gift-wrapped in beautiful scenery. Sidney is located 26km (16 miles) north of Victoria, and approximately 6km (3¾ miles) south of the BC Ferries terminal in Swartz Bay. Washington State ferries, arriving from Anacortes, dock at Sidney.

Getting There

BY CAR AND FERRY If you're driving out of Victoria, head north on **Blanshard Street,** which becomes **Hwy. 17,** or take BC Transit bus nos. 70, 72, or 75 from downtown Victoria. If you're driving from Swartz Bay (BC Ferries terminal), Sidney is a 6km (3³/₄-mile) drive south on **Hwy. 17.** BC Ferries (© **888/223-3779** or 250/386-3431; www.bcferries.com) runs a passenger- and car-ferry service between Swartz Bay and **Tsawwassen,** on the mainland.

June through August, crossings are every hour on the hour, from 7am to 11pm. September through May, crossings are every other hour. Additional ferries are often scheduled during holiday periods. One-way fare is C$13 for adults, C$6.50 for children 5 to 11, and C$43 for a standard-size vehicle. BC seniors travel free Monday through Thursday, except on holidays.

BY FERRY The Washington State Ferry terminal is located in Sidney, at 2499 Ocean Ave. (© **888-808/7977** or 206/464-7977; www.wsdot.wa.gov/ferries). Ferries sail once a day, mid-morning, between Sidney and Anacortes. Crossing time is 3 hours. Summer vehicle reservations are highly recommended, and must be made by 5:30pm the day prior to travel. One-way passenger fares during the high season (May to early Oct) are C$18 for adults, C$14 for students 6 to 18 years, C$9 for seniors, and C$60 for a standard-size vehicle. Fares are lower in the off season (Oct 2–May 2).

Visitor Information

The Sidney Chamber of Commerce operates two visitor information centers on the Saanich Peninsula. One is located at 10382 Pat Bay Hwy., Sidney, BC V8L 3S3 (© **250/ 656-0525;** www.peninsulachamber.ca). It is open year-round, Monday through Friday, from 8:30am to 5:30pm. The other information center is located in Sidney, opposite the Washington State Ferry terminal, at A-2295 Ocean Ave. (© **250/656-3260;** mailing address is 10382 Pat Bay Hwy., Sidney, BC V8L 3S3). The center is open April through October 15, Monday through Saturday, from 10:30am to 12:30pm, to coincide with ferry arrivals, and closed October 16 through March.

THE TOP ATTRACTIONS

British Columbia Aviation Museum You'll want to dig out your bomber jacket for a visit to this hangar on the edge of the Victoria International Airport. It's a working museum that illustrates the province's aviation history. Volunteers restore vintage aircraft to add to the collection, which already has several reconditioned vintage airplanes, helicopters, and kit planes. Most are in working order. Look for a 1930s Bush Plane, an A26 World War II Bomber, a Gibson Twin (built in Victoria in 1911), a replica of the Chanute Glider, built in 1897, a Bell 47 Helicopter (best known as the busy MedEvac-type chopper in *M.A.S.H.*), and more. This may not stack up to the great aviation museums in Europe, but for aviation nuts or for a family looking to wile away an hour or two, it's an enjoyable attraction.

1910 Norseman Rd. © **250/655-3300.** www.bcam.net. Admission C$7 adults, C$5 seniors, C$3 students. Children 11 and under free, but must be accompanied by an adult. Summer daily 10am–4pm; winter daily 11am–3pm. Closed Dec 25. Take the airport turnoff from Hwy. 17. The museum is on your right as you approach the airport. Bus: 70 (Airport Bus).

SOUTHERN VANCOUVER ISLAND

6

THE SAANICH PENINSULA

Butchart Gardens ★★★ Converted from an exhausted limestone quarry back in 1904, Butchart Gardens is an impressive place: 20 hectares (50 acres) of gardens and not a blade of grass out of place! Just shows what having 50 gardeners can do. Every flower blooms so as to be a perfect match to the others in height, color, and tone, including the 300,000 bulbs that bloom in spring. On summer evenings, the gardens are illuminated with soft colored lights. Musical entertainment is provided June through September, Monday through Saturday evenings. In July and August, watch for fireworks every Saturday night, and in December, enjoy lavish displays of Christmas lights. An excellent lunch, dinner, and afternoon tea are offered in the **Dining Room Restaurant;** more casual fare is served in the **Blue Poppy Restaurant.** The gift shop sells seeds for some of the plants on display. If you're not traveling by car, your best bet is to take a Grayline Tour (see "Organized Tours" in chapter 5) that includes admission (C$52) and an optional add-on Grand City Tour (C$69). In the summer, Grayline also offers an hourly shuttle (C$15 round trip) between the gardens and downtown Victoria. Plan your visit for post-3pm to avoid the more intense crowds.

800 Benvenuto Ave., Brentwood Bay. ✆ **866/652-4422** or 250/652-4422. Dining reservations: ✆ **250/652-8222**. www.butchartgardens.com. Admission C$27 adults, C$14 children 13–17, C$3 children 5–12, free for children 4 and under. Daily 9am–sundown (call for seasonal closing time). Take Blanshard St. (Hwy. 17) north toward the ferry terminal in Saanich, then turn left on Keating Crossroads, which leads directly to the gardens. Parking is free. Bus: 75. Grayline shuttle leaves from Victoria Bus Station hourly. Call for exact times ✆ **250/388-6539**.

Sidney Historical Museum If you're an ambler who loves funky detours, this attraction is bound to delight. Tucked away in the basement of the 1939 post office building, the tiny museum is lovingly tended by volunteers and includes a surprisingly varied range of monthly exhibits, from toys and quilts to model railways and radio-controlled boats. It also has a number of historical photographs and artifacts portraying the early lives of Coast Salish, European, and Asian local peoples. A half-hour visit will probably suffice unless you hit upon an exhibit of personal interest and get talking to one of the knowledgeable, and enthusiastic, curators.

2423 Beacon Ave., Sidney. ✆ **250/655-6355**. www.sidneymuseum.ca. Admission by donation. Suggested: C$2 adults, C$5 groups. Daily 10am–4pm. Closed Dec 25. Take Hwy. 17 to Sidney, turning right down Beacon Ave., to 4th St. Bus: 70 from downtown or Swartz Bay.

Victoria Butterfly Gardens ★★ (Kids Hundreds of exotic species of butterflies flutter through this lush tropical greenhouse, from the tiny Central American Julia to the Southeast Asian Giant Atlas Moth (its wingspan is nearly a foot). Pick up an identification chart before you enter so you can put names to the various flying wonders around you. Then wander freely through the gardens. Along the way, you'll encounter naturalists happy to explain butterfly biology, who pepper their speech with slightly bizarre factoids, such as "Butterflies taste with their feet," and "If a human baby grew at the same rate as some caterpillars, it would weigh 8 tons in only 2 weeks." Hmm. Food for thought. If you're visiting between November and February, you need to make a reservation to see the gardens. A good way to see the gardens is in combination with the Butchart Gardens (see listing above). Together, they make a full day's excursion.

1461 Benvenuto Ave., Brentwood Bay. ✆ **877/722-0272** or 250/652-3822. www.butterflygardens.com. Admission C$12 adults, C$11 seniors and students, C$6.50 children 5–12, free for children 4 and under. 10% discount for families. Mar–May and Oct daily 9:30am–4:30pm; June–Sept daily 9am–5:30pm. Closed Nov–Feb. Bus 75.

Got Extra Time?

If the ferry schedules don't co-operate, **Island Camping** (📞 250/656-4826; www.islandcamping.ca) operates an 11-passenger water-taxi service out of Sidney to your gulf island of choice. The service is great for day visits, touring, or for transport to a "base-camp" beach for kayaking. Trips cost C$140 per hour, generally split among the number of passengers. For a point of reference, Pender Island is a half-hour boat ride from Sidney.

PARKS & BEACHES

Located off Hwy. 17 in Saanich, **Elk Lake/Beaver Lake Park** is a lovely place to spend an afternoon. The park's big draw is a 240-hectare (593-acre) freshwater lake rimmed by four beaches, with plenty of play areas and picnic tables. The lake provides for all sorts of aquatic recreation, and is a particularly good place for beginner windsurfers. It is also home to the University of Victoria Rowing Club, and the site of the annual international boat races, one of the five top rowing events in the world. Nearer to Victoria, off Cordova Bay Road, is **Mount Douglas Park,** a 10-hectare (25-acre) park in its natural state. The park is located 8km (5 miles) northeast of Victoria at the north end of Shelbourne Street. Another 1.5km (1 mile) up Churchill Drive brings you to the summit parking lot, and to several great viewpoints of the surrounding area. There are several **easy hiking trails** to the mountaintop. These include the **Irvine Trail** off Cordova Bay Road, and the **Merriman Trail** (it has an easy start but takes a little scrambling near the top). Both trails are well signposted from the road.

The lower park can be accessed near the intersection of Ash and Cordova Bay roads. A trail to the beach leads down from a large parking lot. There's also a playground and picnic area. For a fairly level, easy walk, look for the **Norn Trail,** which roughly parallels Cordova Bay Road, and takes you through some very tall Douglas firs.

WHERE TO STAY

Brentwood Bay Lodge & Spa ★★   Nestled among arbutus trees at the water's edge, this sophisticated boutique resort is a showcase for West Coast style with picture windows; rust-colored cedar and steel-framed terraces; and interior spaces that combine subtle browns, greens, and stone-floor finishes, along with handmade light wood furniture, fir wood beams, and high-gabled ceilings. Each of the 33 suites has a balcony or patio view of the inlet, forested peaks, and marina; gas fireplaces; hand-crafted furnishings; and local art. The rooms' spa-like bathrooms feature hard-to-resist double-jetted tubs, and shuttered windows let you sit in the tub and bask in the views. This is only outdone by the spa itself—a lavish affair. There's a fine-dining restaurant that offers an ever-changing gourmet menu of primarily local seafood and regional game, a sushi-saki bar, and a marine pub serving distinctive craft beers alongside upscale comfort foods. The chunky roast chicken brick-oven pizza with wild mushrooms is a favorite. As the region's only five-star oceanfront resort, service matches the excellent facilities, which are in the midst of an expansion phase. Six oceanfront, two-bedroom villas are set to open in late 2009, each one including a 12m (40-ft.) boat slip. The hotel is a licensed PADI dive center and has an eco-marine center with kayak rentals and charters.

849 Verdier Ave. (on Brentwood Bay), Victoria, BC V8M 1C5. 📞 **888/544-2079** or 250/544-2079. Fax 250/544-2069. www.brentwoodbaylodge.com. 33 units (some with fireplaces and hot tubs). Mid-June to mid-Oct

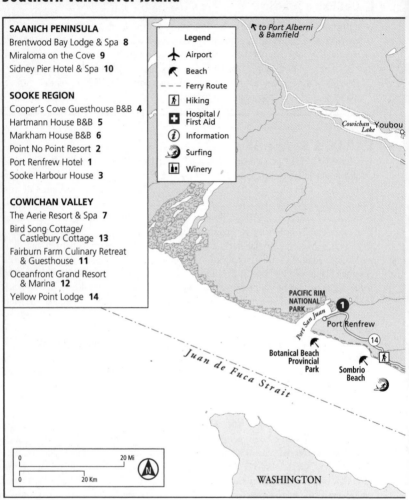

SAANICH PENINSULA
Brentwood Bay Lodge & Spa **8**
Miraloma on the Cove **9**
Sidney Pier Hotel & Spa **10**

SOOKE REGION
Cooper's Cove Guesthouse B&B **4**
Hartmann House B&B **5**
Markham House B&B **6**
Point No Point Resort **2**
Port Renfrew Hotel **1**
Sooke Harbour House **3**

COWICHAN VALLEY
The Aerie Resort & Spa **7**
Bird Song Cottage/
    Castlebury Cottage **13**
Fairburn Farm Culinary Retreat
    & Guesthouse **11**
Oceanfront Grand Resort
    & Marina **12**
Yellow Point Lodge **14**

Legend
✈ Airport
✦ Beach
- - - Ferry Route
🚶 Hiking
✚ Hospital /
    First Aid
ⓘ Information
🏄 Surfing
🍷 Winery

↖ to Port Alberni
& Bamfield

Cowichan Lake   Youbou

PACIFIC RIM
NATIONAL
PARK
Port San Juan
Port Renfrew
14

Botanical Beach
Provincial
Park
Sombrio
Beach

Juan de Fuca Strait

WASHINGTON

0   20 Mi
0   20 Km
N

C$379–C$399 double, C$699 1-bedroom suite; mid-Oct to mid-June C$179–C$299 double, C$399–C$499 1-bedroom suite. AE, MC, V. Free parking. Take Pat Bay Hwy. north to Keating Crossroads, turn left (west) to Saanich Rd., turn right (south) to Verdier Ave. **Amenities:** Restaurant; pub; cafe; heated outdoor pool; full service spa; Jacuzzi; concierge; limited room service; laundry; dry cleaning; nonsmoking facilities; Wi-Fi. *In room:* A/C, TV/DVD, dataport w/high-speed Internet, Wi-Fi, minibar, coffeemaker, hair dryer, iron.

Miraloma on the Cove ★   With stunning West Coast scenery and the sophistication of a European boutique hotel, this inn is now a part of the Bellstar Resort Group. It features warm, honey-toned woodwork and atrium-style architecture for glimpses of sky, and many of the studio, one- and two-room suites have views. All rooms feature local art; locally made furniture and custom-made linens; gas fireplaces; impressive en suite

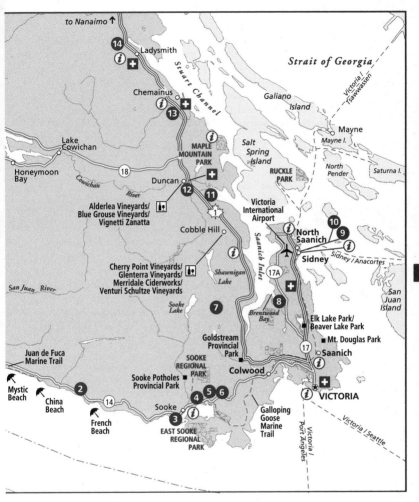

bathrooms (complete with heated towel racks and floors); flatscreen TVs; gleaming, fully appointed kitchens; and decks. The superior suites also have washer/dryer facilities. **The Latch,** one of the region's destination restaurants (see "Where to Dine," below), is right next door and serves as the hotel's dining room.

2326 Harbour Rd., Sidney, BC V8L 2P8. (✆) **877/956-6622** or 250/656-6622. Fax 250/656-6212. www. miraloma.ca. 22 units. July to mid-Sept C$155–C$249 studio, C$205–C$379 1-bedroom, C$382–C$449 2-bedroom; mid-Sept to June C$105–C$209 studio, C$161–C$339 1-bedroom, C$265–C$399 2-bedroom. Rates include continental breakfast. Extra person C$25. Spa, dining, and eco-adventure packages available. AE, DC, MC, V. Free parking. **Amenities:** Restaurant next door; lounge; free mountain bikes; concierge; business center; massage. *In room:* A/C, TV/DVD w/pay movies, dataport, high-speed Internet, minibar, fridge, coffeemaker, hair dryer, iron.

(Finds) Cider by the Sea

Sea Cider's beautiful setting by the sea (2487 Mt. St. Michael Rd., Saanichton; ✆ **250/544-4824;** www.seacider.ca) is the stuff of novels and worth the winding drive to get there. Part of the peninsula wine lands, with a half dozen estate wineries, this vibrant, sprawling apple orchard grows more than 50 varieties of apples and is a great place for a pre-ferry stopover and a casual date. Cider tastings are well paired with charturie plates; Sea Cider's first cases were only produced in 2007. En route there, watch for roadside stalls with honesty boxes, selling everything from help-yourself manure to ducks' eggs and fields of pick-all-you-can tulips.

The Sidney Pier Hotel & Spa   You can't beat its location right downtown, on the waterfront with views of Mt. Baker in Washington State. That's why you should spend the extra dollars for a room on the ocean side, not facing the town, especially if you indulge in one of the few promenade one-bedroom suites. These have WOW factor. All rooms, however, feel spacious, with expansive windows, clean-styled contemporary furnishings including "sink-into" swivel chairs as well as touches like heated towel racks, and waste bins divided into four recyclable options. The spa, Haro's restaurant, and the coffee shop are all worth visiting, especially the latter, which has become a local haunt for its frothy coffees and home-baked scones, despite the fact that those same locals were chagrined by the redevelopment of their sleepy waterfront. The hotel opened in 2007, but still exudes an air of youthful inexperience, made up for by a sometimes overly helpful and enthusiastic service attitude.

9805 Seaport Place, Sidney, BC V8L 4X3. ✆ **866/659-9445** or 250/655-9445. Fax 250/655-0715. www. sidneypier.com. 55 units. Mid-June to late Sept C$179–C$229 double, C$259–C$489 suite; Oct–Mar C$139–C$189 double; C$219–C$449 suite; Apr to mid-June C$159–C$209 double, C$239–C$469 suite. Weekly and monthly rates available. Extra person C$25. AE, DC, MC, V. Free parking. Pets welcome (C$30). **Amenities:** 2 restaurants; lounge; spa; concierge; free shuttle to airport/ferry; library; Wi-Fi. *In room:* A/C, TV/DVD w/pay movies, Internet, fridge (some with freezer), coffeemaker, hair dryer, iron.

WHERE TO DINE

Deep Cove Chalet FRENCH   A local favorite for special occasions, this charming 1914 chalet was originally the terminus building of the British Columbia Electric Railway. Perched on a grassy bank overlooking a beautiful inlet, the restaurant offers top-notch service; a superb menu that emphasizes local seafood, lamb, and game; and a cellar that boasts some 18,000 bottles in its reserve, some dating from 1902. It even has its own fledgling vineyard. If you're looking for a classic fine-dining experience, the chalet makes the drive worthwhile, especially on a sunny day. The a la carte menu selections can add up to be pricey (La Soupe aux Truffles is C$45); four-course prix-fixe dinners won't break the bank and feature items such as roast caribou, Dungeness crab, and sometimes a terrific selection of caviars from Russia, China, and France.

11190 Chalet Drive Rd., Sidney ✆ **250/656-3541.** Reservations recommended for Sunday brunch and dinner. Lunch C$23; dinner C$26–C$38; brunch C$30. Prix-fixe dinner C$58–C$75. AE, MC. Wed–Sun noon–2:30pm; Tues–Sun 5:30–9:30pm.

Dockside Grill PACIFIC NORTHWEST   You can't dine nearer to the water than this—perched on the pier, virtually on top of Van Isle Marina though easily missed from the road since all you'll see is a parking lot. View windows give the room a contemporary ambience, although in summer the heated and covered patio is the favored spot. The menu focuses on local and seasonal items: The Shellfish Steamer pots are a must for zest-loving palettes, as is the Cowichan Valley chicken cooked with minted quinoa, lemon yogurt, and braised bison shortribs. The artisan cheeses and homemade breads, desserts, and ice cream are all delicious. If you're not up to a full meal, at least treat yourself to the latter.

2320 Harbour Rd., Sidney. ⓒ 250/656-0828. Lunch C$14; dinner C$18–C$26. AE, MC, V. Mon–Sun 11:30am–2:30pm and 5–11pm; Sun 10:30am–2:30pm.

The Latch WEST COAST   Built in the 1920s for then Lieutenant-Governor Walter C. Nichol, The Latch was once a summer retreat for dignitaries and debutantes. The restaurant's small dining rooms still retain an intimate heritage feel, and although the antiques hark back to that era, the food certainly does not. New West Coast flavors are prepared in a classic Tuscan style with an emphasis on local produce. House specialties include veal scaloppini served in white-wine lemon sauce, and the Seafood Platter featuring halibut, king crab, salmon, and prawns. The Latch creates its own artisan breads and is known for its homemade Italian ice cream. This restaurant is an excellent choice for romantic, candlelight dining. The Latch also has six sumptuously decorated guest rooms upstairs; they're popular, however, so if you're thinking of staying overnight, advance reservations are recommended.

2328 Harbour Rd., Sidney. ⓒ 250/656-4015. www.latchinn.ca. Reservations recommended on weekends. Main courses C$19–C$36. AE, DC, MC, V. Daily 5–10pm.

2 THE SOOKE REGION

To the west of Victoria lies Southern Vancouver Island's wild side. Within a couple hours' drive of the city, you are met with windswept beaches and trails through old-growth forest. Whether you're an urbanite looking for a spectacular afternoon side trip, a soft adventurer, or a hardy hiker, this drive along **Hwy. 14,** toward Port Renfrew, delivers. The trip from Victoria to Port Renfrew is 107km (66 miles), but the winding and scenic road is slow; allow a good 2 hours just for travel time, and a full day if you really want to enjoy the ride. Better still, make the tranquility of Sooke your home base. Just 32km (20 miles) out of Victoria, you're on the edge of outdoor-adventure country. Sooke is one of those wish-you-were-here coastal towns. Its name is derived from the first inhabitants of the region, the T'sou-ke band. The "e" in both T'sou-ke and Sooke is silent, just like the morning mist that lingers over the harbor.

ESSENTIALS
Getting There
BY CAR   Driving from Victoria, take **Douglas Street** north and follow the signs to **Hwy. 1,** toward Sooke. Take the **Hwy. 14 (Island Hwy) exit** at **Colwood,** and you're on your way. Hwy. 14 follows the coast all the way through Sooke, and along to Port Renfrew. Remember to get gas in Sooke; it's the last gas station before Port Renfrew. Sooke is a 32km (20-mile) drive west from Victoria; Port Renfrew is 74km (46 miles) west from Sooke.

BY BUS   Board at the Western Exchange on Hwy. 14 (Island Hwy.) at Colwood (about 20 min. out of Victoria). Take **bus no. 50** (get a transfer), then **bus no. 61** to Sooke. Depending on traffic, the trip can take up to an hour from Victoria, and because of the transfers it might be a frustrating journey, especially as once you're in Sooke, you'll be tempted to explore farther along the coast.

Visitor Information

Head to the **Sooke Region Museum Visitors and Information Centre,** 2070 Phillips Rd. (right off Sooke Rd./Hwy. 14) (© **866/888-4748** or 250/642-6351). It's open July through August daily from 9am to 5pm. It keeps the same 9am to 5pm hours from October to May, but it's closed Mondays. The staff here is knowledgeable and very enthusiastic, with all kinds of ideas for places to stay and things to do, particularly when it comes to both soft- and rugged-adventure activities. There are options for self-guided explorations or escorted tours. The center is wheelchair accessible.

THE TOP ATTRACTIONS

Adrenaline Zip Adventures   This region is all about eco-experiences, and one of the most exhilarating is zipping between the treetops covering some 40 hectares (100 acres) of rainforest. With a minimum age of 5 years, riding the wires is a great family excursion, albeit at 46m (150 ft.) off the ground. Lines run between 40 and 305m (150–1,000 ft.) in length, and getting to the staging platforms is fun, too, via a 10-minute ATV ride and across two suspension bridges. The company provides a shuttle service to/from Victoria (C$10 per person, round-trip) and has partnered with **Sooke Coastal Explorations** (© **250/642-2343;** www.sookewhalewatching.com) for whale-watching and **Rush Adventures** (© **250/642-2159;** www.rush-adventures.com) for ocean-kayaking adventures, whereby you earn a 10% to 15% discount if you experience all three activities in the same season. Dutch courage can be absorbed at the 17-Mile Pub nearby, though you would be better advised to hold off any alcohol until post-zip.

5128 Sooke Rd. (next to the 17-Mile Pub). © **866/947-9145** or 250/642-1933. www.adrenalinezip.com. Admission C$75 adults and C$65 17 and under (minimum age 5 years). Apr to late Oct daily 9am–6pm, to 7pm on weekends. Reservations recommended.

Fort Rodd Hill & Fisgard Lighthouse National Historic Site (Kids)   The Fisgard Lighthouse is the oldest lighthouse on Canada's west coast. From its vantage point atop a volcanic outcrop, it has guided ships toward Victoria's sheltered harbor since 1873. Although the beacon has long been automated, the site has been restored to its original appearance, and the lighthouse, which you can climb, houses some displays that show how keepers lived some 100 years ago. The surrounding park is filled with old military installations: camouflaged searchlights, underground armories, and guns dating from the 1890s, which, in more than half a century, have never fired a shot in anger. Canada has designated it a National Historic Site. This is a great attraction to pass an hour or so; longer if you're tossing a Frisbee, picnicking, or beachcombing.

603 Fort Rodd Hill Rd. © **250/478-5849.** www.pc.gc.ca. Admission C$4 adults, C$3.50 seniors, C$2 children 6–16, C$10 family pass, free for children under 6. Mar–Oct daily 10am–5:30pm, Nov–Feb daily 9am–4:30pm. Follow Hwy. 1 out of Victoria, taking the Colwood exit (#10) onto Hwy. 1A. Continue for 2km (1¼ mile), turn left at the 3rd traffic light onto Ocean Blvd. Follow the signs to the sites.

Sooke Region Museum   Fittingly, the museum is housed in Moss Cottage (built in 1870), Sooke's oldest building and somewhat of a museum piece itself. Sharing space with the Visitor Information Centre (see "Essentials," above), the museum houses a charming, compact collection of diorama exhibits and pioneer memorabilia. On summer weekends, an interpretive guide in the character of "Aunt Tilly," the original owner of Moss Cottage, will chat with visitors while bustling about doing her household chores. A 30-minute stop here is well worth the extra time while you're picking up information on the area.

2070 Phillips Rd. (right off Sooke Rd./Hwy. 14). © **250/642-6351.** Admission by donation. Suggested: C$2. July–Aug daily 9am–5pm; Sept–June Tues–Sun 9am–5pm.

HIKING TRAILS

Whether you like to cycle, hike, horseback ride, or just stroll, the **Galloping Goose, Lochside,** and **Peninsula trails** are the places to be. Laid out like a green ribbon from Sidney and the Saanich Peninsula to Sooke, their 100km (62 miles) of pathways link the region's parks to form a chain of greenspaces. Named for the gawky and noisy gas rail car that carried passengers between Victoria and Sooke in the 1920s, the popular **Galloping Goose Trail** follows the abandoned rail beds and trestles of that railway legacy. **Leechtown,** once the site of a gold-mining community, marks the westernmost reach, and terminus, of "The Goose," as it's affectionately called. For more information on the Galloping Goose and Peninsula trails, many of which make for easy half-day outings, contact the **Capital Region District Parks,** at © **250/478-3344.**

Stretching 47km (29 miles) along the near-wilderness coastline from **China Beach** to **Botanical Beach** is the **Juan de Fuca Marine Trail.** A neighbor to the famed (and very strenuous) West Coast Trail (see below), the less demanding Juan de Fuca Marine Trail offers similar scenic beauty, yet can be completed as a comfortable, albeit strenuous, 4- or 5-day trek or as several 1-day hikes from different trail heads. It isn't easy going, though—you'll be hiking through muddy trails, over fallen trees, across suspension bridges, and along wilderness beaches. If you're not up to the full distance, each of the four main trail heads at China Beach, Sombrio Beach, Parkinson Creek, and Botanical Beach offers parking lots that allow day hikes and smaller family hikes down to the beach. If you're more interested in the 4- or 5-day trek, you can start at either **Botanical Beach** or **China Beach.** Because this is a wilderness trail, conditions are always changing, so check the trail-head information centers for updates. Be sure to wear proper footwear and appropriate clothing. Campsites are regularly spaced along the trail. A great online resource is www.vancouverislandoutdoors.com. The site has maps, photos, safety pointers, and camping information for the Juan de Fuca Marine Trail. *Note:* As you hike, watch for orange balls that mark exits from the beach to the trail. Be aware, however, that beaches may be cut off from the trail during high tides and storms.

Of all the trails on Vancouver Island, the **West Coast Trail** is the most famous. It is known as one of the most extreme, rigorous, and beautiful trails in the world. With its easternmost trail head just outside of Port Renfrew, the West Coast Trail is virtually the town's only raison d'être. Now a part of **Pacific Rim National Park,** the trail originally was constructed for the rescue of mariners shipwrecked along the rugged west coast, appropriately referred to as the "graveyard of the Pacific." Running approximately 75km (47 miles) north between Port Renfrew and Bamfield, it takes an average of 5 to 7 days to complete, and is a challenge for even the most experienced hikers. For more information about the West Coast Trail, check out www.westcoasttrailbc.com. See chapter 7 for more on the West Coast Trail and Pacific Rim National Park.

PARKS & BEACHES

Goldstream Provincial Park is a favorite escape for Victoria residents and visitors alike. Picnic beneath 600-year-old red cedars (the best spot is near the parking lot), or hike through beautiful rain forest. Watch out for old mine shafts where, in the late 1800s, prospectors mined for gold (hence the park's name); or try panning for gold yourself in the river. All you need is a 30.5 or 38cm (12- or 15-in.) steel pan, and a whole lot of patience. You can take several easy loop hikes that explore a range of ecosystems: deep forests of Douglas fir, dry upland ridges with arbutus and Garry oak, and a salt marsh estuary at the head of Saanich Inlet. Favorite hikes include the 419m (1,375-ft.) climb up the Mount Finlayson Trail. Although only a 1km (.5-mile) ascent, the hike is very steep and rigorous enough that you should allow 3 hours for the round trip. The Upper Goldstream Trail is much easier, and although approximately the same distance, most hikers complete the return in half the time. This trail takes you through some of the oldest and biggest Douglas firs in the park, and at the end, you're rewarded with water-falls. It's a good choice for kids, but not those in strollers. From mid-October through November, thousands come to Goldstream Provincial Park to watch salmon spawn, while in December and January, they come for the Bald Eagle Count (see the "Calendar of Events," in chapter 3). Many areas of the park are wheelchair accessible. For information on Goldstream Provincial Park and all other provincial parks on the South Island, contact BC Parks (© 250/391-2300; www.env.gov.bc.ca/bcparks). The park's Freeman King Visitor Centre (© 250/478-9414; www.naturehouse.ca) is open daily from 9am to 4:30pm and offers a nature house and year-round guided walks, as well as programs geared to children. Interested in camping in the park? Choose from among 173 sites. Reserve through Discover Camping (© 800/689-9025 or 604/689-9025; www.discover camping.ca).

In Sooke, you'll find **Sooke Potholes Provincial Park,** featuring an unusual rock formation, over which the Sooke River flows onto a series of ledges and waist-deep swim-ming holes, and from there into rock pools below. In summer, the chilly waters are just warm enough to attract a swarm of swimmers. The park has picnic facilities, while easy hiking trails are firm under foot. A network of over 50km (31 miles) of trails can be found in **East Sooke Regional Park**, lacing through the park's 1,421 hectares (3,511 acres) to beaches, secluded coves, forested areas, petroglyphs, and an abandoned copper mine. In the heart of the park, stumps of Douglas fir and red cedar, some measuring 2 to 3m (6½–10 ft.) in diameter, hold clues to the era when loggers felled their riches with the springboard, axe, and crosscut saw. One of these trails, the **East Sooke Coast Trail,** is considered a premier day hike. Though it covers only 10km (6.2 miles), the trail is rough, winding, and a challenging 6- to 8-hour trip. You can access East Sooke Regional Park at **Aylard Farm,** off Becher Bay Road (popular with picnickers and those looking for easy excursions); at **Anderson Cove** (for hikers heading to Babbington Hill and Mount Maguire); or at **Pike Road,** off East Sooke Road, an old logging road that winds through forest to meadow and beach. Information posted at these trail heads will help you choose a trail suitable to your hiking ability. Many trails are wheelchair accessible. As you wind your way west along Hwy. 14 (also known as the West Coast Rd.) toward Port Renfrew, you'll pass a series of beaches—many of which are worth pulling over to explore. Some are more accessible than others, and trails often link one stretch of sand to another, but sometimes only at low tide. *Note:* If you park your car, remove all valuables. Thefts are common; rental cars are favored targets.

The first beach you'll come to, ironically, is called **Second Beach,** a small sand and cobblestone beach, subject to strong storm and tidal action. At low tide, it's possible to walk along the beach to **Jordan River,** a popular wintertime surfing and windsurfing area, or to **China Beach,** where fine sand makes an ideal spot for picnicking, building sandcastles, wading, and relaxing. There's a hidden waterfall at the west end of the beach.

ⓜ Moments   Recipe for Gold Panning

Goldstream Park got its name during the 1860s gold rush for the gold the river contained. There is still gold in them thar waters, and panning for gold flecks can be a fun family activity if you've youngsters in tow. With patience, you'll probably produce some tiny flecks – enough to cover your pinky fingernail.

Ingredients
- One darkened gold pan, preferably 30.5 to 38cm (12–15 in.) (most hardware stores have suitable pans which you can darken by placing it over a burner or in a campfire in order to see the gold flecks more clearly).
- Oodles of patience

Location
- Rivers or streams with gravel bars
- Downstream of large boulders
- On the inside of a river bend
- In the middle of heavy water run-off
- On and around tree roots

Method
- Using the pan, scoop up a thin layer of silt from under water.
- Pick out large stones and break up lumps of mud.
- Hold pan level with both hands; rotate it with a swirling motion.
- Tilt the pan slightly downward to carefully discard the dirty water, sand, and gravel (heavier gold will settle to the bottom of the pan).
- Rotate the pan with increasingly lighter material by raising and lowering the pan's lip so water will flow over it.
- Continue this process until nothing but heavier minerals—and possibly gold—are left.

From the parking lot, follow the wide gravel trail through lush forest to the beach itself. The trail is easy to navigate, and therefore suitable for children as well as older travelers. It takes about 20 minutes one-way; watch for some steep sections. China Beach is the southern terminus of the Juan de Fuca Marine Trail. Camp overnight in your vehicle (it's allowed), or at one of the beach campsites.

Getting to **Mystic Beach** involves a fairly strenuous, 2km (1.2-mile) hike along a steep rainforest trail, which can take up to 45 minutes to complete. But you'll be rewarded by a sandy beach surrounded by sandstone cliffs, shallow waves, and a waterfall. If you can manage it, the trip is worth making. Beachfront campsites are available, but pit toilets are the only amenity. Bring your own water, or if you take water from the streams, remember to purify it. Farther along is **French Beach,** a sand and gravel beach that's a hot spot from which to watch for passing grey **whales.** Picnic tables and an adventure playground are located on an open, grassy area between the parking lot and beach, making this a good family destination. Sixty-nine campsites are right on the beach. The winds, breakers, and rollers of the Pacific Ocean make **Sombrio Beach** a favorite spot for surfers. An old logging road winds down from Hwy. 14 to a large parking lot. From there, it's an easy 10-minute walk to the beach. Sombrio Beach is another entry route to the Juan de Fuca Marine Trail. Overnight camping in your vehicle is allowed, and there are a number of beach sites. But the real treasure is **Botanical Beach Provincial Park**, about 4km (2½ miles) south of Port Renfrew. A terrific place for kids, it's one of the richest intertidal zones on North America's west coast, and a magnet for avid poolies, who gather to enjoy the ocean's bounty. Over the millennia, tidal action has carved out spectacular pits and pools that have filled with purple sea urchins, gooseneck barnacles, fiery red blood stars, and other marine flora and fauna. Check local tide tables: A low tide of 1 meter (3¾ ft.) or less is best for viewing. In spring and fall, watch for passing grey whales. Camping is prohibited at this park.

For information about camping at any of these beaches, and to reserve campsites, contact **Discover Camping** (© 800/689-9025 or 604/689-9025; www.discovercamping.ca).

PORT RENFREW

Port Renfrew is a sleepy fishing village quite literally at the end of the road (Hwy. 14), and unless you're heading to the West Coast Trail (see "Hiking Trails," above, and chapter 7), there aren't a whole lot of reasons to stay. Most accommodations are geared to hikers, and include a complete range of camping facilities for both tents and RVs. You might want to try the **Port Renfrew Recreational RV Retreat** (© 250/647-0058). Thirty-three full RV hookups are each C$35 per night; 6 tent sites are C$20 per night. The **Port Renfrew Hotel,** beside the community wharf at the end of Parkinson Road (© 250/647-5541; www.portrenfrewhotel.ca, is a bit more upscale, with 11 well-appointed waterfront cabins and four motel-style studio rooms, starting at C$199 (25% less in low season), as well as a decent restaurant and pub—a good pit stop before turning the car around for the drive back to Sooke.

WHERE TO STAY

Coopers Cove (Finds)   This guest house is a real find for foodies. The owner, Angelo Prosperi-Porta, is an ex–Olympiad chef, and his culinary school and interactive dinners are legendary. They've even been featured on Oprah! Few places let you muse over dinner preparations—with an option to participate—as an elaborate, multi-course, dinner is created before your very eyes. Guest rooms are tasteful also, with downy, soft duvets on comfortable king- and queen-size beds; warm pine furniture: and touches like homemade truffles on your pillow to sweeten the night. All rooms have water views and a fireplace. Although you don't have to love food to enjoy your stay, the culinary packages are where this inn excels. Suffice it to say, breakfast, too, is the mother-of-all meals, with home-baked croissant, bread, yogurt, cheese, and edible flower garnishes.

5301 Sooke Rd., Sooke, BC V0S 1N0 © 877/642-5727 or 250/642-5727. Fax 250/642-5749. www. cooperscove.com. 4 units. C$167–C$225. Culinary packages available. AE, MC, V. **Amenities:** Golf nearby; hot tub; in-room massage; Wi-Fi. *In room:* Fridge, hair dryer.

Hartmann House B&B ★   Hartmann House is at its best in spring: shrouded by wisteria and surrounded by hydrangeas, peonies, rhododendrons, azaleas, and other flowering plants. It has a stunning English country garden–style setting (that's very private), with distant views of the water. Inside is just as welcoming. The cedar finish throughout the home adds warmth and character, and is accented by a roaring fire and overstuffed rattan couches. These touches extend into each of the two private, self-contained and spacious suites, each with its own entrance, private veranda, and oversize whirlpool tub. You can expect complimentary chilled wine waiting for you upon arrival

(M)Moments   Ocean Potions

Seaweed is so abundant in Sooke that local entrepreneur Diane Bernard has parlayed its byproducts into much more than a cottage industry. Better known as *The Seaweed Lady,* she is up-to-speed on all the latest scientific research on seaweed's medical and nutritional properties, and supplies many of the region's leading restaurants, as well as a line of highly effective spa products. Catch up with her on the beach most mornings for a seaweed tour that is an experiential eye-opener on the glories of some of the fastest growing, and most nutritious, plants in the world. Call **Outer Coast Seaweeds** (© **877/713-7464**) for tour information; it's a wet and slippery walk, so galoshes and walking sticks are provided.

alongside Belgian chocolates and a fruit and cheese plate. Breakfast is delivered to your door through a butler's pantry. A truly one-of-a-kind romantic retreat.

5262 Sooke Rd., Sooke, BC V0S 1N0. © **250/642-3761.** Fax 250/642-7361. www.hartmannhouse.bc.ca. 2 units. May–Oct C$195–C$225; Nov–Apr C$175–C$195. Rates include full breakfast. V only. No pets. Nonsmoking. **Amenities:** Golf nearby; Wi-Fi. *In room:* TV/DVD, fridge, microwave, hair dryer, Jacuzzi, fireplace.

Markham House B&B and Honeysuckle Cottage ★★   Nestled into a 4-hectare (10-acre) hillside, this Tudor-style home is bordered by towering firs and flowering perennials. A golf tee and bocce ball court are set up on the lawns, and intriguing pathways lead to mossy bluff lookouts. Guests enjoy afternoon tea on the veranda or in the old English-style living room filled with antiques. Each guest room has all the trimmings necessary for cocooning: featherbeds, duvets, and comfortable sofas, as well as luxurious bathrobes and double Jacuzzis. There's a separate 56-sq.-m (600-sq.-ft.) cottage tucked away in the woods that has its own private deck, outdoor Jacuzzi, woodstove, full kitchen, and barbecue. It's the ultimate "we want to be alone" couple's getaway.

1853 Connie Rd., Victoria, BC V9C 4C2. © **888/256-6888** or 250-642-7542. Fax 250-642-7538. www.markhamhouse.com. 3 units, 1 cottage. C$120–C$195 guest room; C$250 cottage. Extra person C$25. Special packages and off-season discounts available. AE, DC, MC, V. **Amenities:** Lounge; golf nearby; hot tub; Wi-Fi. *In room:* TV/DVD/VCR, hair dryer.

Point No Point Resort   It's the ultimate getaway—a private cabin, the ocean as your front yard, and 16 hectares (40 acres) or so of wilderness "out the back." Since this waterfront resort has been in business more than 50 years, the size and relative quality of the cabins vary depending on when they were built. Some are large enough for families; others are romantic retreats that are as private as they are cozy. All have wood-burning fireplaces, full kitchens, private bathrooms, stunning ocean views, and a strip of private beach, which includes a beach house and fire pit. Lunch and traditional tea are served daily in a central teahouse overlooking the Juan de Fuca Strait. Bring a flashlight and ask for a cabin away from the generators, which can hum all night. Dinner is served Wednesday through Sunday. Portions are on the large side (share if you have a small appetite) and include items such as grilled salmon, crusted chicken with morel sauce, crepes overstuffed with pork, caramelized onions, and gorgonzola.

(Finds) Fine Fermentation

Tugwell Creek Honey Farm & Meadery (8750 West Coast Rd.; ℂ **250/642-1956**) uses its 150 hives and the oldest art of fermentation to create all manner of honey products, including several varieties of honey wine, better known as mead. Once enjoyed by royalty and peasants alike, mead was purported to bestow the drinker with courage, wisdom, and strength—perhaps that's why Tugwell retails almost 3,000 bottles a year. You can test that theory: The Meadery's tasting room and shop are open every afternoon Wednesday through Sunday during the summer and on weekends October to April, except when it closes in January.

1505 West Coast Hwy. (Hwy. 14), Sooke, BC V0S 1N0. ℂ **250/646-2020.** Fax 250/646-2294. www.point nopointresort.com. 25 cabins, 10 w/Jacuzzi and private deck. C$180–C$270. 2-night minimum stay on weekends; 3-night minimum stay July–Aug, holiday weekends, and Christmas. AE, MC, V. Free parking. Small pets accepted (C$10). **Amenities:** Restaurant. *In room:* Kitchen, fireplace.

Sooke Harbour House ★★★   Poised on the end of a sand spit, this little inn is a celebrity hideaway for Hollywood types such as Gillian Anderson, Robert DeNiro, and Richard Gere. The ambience is understated elegance with a friendly, yet completely unobtrusive, staff. An eclectic blend of antiques, original art, and whimsical crafts is showcased throughout the inn. In fact, the collection is one of the largest public art displays on Vancouver Island. Each of the 28 guest rooms is decorated in a unique way, though they all express a Northwest theme. All have wood-burning fireplaces, exquisite views, and all but one have sundecks. Many have Jacuzzis and showers with beautiful stained-glass doors. Speaking of showers, guests will find rooms well equipped if the day is rainy; umbrellas, rubber boots, and rain jackets are provided for all. And if the sun is shining, take time to wander the gardens, a trove of edible wildflowers, herbs, and display blooms. The experience wouldn't be complete without enjoying a meal at the **Sooke Harbour House** restaurant, which is the best in the region (see "Where to Dine," below). If you're not a guest at the hotel, dining here often means making a reservation weeks in advance, especially in summer. Be sure also to try the **Sea-renity Spa;** it offers an excellent range of massage and aesthetic services. Among the spa's specialties are seaweed treatments, many of which have been created for Sea-renity

1528 Whiffen Spit Rd., Sooke, BC V0S 1N0. ℂ **800/889-9688** or 250/642-3421. Fax 250/628-6988. www. sookeharbourhouse.com. 28 units, 23 w/Jacuzzi. May–Sept C$395–C$650 double; Oct–Apr C$305–C$575 double. Rates include breakfast and picnic lunch. Off-season discounts available. Children 12 and under stay free in parent's room. DC, MC, V. Free parking. Take Island Hwy. to the Sooke–Colwood turnoff (junction Hwy. 24), continue on Hwy. 14 to Sooke, turn left onto Whiffen Spit Rd. Pets accepted (C$20). **Amenities:** Restaurant; spa; 24-hr. room service; babysitting; Wi-Fi. *In room:* Coffeemaker, hair dryer, iron, steam shower, bottle of port.

WHERE TO DINE

Mom's Cafe (Finds   CASUAL FOOD   Tucked away by the community hall in downtown Sooke, Mom's Cafe is the quintessential 1950s diner, complete with juke boxes at the booths and its fair share of bric-a-brac (you just know Mom never throws anything away). It serves up excellent home cooking, and is considered one of the top 10 diners in British Columbia. Mom's is always packed with locals and visitors alike. Mom's home-made dessert pies are absolute musts.

2036 Shields Rd., Sooke. ✆ **250/642-3314.** Main courses C$8–$C15. MC, V. Sun–Thurs 8am–8pm; Fri–Sat 8am–9pm. Drive into Sooke on Hwy. 14; take the first right after the traffic light at Murray Rd.

Six Mile Pub PUB FARE   You'll find a good variety of brews on tap, and tasty food seasoned with fresh herbs from the pub's own garden—burgers as well as some higher-end dishes such as fresh halibut with risotto, braised lamb shank, and beef tenderloin. Part of a franchise, the Six Mile Pub is one of several "mile" pubs you'll find along Hwy. 1A, all of them, to some degree, incorporating an oak-beamed, fireside ambience of yesteryear. Most were once mile-measured stops for stagecoaches that traveled up-island from Victoria. This pub has a particularly rich history. The building dates to 1855, and it was the hub for provincial bootleggers during Prohibition. Since Victoria continued the ban on booze until the early 1950s, "mile houses," as they were known, were the only places Victorians could get a tot outside of the city. Today, the Six Mile Pub has broad appeal and a loyal local following.

494 Island Hwy., Victoria ✆ **250/478-3121.** Main courses C$7–C$28. MC, V. Sun–Thurs 11am–midnight; Fri–Sat 11am–1am. Follow Hwy. 14 to Six Mile Rd.

Sooke Harbour House ★★★ GOURMET WEST COAST   The cuisine has seduced thousands of palates, and the restaurant's award-winning wine cellar is regarded as one of the best on the West Coast. Chef Edward Tuson's imaginative menu focuses on local seafood and organically grown produce, much of it harvested from the over 200 edible herbs, greens, flowers, and vegetables grown on the premises. Their culinary transformation creates predominately seafood dishes such as creamy broccoli soup with smoked sablefish and daylily oil, or yellow split pea–crusted lingcod with a carrot-and-mint emulsion. Even the sorbets are a cornucopia of flavors served together: green apple and mint; yellow plum and anjoy bear black currant. The food is so good here that your best bet is the multi-course gastronomic adventure tasting menu, which allows you to sample as much as possible. These are C$120; add C$80 or more if you choose the wine pairings. The four-course set menu is an excellent value at C$75, and includes a vegetarian option. Dinner is by reservation only, at least 3 days in advance (but you'd be better off calling 3 weeks in advance in the summer). Breakfast and lunch are served for hotel guests only.

In Sooke Harbour House, 1528 Whiffen Spit Rd., Sooke. ✆ **250/642-3421.** Reservations required. Main courses C$35; set menu C$47–C$75. DC, MC, V. Daily in summer 5–9:30pm; closed Tues and Wed in winter. Take Island Hwy. to the Sooke–Colwood turnoff (junction Hwy. 24), continue on Hwy. 14 to Sooke, and turn left onto Whiffen Spit Rd.

Stick in the Mud   Eighty percent of coffee in North America is sold before 10am, which is why this hole-in-the-wall opens early, and closes mid-afternoon. If you've made an early start out of Victoria, this is the place to catch up on a breakfast of fresh baked goodies and a quality caffeine boost. Barista/owner David Evans lives and breathes a passion for the bean, refusing to serve any dark roasts, any coffees roasted more than a week ago, and certainly no drips. If you're serious about your coffee, meet a connoisseur. Just get there early.

6715 Eustace Rd. ✆ **250/642-5635.** Main courses C$4. MC, V. Daily 6:30am–3:30pm.

Totem Poles

Representing history and tradition, and full of symbolism, totem poles are some of the most fascinating examples of aboriginal art. In the Pacific Northwest, they are carved from mature cedar trees with skills that have been handed down from one generation to the next. In the past, a totem was created for a specific purpose: to tell a story, to honor a deceased elder, or to record a link to the spirit—human beings that were, and still are, so much a part of aboriginal culture. Most important, a totem is the emblem of tribal unity; through its imagery, a totem conveys a tribe's ancestry, prestige, and accomplishments. Contrary to popular belief, totem figures were not Gods, and they were never used to ward off evil spirits.

Symbols are called crests, and nearly always reflect a link between human and nature (usually an animal). For example, some Northwest Coast families claim as a crest the Thunderbird, who descended from the sky to take off his animal clothing and become their human ancestor.

Today, both Native and non-native people carve totem poles, which are a source of pride and tradition for the people in the Pacific Northwest.

Some common totem symbols:

- Bear – Strength, teaching, motherhood
- Eagle – Powerful leadership and prestige
- Frog – New life, communicator
- Hummingbird – Love, beauty, a Spirit messenger
- Killer Whale – Traveler and guardian
- Otter – Trusting, inquisitive, a loyal friend
- Owl – Wisdom
- Raven – Knowledge, bringer of the Light
- Salmon – Dependable, a good provider
- Sun – Healing energy; guardian of the Day

3 EN ROUTE TO NANAIMO: THE COWICHAN VALLEY

This blood pressure–lowering trip north along Vancouver Island's east coast to Nanaimo can take you from 1½ hours to all day, depending on how many stops you make. The **Cowichan Valley** is an ideal side trip if you're staying in Victoria, and a wonderful meander through rich, rolling countryside. The more direct route is along the Trans-Canada Highway (Hwy. 1), over the mountain hump of the **Malahat,** and down through the Cowichan Valley. The Quw'utsun' people call the valley the Warm Land, and with good reason: Here, you'll find many small, family-owned farms and orchards selling homemade products such as jams, candles, and soaps. You can also visit estate **vineyards** featuring award-winning wines, as well as potters' studios, craft stores, and galleries. Many artisans work out of their homes, and, other than the annual open-house tour (usually the second week of July), they may not work regular hours. Your best bet is to pick up a map from the Victoria or Duncan visitor information centers or download it from www.visionsarttour.ca and either take your chances, or phone ahead for appointments.

One detour of interest is the city of **Duncan,** nicknamed **"City of Totem Poles"** for its impressive collection of, you guessed it, totem poles! This part of the world is famed for its residents' carving skills, yet most historic totem poles are in museums or stand in abandoned villages reclaimed by nature. In the 1980s, the mayor of Duncan commissioned local First Nations artists to carve new totem poles, and today, the city showcases one of the world's largest collections of modern totem carving. If you're just driving through Duncan, catching sight of them can be a bit hit-or-miss, however, as many are on side streets. The best suggestion is to follow the **yellow shoeprints** on the pavement, or take a free **walking tour** that starts at the **Cowichan Valley Museum,** in the VIA Rail station, at Station Street and Caan Avenue. Call ℂ **250/715-1700** for information. You can also check in at the **Duncan-Cowichan Visitor Information Centre,** 381A Trans-Canada Hwy., Duncan, BC V9L 3R5 (ℂ **250/746-4636**).

Another worthwhile detour is the town of **Chemainus.** When the building of the Trans-Canada Highway bypassed Chemainus and the local lumber mill slowed to a virtual standstill, the town turned its declining fortunes around by painting the exteriors of its quaint buildings. Today, more than 300,000 visitors stop each year to see the 39 murals and 13 sculptures, particularly in July and August each year, when more are added. If you do decide to make a stop in Chemainus, stay in one of the heritage B&Bs (see "Where to Stay," below). Spend the evening at the **Chemainus Theatre,** 9737 Chemainus Rd. (ℂ **800/565/7738;** www.chemainustheatrefestival.ca). Year-round, this troupe offers professional live theater in the town's most eye-catching building, a late-19th-century opera house. Past shows have included quality productions of *The Miracle Worker, South Pacific, My Fair Lady,* and *Lost in Yonkers.* Every December, there's a seasonal family show. Tickets range from C$14 for the preview to C$40; C$49 to C$63 for the dinner-theater package. The **Visitor Information Centre** is housed in an old railroad car at 9796 Willow St. (ℂ **250/246-3944**).

ESSENTIALS
Getting There
BY CAR   Take Douglas Street north out of Victoria, which becomes Hwy. 1 (the Trans-Canada Hwy.). From here it's about 111km (69 miles) to Nanaimo.

BY BUS   **Laidlaw Coach Lines** operates between Victoria and Nanaimo, with various stops along the way. Schedules and reservations are handled by **Greyhound Canada** (ℂ **800/663-8390** or 604/482-8747; www.greyhound.ca). There are six departures a day from Victoria, from 5:45am to 7pm. Fares are C$19 for adults, C$17 for seniors, and C$9.50 for children 5 to 11. The trip between Victoria and Nanaimo takes 2 to 2½ hours.

BY TRAIN   **The Malahat,** run by VIA Rail (ℂ **888/842-7245;** www.viarail.com), operates a daily service between Victoria and Courtenay. One-day sightseeing trips from Victoria include stops in Chemainus, Duncan, and Nanaimo. Trains depart from Victoria's VIA Rail station, at 450 Pandora Ave. One-way fares are C$28 adult, with discounts for youth, student, and senior travelers. Seniors should check into buying one ticket and travel with a companion for free promotions. Travel time between Victoria and Courtenay is about 4¼ hours.

Obtain maps and information at the **Tourism Victoria Information Centre,** 812 Wharf St., Victoria, BC V8W 1T3 (📞 **250/953-2033;** www.tourismvictoria.com). The center is open May and June daily from 9am to 8pm; July and August daily from 9am to 9pm; September through April daily from 9am to 5pm. You can also contact **Tourism Vancouver Island,** 501-65 Front St., Nanaimo, BC V9R 5H9 (📞 **250/754-3500;** www.islands.bc.ca). The center is open year-round, Monday through Friday from 8:30am to 5pm.

THE TOP ATTRACTIONS

BC Forest Museum Park/BC Forest Discovery Centre (Kids)   An affiliate of the Royal BC Museum, this is a fabulous learning and nature experience for the entire family. Focusing on forestry practices and preservation, the museum features an exhibit on the history of logging, a miniature town, a logging camp, a sawmill, a fire-watching tower, and a ranger station. Don't miss the 20-minute ride on a full-size steam train; it's included in the ticket price and is a lot of fun. Expect to stay for 1¹/₂ hours, allowing an additional half-hour for the train.

2892 Drinkwater Rd., Duncan. 📞 **250/715-1113.** www.bcforestmuseum.com. Admission C$14 adults, C$12 seniors and students, C$9 children 5–12, free for children 4 and under; C$50 family pass. May to Oct daily 10am–5pm. Closed Nov to Apr. Take Hwy. 1 past Duncan, watching for the double-span bridge over the Cowichan River. The center is approximately 3km (1³/₄ miles) past the bridge, off the highway to the right, after the fourth set of traffic lights at Beverley St.

Quw'utsun' Cultural Centre ★★   The Cowichan were the original inhabitants of the valley that now bears their name. Their culture and way of life are creatively illustrated at the Cowichan Native Village. Storytelling, dancing, and traditional feasting are some of the activities here. Go on a guided walking tour of the village, which includes several modern longhouse structures; talk to carvers as they work, or enjoy the excellent multimedia theater presentation that retells the Cowichan myth and history. A visit takes about an hour, though you might want to stop longer to try some authentic native cuisine in the Riverwalk Café. The art gallery is the best place in the valley to buy the famous bulky, durable Cowichan sweaters, knitted with bold motifs from hand-spun raw wool.

200 Cowichan Way, Cowichan. 📞 **877/746-8119** or 250/746-8119. www.quwutsan.ca Admission C$13 adults, C$11 seniors and students, C$2 children 12 and under; C$25 family pass. May–Sept daily 10am–5pm; Oct–Apr Mon–Fri 10am–4pm.. Take Hwy. 1 past Duncan, cross the double-span bridge over the Cowichan River and take Cowichan Road East en route to Duncan Mall.

MEANDERING AMONG THE WINERIES

The wine scene in British Columbia just keeps getting better in quality and variety, and although the vineyards on Vancouver Island are young compared to those found in the province's interior, they are beginning to produce some excellent vintages. As you make your way north through the Cowichan Valley toward Nanaimo, you might want to consider a stop at any one of the worthy wineries that dot the route northward from Victoria. Touring is as easy as following the burgundy-and-white Wine Route signs.

The first pocket of wineries along the route is in Cobble Hill, south of Duncan. **Cherry Point Vineyards,** 840 Cherry Point Rd., RR#3, Cobble Hill (📞 **250/743-1272;** www.cherrypointvineyards.com), is one of the most prominent Cowichan Valley wineries, with national awards to prove it. Run by the Cowichan tribes, Cherry Point's California-like vineyards produce some of the finest Gewürztraminer in the country, and its Solerra blackberry dessert wine has become equally sought after. Try it with locally made Shawnigan Lake chocolates—yes, chocolate and wine are on the must-taste list. The

Crush Wine Tours (© **877/888-5748** or 250/888-5748; www.crushwinetours. com) offers a variety of meandering tours that range from 3-hour adventures around the Peninsula (C$79 per person) to 6-hour excursions though the Cowichan Valley (C$139). Tours are led by a seasoned sommelier, so if you're serious about your grape, these tours serve to educate. **Travel with Taste** (© **250/385-1527;** www.travelwithtaste.com) also offers a variety of culinary adventures including visits to working farms, cheese-makers, a handcrafted organic gin distillery, and wineries, along with a gourmet lunch (C$195 per person Cowichan Valley; C$225 per person Saanich Peninsula). They also offer customized multi-day tours that are more akin to gastronomic safaris. See Victoria (chapter 5) for information on the city's only Urban Culinary Walking Tour.

tasting room is a Swiss-style chalet (open year round), which opens up into a quaint bistro and patio where lunches are served April to December. The artwork of local and Native artists adorns the walls.

Many of the other Cowichan-area wineries are much smaller than Cherry Point, and some choose not to host formal tours. Still, visitors are welcome to drop by, and it's not uncommon to meet an owner working in the vineyard as you roll up a dusty driveway. In fact, the locals often refer to vineyards as "farms" to illustrate their working nature—tractors, manure heaps, and all. One example is just minutes away. As small as it is, **Glenterra Vineyards,** 3897 Cobble Hill Rd., Cobble Hill (© **250/743-2330**), produces award-winning wines. Their Vivace is exclusively from their own estate-grown grapes. Also, try their Pinot Gris and Meritage. Glenterra also has a cozy tasting room and casual eatery, Thistles, that features daily lunch specials of tapas, soups, sandwiches, and good homemade desserts.

Merridale Ciderworks, 1230 Merridale Rd., RR#1, Cobble Hill (© **800/998-9908** or 250/743-4293; www.merridalecider.com), is Canada's only orchard dedicated solely to cider and wine apples. Chat with the cider-makers, tour the apple mills, presses, and fermentation casks, and feel free to wander the orchards around where you'll see fairy figurines going about their business. Kids love them. Visit in April and you'll see the orchard in magnificent bloom; turn up in October through November to watch the fragrant press. In 2008, it released its first cases of fruit brandies; a calvados-style brandy from cider apples is slated to makes its debut in 2010. The cozy bistro, La Pommeraie, offers authentic country-style cooking and a virtual showcase of gourmet pizzas, artisan breads, and fruit pies from its brick-oven bakery, Flour Water Salt. It is open daily for lunch. **Venturi-Schulze Vineyards,** 4235 Trans-Canada Hwy., RR#1, Cobble Hill (© **250/ 743-5630;** www.venturischulze.com), is the smallest winery in the Cowichan Valley, and it's truly a family affair, centered on the 100-year-old farmhouse. The winery, built partially underground, paved the way to convert the old winery into a vinegary. All wines and gourmet vinegars are grown, produced, and bottled on the property.

Another group of wineries worth visiting is found near Duncan. **Alderlea Vineyards,** 1751 Stamps Rd., RR#1, Duncan (© **250/746-7122**), is located on a picturesque 4-hectare (10-acre) site. Creating wines from grapes grown only in their own vineyard, Alderlea produces an excellent Bacchus, Pinot Gris, Hearth (a port-style dessert wine),

Pinot Auxerrois, and Angelique blend. **Blue Grouse Vineyards,** 4365 Blue Grouse Rd., Duncan (© 250/743-3834; www.bluegrousevineyards.com), is one of the founding estate wineries on Vancouver Island, and is renowned for its exclusive premium wines. All are 100% estate grown and produced on what are purported to be the warmest 4 hectares (10 acres) in the valley. Because of this, the Pinot Gris has a slightly pinkish tone and, along with their Ortega, Pinot Noir, and exclusive Black Muscat, is an award-winner. Wine tastings are held in a comfortable European-style tasting room overlooking the valley. In summer, picnic tables under the arbor are perfect for a savory lunch. **Vignetti Zanatta,** 5039 Marshall Rd., RR#3, Duncan (© 250/748-2338; www.zanatta.ca), is one of the oldest vineyards on Vancouver Island. Wines here are made by an old-world Italian method using grapes grown only on the property. Try the Ortega, a dry, fruity white wine; or the Glenora Fantasia, a sparkling wine. The Pinot Grigio, Pinot Nero, and special Damasco are all worthwhile. Plan to stop for lunch or dinner at **Vinoteca** (see "Where to Dine," below), featuring many foods grown on the Zanatta 49-hectare (121-acre) farm. Touring maps are available at most visitor centers and from www.islandwineries.ca.

WHERE TO STAY
On The Malahat
The Aerie Resort & Spa ★★★   An acclaimed member of the Relais & Châteaux group of hotels, the Aerie is a magnificent Mediterranean-style mansion reminiscent of grand homes in Southern Europe. Surrounded by 4 hectares (10 acres) of meticulously kept grounds, this hotel offers a breathtaking view of the Olympic Mountains and the Gulf Islands that alone is worth the trip, especially if you arrive by helicopter (there's a helipad amid the landscaped gardens). Rooms and suites are individually designed (some are multilevel); most feature Persian and Chinese silk carpets, fireplaces, Jacuzzis, decks, and four-poster queen- or king-size beds. Inspired touches include fresh flowers, terry-cloth robes, CD players, and Bernard Callebaut chocolates hand-dipped by the renowned chocolatier based in Banff, Alberta. The Villa Cielo, set above the main building, is the Aerie's pièce de résistance, offering the ultimate in luxury and space. Suites range in size from 70 to 130 sq. m (753–1,399 sq. ft.) with views that are a stunning 549m (1,801 ft.) high. The hotel's restaurant is not to be missed (see "Where to Dine," below), and the spa is also a top-ranked part of the Aerie experience. And bird-watchers take note: One of the hotel's best packages (especially in view of its name) is the Audubon, which includes a full day with Pacific Northwest Raptors, the only falconry/raptor educational facility of its kind in the Pacific Northwest.

600 Ebadora Lane (P.O. Box 108), Malahat, Victoria, BC V0R 2L0. © 800/518-1933 or 250/743-7115. Fax 250/743-4766. www.aerie.bc.ca. 35 units. C$139–C$319 double; C$249–C$499 suite; C$450–C$675 villa. Packages available. AE, DC, MC, V. Free parking. Take Hwy. 1 to the Spectacle Lake turnoff; take the first right and follow the winding driveway. **Amenities:** 2 restaurants; bar; outdoor tennis court; fitness room; spa; Jacuzzi; sauna; concierge; 12-hr. room service; laundry; dry cleaning. *In room:* A/C, LCD TV, dataport, Wi-Fi, minibar, coffeemaker, hair dryer, iron.

In Duncan
Fairburn Farm Culinary Retreat & Guesthouse ★★   This one-of-a-kind inn offers guests an idealized farm experience—you can be coddled, enjoy exquisite culinary fare, and at the same time explore at your leisure this working farm, orchard, vineyard, and dairy. The farm's resident, and North America's only, herd of genuine European River Water Buffalo produces yogurt, ice cream, and mozzarella. Built in the 1880s, the rambling but upgraded farmhouse has high ceilings, antique moldings, tiled fireplaces, and a broad columned porch that overlooks 53 hectares (131 acres) of gardens and meadows, with

mountain slopes visible in the distance. Each of the three large, year-round guest rooms is individually decorated with fine Italian linens and original art. Two have fireplaces. A renovation of a 1930s caretaker's cottage has created an additional two rooms in the summer; they're not as fancy, but if food is your motivation for being here, then these represent great savings. The two-bedroom cottage, too, is only available during the summer months. It includes a fully equipped kitchen, and with its simpler furnishings is ideal for families. Fairburn's showcase kitchen is the source of its reputation, and is where guests enjoy cooking lessons, bread-making demonstrations, and other culinary programs such as the participatory lavish Saturday dinners. Food programs reflect seasonal cycles, so call ahead of your stay to check the schedule. Breakfast, which is included in the room rate, is a homemade farm-fresh feast. These folks also rent out a fully furnished Victoria apartment, located on the top floor of a renovated 1912 home in Fernwood, only minutes from downtown Victoria.

3310 Jackson Rd., Duncan, BC V9L 6N7. ©/fax **250/746-4637.** www.fairburnfarm.bc.ca. 6 units, 1 cottage. Nov–May C$130–C$165 double; Oct 1–15 and April–May C$145-C$175 double; Jun–Sep C$165–C$190 double. Extra person C$20. MC, V. **Amenities:** Lounge, Wi-Fi. In room: Hair dryer, no phone. Closed mid-Oct to mid-Nov.

In Chemainus

Bird Song Cottage/Castlebury Cottage These separate bed-and-breakfasts adjoin one another, but could hardly be more different. Both have overindulged in the whimsy department, yet somehow have come out on the winning side. For example, Bird Song is filled with so much Victorian bric-a-brac that it's actually quite enchanting and theatrical. The recorded sound of birds trilling is a bit over the top; but then so is the all the architectural gingerbread. Next door, Castlebury Cottage exemplifies medieval romantic fantasy, with its vaulted ceilings, mullioned casement windows, and antique wrought-iron wall-lamp sconces. There's even a full-size suit of armor standing in one corner. The kitsch extends to the guest rooms too: Oversize beds (some four-poster) are covered in satin cushions, windows are framed with lacy chiffon, and chairs are upholstered in velvet. Bathrooms are on the small side, but anything larger would detract from the Camelot-like ambience. These places might be too over the top for some people—but just think of the stories (and photos) you could take back home.

9909 Maple St., Chemainus, BC V0R 1K0. © 250/246-9910. Fax 250/246-2909. www.birdsongcottage. com. 3 units, one cottage. C$125–C$145 Bird Song Cottage; C$140–C$280 Castlebury Cottage. 2-night minimum stay on weekends. Rates include breakfast and afternoon tea. Extra person $25. MC, V. **Amenities:** Lounge. In room: Bird Song has TV/VCR/DVD, hair dryer, no phone; Castlebury has TV/VCR/DVD, full-service kitchen, fireplace.

In Ladysmith (Near Chemainus)

Yellow Point Lodge Yellow Point Lodge began operating in the 1930s, and its blend of summer camp and luxury resort has remained a perennial favorite, especially with families. The main lodge has an enormous lobby, a huge fireplace, and a dining room with communal tables. Meals—good, home-style cooking such as prime rib and Yorkshire pudding, roast turkey and mashed potatoes, and a terrific seafood buffet on Friday nights—are included and served at set times. There are a number of comfortable hotel-like guest rooms in the lodge, all with ocean views. Away from the lodge, self-contained cabins range from rustic, barrack-style accommodations with shared bathrooms and beach cabins with no running water to luxurious one-, two-, and three-bedroom cottages; some are on the lodge's private beach, most are tucked in between the trees. The lodge is surrounded by 67 hectares (166 acres) of private, mostly first-growth coastal rain forest, with over 2.4km (1¹/₂ miles) of waterfront facing the Gulf Islands.

3700 Yellow Point Rd., Ladysmith, BC V0R 2E0. ℭ 250/245-7422. Fax 250/245-7411. www.yellowpoint lodge.com. 53 units. May to mid-Oct and winter weekends C$189–C$200 lodge rooms, C$162–C$202 cabins, C$127 barracks; rates 10% lower mid-Oct to Apr weekdays. Rates include all meals. AE, MC, V. Children 13 and under not accepted. No pets. **Amenities:** Restaurant; 2 outdoor tennis courts; Jacuzzi; sauna; kayaks; bikes; hiking. *In room:* Fridge (some rooms), coffeemaker (some rooms), no phone.

In Cowichan Bay

Oceanfront Grant Resort & Marina   Every one- and two-bedroom suite faces the water, and all have been refurbished in the last few years. Out with drab and neutral; in with Italian marble floors, handcrafted furniture, upgraded and contemporary kitchens, and exceptionally comfortable king- and queen-size beds. Some rooms have fireplaces and views of the marina below. Oceanfront has a good steak and seafood restaurant that adds a sushi twist at the weekends. It also features wines from every single winery in the Cowichan Valley, as well as international labels. The marina provides kayak rentals and boat charters.

1681 Cowichan Bay Rd., Cowichan Bay, BC V0R 1N0. ℭ **800/663-7897** or 250/701-0166. Fax 250/701-0126. www.thegrandresort.com. 57 units. Mid-Apr to Sep C$189–C$239 1-bedroom, C$219–C$269 2-bedroom; mid-Oct to mid-Apr C$99–C$239 1-bedroom, C$169–C$189 2-bedroom. Extra person C$20. Children 12 and under stay free in parent's room. AE, MC, V. Free parking. **Amenities:** Restaurant; bar; heated indoor pool; golf nearby; gym; tanning bed; hot tub; boat rental; concierge; beer and wine sales. *In room:* TV, DVD, coffeemaker, fridge, hair dryer, iron.

WHERE TO DINE
On & Over The Malahat

The Aerie ★★★ WEST COAST/FRENCH   The entire setting of the Aerie is overwhelmingly beautiful (see "Where to Stay," above), and the elegant restaurant takes full advantage of its sky-high location, which sets the stage for equally impressive food. Menus items might appear overly fancy French in their description, but press on. The wonderful array of locally sourced products has a zesty French flair. Think items such as Dungeness crab beignet with avocado salpicon and shellfish bisque; or Cowichan Bay duck breast with seared foie gras and superbly matched with cherry marmalade pithiviers (miniature puff pastry pies), corn puree, and vichy carrots. The pan seared arctic char is equally unexpected because of the accompanying quenelle of slow-cooked potatoes, mild curry butter, and citrus vanilla oil. The six-course **tasting menu,** paired with exquisite wines, is highly recommended. Did we mention that the wine cellar has a 6,000-bottle inventory? This is a destination restaurant few Victorians miss, and you won't want to either.

600 Ebadora Lane, Malahat. ℭ **250/743-7115.** Reservations required. Lunch C$17; dinner C$36; 6-course prix-fixe dinner C$110; C$150 with pairings. AE, MC, V. Daily noon–2pm and 5:30pm-9pm. Take Hwy. 1 to the Spectacle Lake turnoff; take the first right and follow the winding driveway.

Amuse Bistro ★★★ WEST COAST/FRENCH   Just over the Malahat en route to Shawnigan Lake lies a tiny destination restaurant set in what used to be a private home. You're greeted like a houseguest, and you will walk to the rear of the building with its open kitchen before heading upstairs into the living room that now seats about 20. In summer, the patio doubles capacity. The food is superlative and puts a French inspiration into local ingredients, with a different amuse-bouche offered at every meal. If that serves to awaken the palette, other dishes will do no less. Look for items like pan-seared medallions of farm-raised pork tenderloin with caramelized apples and pan juices, finished with organic

---

Moments **Picnic Supplies**

There's no better place to pick up simple but delicious picnic supplies than Cowichan Bay's seaside village, especially if you're planning to spread a blanket at one of the wineries. **True Grain Bread** (1725 Cowichan Bay Rd.; ✆ **250/746-7664;** www.truegrain.ca) bakes organic, handcrafted breads, croissants, cookies, pretzels, and rolls using heritage wheats, natural leavens, sea salt, alternative grains, and freshly stone-milled products. At **Hilary's Artisan Cheese & Deli** next door (Village Store; 1737 Cowichan Bay Rd.; ✆ **250/748-5992;** www.hilarys cheese.com), you'll find farm-fresh, aromatic fromages as well as over 100 specialty cheeses, cold cuts, and homemade deli items. And to see you on your way? The **Udder Guy's Old Fashioned Ice Cream** (1721 Cowichan Bay Rd.; ✆ **250/954-5555**) has the best flavors on the island. Ingredients are fresh with no artificial additives. Strawberry Extreme is made with local berries and real coconut, shredded and roasted on site, that are sublime.

---

black currants, purple heritage carrots, rainbow Swiss chard, golden beets, Russian blue potatoes, and Egyptian walking onions. The roasted squash bisque is wonderfully flavored with a swirl of buerre noisette rather than the ubiquitous Indian spices, and the warm gingerbread gateau, dolloped with lemon preserve, is accompanied by a red wine–pocked pear and spiced ice cream. In addition to an a la carte menu, there are three-, four-, or five-course table d'hote menus (C$36–C$59); add about C$30 for wine pairings.

753 Shawnigan-Mill Bay Rd., Shawnigan Lake. ✆ 250/743-3667. www.amusebistro.com. Reservations recommended. Dinner C$19–C$32; brunch May–Sept only C$23. MC, V. Wed–Sun from 5pm; May–Sept 10am–2pm and 5–10pm.

In Cowichan Bay

Crow & Gate PUB FARE   This classic Tudor-style pub was built in 1972 yet looks like it was plucked out of Cornwall, with its stone and timbered walls, leaded-glass windows, and low-slung ceilings. Even the hand-painted sign is just like the old pub signs you still find in England. Surrounded by a working farm, this popular watering hole offers the best of British pub fare, including traditional Ploughman's Lunch, roast beef and Yorkshire pudding, pasties, and shepherd's pie. There's a flower-laden patio in summer.

2313 Yellow Point Rd. ✆ 250/722-3731. www.crowandgate.com. Reservations recommended for dinner. Main courses C$9–C$17. MC, V. Daily 11am–11pm.

Masthead Restaurant WEST COAST   In the late 1800s, the building was a stopover inn for those making the arduous wagon journey north from Victoria. When the railway arrived, the entire main floor became a machine shop, and now, in its current incarnation, it's a bright and airy dining room that serves up some of the region's best West Coast cuisine. Much of it has local origins: the Queen Charlotte Coho Salmon; Fanny Bay oysters; Cowichan Valley venison, chicken, and pork; and Salt Spring Island mussels. Most dishes are prepared without too much filigree: Grilled tenderloin with béarnaise sauce has just a touch of bacon, and venison is simply flavored with sautéed mushrooms and a mustard demiglaze. The fancy fixings, however, do come as side garnishes such as a potato croquette stuffed with figs, goats cheese, and a ginger puree. The three-course table d'hôte is good value for taste experiences and dollars spent. Masthead has dibs on select limited editions produced annually by some Cowichan Valley Estate wineries, so you can expect to discover hard-to-find labels here like Venturi Schulze's Millefiori and Pinot Noir. Some of these are so in demand that they must be ordered two harvests in advance.

1705 Cowichan Bay Rd., Cowichan Bay. 📞 **250/748-3714.** www.themastheadrestaurant.com. Reservations recommended. Main courses C$19–C$29; 3-course menu C$30. MC, V. Daily from 5pm.

Rock Cod Café FISH & CHIPS   Perched above the water, this busy cafe overlooks busy fishing docks and serves the best fish and chips in the area. After all, when the fish is pulled straight off the boats and put right into the pan, what would you expect? Check out the specials board: It's crammed with value-priced items based on whatever those boats bring in, as well as burgers, salads, and pasta dishes. This is a great place for takeout, especially family packs, or simply to fuel up for a stroll around the harbor.

1759 Cowichan Bay Rd. 📞 **250/746-1550.** www.rockcodcafe.com. Main courses C$7–C$15. MC, V. Daily 8am–8pm.

Around Duncan

The Genoa Bay Café PACIFIC NORTHWEST   Genoa Bay, a 20-minute drive from Duncan, was named by Giovanni Baptiste Ordano in 1858. The bay reminded him of his home in Italy and still retains a picturesque charm. The cafe is part of the marina complex and is always busy with sea-faring folks and locals. Although the menu leans to seafood, exquisitely prepared, you'll find items such as BBQ ribs, slow-roasted in apple and sun-dried cranberry BBQ sauce, and a rack of lamb with pesto and mango chutney glaze—an absolute winner. In the fall and winter months, tapas dishes are offered—a clever way to monitor purchases and portion controls during the slower season. Any time of year, however, it's fish that really tops the charts—mouth-watering halibut and candied smoked salmon in white-wine cream sauce, calamari with roasted-red-pepper pesto dip, or sole and scallops with a mango Thai chili sauce. The island's daily newspaper rated the chocolate-pecan pie the best of the island.

5100 Genoa Bay Rd., Genoa Bay Marina, Genoa Bay. 📞 **800/572-6481** or 250/746-7621. www.genoabay marina.com. Reservations recommended. Main courses C$19–C$31. MC, V. Daily 5:30–10pm; lunch Thurs–Sun 11:30am–2:30pm.

Vinoteca ★★ LIGHT DINING   A combination wine-tasting room and tapas bar, Vinoteca is set amid the family-owned and -operated Vignetti Zanatta vineyards (see "Meandering Among the Wineries," earlier in this chapter). The 1903 farmhouse has been lovingly restored and is a restful place to dine or sip your afternoon away. The menu reflects the family's Italian heritage, incorporating food that is grown either on the farm or locally. A great place for a light meal, here you'll find items such as marinated vegetables, bruschetta, as well as a daily fresh pasta selection (the chicken confit cannelloni is very good), and more substantial dishes such as espresso-marinated duck breast. What make the food outstanding are unexpected combinations: a salad of melon, smoked rout, arugula and capers, and shellfish poached in coconut milk and served with saffron rice. All are complemented by wines from their vineyards.

5039 Marshall Rd. (near Glenora, south of Duncan). 📞 **250/709-2279.** Reservations recommended for dinner. Lunch C$11–C$16; dinner C$14–C$30. MC, V. Wed–Fri noon–2:30pm; Sat–Sun noon–4pm; closed Mon–Tues. Closed Dec–Mar. Take Miller Rd. exit off Hwy. 1 to stop sign. Turn left onto Miller Rd., right on Koksilah Rd., and left onto Miller Rd. again. Turn left on Glenora; the vineyards are at the junction of Glenora and Marshall rds.

7

Central Vancouver Island

The central part of Vancouver Island showcases some of the best of British Columbia's natural attractions—it's a real haven for eco-adventurers. And it's so diverse that much of it is also geared to family fun. Nanaimo, the island's second-largest city and the gateway to the region, is the arrival point for visitors traveling by ferry from the mainland. Families usually head for the neighboring communities of Parksville and Qualicum Beach, where sandy beaches, warm water temperatures, tranquil lakes, and exceptional golf courses prevail. They are year-round vacation destinations, and are increasingly attractive to active retirees; few can resist the more than 2,000 hours of sunshine the townships receive each year.

Things begin to change, however, as you head inland, cutting across the island to the west coast. Here lie the deep Douglas fir forests of **Cathedral Grove,** and the mill town of **Port Alberni,** from which you can explore the region's protected inlets. And once you reach the west coast, well, the changes in scenery are dramatic. The shores are windswept and wild. Fishing villages like **Tofino** ("Tough City") and **Ucluelet** (Yew-*kloo*-let) are home base to kayakers, hikers, surfers, naturalists, and photographers, who flock to explore **Pacific Rim National Park,** the Broken Group Islands, and Clayoquot Sound. Here you can discover some of the most pristine and accessible coastline in the province.

---

1 NANAIMO

With a population close to 80,000, Nanaimo is quickly shedding its industrial roots. Once the center of vast coal-mining operations, Nanaimo developed into rather a parochial community. This image is finally beginning to change. Although its suburban environs are pretty nondescript, a small downtown nucleus is smartening up into a hip and pedestrian-friendly area where old buildings such as a century-old firehall-turned-restaurant are finding new leases on life. The city's fathers mean business: 21 of 58 heritage commercial buildings have received grants for renovations since 2001, and more than 400 condominium units have been developed in the last two years alone. Around the revamped harborfront you'll find a number of galleries, intriguing shops, and quality restaurants to enjoy. The Port of Nanaimo Centre opened in 2008, as the new home of the Nanaimo District Museum, an open-air community plaza, and the new convention center. Other news includes: Vancouver Island University's recent upgrade from a community college, a reflection of the school's increasing growth and stature; plans for a cruise-ship terminal; and expansion of the airport so it can handle bigger jets—important if Nanaimo is to become a visitor destination. Add to this the rapidly rising condo developments along the downtown waterfront, and Nanaimo's designation in 2008 as a "Cultural Capital of Canada," and it all points to an up-and-coming city on the fast track to adulthood.

Naming Nanaimo

Pronounced "Na-*nye*-mo," the city's name originated when the first white settlers tried to adapt a Coast Salish world "Snu-Ney-Muxw" meaning "The Meeting Place," into English. It was originally called Colvilletown.

ESSENTIALS
Getting There

BY CAR Nanaimo is located right off the Trans-Canada Highway (Hwy. 1), 111km (60 miles) north of Victoria.

BY PLANE The **Nanaimo Airport** (© 250/245-2157) is 18km (11 miles) from downtown Nanaimo. **Air Canada Jazz** (© 888/247-2262 or 800/661-3936) operates seven flights daily between Nanaimo and Vancouver. There are also several harbor-to-harbor flights among Vancouver, Nanaimo, Victoria, and Seattle. These seaplane carriers include **West Coast Air** (© 800/347-2222 or 604/606-6888; www.westcoastair.com), **Harbour Air** (© 800/665-0212 or 250/714-0900; www.harbour-air.com), and **Kenmore Air** (© 877/359-5366 or 425/486-1257; www.kenmoreair.com).

BY BUS **Greyhound/Island Coach Lines** (© 800/661-8747 or 250/385-4411) operates from Victoria to Nanaimo, Tofino, and Port Hardy. One-way fares from Victoria to Nanaimo are C$19 for adults. Fares for seniors are 10% less; fares for children 5 to 11 are 50% less.

BY TRAIN The Malahat, operated by VIA Rail (© 888/842-7245; www.viarail.com) has daily service between Victoria and Courtenay. One-day sightseeing trips from Victoria include stops in Chemainus, Duncan, and Nanaimo.

BY FERRY BC Ferries (© 888/BCFERRY [223-3779], 888/223-3779, or 250/386-3431; www.bcferries.com) runs between **Horseshoe Bay** in West Vancouver, and **Departure Bay,** in Nanaimo, as well as between **Tsawwassen** and **Duke Point,** in Nanaimo. The latter is used primarily by trucks and commercial vehicles, but if you're traveling by car (Duke Point is 16km/10 miles south of Nanaimo and is not served by public transit), it's a good alternative to the very busy Horseshoe Bay–Departure Bay routing. Fares for either route are C$13 adult and C$43 per standard vehicle.

Visitor Information

Tourism Nanaimo is located at Beban House, 2290 Bowen Rd., Nanaimo, BC V9T 3K7 (© 800/663-7337 or 250/756-0106; www.tourismnanaimo.com). A summer-only information center operates at the Pioneer Waterfront Plaza near the Bastion. Tourism Vancouver Island is also based in Nanaimo, at 501-65 Front St., Nanaimo, BC V9R 5H9 (© 250/754-3500; www.islands.bc.ca).

Getting Around

BY CAR Be alert to street signs; Nanaimo's roads go off at angles and change names along the way. For example, Bastion Street becomes Fitzwilliam Street (once Nanaimo's red-light district), which becomes 3rd Street, which leads to the Parkway before becoming Jingle Pot Road, named for the time when miners walked the route to work, "jingling" their lunches in metal pails along the way. Street parking is ample, and most hotels have secured underground parking.

BY PUBLIC TRANSPORTATION **Nanaimo Regional Transit System** (✆ 250/390-4531; www.rdn.bc.ca) provides public transport through Nanaimo's suburbs, mainly residential areas and a couple of strip malls. From a visitor's standpoint, they're buses that go nowhere unless you're heading up to Parksville and Qualicum. Fares are C$2.25 for adults and C$2 for seniors and youths. If, for some reason, you're out in the boonies where there are few official stops, you can flag one down.

BY TAXI For cab service, call **AC Taxi** (✆ 800/753-1231 or 250/753-1231; www.actaxi.ca) or **Swiftsure Taxi** (✆ 250/753-8911). You would be lucky to find a taxi hanging around the bus station or a downtown hotel; better to call ahead.

Exploring Nanaimo

The best thing about Nanaimo is its **Pioneer Waterfront**—refurbished with multi-level walkways, banks of flowers, marina restaurants, and gift shops—some touristy, others worthwhile. On most summer days, the walkways have a mix of one-person stalls selling paintings, junk jewelry, and carvings; and come Friday, they're joined by local farm vendors selling fresh produce, homemade jams, and baked goods. The Harbourside Walkway actually extends all the way to Departure Bay, 4km (2½ miles) away, and is a popular route for joggers. The waterfront is anchored by the **Bastion,** Nanaimo's oldest building and the only remaining fort structure of its type in North America. Getting around the harbor waters is most fun aboard the stylized 12-passenger shuttles run by **Nanaimo Harbour Ferry** (✆ 250/619-5759; www.nanaimoharbourferry.com); the same folks run the shuttles around Victoria's harbor. Catch a ride from Fisherman's Market Pier for a 45-minute tour (C$17 per adult; C$15 seniors/students; C$9 children 12 and under), or hop over to Newcastle Island (C$8).

The **Old City Quarter** is also undergoing a facelift. Although only a 3-block area, it's where you'll find some good restaurants, and specialty gift shops, such as **Flying Fish Giftware,** 180 Commercial St. (✆ 250/754-2104), for handmade crafts, housewares, and whimsical items; **Shanghai Tea Emporium,** 13B Commercial St. (✆ 250/753-9957); and the **Artisan's Studio,** 70 Bastion St. (✆ 250/753-6151), a co-op gallery run by and featuring the work of local artists. **Hill's Native Art,** 76 Bastion St. (✆ 250/755-7873), is a reputable place for quality First Nations art. Just be aware that the "new" historic district backs onto the older area that still sports a couple of seamy clubs.

Fun Facts **Castaways Find a New Home**

You'll be forgiven if you do a double take. Yes, that's the real SS *Minnow* from the classic TV show, *Gilligan's Island*. Now residing in Nanaimo Harbour, the iconic 46-year-old Wheeler Express Cruiser has been totally refurbished and, although privately owned, it is used for charity events and special occasions such as the Bathtub Races. The show—featuring the hapless Gilligan stranded on an island with Skipper, the Millionaire and his Wife, the Professor, Ginger, and Mary Ann—stopped production in 1967, but still lives on in endless reruns.

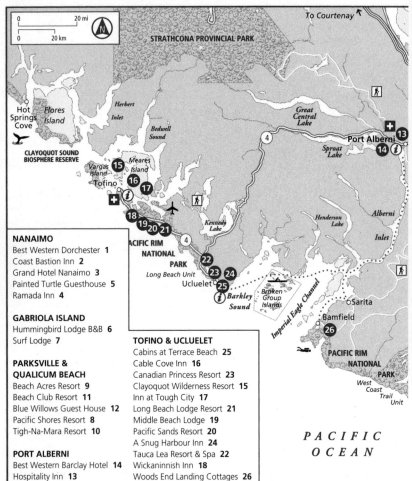

0 20 mi
0 20 km

To Courtenay

STRATHCONA PROVINCIAL PARK

Herbert
Inlet

Great
Central
Lake

Hot
Springs
Cove

Flores
Island

Bedwell
Sound

Sproat
Lake

Port Alberni

13

14

CLAYOQUOT SOUND
BIOSPHERE RESERVE

Vargas
Island

Meares
Island

Tofino

15

16 17

Alberni

Henderson
Lake

Inlet

18

19 20 21

Kennedy
Lake

PACIFIC RIM
NATIONAL
PARK
Long Beach Unit
Ucluelet

4

22

23 24

25

Barkley
Sound

Broken
Group
Islands

Imperial Eagle Channel

Sarita

Bamfield

26

NANAIMO
Best Western Dorchester 1
Coast Bastion Inn 2
Grand Hotel Nanaimo 3
Painted Turtle Guesthouse 5
Ramada Inn 4

GABRIOLA ISLAND
Hummingbird Lodge B&B 6
Surf Lodge 7

PARKSVILLE &
QUALICUM BEACH
Beach Acres Resort 9
Beach Club Resort 11
Blue Willows Guest House 12
Pacific Shores Resort 8
Tigh-Na-Mara Resort 10

PORT ALBERNI
Best Western Barclay Hotel 14
Hospitality Inn 13

TOFINO & UCLUELET
Cabins at Terrace Beach 25
Cable Cove Inn 16
Canadian Princess Resort 23
Clayoquot Wilderness Resort 15
Inn at Tough City 17
Long Beach Lodge Resort 21
Middle Beach Lodge 19
Pacific Sands Resort 20
A Snug Harbour Inn 24
Tauca Lea Resort & Spa 22
Wickaninnish Inn 18
Woods End Landing Cottages 26

PACIFIC RIM
NATIONAL
PARK
West
Coast
Trail
Unit

PACIFIC
OCEAN

THE TOP ATTRACTIONS

The Nanaimo Bastion The white, fortified tower was built by the Hudson's Bay
Company in 1852 to protect its Nanaimo trading post. At that time, Haida Indians traveled down from the northerly Queen Charlotte Islands and mounted a series of raids. Its
three floors house a hands-on exhibit that explores early life in Nanaimo: On the first
floor is The Company's Clerk's Office displaying coal-mining gear of the time; The Arse-
nal on the second floor (in summer, the Bastion Guards recreate the firing of the noon
cannon daily at 11:45am); and the third-floor Refuge, once used in times of danger, now
has displays on blacksmithing, homemaking, and farming.

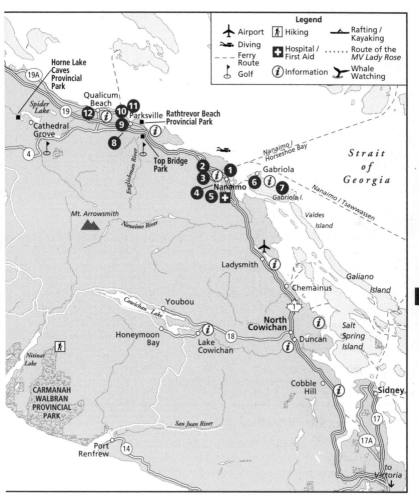

Legend

✈ Airport   🚶 Hiking   🛶 Rafting / Kayaking
🤿 Diving   ➕ Hospital / First Aid   ⋯ Route of the MV Lady Rose
‐‐ Ferry Route   ⛳ Golf   ⓘ Information   🐋 Whale Watching

Bastion & Front St., on Pioneer Waterfront Plaza. © **250/753-1821.** www.nanaimomuseum.ca. Admission C$1. May–Sept daily 10am–4pm.

Nanaimo District Museum   Since moving to its new location at the Port of Nanaimo Centre last year, things are still in a state of flux, with all exhibits being redesigned and reinstalled. Among those complete to date is an exhibit that gives a good overview of the history of Nanaimo's waterfront. In 2009, you can expect to see a coal miner's tunnel and First Nations Gallery, including a re-creation of a Salish Indian village (the Snuneymuxw—the "Nanaimo people"). The old miner's cottage and restored 1890s locomotive remains in the museum's original location in Piper's Park, accessed by climbing two steep flights of stairs. Make your own petroglyph rubbings for an unusual souvenir or find Snuneymuxw wooden carvings in the gift shop.

100 Museum Way, Port of Nanaimo Centre. ℂ **250/753-1821;** www.nanaimomuseum.ca. Admission C$2 adults, C$1.75 seniors, C75¢ children 6–12. Mid-May to Labor Day daily 10am–5pm; after Labor Day to mid-May Tues–Sat 10am–5pm.

OUTDOOR ACTIVITIES

SCUBA DIVING   Jacques Cousteau called the waters around Nanaimo "the best temperate water diving in the world, second only to the Red Sea," so suffice to say, scuba diving is big business here. Nicknamed the "Emerald Sea," its water is clear enough to see the likes of giant Pacific octopi, colorful sea anemones, and herds of marine mammals that appear to just "hang around" for entertainment. **Dodds Narrows,** between Vancouver Island and Mudge Island, is a particularly hot diving spot. Other areas include **Snake Island Wall** (*Tip:* even if you're not a diver, you can snorkel with the seals on nearby Snake Island), **Gabriola Passage,** and the **largest artificial upright reef in the world.** The reef is made up of a number of sunken wrecks, including the **HMCS *Saskatchewan,*** a 366-foot Canadian Naval destroyer sunk in 1997, and the **HMCS *Cape Breton.*** In 2005, *Rivtow Lion,* a retired deep-sea rescue tug, was added to the reef. The *Rivtow* rests at a manageable depth of about 15m (49 ft.) right in Departure Bay, making it a great dive for those wanting to get a bit more comfortable before heading down deeper to the Cape Breton or Saskatchewan. Together, they have created the largest artificial upright reef in the world.

A good diving operator, which offers guided dives, equipment rentals, and instruction with fast, custom-dive boats, is **Ocean Explorers Diving** (1690 Stewart Ave; ℂ **800/ 233-4145** or 250/753-2055; www.oceanexplorersdiving.com). Prices start at C$65 per dive. **The Dive Outfitters** (2205 Northfield Rd.; ℂ **250/756-1863;** www.thediveoutfitters. ca) are also recommended.

BUNGEE JUMPING   Keeping your head above water delivers something quite different, if you've got the nerve, go for it. Set high over the Nanaimo River lies **Wild Play**

Petroglyph Provincial Park ★

It's a wonder more travelers don't stop by. Estimated to be at least 1,000 years old, this park's petroglyphs are an overlooked treasure. Although similar sandstone carvings exists elsewhere on Vancouver Island, including nearby Gabriola, rarely are they found in such concentration and as easily accessible. Look for mythological creatures—sea wolves in particular—and a variety of other symbolic designs resembling bird, human, and fish. For the artistically inclined, an interpretive display of concrete castings taken from the nearby petroglyphs is available to make coffee-table-size rubbings. The originals are just a short distance farther along the walkway on a hill that overlooks Nanaimo Harbour. The Nanaimo Snuneymuxw First Nation community believe that the petroglyphs were carved by Thochwan, who is present among the carvings, having himself been transformed into stone by a supernatural visitor. The park is located on the east side of the Trans-Canada Highway, 4km (2½ miles) south of Nanaimo. Visit www.bcparks.ca for information; or contact **Tourism Nanaimo** (ℂ **800/663-7337;** www.tourismnanaimo.com).

at the **Bungy Zone** (℃ **888/668-7874** or 250/714-7874; www.wildplayparks.com), touted as the "Only Legal Bridge Bungy Jump Site in North America." If free-falling 43m (141 ft.) at speeds of up to 140kmph (87 mph), doesn't appeal, watching the bungy bravehearts is still a thrill. An on-site gift shop sells plenty of bungy paraphernalia, so you can always pretend you dared. Jumps are C$99 and include an I Did It! T-shirt. But that isn't all you'll find here. There's a high-elevation swing that cinches you up in a slingshot-like device (C$90) and a zip-line ride that zips you across a wooded canyon at almost 100kmph (62 mph). The zip trips are also a part of the aerial tree obstacle course called Tree Go that's set some 3 to 15m (9³/₄–49 ft.) high in a Douglas fir forest with suspended bridges, scramble nets, and swinging logs. Although there's a children's-only version of the course, most experiences have a minimum age of 12 years old. Tree Go prices range from C$20 to C$40. Bungy Zone is a great spot for teenagers who are looking for an adrenaline rush.

GOLF   **Nanaimo Golf Club** (2800 Highland Blvd.; ℃ **250/758-6332;** www.nanaimo golfclub.ca) is a pretty, 6,700-yard course; green fees March to September are C$72, with reduced rates off-season. **Cottonwood Golf Course** (1975 Haslam Rd.; ℃ **250/ 245-5157;** www.cottonwoodgolfcourse.com) is an 18-hole, par-72 course with panoramic views of the coastal mountains. Green fees range from C$40 to C$48.

HIKING   One of Nanaimo's lesser-known trails is the 2km (1.2-mile) **Cable Bay Trail.** You hike through a serene forest to Cable Bay Bridge, where you can beachcomb or observe migrating sea lions (Oct–Apr). The trail is an off-leash (dog-friendly) area. **Park-way Trail,** which runs alongside Hwy. 19, links Aulds Road to Chase River. The 20km (12-mile) paved and tree-lined span is best suited for long-distance cyclists and joggers. It leads to Buttertubs Marsh, Colliery Dam, Bowen Park, and the Harbourfront Walk-way via the Millstone Trail. Because the **E&N Trail** is paved and level, it's a magnet not only for walkers, but for in-line skaters, bikers, and skateboarders too. The 8km (5-mile) paved trail parallels the E&N Railway tracks and the old Island Hwy. 19A from Rosehill Avenue to Mostar Road and is the best option for "wheels." **Tracks Outdoor Adventures** (2130 Akenhead Rd.; ℃ **250/754-8732;** www.tracksoutdooradventures.com), offers a variety of guided hiking excursions, from a heritage stroll through downtown Nanaimo to treks through rain forests, around Newcastle Island, and more.

KAYAKING   Nanaimo's sheltered waters make them ideal for kayakers, whether pad-dling over to Newcastle Island or taking a full day (even multi-day) excursion over to the

---

ⓕun Facts   Tubs Ahoy!

For more than 40 years, daredevils have raced across the Georgia Strait in one- and two-man craft. In the early days, vessels were old claw-foot tubs fitted with engines. Often, they sank in the harbor. In fact, these days the first racing tub to sink now wins the prestigious Silver Plunger Award. Today, most contestants speed across the whitecaps in sleek-looking, specially designed, high-tech boats, although there are always a handful of wildly creative vessels that hark back to earlier times. The race is the highlight of the week-long Marine Festival held in July, which includes a street fair, a parade, and a spirited atmosphere. For details, visit **www.bathtubbing.com.**

Foodies' Fancy

Edible British Columbia ((C) **604/812-9660;** www.edible-britishcolumbia.com) hosts a series of 2- and 3-night kayaking getaways, where paddling and culinary adventure go hand-in-hand. Professional guides put a gourmet touch on every meal; accommodations choices include camping or intimate lodges. Prices start at C$749 per person, inclusive of transfers from the Nanaimo ferry terminal or seaplane landing to the launch site near Nanaimo.

Gulf Islands. **Adventuress Sea Kayaking** (3225 Uplands Dr.; (C) **866/955-6702** or 250/755-6702) runs several half-day and full-day excursions to the surrounding islands, starting at C$60 per person, including all gear. **Wildheart Adventure Tours** (1560 Brebber Rd.; (C) **250/722-3683**) also offers guided trips, including multi-day camping adventures starting at C$500.

PROTECTION ISLAND

This island is actually a part of the City of Nanaimo and sits like a protecting arm a kilometer offshore in Nanaimo Harbour. As close as it is, this tiny island, about 5km (3 miles) in circumference, is almost a place time forgot. With about 200 homes, and a pirate theme that runs rampant (Capt. Morgan's Boulevard, Smugglers Lake, and Pirate Lane), it has no schools, churches, post office, stores, or other businesses, and virtually no cars. Island transportation is by foot, bike, or golf cart. Ferries—actually converted lifeboats—make the 10-minute run from the mainland from 7am to 10pm, on the hour. Even the pub, the **Dinghy Dock** (Canada's only floating pub/restaurant; (C) **250/753-2373**), keeps ferry hours, with last call in time for mainlanders to catch the 10pm ferry home to Nanaimo. At low tide, hikers can even wade across Pirate's Causeway to Newcastle Island.

NEWCASTLE ISLAND

Originally settled by the Coast Salish, then mined for coal and sandstone, and later a resort island for Canadian Pacific Steamship Company, **Newcastle Island Provincial Park** ((C) **250/754-7893;** www.newcastleisland.ca) has largely reverted to its natural state, though you can still see remnants of the 1850s coal mine, sandstone, and pulp stone quarries (the sandstone columns of the US Mint in San Francisco were quarried and shaped here), and two Salish First Nations villages. Many visitors kayak over from the mainland; others make the 10-minute crossing with **Nanaimo Harbour Ferry** ((C) **250/753-5141;** www.nanaimoharbourferry.com), which runs trips daily on the hour from 10am to 9pm in July and August; until 5pm the rest of the year. The round-trip fare is C$8 adults, C$4 seniors and children; bikes are C$2. As a protected marine park, it has a network of hiking and cycling trails and 18 campsites (C$15 per night) with toilets, showers, fire pits, and wood.

Trail lengths vary, but if you're up to walking 2 to 4km (1.2–2.5 miles), the **Mallard Lake Trail,** the **Channel Trail,** and the **Shoreline Trail** are among the most rewarding. The Mallard Lake Trail takes you through the forested heart of the island to a freshwater lake; you can return via the Channel Trail that follows the shoreline across from the mainland and past an old sandstone quarry. The Shoreline Trail is on the opposite (ocean) side of the island overlooking Nanaimo, and winds itself up to Kanaka Bay

Beach. If you've the energy, continue on to viewpoints at McKay Point and Giovando Lookout before hiking back past an old mine shaft and joining the Channel Trail back to the ferry docks. The entire perimeter hike is 7.5km (4.7 miles). There are interpretive signs along the way as well as a visitor center, snack bar, and gift shop.

WHERE TO STAY

Best Western Dorchester Hotel   This Best Western is not only a cut above most Best Westerns, it's the best value for the money in terms of services, quality, and central location in the Old City Quarter. The hotel stands on the site of the original Hudson's Bay Company trading post. Guest rooms may be on the small side, but they are comfortably furnished with quality amenities, and if you opt for a harbor-view room, the vista is more than worth the C$10 extra you'll pay. Book via the Internet and the savings can be substantial. Check out the stunning chandeliers in the lobby and the elaborate columns in the dining room—they came from the opera house that also once stood on this site.

70 Church St., Nanaimo, BC V9R 5H4. © **800/661-2449** or 250/754-6835. Fax 250/754-2638. www.dorchesternanaimo.com. 65 units. C$109–C$199 double. Extra person C$10. Senior, Internet, and seasonal discounts available. AE, DC, DISC, MC, V. Free parking. Pets accepted (C$20 per night). **Amenities:** Restaurant; lounge; golf course nearby; business services; laundry service; same-day dry cleaning; Wi-Fi. *In room:* TV w/movies, dataport, Wi-Fi, coffeemaker, hair dryer, iron.

Coast Bastion Inn   Overlooking the Strait of Georgia, right on the inner harbor, this hotel feels geared to the business traveler. It's taken a while, but finally guest rooms have just undergone a C$5-million refresh: Drab and dull have been replaced with a contemporary look, earth tones, quality linens, and scenic prints. The best feature, however, is still the waterfront views. Some suites have Jacuzzis with upgraded amenities and a lot more space, especially the corner units. The extremely courteous staff seems to enjoy fulfilling every request, whether it's recommending spa services or arranging for bike rentals nearby. Because the hotel is connected to the Port Theatre, which hosts plays and musical concerts from Bruce Cockburn to London Quartets, theater packages are usually the best value in town.

11 Bastion St., Nanaimo, BC V9R 6E4. © **800/663-1144** or 250/753-6601. Fax 250/753-4155. www.coasthotels.com. 177 units. May–Sept C$130–C$200 standard, C$190–C$260 premium; Oct–Apr C$120–C$160 standard, C$180–C$220 premium. Extra person C$10. Senior, AAA, off-season discounts, and packages available. AE, DC, DISC, MC, V. Self-parking C$5.50. Valet parking C$10. Pets accepted (C$10). **Amenities:** Restaurant; lounge; health club; concierge; 24-hr. room service; babysitting; laundry service; same-day dry cleaning; Wi-Fi. *In room:* A/C, TV w/play movies, dataport, Wi-Fi, minibar, fridge, coffeemaker, hair dryer, iron.

Grand Hotel Nanaimo   This is Nanaimo's most luxurious full-service hotel. The facilities, especially the impressive lobby, are bright and modern, and even a shade pretentious for this up-and-coming town. The restaurant would do better if it weren't so focused on "fine dining"; while service staff are friendly, they are dressed in black suits and look ready to serve at a funeral or at a high-end New York hotel. Accommodations range from standard guest rooms to spacious one-bedroom suites with jetted tubs. All have fireplaces and many have balconies. There are 12 fully furnished two- and three-bedroom townhouses for long-term stays. The hotel's location is amidst shopping nirvana; across the street lies Nanaimo North Town Centre, and Woodgrove Centre, the largest mall on Vancouver Island, is five minutes away.

4898 Rutherford Rd., Nanaimo, BC V9T 4Z4. © **877/414-7263** or 250/758-3000. Fax 250/729-2808. www.thegrandhotelnanaimo.ca. 72 units. May–Sept C$129–C$209 double; Oct–Apr C$119–C$189 double. Suites C$229–C$350, year-round. Extra person C$15. Senior discounts available. AE, MC, V. Free gated/

underground parking. **Amenities:** Restaurant; lounge; indoor heated pool; fitness center; limited room service; same-day dry cleaning. *In room:* A/C, TV, high speed Internet/dataport, fridge, coffeemaker, microwave, hair dryer, iron.

Painted Turtle Guesthouse (Value)   A hybrid between an inn and a boutique hostel, this is an affordable alternative with a central location that's hard to beat. Guest rooms are simply furnished and spotlessly clean. All have queen beds; the family suites have additional bunk beds, and some rooms are set up to share, hostel-style. The share-bathroom ratio is about three rooms to one bathroom, and because there are separate lavatories, lineups aren't an issue. The Great Room is bright and inviting, with a large communal kitchen, an eating area, and sofas around a gas fireplace. It can get very social at night—with guitars, singing, or just meeting your fellow travelers who are a mix of backpackers, families on a budget, and active retirees.

121 Bastion St., Nanaimo, BC V9R 3A2. (℃ **866/309-4432** or 250/753-4432. www.paintedturtle.ca. 20 units. C$55–C$75 double. MC, V. **Amenities:** Lounge; full kitchen; coin-op laundry; complimentary high speed-Internet. *In room:* Shared bath, no phone.

Ramada Inn   Although this new hotel sits on one of the main drags to/from the ferry terminal, the angle of the building and quality double-glazing does a good job of keeping things quieter that you would expect. The set-up is like a Holiday Inn Express—clean, comfortable, contemporary, and with all the basic creature comforts. Rates include an extensive continental breakfast, use of a small gym, the business center, and even a small coin-op laundry. Rooms have queen-size beds, but the suites, with king beds and Jacuzzi tubs, have more space and extras such as a DVD player.

315 Rosehill St., Nanaimo, BC V9S 1E3. (℃ **866/928-2009** or 250/716-2009. Fax: 250/716-0011 www. ramada.ca. 65 units. Mid-May to mid Sept C$135–C$155 double, C$175 suite; mid-Sept to mid-May C$125–C$145 double, C$165 suite. AE, MC, V. **Amenities:** Breakfast room; gym; business center; coin-op laundry; complimentary high-speed Internet; Wi-Fi. *In room:* TV, DVD (suites), dataport, Wi-Fi, coffeemaker, iron.

WHERE TO DINE

Central Nanaimo has a surprising number of good dining spots, another indicator that this town is beginning to go places as it attracts more and more urban mainlanders. Tapas are still very "de rigueur" in Nanaimo, and more and more eateries are found on the waterfront and in converted heritage buildings. One example, the **Lighthouse Bistro and Pub,** off Harbourside Walkway at 50 Anchor Way (℃ **250/754-3212**), serves up traditional burgers and grills alongside waterfront views of the seaplanes coming and going. There's also a converted firehall that makes for an unusual dining location. Unfortunately, restaurant tenants keep changing, but check it out because one day, someone is going to fire this place up with great cooking – all puns intended.

Glorious Gelato

Ice cream aficionados take serious heed. **The Buzz** (4515 Uplands Dr., behind Nanaimo North Town Centre; ℃ **250/758-2881**; www.thebuzzcoffeehouse.ca) is a terrific neighborhood coffee house where Salt Spring Gelato ice creams are the real story. Flavor combinations are among the most authentic, naturally delicious presentations you can get. Blood Orange never tasted so citrusly rich, Tiger Butter is melt-in-your-mouth smooth, and the Lemon Lavender is a refreshingly different blend.

Acme Food Company ECLECTIC   Located on one of downtown Nanaimo's busiest corners, this triangular restaurant caters to all tastes with a range of items that leaves no choice unturned, whether you want to build your own pizzas and pastas, or try one of their soups, sushi, grilled salmon, or steaks. Since changing ownership, locals claim it has become inconsistent, but we saw no sign of it. The place is always busy, and the menu still turns out an unexpected, flavorful variation on standards: One of Acme's cheeseburger features blue cheese, sun-dried tomatoes, and roasted garlic; a spicier version comes with Cajun spice and brie. They also offer takeout.

14 Commercial St. © 250/753-0042. www.acmefoodco.ca. Reservations recommended. Main courses C$8–C$23. MC, V. Daily 11am–midnight.

Fox & Hounds ★★ (Finds) ENGLISH PUB   This is the best of merry old England. British food is served all day, and there's beer on tap and roast dinners every Sunday; they even stock English sodas such as Tango and Ribena. Easily recognized by the bright red phone booth at its entrance, this restaurant-pub is located just 2 blocks up from the Old City Quarter and is worth the uphill climb. The decor is classic English pub, with a well-stocked bar, a chalkboard menu the size of a door, prolific oil paintings of the English countryside, and a fireplace mantle to cozy up to. Plates are heaped with hearty pub grub, all of which is excellent: The steak and kidney pie has good sized mouthfuls of meat, and you can actually find a decent amount of kidneys. The chicken and vegetable pie is equally good, as is the cottage pie, chicken curry, cod and chips, and oven-baked rice pudding. You don't have to be a Brit to appreciate the quality and value-for-money here, though there are a fair number of English accents in the crowd.

247 Milton St. © 250/740-1000. Main courses C$10–C$24. MC, V. Daily noon–10pm.

Mahle House PACIFIC NORTHWEST   Built in 1904, Mahle (pronounced "Molly") House is a lovingly restored delight overlooking an enclosed English-style garden. This family-owned restaurant has been a local favorite for more than 20 years, and the menu changes weekly. Items may include marinated duck with peanut-crusted prawns and a coconut curry sauce, roasted pork tenderloin with ancho chili, harrisa rice and black beans, or free-range chicken stuffed with Dungeness crab and a lemongrass sauce. Everything comes from local suppliers, while the herbs used to season these dishes come from the restaurant's own garden. Special evenings include wine tastings; "Tapas Thursdays"; "Adventurous Wednesdays," featuring a multi-course meal for C$40 (C$58 with wine); and a three-course Sunday dinner for C$35. The wine list is extensive, and has been a Gold Medal winner in the Vancouver International Wine Festival.

2104 Hemer Rd., at Cedar (10 min. south of Nanaimo). © 250/722-3621. Reservations recommended. Main courses C$18–C$32. MC, V. Wed–Sun 5–10pm; closed Mon–Tues.

Modern Cafe NEW CANADIAN   Open for breakfast, lunch, dinner, and tapas, suffice to say that the menu is extensive. Breakfasts are huge, lunches include great midday selections such as tempura halibut burgers, chowders and soups, and a New York–steak sandwich (though this is not a steakhouse, per se, so steak probably shouldn't be your first choice here). Dinner ups the ante to include an excellent vegetarian crepe served on a yam puree, a slow-cooked oven-roasted pork, and a variety a tasty rice bowls. The interior features brick decor and rotating art on the walls, and some of the best seats in the house are on the window counters—the people-watching is excellent, especially accompanied by one of the tapas plates. Coconut prawns, Navajo fried bread, and Yam fries are top choices.

221 Commercial St. © 250/754-5022. Main courses C$8–C$15 lunch; C$10–C$24 dinner. MC, V. Daily 8am–10pm.

Nanaimo's Best Dessert, Bar None

The Nanaimo Bar—a sweet three-layered confectionery of chocolate, custard cream, and graham wafers, may be known internationally, but its origins remain a mystery. Some legends trace its roots to Nanaimo's coal-mining days when families of miners sent care packages that often included the rich custard treat. Other accounts say Dutch settlers brought the recipe over in the early 1900s. Local historians figure the Nanaimo Bar was most likely inspired by a recipe in a 1952 *Woman's Auxiliary to the Nanaimo Hospital Cookbook*.

Red Martini Grill TAPAS   A casual, jazz-style bistro that is a clever conversion of two side-by-side storefronts where the more light-filled front room is geared for daytime dining (breakfast and lunch), and the moody back-room, aka "The Red Room," is for romantic trysts and live music. The tapas selection is large enough to suit every taste, with everything from chicken satay and coconut prawns to apricot- and date-stuffed pork tenderloin, all to be savored alongside imaginative martini mixes. There's jazz and blues Thursday through Saturday (get there by 7:30pm to snag a booth) and an "all jammers welcome" night on Wednesday, which is about as fun and impromptu as music gets. Remember, Nanaimo is Diana Krall's hometown, so you know the area generates talent!

1075 Front St. ℂ **250/753-5181**. www.redmartinigrill.ca Tapas C$5–C$9; main courses C$12–C$23. AE, MC, V. Tues–Sun 9:30am–midnight; Mon 9:30am–3pm.

Wesley Street Cafe ★ PACIFIC NORTHWEST   This is a small, charming restaurant. Dining options progress from a casual lunch that includes gourmet soups and sandwiches to a more sophisticated dinner menu that offers items such as roast quail with an exotic mushroom stuffing, pumpkin seed–crusted rockfish with spot prawn risotto, and a carrot ginger soup sweetened with a dash of honey that creates a great amuse-bouche. The chef is more than willing to adapt menu items to accommodate allergies. Monday through Thursday, there's a great-value three-course dinner for C$30 alongside an enormous wine list featuring many of the better BC labels. Dine inside or, in summer, opt for the flower-covered patio.

321 Wesley St., Nanaimo. ℂ **250/753-6057**. www.wesleycafe.com. Lunch C$12–C$21; dinner C$25–C$31. AE, MC, V. Tues–Sat 11:30am–2:30pm and 5:30–10pm; closed Sun–Mon.

Zougla   While there's nothing extraordinary about this restaurant, it's a really safe bet for a nice meal. The decor is conservative, and the extensive menu is mainstream, with a nod to the Greek owner-chef. Some might argue the range is overly ambitious, but you can't go wrong with calamari, souvlaki, or the rack of lamb. And the daily sheets are always good value. For lunch they include burgers, quesadillas, and Greek classics, such as an excellent moussaka. Dinner goes more upscale with steak and lobster, chicken topped with prawns and scallops, and a grilled halibut with a homemade Mediterranean-style sauce.

2021 Estevan Rd. ℂ **250/716-3233**. Reservations recommended. Main courses C$8–C$20 lunch; C$21–C$37 dinner. MC, V. Mon–Sat 11am–10:30pm; Sun 4–10pm.

2 GABRIOLA ISLAND

Although only a 20-minute ferry ride from Nanaimo Harbour, **Gabriola Island** feels a world away from the bustle of Vancouver Island. Known as the "Queen of the Gulf Islands," Gabriola provides a little of everything: sandy beaches, kayaking, canoeing, fine restaurants, artisans' studios and galleries, petroglyphs, and tide pools.

ESSENTIALS

Getting There

BC Ferries operates a vehicle and passenger ferry between Gabriola Island and Nanaimo with crossings leaving almost every hour from 6am to 11pm. Sailing time is 20 minutes. Passage is C$8 per person, C$21 per vehicle, and C$2 per kayak. Bicycles are carried free of charge.

If you're getting to the island by your own boat, you can find moorage, services, and lodging at **Silva Bay Marina** (© 250/247-8662; www.silvabay.com) and **Pages Marina** (© 250/247-8931; www.pagesresort.com), where you can buy groceries, fishing licenses, and tackle; as well as rent bicycles, scooters, mopeds, kayaks, and diving gear.

Getting Around

Most people bring their cars or bikes, but if you do decide to come on foot but want to tour, call Island Cabs (© 250/247-0049). Gabriola is an easy island to navigate with a main circular road, appropriately called South Road and North Road depending on which side of the island you are on, that leads to a number of side trips. If time is of the essence, there are some pastoral roads crossing the island's midsection. Like many of the Gulf Islands, but perhaps more so on Gabriola since its more northerly location has protected it from big-city influences and people, hitchhiking is regarded as safe and dependable, particularly among islanders themselves.

Visitor Information

The Island has a first-rate Visitor Information Centre, located at **Folklore Village Centre** (© 250/247-9332; www.gabriolaisland.org), which is not "folksy" at all, but quite a swish shopping mall housed in the recycled Folklife Pavilion from Expo '86.

EXPLORING THE AREA

Overall, Gabriola Island has a whimsical atmosphere, which you grasp as soon as you get off the ferry and come across tongue-in-cheek wood creations and sculptures scattered all over the island. The artistic center of the island is at **Gabriola Artworks** (575 North Rd.; © 250/247-7412; www.gabriolaartworks.com), a two-level, 279-sq.-m (3,003-sq.-ft.) gallery of work by local talent. You can also pick up a studio tour map and travel to various at-home galleries; open hours vary, so this self-drive choice might lead you down the odd garden path. Gabriola is also home to the **Silva Bay Shipyard School** (3200 Silva Bay Rd., © 250/247-8809; www.boatschool.com), Canada's only traditional wooden boat-building school. Visitors are welcome to view works-in-progress every Friday afternoon from 2 to 4pm.

The island's biggest natural attraction is the **Malaspina Galleries,** an amazing series of sandstone formations carved by the surf into unusual caves and caverns. Most beaches are protected, providing excellent tidal pools and safe swimming, especially at **Drumbeg Park,** where the sun heats the sandstone rocks enough to dry your towels. Scuba divers

Fun Facts   A Marmot Moment

The Vancouver Island marmot is rarer than even the giant panda. It is found only on Vancouver Island, and its primary habitat, just outside of Nanaimo, is protected by a special trust organization. In the mid-1980s, the population was estimated to be over 300 animals; today the count is half that number, making them one of the rarest and most endangered mammals in the world.

also use this area, as it provides shore-based access to nearby **Gabriola Passage.** Other recreational activities include biking and kayaking. Helpful charter contacts include **Silver Blue Charters** (✆ **250/247-8807** or 250/755-6150 [boat phone]; www.silverbluecharters.com) for sea-fishing excursions, **Jim's Kayaking** (✆ **250/247-8335;** www.jimskayaking.com) for rentals and guided paddles, and **Gabriola Cycle & Kayak** (✆ **250/247-8271;** www.gck.ca) for bike rentals. For moped and scooter rentals (C$69/day), contact **Silva Bay Resort & Marina** (3383 South Rd.; ✆ **250/247-8662;** www.silvabay.com).

WHERE TO STAY AND DINE

Hummingbird Lodge B & B ★★   This lodge is a gorgeously hand-built 465-sq.-m (5,005-sq.-ft.) home made up of the cedar and alder trees from the area. Rooms are clean and comfortable, decorated with island art. High and vaulted ceilings seem to bring the outdoors in, especially with floor-to-ceiling windows and over 186 sq. m (2,000 sq. ft.) of open and covered decks. The sunroom is especially sunny, and home to a variety of instruments—a piano, guitars, and a banjo (as well as a comprehensive musical CD library), to strike the right chord. The lodge is private and near to secluded, sandy Whalebone Beach.

RR#1 Site 55 C–54, Gabriola Island, BC V0R 1X0. ✆ **877/551-9383** or 250/247-9300. www.hummingbird lodgebb.com. 3 units. Mid-June to mid-Sept C$129–C$149 double; mid-Sept to mid-Oct and mid-May to mid-June C$119–C$139; mid-Oct to mid-May C$99–C$119. MC, V. Nonsmoking facilities. **Amenities:** Lounge; dining room; kitchenette; fridge; microwave; hot tub; massage; BBQ grill; sunroom. *In-room:* Hair dryer, no phone.

Silva Bay Bar & Grill CASUAL   This is really the only show on the island. Located at the Silva Bay Marina, it's the best place to savor a sunset and to nibble your way through an extensive menu. Many dishes are designed for sharing over an on-tap ale. Although it's primarily a pub-style restaurant, there's also a fully licensed area where families are welcome. In summer, tables extend along the dock overlooking the marina, and there's a BBQ deck for grills and salads.

3383 South Rd., in the Silva Bay Resort and Marina. ✆ **250/247-8662.** Menu items from under C$10; main courses around C$22. MC, V. Daily noon–9pm; Sun brunch 11am–2pm.

Surf Lodge   In spite of two walls of windows in the great room, the cedar siding throughout this lodge takes woodsy to the extreme, especially when set against the impressive floor-to-ceiling river-rock fireplace. Guest rooms and cabins also sport wood everywhere, but with a whitewash finish that gives them a bright, clean look. In the last year, all the floors, bathroom tilework, and textiles have been upgraded, as have the linens. Most rooms have ocean views, some with a window seat. The three self-contained cabins are ideal for families. The pub and dining room are both rather characterless, save for the stunning views.

885 Berry Point Rd., Gabriola, BC V0R 1X1. ℂ **250/247-9231.** Fax 250/247-8336. www.surflodge.com. 9 units (6 rooms and 3 cabins). Mid-May to Sept C$115–C$125 room, C$145–C$185 cabin; Oct to mid-May C$92–C$108 room, C$116–C$148 cabin. Pets not accepted. MC, V. **Amenities:** Lounge; pub. *In room:* TV (cabins), kitchenettes (cabins), no phone.

3 PARKSVILLE & QUALICUM BEACH

There was a time when Parksville and Qualicum Beach were sleepy seaside towns that swelled with family vacationers every summer. Now that activity happens year-round. Oceanside, as the region is now called, is bursting with development for vacationers— with a whopping 33 resorts, hotels, and motels; nearly 30 B&Bs; and more than 30 vacation rentals—and for the waves of retirees making this golf mecca their year-round home; not to mention young families finding an affordable alternative to expensive urban neighborhoods. In the past 2 decades, the area's population has nearly tripled, and is expected to double again by 2016. The climate doesn't hurt, either. Mild temperatures and the island's lowest annual rainfall have earned it the moniker of Canada's Riviera.

As a consequence, much of Parksville's original park-like attributes have been overtaken by used car lots and motels that now line the highway through town, giving it a strip-mall-like air. It does redeem itself, however, with its expansive beaches— picked by *Better Homes & Gardens* as being among North America's most family-friendly—and waterfront resorts. In fact, once through downtown Parksville, the Oceanside shoreline along Hwy 19A opens up vistas to mountains and oceans, lush parks, formal gardens, and quaint shops and galleries. The Oceanside area extends beyond Parksville and Qualicum to include Horne Lake, Bowser, and Deep Bay, all sharing the same stretch of magnificent beach and among them offering activities such as swimming, nature hikes, golf, tennis, and spelunking.

ESSENTIALS
Getting There
BY CAR Parksville and Qualicum Beach are located 36km (22 miles) north of Nanaimo, off Hwy. 19.

BY BUS Greyhound/Island Coach Lines (ℂ 800/661-8747 or 250/385-4411) offers service between Nanaimo and Parksville/Qualicum Beach along the Hwy. 1–Hwy. 19 corridor. One-way fares are C$6.50 for adults. Fares for seniors are 10% less; fares for children 5 to 11 are 50% less.

BY TRAIN VIA Rail's **Malahat** (ℂ 888/842-7245; www.viarail.com) stops in Parksville and Qualicum Beach on its daily trip from Victoria to Courtenay.

BY AIR **KD Air** (ℂ 800/665-4244, 604/688-9957, or 250/752-5884; www.kdair. com) offers several daily flights from Vancouver to the Qualicum Beach Airport, for C$250 round-trip, with discounts for seniors and children.

Visitor Information
The **Parksville Visitor Information Centre** is at 1275 East Island Hwy. (P.O. Box 99), Parksville, BC V9P 2G3 (ℂ **250/248-3613;** www.chamber.parksville.bc.ca). The **Qualicum Beach Visitor Information Centre** is at 2711 West Island Hwy., Qualicum

7

Mark Your Calendar

April: **The Brant Festival** celebrates the arrival of thousands of migrating Brant geese. With more than 250 species of birds making their home in the coastal estuaries, the Qualicum Beach area is a premier destination for both serious ornithologists and amateur birders. Call ✆ **866/288-7878** for information.

August: Ebbing tides can expose up to a kilometer of shore, leaving large, shallow pools in the sand, perfect for sandcastle-building and collecting sand dollars. In fact, the sands are so good that they host Parksville's **International Sandcastle Competition,** during which competitors race—between tides—to create award-winning sculptures. Call ✆ **250/248-4819** for information or visit www.parksvillebeachfest.ca.

September: The Qualicum Beach Harvest of Music brings together musicians from all over the world for a 9-day multicultural festival of music from Gypsy jazz to Japanese taiko drumming. Performances and workshops take place at Qualicum Beach Civic Centre, the Old School House, and other small venues. Call ✆ **250/752-6133** or check www.theoldschoolhouse.org for information.

Beach, BC V9K 2C4 (✆ **250/752-9532;** www.qualicum.bc.ca). Another resource is available at www.visitparksvillequalicumbeach.com.

EXPLORING PARKSVILLE & QUALICUM BEACH

Of the two communities, Parksville is by far the more developed, both in terms of commercial businesses and in its destination resorts (see "Where to Stay," below), which have all contributed to its reputation as Canada's Riviera. Although Parksville is a haven for fast-food junkies, these are countered with a growing number of quality restaurants and specialty activities. For example, if you're a cheese aficionado, check out **Little Qualicum Cheeseworks** (403 Lowry's Rd., Parksville; ✆ **250/954-3931;** www.cheeseworks.ca). From June to September, there are guided tours and hayrides around the farm, as well as a small gift shop that's open year-round, where you can taste and purchase their artisan cheeses. Although based in Parksville, **Pacific Rainforest Adventure Tours** (215 Chestnut St.; ✆ **250/248-3667;** www.rainforestnaturehikes.com) provides easy walking half-day and full-day sightseeing and nature tours (suitable for seniors) to various destinations in the region, such as **Cathedral Grove; Pacific Rim National Park**; and **Green Mountain,** home to the endangered Vancouver Island marmot. This particular tour takes you by the Nanaimo River through a working forest and requires you to book a year in advance to receive a special permit.

Qualicum lies about 10 minutes north of Parksville, and although it overlooks the same stretch of beach, it is far more genteel. While here, follow the Art Walk to galleries and artisan studios and browse the shops in the town center, which is actually set a few kilometers from the beach and has a garden village ambience—perhaps because Qualicum residents are passionate gardeners, having earned their community the coveted Four Blooms Award in a province-wide annual Communities in Bloom competition. Take time to visit the **Old School House** (122 Fern Rd. W.; ✆ **250/752-6133;** www.theold schoolhouse.org), which exhibits the works of potters, weavers, painters, and other local

artists. It also holds frequent workshops, classes, and Sunday afternoon concerts as well
as jazz gatherings on Tuesday evenings.

ATTRACTIONS

Milner Gardens & Woodland ★★ Once the personal retreat of Queen Elizabeth and Prince Phillip, these princely gardens by the sea are now open to the public. After you've toured the Cotswolds-style house, put on your wellies and get set for a fabulous garden walk through a 4-hectare (10-acre) artist's garden within a 24-hectare (59-acre) old-growth Douglas-fir forest. It's a living laboratory of rare and unusual plants, combining avenues of rhododendrons (more than 500), indigenous plants, and rare and exotic species with towering Douglas firs. The ocean views are breathtaking, but then, you would expect nothing less for royals. Afternoon tea is served.

2179 W. Island Hwy., Qualicum Beach. ℂ **250/752-6153.** www.milnergardens.org. Admission C$10 adults; C$6 students. May–Sept daily 10am–5pm; Apr and Oct Thurs–Sun 10am–5pm. Closed Nov–Mar.

Paradise Fun Park It's commercial, perhaps overrated, but if you're traveling with young children, it's one of the few places that is a one-stop-shop for activities that include a miniature golf course with its full-rigged pirate galleon, a treasure cave and water mill, bumper-boat rides (equipped with water canons), and a games pavilion. Kids will want to make a day of it and as a break from the beach, it serves its purpose. The park also features an RV park and motel.

375 W. Island Hwy., Parksville. ℂ **250/248-6612.** www.paradisefunpark.net. Activities C$5–C$7, with combination tickets C$13–$15. Mar to mid-Oct daily 9am–dusk. Closed Nov–Feb.

REGIONAL, PROVINCIAL & NATIONAL PARKS

Rathtrevor Beach Provincial Park ★★ is a family-oriented park that has special nature displays, interpretive walks, and safe sandy beaches. The interesting sandstone formations on the beach, gentle tides, and forested campsites make this one of the most popular camping areas in the province (see "Camping," below). Located approximately 5km (3 miles) up Englishman River from Rathtrevor Provincial Park, **Top Bridge** is designated "Mountain Bike Park" and is extremely popular with bikers from all over the world for its purpose-built trails deep in the forest. Nearby **Englishman River Falls Park** is one of the prettiest parks in the region, with camping, picnic areas, swimming, and easy hiking. There are two spectacular waterfalls in the midst of the forest; during the summer a crystal-clear pool at the base of the lower falls turns into one of the best swimming holes in the area. Come fall, Englishman River fills with the return of spawning salmon, and throughout the year the area serves as a protected estuary for more than 250 species of resident and migrating birds.

Just east of Parksville on Hwy. 4, the **Mt. Arrowsmith Regional Park** offers several moderate to difficult hiking trails from the **Cameron Lake** picnic area. The moderately easy hiking trail up to the 1,818m (5,965-ft.) summit follows, in part, an old logging

---

(Fun Facts) How Come Qualicum?

The name Qualicum comes from *squal-li,* "chum salmon" in the language of the Pentlatch people who once fished here but were devastated by smallpox in the late 1700s.

Teeing Up

There are six golf courses in the Parksville–Qualicum Beach area, and over a dozen within an hour's drive. All have a driving range, clubhouse, and pro shop. From April to October, green fees average C$70 for adults; from November to March, they average C$40 for adults. Twilight rates and discounts for children 18 and under are offered year-round. *Tip:* The greens can be deceptive, but as a general rule they break toward the ocean.

The **Eaglecrest Golf Club,** 2035 Island Hwy., Qualicum Beach (© **250/762-6311;** www.eaglecrestgolfclub.ca), is an 18-hole, par-71 course with an emphasis on shot-making and accuracy.

Fairwinds, just east of Parksville at 3730 Fairwinds Dr., Nanoose Bay (© **888/781-2777** or 250/468-7666; www.fairwinds.bc.ca), is a challenging 18-hole, par-71 course with ocean views and lots of trees.

Pheasant Glen Golf Resort, 1025 Qualicum Rd., Qualicum Beach (© **877/407-4653** or 250/752-8786; www.pheasantglen.com), has a 6,628-yard, par-72 championship-length links-style course; holes 16, 17, and 18 are reputed to be three of the toughest finishing holes in BC.

The long established **Qualicum Beach Memorial,** 469 Memorial Ave., Qualicum Beach (© **250/752-6312;** www.golfqualicum.ca), has 9 holes, stunning ocean views, a pro shop, and a restaurant.

Morningstar Golf Club, 525 Lowry's Rd., Parksville (© **800/567-1320** or 250/248-2244; www.morningstar.bc.ca), is an 18-hole, par-72 championship course with seaside links and fairways running in and out of the woods.

Arrowsmith Golf and Country Club, 2250 Fowler Rd., north of Qualicum Beach (© **250/752-9727;** www.golfarrowsmith.com), is a family-oriented course with 18 holes and a par-61 rating.

railway. The climb passes through a series of climatic zones, each with different vegetation and forest cover. The view from the slopes and high alpine meadows of Mount Arrowsmith overlooks the entire Strait of Georgia. Allow 6 to 7 hours for the round-trip. For something completely different, consider kayaking out from the Parksville-Qualicum shores to **Jedediah Marine Park,** located between Lasqueti Island and Texada Island in the Sabine Channel of the Strait of Georgia. Accessible only by boat, this recently created park was originally homesteaded in the late 1800s. The island is now inhabited by wild goats and sheep. The island has no amenities, but the settlers' cabins and outbuildings are maintained in their original condition so visitors can see how people lived on the coast before roads and electricity.

If you prefer to stay on land, **Spider Lake Park** is a smaller day-use park on the lake located just off the Horne Lake Road. Stocked with small-mouthed bass and trout, the lake has excellent fishing and a warm, safe, sandy beach to launch kayaks and canoes. No motorized watercraft are allowed, so it attracts swimmers as well as anglers. Many visitors bypass Spider Lake, however, in favor of Horne Lake Regional Park that sits at the west end of Horne Lake, adjacent to Horne Lake Caves Provincial Park (see below). This 105-hectacre (259-acre) regional park includes about 3km (1³/₄ miles) of lakefront and another 2km (1¹/₄ miles) of riverfront along the Qualicum River. Offering both wooded (C$17) and lakefront (C$22) campsites, it's an excellent base for family camping with day-use picnicking and swimming, canoeing, rock climbing, and spelunking activities, as well as evening and daily nature programs. Call ✆ **250/927-0053** for camping reservations.

Note: To reach the Horne Lake area from Hwy. 19, take the Horne Lake Road exit (#75) and follow the signs. It's about a 13km (8-mile) drive on a mainly gravel road, which can get deeply rutted after a rainfall. Also, logging trucks use this road 7 days a week, so drive carefully—there are some narrow blind corners.

Horne Lake Caves Provincial Park ★★★

This is one of Vancouver Island's best outdoor-adventure destinations. Nestled in the mountains of the Beaufort Range, beside a lakeside park with camping and canoeing, Horne Lake Caves attracts spelunkers for half- or full-day adventures. Getting to the park is a bit of an adventure in itself. Take the **Horne Lake exit** off **Hwy. 19** (the Island Hwy.) or **19A,** and follow the signs for 12km (7¹/₂ miles). Drive with your headlights on, and watch out for logging trucks.

Two caves are open year-round for self-guided tours, although you must bring at least two sources of light, and helmets are recommended. In summer, you can rent these from the **park office.** The park also offers a number of guided tours, catering to everything from easygoing family fun to extreme experiences. The 1¹/₂-hour **Family Cavern Tour** is the easiest of these tours, and the most popular. It starts with a short uphill hike through the forest to the cave entrance, which leads to a haven of beautiful crystal formations and ancient fossils. This tour costs C$21 for adults, C$17 for children 11 and under. The 3-hour **Spelunking Adventure** is a shade more challenging, involving some tight passages and lots of cave scrambling. It costs C$54 for adults, C$45 for children 11 and under. The minimum age for this is 8 years old. For real diehards, there's a 5-hour **Extreme Rappel** tour. It includes instruction in basic rock climbing and roping, which you'll need to rappel down a seven-story waterfall known as the "Rainbarrel." Sturdy footwear and warm clothing is a must, although previous climbing experience is not. The tour costs C$149 per person. Two-hour **Outdoor Rappel** clinics are available, and strongly recommended for those without recent rappel experience. The clinic cost is C$40. *Note:* You must be 15 years or older and sign a liability-waiver form to participate in the more extreme tours. Although you might get lucky and find space on one of the many daily family cavern tours, advance reservations are required for all tours, year-round. Call ✆ **250/248-7829** for reservations or visit www.hornelake.com.

CAMPING

Located next to 2km (1¹/₄ miles) of sandy shore, Rathtrevor Beach Provincial Park offers 200 tent and RV forested sites, with showers, firewood, a sani-station, and interpretive programs. Reservations are a must; beachfront sites are obviously the hot favorites, but all sites are really well maintained with a natural, surprisingly private, landscape. Most folks are just grateful to be in. There's a 1-week-stay limit and usually a lineup of tenters and RVs in front of the park gate as early as 8am, waiting for cancellations. The early birds are often successful in securing a spot. Alternative camping space is at Englishman River Falls Provincial Park (13km/8 miles from Rathtrevor)) and Little Qualicum Falls Provincial Park (24km/15 miles from Rathtrevor). All these parks accept reservations. Rates are C$17 to C$24 per night. Contact Discover Camping (✆ **800/689-9025** for reservations; www. discovercamping.ca). Also, see "Horne Lake Caves Provincial Park," above.

Beach Acres Resort ★ (Kids) Reminiscent of the great family resorts of days gone by, this forested, waterfront resort entices families to return summer after summer to catch up with old friends and to make new ones. Located on Parksville's Rathtrevor Beach, the resort offers 9 hectares (22 acres) of family fun with a carefree, summer-camp atmosphere. Children's programs include everything from scavenger hunts to sandcastle contests, and there's a supervised indoor swimming pool. While the children have fun, Mom and Dad can relax in the Jacuzzi, or challenge each other to a tennis match. Accommodations-wise, guests can choose among cottages in a forest setting with country-style furniture, one-and two-bedroom Tudor-style cottages on the beach, or oceanview town houses that sleep up to six people. All have full kitchens and either gas or wood-burning fireplaces. The resort has a roster of rentals such as high chairs, playpens, and BBQs. Because it's so hyper-busy in summer, try booking the shoulder season (with kids); or low season for a romantic getaway.

25-1015 East Island Hwy., Parksville, BC V9P 2E4. *C* **800/663-7309** or 250/248-3424. Fax 250/248-6145. www.beach-acres.com. 55 units. June–Sept and holidays C$165–C$405; Oct–May C$135–C$225. Mid-week, weekly, and monthly rates available. 2-night minimum stay July–Aug and holidays. AE, MC, V. **Amenities:** Large heated indoor pool; 3 tennis courts; 1 outdoor basketball court; 1 outdoor volleyball court; Jacuzzi; sauna; children's programs; coin-op washers and dryers. *In room:* TV, kitchen, fridge, coffeemaker, iron, fireplace, Wi-Fi.

Beach Club Resort Open since summer 2008, this upscale lodge and resort-home complex lies on the former site of Parksville's historical Island Hall, which, when it opened in 1917, was one of Vancouver Island's most prestigious resort destinations. Guests have included Queen Elizabeth II. This new West Coast–style resort (i.e., lots of wood and windows) has incorporated much of the Hall's memorabilia in the main areas, and the decor has done much to bring the outdoors to the inside. The carpets mimic sand, and the custom design drapes, furnishings, and quality local art have a very upscale, beachy feel. Suites are a mix of spacious studios, as well as one- and two-bedroom units with full kitchens, laundry facilities, and fireplaces.

181 Beachside Drive, Parksville, BC V9P 2H5. *C* **888/760-2008** or 250/947-2101. Fax 250/947-2122. www.beachclubbc.com. 149 units. July–Sept C$169–C$289 double; Oct–Feb C$109–C$249 double; Mar–June C$119–C$259 double. Extra person C$20. Children 16 and under stay free in parent's room. AE, MC, V. **Amenities:** Restaurant; bar; indoor pool; fitness center; spa; concierge; room service; Wi-Fi; free underground parking. *In room:* TV, DVD, Wi-Fi, kitchen (some), fridge, coffeemaker, iron, fireplace (some).

Blue Willow Guest House British owners add an authentic touch to this English-styled B&B, much of which is covered with bowers of clematis and climbing roses. For some, the chintz-covered furniture, lacy white curtains, and wreaths of dried flowers might feel a bit twee, but the hardwood floors, leaded-glass windows, and high-beamed ceilings create a cozy ambiance. The small conservatory is the perfect spot for breakfast. The separate Garden Cottage is the best choice if you're traveling with children or another couple. It has two bedrooms that share a bathroom as well as an alcove with a twin bed.

524 Quatna Rd., Qualicum Beach, BC V9K 1B4. *C* **250/752-9052.** Fax 250/752-9039. www.blue willowguesthouse.com. 3 units. Mid-Apr to mid-Oct C$130–C$140 double; mid-Oct to mid-Apr C$120–C$130 double. Extra person C$30–C$50. MC, V. Pets not accepted. **Amenities:** Library lounge with TV; DVD; coffeemaker; conservatory. *In room:* No phone.

Pacific Shores Resort and Spa Adjacent to the Nature Trust Bird Sanctuary and part of the Englishman River Estuary, the resort is set on a landscaped 5.5 hectares (14 acres). There are 102 two-bedroom suites that become studios or one-bedroom suites on

demand by opening up or shutting off connecting doors, thereby creating quite a mix of
accommodations. Studio suites are like a contemporary hotel room; when configured into one- and two-bedroom units, they offer full kitchens, fireplaces, washers/dryers, and all the home-away-from-home amenities you need. The resort is popular with families in summer, which is good if you're traveling with children and looking to keep them involved with their peer group, but disastrous if you're seeking a romantic getaway. Family areas include a thermally heated outdoor pool, a picnic and BBQ area, and an outdoor playground. **The Aquaterre Spa** provides respite for harried adults; **The Landing West Coast Grill** (see "Where to Dine," below) is worth a visit. Because this complex is a part of the Avia West Vacation Group (✆ **866/986-2222;** www.aviawest.com), you may want to ignore some of the Internet discounts and make your reservations direct with the resort. The discounts often have strings attached, like having to listen to the sales pitch for a timeshare.

1600 Stroulger Rd., Nanoose Bay, BC V9P 9B7. ✆ **866/986-2222** or 250/468-7121. Fax 250/468-2001. www.pacific-shores.com. 102 units. Jul–Aug C$110–C$175 studio suite, C$255–C$345 1- and 2-bedroom condos, C$500 3-bedroom condo; Sept to mid-Oct and mid-Mar to June C$100–C$160 studio suite, C$210–C$270 1- and 2-bedroom condos, C$450 3-bedroom condo; mid-Oct to mid-Mar C$80–C$140 studio suite, C$145–$250 1- and 2-bedroom condos, C$360 3-bedroom condo. AE, MC, V. Free parking. **Amenities:** Restaurant; large indoor pool; health club; spa; Jacuzzis; sauna; free kayaks and canoes; babysitting; laundry service; Internet access; Wi-Fi; convenience store and deli; outdoor children's play area. *In room:* TV/VCR/DVD, dataport, Wi-Fi (some), kitchen, fridge, coffeemaker, iron.

Tigh-Na-Mara Seaside Resort & Spa ★★ 〖Kids〗 Romantic family getaways might sound like an oxymoron, but not here at Tigh-Na-Mara, Gaelic for "the house by the sea." Established in the 1940s on an 11-hectare (27-acre) forested waterfront beach near Rathtrevor Beach Provincial Park, this time-honored resort just keeps getting better. Romantics gravitate here for the Grotto Spa; it's the largest spa in British Columbia and offers a mineral pool and exceptional spa services such as massages and hair and skin care. Tigh-Na-Mara also has a diverse range of quality accommodations; guests can stay in intimate one- or two-bedroom log cottages in a forest setting, luxuriate in special spa suites, splurge on the lavish oceanview condominiums (many with Jacuzzis), or enjoy lodge-style standard rooms. All guest accommodations have fireplaces, and some have kitchen facilities. The three- and four-room cottages can sleep up to eight. Families flock to Tigh-Na-Mara for its supervised child-friendly programs as much as for its stunning location. Activities are numerous and even include "parents' nights out" every Tuesday and Thursday when children are entertained with movies and the like. The lodge has a sushi and jazz lounge, and a welcoming cedar-paneled **Cedar Restaurant** featuring Northwest cuisine alongside BBQs in summer, and a children's menu.

1155 Resort Dr., Parksville, BC V9P 2E5. ✆ **800/663-7373** or 250/248-2072. Fax 250/248-4140. www. tigh-na-mara.com. 210 units, some with fireplace. July–Aug C$159–C$199 lodge rooms, C$179–C$299 oceanview studios and suites, C$239–C$359 cottages and spa bungalows; May, June, and Sept C$149–C$189 lodge rooms, C$159–C$259 oceanview studios and suites, C$189–C$309 cottages and spa bungalows; Oct–Apr C$119–C$159 lodge rooms, C$129–C$209 oceanview studios and suites, C$169–C$289 cottages and spa bungalows. 3- to 7-night minimum stay July–Aug. Seasonal and spa packages available. AE, DC, MC, V. Pets accepted Sept–May. **Amenities:** Restaurant; lounge; large heated indoor pool; 1 outdoor tennis court; exercise room; Jacuzzi; sauna; paddleboat rentals; mountain bike rentals; business center with Wi-Fi; babysitting. *In room:* TV, Wi-Fi (C$10), kitchen, fridge, coffeemaker.

WHERE TO DINE

Beach House Cafe WEST COAST Located right at the water's edge, the fully licensed Beach House Cafe is a local favorite, serving good food without a lot of frills. Its bistro-style atmosphere carries through from an easy soup-and-sandwich lunch to a casual, intimate dinner. Some lunch items are repeated at dinner, although in the evening, you'll be treated to house specialties, such as a bouillabaisse loaded with local seafood. Homemade pies, whether savory steak-and-mushroom or sweet rhubarb-and-strawberry, are a must. It's a tiny place that fills up quickly, so if you make reservations, be on time.

2775 West Island Hwy., Qualicum Beach. [tel[**250/752-9626.** Reservations recommended on weekends. Main courses C$10–C$20. MC, V. Daily 11am–2:30pm and 5–8:30pm; daily 11am–10pm July–Aug.

Kalvas EUROPEAN   Inside the rustic-looking log cabin is an intimate dining room that locals favor as a special-occasion restaurant. The menu specializes in seafood and traditional German dishes. Consequently, you can't go wrong with sole amandine, the salmon Oscar (poached, topped with shrimp and hollandaise sauce), and wiener schnitzel, which is just about as good as it gets. The menu also has a wide range of steaks and pastas, and an excellent oyster and live crab bar—the latter is simply steamed and served with drawn butter. Be sure to ask for the house-made spaetzles.

180 Molliet St., Parksville. Ⓒ **250/248-6933.** Reservations recommended. Main courses C$12–C$60. MC, V. Daily 5–10pm.

The Landing West Coast Grill WEST COAST   With so many seaside resorts lining these expansive beaches, it's hard to know which ones, if any, have decent restaurants that are open to the public. This is one of them. Despite an outdoor heated patio, wine bar, and terrific ocean views, it's the 23,000-liter (6,000-gallon) curvaceous saltwater aquarium wall that will really catch your eye. Food focuses on seafood that is refreshingly simple in its preparation: a tuna dish served with warm tomato vinaigrette, mushroom risotto and grilled halibut with cilantro salsa, as well as local produce such as dry-rubbed, slow-smoked port back ribs; wood-smoked chicken confit; and a good vegetarian selection.

At Pacific Shores, 1600 Stroulger Rd., Nanoose Bay. Ⓒ **888/640-7799** or 250/468-2400. www.landing grill.com. Main courses C$14–C$37. AE, MC, V. Mon–Fri 11am–9pm; Sat–Sun 10am–10pm.

Shady Rest Waterfront Pub & Restaurant CANADIAN   There's been an eatery here since 1924, although today's contemporary look neither hints to its heritage nor detracts from the real show—the beachside vistas. With skylights and a wall of windows fronting the beach, this restaurant offers a view to every seat in the house, although in warmer weather you'll probably prefer a spot on the deck. Open for breakfast, lunch, and dinner, its menu items are no-frill classics such as steak and prawns, fish and chips, stir fries, schnitzels, pasta, and pizzas. It does these well for lunch and dinner, but the evening menu's fancier items are a bit hit-or-miss. Ask your waitress to be honest about the specials to avoid disappointment. Weekend brunches are the winners with various Benedicts (the sauces can be a bit heavy handed, so ask for these on the side), scrambles, and skillets.

3109 W. Island Hwy., Qualicum Beach. Ⓒ **250/752-9111.** www.shadyrest.ca. Reservations recommended for restaurant dinner. Main courses C$10–C$25. MC, V. Mon–Fri 11am–9pm; Sat–Sun 8am–9pm; pub open Fri–Sat to 1am.

Triskell Restaurant & Creperie FRENCH   When Triskell's husband-and-wife team closed up their Victoria creperie and relocated here, they brought with them a loyal following that makes the trip up to Parksville worth it just for the crepes. The small dining room, with white linens and whitewashed walls with prints of the French countryside, hints at the French-influenced menu. In addition to savory and sweet crepes, there's a range of local fresh fish, game, beef, and lamb dishes. Specialties include a mussels pate, a tasty rabbit braised in a Beaujolais and apricot sauce, and a Callebaut chocolate mousse.

As might be expected from a French restaurant, the wine list includes an excellent selection from France as well as from Australia, Chile, and British Columbia.

220 West Island Hwy., Parksville. (*C* **250/248-2011.** Main courses C$18–C$25. MC, V. Tues–Sat 4:30–9:30pm.

4 HEADING WEST: PORT ALBERNI & BAMFIELD

Jump into your vehicle, hit the accelerator, and begin a memorable voyage from the east to the west side of central Vancouver Island. The trip is about 200km (124 miles) and takes about 3 hours to drive. En route, you'll pass through **Coombs,** a farming community with a good selection of country crafts boutiques. The **Old Country Market** ★ (2310 Alberni Hwy.; (*C* **250/248-3349**), complete with goats on the roof, is a Kodak moment and a chance to stretch your legs, buy a delicious ice cream, or pick up picnic supplies. There's also an intriguing gift-for-yourself emporium with teapots, marmalades, imported clothes, and baskets. The market has become such a landmark that an entire landscape has sprouted up in the environs, a haphazard collection of gift and souvenir stores, many of which might be fun to browse. If you can put up with the squawking, drop by the **World Parrot Refuge** (2116 Alberni Hwy.; (*C* **250/248-5194** or 250/951-1166; www.worldparrotrefuge.org) and its sanctuary for more than 400 previously owned parrots. Admission is by donation.

As you near the west coast, you pass waterfalls beneath a canopy of rain forest. **Port Alberni** is another stopover that's an interesting detour for a quick lunch and a wander, but unless you're taking a trip on the **MV** *Lady Rose* to Bamfield, there's no draw to stay overnight. **Bamfield,** on the other hand, is a delightful diversion that's worth at least a day trip, if not an overnight stay. Reached only by boat, this village is built on boardwalks, with lovely coves, homes, and B&Bs tucked into the surrounding inlets.

ESSENTIALS
Getting There

BY CAR   From Nanaimo, take the Island Highway (Hwy. 19) 52km (32 miles) north toward Parksville. Just before you hit Parksville, take the turnoff for Hwy. 4, which leads west to Port Alberni and on to the coastal towns of Tofino and Ucluelet. It's a good idea to leave Nanaimo in the morning to avoid having the afternoon sun in your eyes as you drive west (and to return in the afternoon so that the sun is behind you as you head east). A secondary highway, Hwy. 4 is narrow in places, as well as winding, slippery, and mountainous. Night driving isn't recommended. If you plan to drive straight through to Tofino or Ucluelet, gas up in Nanaimo. Gas stations are scarce along Hwy. 4.

BY BUS   Greyhound/Island Coach Lines ((*C* **800/661-8747** or 250/385-4411; www.greyhound.ca) operates regular daily service between Victoria and Tofino–Ucluelet, departing at 8:30am and arriving in Tofino about 2:30pm. The bus stops in Nanaimo to pick up passengers arriving on the Vancouver ferry (the bus station is a 10-minute cab ride from the ferry docks). Fares from Victoria to Tofino are C$62; from Nanaimo to Tofino are C$38; and from Nanaimo to Port Alberni are C$18. **The Tofino Bus Company** ((*C* **866/986-3466;** www.tofinobus.com) also runs a daily service from Vancouver and Victoria to Tofino–Ucluelet. From Vancouver the one-way (hotel-to-hotel) adult fare is C$65 (including ferry crossing); from Victoria, C$64; from Nanaimo, C$18. Nanaimo to Port Alberni is also C$18. Discounts of about 10% apply to seniors, youths, and international hostel members; children are half price. Because Greyhound bases its rates on mileage bands, it is locked into certain price parameters, making some routes more (or less) expensive than competing carriers.

BY TRAIN VIA Rail's **Malahat** (© 888/842-7245; www.viarail.com) stops in Parksville and Qualicum Beach on its daily trip from Victoria to Courtenay.

BY AIR KD Air (© 800/665-4244, 604/688-9957, or 250/752-5884; www.kdair.com) offers several daily flights from Vancouver to Port Alberni via Qualicum Airport and then bus transportation for C$285 round-trip. One-way fares are C$175, with discounts for seniors and children.

BY FERRY Although a somewhat unconventional ferry, Lady Rose Marine Services (© 800/663-7192 or 250/723-8313; www.ladyrosemarine.com), runs two packet freighters from Port Alberni to different points on the island's west coast, including a trip to Ucluelet. Call for seasonal sailing times and costs.

Visitor Information

For more information on Port Alberni, the Alberni Valley Chamber of Commerce runs a **Visitor Information Centre** at 2533 Port Alberni Hwy., Port Alberni, BC V9Y 7L6 (© 250/724-6535; www.avcoc.com).

EXPLORING THE AREA

Located midway between Parksville and Port Alberni in MacMillan Provincial Park is the world-renowned **Cathedral Grove.** If you've time, don't simply drive through; take an hour or two to follow the winding interpretive trail system through the 1,000-year-old forest of Douglas fir, western hemlock, grand fir, and western red cedar. The trees stand so tall you'll feel like you're standing inside of a cathedral; hence the name. This day park gives you a sense of what Vancouver Island and the West Coast looked like before the arrival of European settlers. To see where many trees like these end up, you need look no farther than Port Alberni.

Port Alberni is a hard-working little town of nearly 20,000. Along the waterfront, logs are milled into lumber, pulp, and paper. Smoke from the mills spews up into the low-lying clouds that cling to the surrounding mountains. On a dull day, the entire town is grey with nary a hint of the fabulous views that a sunny day brings. Port Alberni is currently trying to revitalize its rather industrial facade, and its self-professed nickname "Positive Port Alberni" is beginning to show dividends, with sprawling urban development rising up the hill from the water, including two Wal-Mart outlets.

If you need to break the drive to the coast, head down to the redeveloped **Harbour Quay** area at the foot of **Argyle Street,** and you'll find restaurants and gift shops amid the cackle of seagulls and the full-throated honk of ship's horns. There's a **Maritime Discovery Centre** (© 250/723-2181; www.alberniheritage.com) housed in a lighthouse replica at the end of the pier; it tells the story of Port Alberni's seafaring past. Alberni's land-based history is shown at **The Alberni Valley Museum** (4255 Wallace St.; © 250/723-2181; www.alberniheritage.com), which displays local Nuu Chah Nulth art and pioneer artifacts. Admission to both museums is by donation. And, thanks to money the provincial government gave in 2008 to help celebrate British Columbia's 150th birthday, Port Alberni has created a Spirit Square as a venue for festivals, events, and people gathering. Garden enthusiasts can head for **Rollins Art Centre and Gardens** (3061 8th Ave.; © 250/724-3412; www.portalberniarts.com), a combination fine-arts gallery and gardens,

World's Largest Flying Boat

The Mars are known as the world's largest flying boats, capable of scooping up 24,500 kilograms (27 tons) of water at any one time beneath their 61m (200-ft.) wingspan. There are only two active Mars Tankers left in the world; both are based on Sprout Lake in Port Alberni.

including a traditional Japanese garden that was a gift from Abashiri, Port Alberni's sister city.

Aviation fans might want to stop at the **Home of the Mars Water Bombers,** the largest water-bombing plane in the world, headquartered at lovely **Sproat Lake** nearby.

In summer, you can head over to the restored Port Alberni **railway station** (built around 1912) and board an antique locomotive for the 35-minute ride up to the McLean Mill National Historic Site. Upon request, the train also makes a stop at the **Case and Warren Winery** (6253 Drinkwater Rd.; ✆ **250/724-4906**) for a tour and tasting. Originally used by the Esquimalt and Nanaimo (E&N) Railway to transport logs and lumber between the mills and the harbor, the fully restored steam train now carries passengers. It operates two rides a day, Thursday through Monday. Call ✆ **250/723-2181** for fares, which include admission to the McLean Mill (see listing below) and schedules.

A truly unique way to experience the area is a day trip with **Lady Rose Marine Services** (✆ **800/663-7192** Apr–Sept, or 250/723-8313; www.ladyrosemarine.com), which operates **MV** *Lady Rose* and **MV** *Frances Barkley*, packet freighters that transport supplies to some of British Columbia's far-flung coastal communities along Barkley Sound and the Alberni Inlet. Passengers observe life aboard a coastal freighter first-hand as it delivers all manner of cargo: from newspapers and groceries bound for general stores to equipment for logging camps—even laundry. For some residents scattered along this coast, the MV *Lady Rose* and the MV *Frances Barkley* are their only links to civilization. The scenery, of course, is spectacular. Kayakers and canoeists en route to the **Broken Group Islands** take the MV *Lady Rose* to a base camp at Sechart. Hikers bound for the **West Coast Trail** and day trippers can catch a ride to **Bamfield,** a picturesque fishing village just north of the trail head (see "A Side Trip to Bamfield," below). In summer, there are also day trips through the Broken Groups Islands to Ucluelet. Wear sensible shoes and bring warm, windproof clothing, because the decks are open and weather on the coastal waters can be temperamental. Basic food such as egg and bacon sandwiches is available on board in a tiny galley-restaurant. The freighters depart at 8am, year-round, from **Harbour Quay** on Tuesday, Thursday, and Saturday, returning to Port Alberni at about 5pm. From June through September, there are additional 8am sailings to Ucluelet, via Sechart near the Broken Group Islands, on Monday, Wednesday, and Friday, returning to Port Alberni at about 7pm, as well as an extra sailing on Sunday to Bamfield, again via Sechart to drop off/pick up kayakers.

Adult fares to Bamfield are C\$32, return C\$64; one-way to Ucluelet C\$35, return C\$70; and one-way to Sechart C\$32, return C\$64. If you're staying in Ucluelet, the trip to Sechart is a fun excursion at C\$48 round-trip. Fares are half price for children 8 to 15. Children 7 and under ride free. Reservations are required.

Butterfly World and Orchid Gardens   It's not quite to the standard of Butterfly Gardens near Victoria, but it's still a worthwhile detour. Outside, the gardens are planted to attract wild native butterflies, while inside are more exotic varieties, as well as a display of creepy crawly bugs (a kid's dream), and an aviary of exotic birds, including multi-colored finches. An Orchid Garden featuring hundreds of orchids from around the world is the largest indoor exhibit of its kind in Canada. Thirty minutes should be sufficient for a visit, longer if you love orchids or have bug-crazy children in tow.

1080 Winchester Rd. ✆ **250/248-7026.** www.nature-world.com. Admission C$11 adult, C$10 senior, C$6 student, C$5 children 4–12 years. Mid Mar–mid Sept daily 10am–5pm.

McLean Mill National Historic Site   Built in 1926, this is the only family-run steam-driven sawmill in Canada and is a township all on its own. More than 30 buildings include an operational mill, bunkhouse accommodations for the 20-odd millworkers who once worked here, and a schoolhouse for the workers' children, as well as a steam donkey (an antiquated steam engine that powered winches), logging trucks, and lumber carriers. Although only operational in summer, it's a place where visitors are welcome to wander year-round. Located on Smith Road, off Beaver Creek Road, west of Port Alberni, the site is easiest to reach by train (see above). Allow $3^1/_2$ hours for the entire experience—more if you're a hiker or mountain biker. The Mill happens to be the hub for a network of trails for hikers and mountain bikers alike. The best trail is the Log Train Trail, an easy to moderate 26km (16-mile) linear trail that travels alongside the historic site.

5633 Smith Rd. ✆ **250/723-1376.** www.alberniheritage.com. Mid-June to Labor Day Thurs–Mon 10:30am–5:15pm. Train departs from E&N Station (3100 Kingsway) 10am and 2pm; from McLean Mill 1pm and 5:15pm. C$29 adults, C$22 seniors and youth, C$9.95 child, C$75 family pass that includes 2 adults and 3 children.

WHERE TO STAY

There are a lot of seedy dives in Port Alberni, so if you're staying overnight here, most likely because you're catching an 8am sailing aboard *Lady Rose*, you want to stick to tried-and-true hotels. These two recommendations are standard, each with downtown locations and offering a comfortable night's rest.

Best Western Barclay Hotel   This is as close to the waterfront as you can get, and within walking distance of all its activities. Guest rooms are on the small side, but pleasantly furnished with appealing blue-toned fabrics and warm woods. Suites have fridges, microwaves, and coffeemakers. The **Stamps Cafe** serves casual fare. If you're looking for something more lively, there are no fewer than 22 TV screens in **Pastimes Sports Bar and Grill.**

4277 Stamp Ave., Port Alberni, BC V9Y 7X8. ✆ **800/563-6590** or 250/724-7171. Fax 250/724-9691. www.bestwesternbarclay.com. 86 units. May–Sept C$129–C$199 double; Oct–Apr C$99–C$179 double. Off-season discounts available. Extra person C$10. Children 17 and under stay free in parent's room. Pets accepted (C$10). AE, DC, DISC, MC, V. Free parking. **Amenities:** Restaurant; pub; sports bar; small heated outdoor pool (May–Oct); exercise room; Jacuzzi; sauna; Wi-Fi. *In room:* A/C, TV, dataport, Wi-Fi, coffeemaker, hair dryer, iron.

Hospitality Inn   A cozy fireplace in the lobby welcomes guests to this modern Tudor-style inn that is set away from the waterfront, a few minutes' drive down the hill. There's an upbeat, executive feel to the chocolate-brown and beige decor, and services include all the standard amenities such as fair-size rooms, comfortable beds, and nothing-to-write-home-about bathroom toiletries. The Inn is as geared to business travelers as it is to families, an arrangement that co-exists since each travel group travels at different times—so when kids want to take a dip in the new pool, it's usually not to the chagrin of the

A Side Trip to Bamfield ★★

With its flowing high street, **Bamfield** (© **250/728-3006;** www.bamfield chamber.com) is the Venice of Vancouver Island, and although this isolated community can be reached from Port Alberni via a 102-km (63-mile) unpaved road, most people arrive by boat or floatplane (see "Exploring the Area," above). Bamfield's high street is lined with marine suppliers and quirky boardwalks that join weather-beaten houses, stores, and resorts. Crossing the street means hitching a ride with a local boat owner or hailing a water taxi. Day-trippers off the MV *Lady Rose* have just enough time to meander the boardwalks, buy a carving from a soapstone studio, and maybe enjoy a drink at the historic **Bamfield Inn** (Customs House Lane; © **250/728-3354**) before the return trip to Port Alberni.

Outdoor enthusiasts tend to linger, using Bamfield as a base for fishing, diving, or kayaking. **Broken Island Adventures** (© **888/728-6200** or 250/728-3500; www.brokenislandadventures.com) offers customized diving excursions in Barkley Sound, kayak rentals, and kayak and wildlife-viewing tours. Check out the **Bamfield Marine Sciences Centre** (100 Pachena Rd.; © **250/728-3301;** www.bms.bc.ca), a stellar local attraction with programs and hands-on displays, as well as a new presentation venue that in July hosts an annual music festival of some of the world's finest young musicians. There are scenic hiking trails to Brady's Beach, Cape Beale, Pachena Lighthouse, Keeha Beach, and Tapaltos Beach. Hikers heading for the West Coast Trail use Bamfield as a pit stop before or after a week in the rugged coastal wilderness (see "Pacific Rim National Park," below). **The Hook and Web Pub** (© **250/728-3422**) is a good place to eavesdrop on their harrowing stories of survival. If you just want to get away from it all, **Woods End Landing Cottages,** 168 Wild Duck Rd., Bamfield, BC V0R 1B0 (© **877/828-3383** or 250/728-3383; www.woodsend.travel.bc.ca), offers comfort and character. **The Great Canadian Adventure Company** (© **888/285-1676;** www.adventures.ca) offers an easy hiking tour on remote Tapaltos Beach. It starts with a 2-hour drive along the logging road to Bamfield before you hit the trail for an hour's hike through rainforest to the beach, where you can enjoy a picnic lunch and some beachcombing.

corporate guest. There's an on-site liquor store, and the hotel sells fishing licenses. The **Harvest Restaurant** specializes in home-style cooking, while **Polly's Pub** serves a lighter menu and traditional pub fare.

3835 Redford St., Port Alberni, BC V9Y 3S2. © **877/723-8111** or 250/723-8111. Fax 250/723-0088. www.hospitalityinnportalberni.com. 50 units. June–Sept C$119–C$139 double; Oct–May C$99–C$119 double. Extra person C$10. Family plan, AAA and seniors discounts, and off-season discounts available. AE, DC, MC, V. Free parking. Pets accepted (C$10). **Amenities:** Restaurant; pub; pool; exercise room; hot tub; limited room service; babysitting; laundry service; dry cleaning; fish freezer; Wi-Fi. *In room:* A/C, TV, dataport, coffeemaker, hair dryer, iron, fridge and microwave (upon request), Wi-Fi.

5 TOFINO, UCLUELET & PACIFIC RIM NATIONAL PARK

The scenic drive through the center of Vancouver Island is only a taste of what's to come once you reach the wild coast of Western Canada. Here, the Pacific Ocean rollers crash against the shore, beaches stretch for miles, and the mist clings to the rainforest like cobwebs. Most of what you'll see is part of **Pacific Rim National Park.** In winter, you'll witness some of the best storms in the world—as dramatic and angry as a Turner landscape. In summer, families play alongside surfers, kayakers, and others enjoying this Valhalla for outdoor activities. **Tofino** has long been the commercial center of the region and as such, has many more services to offer visitors, including a sushi restaurant and decent, albeit small, shops and galleries. Tofino is the gateway to **Clayoquot Sound,** North America's largest remaining expanse of low-elevation old-growth temperate rainforest and a UNESCO World Biosphere Reserve. It's a "living laboratory," where you'll find isolated resorts and cabins clinging to the edge of the wilderness, and bears scavenging the shoreline for tasty delicacies, flipping rocks like flapjacks. Unfortunately, Tofino becomes so busy in summer that its popularity is eroding its charm.

For many, the town of **Ucluelet,** 42km (26 miles) away, is a quieter haven. Although a little rougher around the edges, here you can link up with the Wild Pacific Trail, and find B&Bs that are truly away from the madding crowd—although judging from new developments, it's only a matter of time until eco-adventurers and urban escapees start to influence the wilderness here too. Wherever you decide to stay, to get from A to B you really do need a set of wheels, or strong legs, to explore the area more fully. If driving, be careful. Black bear and deer are common, and at times, the roads can be windy and unexpectedly foggy.

ESSENTIALS
Getting There

BY CAR   From Port Alberni, continue west on Hwy. 4 for about 145km (90 miles) to a T-junction. Turn north to Tofino (34km/21 miles), or south to Ucluelet (8km/5 miles).

BY PLANE   Orca Airways (© 888/359-6722; www.flyorcaair.com) flies year-round between Vancouver and Tofino; one-way fares are about C$190 per adult, with discounts offered on advanced bookings. The airline also offers a Victoria–Tofino schedule during the summer months. **Tofino Air** (© 866/486-3247 or 250/725-4454; www.tofinoair. ca) provides charters and scenic tours. For both carriers, discounts for seniors and children are 5% to 10% off listed price.

BY BUS   Greyhound/Island Coach Lines (© 800/661-8747 or 250/385-4411; www.greyhound.ca) operates regular daily service between Victoria and Tofino–Ucluelet, departing at 8:30am and arriving in Tofino about 2:30pm. The bus stops in Nanaimo and will drop off/pick up at Port Alberni. Fares from Port Alberni to Tofino are C$23 per adult. **The Tofino Bus Company** (© 866/986-3466; www.tofinobus.com) also runs a daily service from Vancouver and Victoria to Tofino–Ucluelet (see section 4, above). From Port Alberni to Tofino–Ucluelet, single adult fare is C$24 and C$20 respectively. The company also runs a shuttle service between the two towns for C$10 each way, which includes the Park. In summer the bus makes four runs per day, which trails off to a once-a-day service October through March.

The **Tofino–Long Beach Chamber of Commerce** is located at 1426 Pacific Rim Hwy. (© **250/725-3414;** www.tourismtofino.com); open hours are March through September, weekdays 11am to 5pm. The **Ucluelet Chamber of Commerce** is at the foot of Main St. (© **250/726-4641;** www.uclueletinfo.com or www.ucluelet.com), and is open July to September, Monday through Friday, 11am to 5pm.

EXPLORING TOFINO

Picturesque Tofino, or "Tough City," is an intriguing combination of old-growth forests, white-sand beaches, and the ever-churning Pacific Ocean. It got its name from a Spanish hydrographer who had a reputation for fights and wild living. But don't let the name's origins scare you. For most of the year, Tofino is a sleepy community, though in the summer it's frenzied. As visitors flock toward the Clayoquot Sound Biosphere Reserve, boat charters, whale-watching companies, fishing boats, and seaplanes create a hubbub of activity in the harbor.

The small high street has a number of junk souvenir shops as well as several galleries showcasing aboriginal art. If you've time for only one stop, it must be Roy Henry Vickers's **Eagle Aerie Gallery**, 350 Campbell St. (© **250/725-3235**). As the first First Nations artist with his own gallery in British Columbia, Vickers and his work both inspire and dominate. The carved wooden door makes an impressive entrance, and the entire gallery feels like a life-revering chapel. First Nations artists carved all woodwork within the gallery, including the rails, canoes, and eagles. A percentage of sales of certain works is given to First Peoples recovery programs. **The Tofino Botanical Gardens** (1084 Pacific Rim Hwy.; © **250/725-1220;** www.tofinobotanicalgardens.com) is a 10-minute drive from downtown Tofino. Wander past garden sculptures on boardwalks and trails that take you through the rainforest to themed clearings, such as a kitchen garden and beds filled with native plants, medicinal herbs, and English and Japanese imports that were introduced to the region by early homesteaders. The gardens are an excellent resource for finding out more about the Clayoquot Sound biosphere. On-site there's a hostel-style field station for up to 34 guests, mostly as shared accommodations, for those who want to immerse themselves in the eco-experience. Two private rooms are C$85 and C$120 per person; the rest are bunk beds at C$32 per bed, sharing four to a room.

SIDE TRIPS FROM TOFINO

An hour's boat ride north of Tofino (even faster by seaplane), **Hot Springs Cove** is the only all-natural thermal hot springs on Vancouver Island. A beautifully maintained, 2km (1¼-mile) boardwalk winds through lush rainforest to the sulfur-scented springs. Wisps of steam rise from water that is 122°F (50°C) at its source and cools as it cascades through a series of pools to the sea. It's a busy place in summer, so if you want to experience the tranquility of the place, get there before 10am.

(Fun Facts) Sandpiper Stopover

In late April, many of the world's 2 to 5 million western sandpipers stop to feed on BC's coastal mudflats, including the Tofino mudflats, en route to Arctic breeding grounds. Single flocks of 100,000 are not uncommon at peak migration.

About Clayoquot

Clayoquot Sound contains the largest remnant of ancient temperate rainforest in the world. With its fjord-like inlets, protected archipelagos, and shores, the rainforest has a complex ecosystem of intertidal zones, extensive mudflats, giant kelp and eelgrass beds, and strong tidal currents. The rich diversity of its habitat serves an equally diverse population of both marine and terrestrial species such as migrating whales and shorebirds, basking sharks, Dungeness crabs, various shellfish, wild salmon, herring, ground fish, otters and sea lions, as well as black bears, Roosevelt elk, marbled murrelets, cougars, wolves, bald eagles, and red-legged frogs.

The Nuu-chah-nulth people have occupied Clayoquot Sound and much of the west coast of Vancouver Island for the past several millennia. Of the Nuu-chah-nulth Nation, the Ahousaht, Tla-o-qui-aht, and Hesquiaht tribes live in Clayoquot Sound. First Nations make up approximately 50% of the population, primarily residing in the communities of Hot Springs, Opitsaht, Esowista, and Marktosis.

Just 30 minutes north of Tofino, **Flores Island** is where to find the 32km (20-mile) **Ahousaht Wildside Heritage Trail,** an easy hike through rainforests and along beaches. Nearby **Meares Island,** a 15-minute water-taxi ride from Tofino, is worth seeing both for its beauty and its devastation from clear-cutting. It's the site of many a tree-hugger-versus-logging-company conflict. **The Big Cedar Trail** is a 3km (1.9-mile) boardwalked path through the forest with a long staircase leading up to the Hanging Garden Tree, said to be 1,500 years old. On **Vargas Island,** the **Ahous Trail** (5km/3.1-mile return) is an old telegraph trail that bisects the island from one magnificent beach to another, taking you through salal, tussocky bog, and hummocks of peat. Many Tofino outfitters offer tours and boat transportation to the islands (see "Outdoor Activities," below, for some recommendations). **Tofino Water Taxi** (© 877/726-5485; www.tofinowatertaxi.com) will get you from point A to point B, including a return shuttle service to Meares Island Big Trees Trail (C$20), and Lone Cone Mountain (C$30), as well as the remote beaches of Vargas Island (C$30).

The traffic that explores **Clayoquot Sound** rises every year in direct correlation to the rise in people's eco-awareness and desire to experience pristine wilderness before it vanishes forever. Even though this is a UNESCO-protected region, the evidence of logging and clearcuts lurks behind many a corner, and the cynics feel that it's only a matter of time until lack of resources will demand another look at this designation. Until then, most of the outfitters in Tofino have the Sound on their list of activities, be it for hiking, fishing, kayaking, or boating. But be warned: The myriad islands that are landmarks to locals can easily blur into each other to the untrained eye, so exploring this region is best, and safest, with a guide. Check "Outdoor Activities," below, for ideas.

EXPLORING UCLUELET

Smaller and less sophisticated than Tofino, Ucluelet (Yew-*kloo*-let) is waking up to the extraordinary magnetism of the surrounding area. It used to be that Ucluelet was Tofino's "ugly little stepsister," but that's changing quickly. It's becoming a year-round resort and tourist destination in its own right. New developments are not only sprucing up the downtown core and harbor—where you'll now find the masts of classic fishing boats bobbing alongside moneyed, modern yachts—but they also promise to boost the town's population from 1,650 to nearly 4,000 over the next decade. Projects either underway or just completed include **Reef Point Cottages** (© **877/726-4425;** www.reefpointcottages. com), **Black Rock Oceanfront Resort** (© **877/762-5011** or 250/726-4800; www. blackrockresort.com), and the $600-million **Wyndansea** oceanfront resort with its marina and Jack Nicklaus–signature course (© **888/898-8568;** www.wyndansea.com). The 150 hectare/370-acre project is one of the largest on Vancouver Island.

At the moment, though, the village is still a modest affair. The village has a couple of **folk art galleries,** and there are numerous picnic areas along the beaches and rocky coast offering spectacular views. These views are best experienced on the **Wild Pacific Trail,** which is reason alone to visit Ucluelet. If you're not hardy enough to take on the West Coast Trail, then this is a good bet. The 14km (8.7-mile) trail is being developed in phases, and will eventually run along the outer coast to Long Beach at Florencia Bay. The first 2.5km (1.5 miles) is a loop that leads along the coastline from **Amphitrite Point** and its **lighthouse** overlooking Barkley Sound to the Broken Group Islands. In winter, storm-watchers come to this headland to see it pounded by 30m (98-ft.) waves, and in March, this is *the* place to gather to watch the annual migration of the gray whales. Boardwalks lead you through rainforest to bluffs high above the ocean, where trees, beaten back by the wind, grow at 90-degree angles. It's an easy path that gets you close to the fury of winter waves or the splendor of summer sunsets. Another section (6km/3.7 miles) has been completed from Big Beach Park to the bike path just outside of Ucluelet. It's a mix of boardwalks, stairs, and gravel paths that follows the edge of the forest. The final section will extend the trail to Halfmoon Bay in Pacific Rim National Park. From there, you'll be able to pick up the Willowbrae Trail, a 2.8km (1.7-mile) loop trail that traces a portion of the pioneer route linking Ucluelet and Tofino. Access to this hike begins from a small gravel lane marked Willowbrae Road, 2km (1¼ miles) south of the Ucluelet–Tofino junction.

ATTRACTIONS

Ucluelet Mini Aquarium (Finds) ★ Housed in a converted container, this mini public aquarium is likely the world's smallest. Displays are gathered from the surrounding waters and put together with imagination, creativity, and an eye to encourage touching, stroking, ogling, and questioning of the student marine biologists in attendance. The presentations are as intriguing as they are informative; did you know an octopus has three hearts, or that a sea star can travel 3kmph (1³⁄₄ mph) on its 10,000 feet? It's the West Coast ocean under a microscope, all of which is returned to the sea in the fall. This is a winner for kids, and will charm curious adults, too.

Main Street Waterfront Promenade (near Whisky dock). © **604/987-6992.** www.uclueletaquarium.org. Admission C$5. May–Sept daily 10am–6pm.

OUTDOOR ACTIVITIES

BIRDING With the rapidly aging baby-boomer generation, less strenuous pursuits like bird-watching have garnered an enthusiastic following. **Just Birding** (© **250/725-2520;** www.justbirding.com) provides guided birding tours for novice and expert birders (sometimes called "twitchers"). Tours range from early bird, half-day excursions to shorebird

Storm-Watching

From November through February, the world's largest ocean unleashes its winter fury with epic proportions, so don your rain gear and get set for a dynamic and exhilarating experience. Breakers roll in as much as 15m (49 ft.) high, and crash against the craggy shore with awesome force. Favorite storm-watching spots are along the Wild Pacific Trail, Big Beach, at the Amphitrite Point Lighthouse located at the Canadian Coast Guard Station, the Wickanninish Centre, and Chesterman Beach.

walks, full-day paddles with eagles, and mountain birding. Rates vary depending on the tour, but start at C$100. The annual Shorebird Festival, in late April, is a big draw.

FISHING   Tofino and Ucluelet are at the heart of the region's commercial fishing industry, and you'll find a number of sport-fishing charters in both marinas. The big draws are salmon, steelhead, rainbow trout, Dolly Varden char, halibut, snapper, and cod. **Jay's Clayoquot Ventures** (564 Campbell St.; ⓒ **888/534-7422** or 250/725-2700; www.tofinofishing.com) is an experienced and reputable company that organizes fishing charters throughout Clayoquot Sound—both deep-sea and freshwater excursions. Salt-water fly-fishing trips start at C$110 per hour for a 5-hour minimum and include equipment and flies; all inclusive, fly-in freshwater fishing trips, overnighting at a remote camp, and generally customized to need, start at C$2,495 for one or two people. **Lance's Sportfishing Adventures** (120 Fourth St.; ⓒ **888/725-6125** or 250/725-2569; www.fishtofino.com) combines fishing trips aboard 24-foot offshore vessels with a visit to Hot Springs—the advantage being you'll enjoy the springs before the crowds. Rates are C$110 per hour for a 6-hour minimum and include all gear. This outfitter also packages overnight deals with Weigh West Marine Resort (www.weighwest.com).

GOLFING   At press time, a Jack Nicklaus–signature golf course is under development as part of the new Wyndasea luxury resort (see "Exploring Ucluelet," above) in Ucluelet. For information, check out www.marinedriveproperties.com (ⓒ **250/726-8406**).

HIKING   Naturalist, biologist, author, and ecologist Bill McIntyre was such a sought-after guide that he now runs a full program of guided beach and rainforest walks, land-based whale-watching tours, and storm-watching hikes through **Oceans Edge** (855 Barkley Cres., Ucluelet; ⓒ **250/726-7099**; www.oceansedge.bc.ca). All excursions are 3 to 6 hours over moderate terrain, and prices vary according to activity; budget around the C$225 mark for a half-day tour. Book well in advance or just hope he has a cancellation when you arrive. Other star hikes include the 3.5km/2.2-mile **Gold Mine Trail** near Florencia Bay, so called for its gold-mining heritage; the partially boardwalked **South Beach Trail** (about 1.5km/0.9 mile); and the even shorter **Schooner Beach Trail,** both of which take you through rainforest before opening up onto sandy beaches.

KAYAKING   Kayaking through Clayoquot Sound is one of the most intimate ways to experience its history, serenity, and natural beauty. The trick is to find an outfitter who can enrich the experience beyond just a paddle. The owners of **Rainforest Kayak Adventures** (ⓒ **877/422-WILD** [9453]; www.rainforestkayak.com) helped set the benchmark for sea-kayak instruction in BC more than 20 years ago and have been guiding the area for almost as long. These are the folks to see if you're looking to guide and instruct

(C$685 to C$1,1550 and up). The **Tofino Sea-Kayaking Company** (320 Main St.; © **800/863-4664** or 250/725-4222; www.tofino-kayaking.com) also offers guided tours, ranging from a 2¹/₂-hour paddle at C$54 to all-day excursions at C$115, as well as daily rentals (C$40 single and C$74 double). If you're based in Ucluelet, **Majestic Ocean Kayaking** (1167 Helen Rd., Ucluelet; © **800/889-7644** or 250/726-2868; www.oceankayaking.com) might be more convenient. They have a range of ecotourism adventures to Barkley Sound, Pacific Rim National Park, and Deer Group Islands. Prices start at C$60 for a 3-hour paddle around Ucluelet Harbour to a full-day trip to Broken Group Islands (including cruiser transport there) at C$235 per person. All-inclusive, multi-day wilderness camping and overnight trips to Vargas Island and others around Clayoquot Sound start at C$250 per day per person. For a blended paddle of environment and authentic First Nations culture, travel with **Tla-ook Cultural Adventures** (© **877/942-2663** or 250/725-2656; www.tlaook.com) where Nuu-chah-nulth First Nations guides take you aboard stylized dugout canoes, sharing their deep-rooted cultural history of the area, and weaving in stories of aboriginal folklore (C$44 for 2.5 hours; C$64 for 4 hours; C$140 for 6 hours).

SURFING   The heavy, constant rollers of the Pacific Ocean against wide expanses of beach have made this one of the world's hot spots for surfing. Whether beginner or experienced, you'll find outfitters to help you catch the wave, year-round. **Live to Surf** (1180 Pacific Rim Hwy.; © **250/725-4463;** www.livetosurf.com) is Tofino's original surf shop and offers rentals of boards and wetsuits as well as daily surf lessons through its Westside Surf School (© **250/725-2404**). Two-hour lessons include all the gear (wetsuit, booties, gloves, and board) and cost C$100 per person, with longer lessons offered for experienced and ultra-fit surfers. **Pacific Surf School** (440 Campbell St.; © **888/777-9961** or 250/725-2155) holds 3-hour lessons (C$79) and provides private tutoring (C$135), and **Surf Sister** (625 Campbell St.; © **877/724-SURF** [7873] or 250/725-4456; www.surfsister.com) is, as the name suggests, geared to women, with its mother–daughter camps and yoga surf retreats (C$75 with a surfboard and C$65 without). **Inner Rhythm Surf Camp** (© **877/393-SURF** [7873]; www.innerrhythm.ca) is based in Ucluelet, and offers 2-hour winter sessions at C$69 per person; and 3-hour summer sessions at C$79.

WHALE-WATCHING   Operating out of Tofino and Ucluelet, **Jamie's Whaling Station** (606 Campell St., Tofino; © **800/667-9913** or 250/725-3919; and 168 Fraser Lane, Ucluelet; © **877/726-7444** or 250/726-7444; www.jamies.com) is a pioneer of the adventure business. It's been around since 1982 and has evolved a full roster of whale-watching, bear-watching, and other wildlife tours. There's a choice of venturing out in 12-passenger Zodiacs—C$79 per adult or C$65 per child—or in the comfort of a 65-foot vessel—C$99 per adult, C$65 per child—complete with snack bar, inside heated seating, and washrooms. A C$2 surcharge is added, contributing to

> **Fun Facts   A Lot of Lions**
>
> More than 2,400 Stellars and California sea lions congregate in Barkley Sound.

local wildlife research and rescue programs and the local bird hospital. *Note:* Jamie's also has a 35-foot cabin cruiser for the 1¹/₄–hour boat ride up to Hot Springs Cove, where you can soak up the waters for a couple of hours before the return trip, either by boat or by seaplane. The boat has space for sea kayaks. **Ocean Outfitters** (421 Main St.;

ℭ 877/906-2326 or 250/725-2866; www.oceanoutfitters.bc.ca) is another option, also featuring zodiac and family travel vessels.

PACIFIC RIM NATIONAL PARK ★★★

Designated a national park in 1970 to protect the significant coastal environment, Pacific Rim National Park presents outstanding examples of coastal rainforest, surf-swept beaches, marine life, and the cultural history of the area's settlement. Composed of three "units," or sections, the **West Coast Trail Unit,** the **Long Beach Unit,** and the **Broken Group Islands,** the park spans 130km (81 miles) of shoreline. You access each unit via a different route. The variety of activities and level of services offered in each unit varies. The Long Beach Unit is the most accessible—a good choice for families and visitors who want to take it a little easier, whereas the West Coast Trail Unit is for no-nonsense hikers with nothing but trekking in mind. Contact the **Pacific Rim National Park Reserve,** P.O. Box 280, Ucluelet, BC V0R 3A0 (ℭ **250/726-7721**) for information.

West Coast Trail Unit

The West Coast Trail is billed as one of the most grueling treks in North America. And when you see experienced backpackers stagger out of its wilderness, muddy, bedraggled, and exhausted, you might think even that is an understatement. This once-in-a-lifetime wilderness adventure attracts 8,000 hikers each year to do battle with the 77km (48-mile) trail between **Port Renfrew** and **Bamfield** along the southwestern coast of Vancouver Island, known as the "graveyard of the Pacific" because of the numerous shipwrecks along the coast. The trail was originally cleared at the start of the 20th century as a lifesaving rail for shipwrecked mariners. It was upgraded in the 1970s, but trekking it still requires much experience, stamina, and strength. At any point on the trail, you may need to balance yourself on a fallen log to cross a deep gully, negotiate steep slopes, climb and descend ladders 25m (82 ft.) at a time, or wade thigh-deep across a river. In fact, hell on the WCT corresponds directly to rain, which can drop 15 centimeters (6 in.) in just 12 hours, turning the trail to mud. More than 100 people are evacuated from the trail every year; one of the main reasons is hypothermia. Bring painkillers and guards for ankle sprains, and be prepared to take a *minimum* of 5 days to complete the trail end to end.

   Tip: If you're not up to the entire challenge, consider taking on the far more accessible 11km (6.8-mile) oceanfront stretch at the trail head near Bamfield. You'll still need your wits (and survival gear) about you, but at least you'll be able to wear the West Coast Trail badge of honor—or part of it, anyway! For peace of mind, such as is possible on this trail, you may prefer to spend the extra money and go with an experienced outfitter such as **Sea to Sky Expeditions** (ℭ **800/900-8735** or 604/594-770l), which offers 9-day guides through the West Coast Trail, starting from C$1,495, and an 8-day hike exploring a part of the Clayoquot region where, from a remote clearing in the rainforest, Annie Rae-Arthur ran a nursery garden and shipped plants across Canada. She was nicknamed Cougar Annie for her handiness with a rifle in defending her lonely lifestyle from hungry cougars.

BOOKING YOUR HIKE   The West Coast Trail is open to hikers from May 1 to September 30. You should reserve up to 3 months ahead, since only 52 hikers are allowed to enter the trail a day: 26 from Bamfield, 26 from Port Renfrew. To reserve, call ℭ **800/ HELLOBC** [435-5622], 800/435-5622, 250/387-1642 (international callers), or 604/435-5622. There is a nonrefundable booking fee of C$25 (per hiker), and a C$129 hiking fee, both payable at time of booking. You also need to register at the park office before you set out, and be at the trail head by noon, or lose your spot. For more information on weather conditions and last-minute options only, call the park's offices (*C* **250/647-5434** (for hikers departing from Port Renfrew) or (*C* **250/728-3234** (for hikers departing from Bamfield; www.pc.gc.ca). ***Note:*** In high season, you may have to wait for up to 3 days, but there are six standby slots per day, filled on a first-come, first-served basis. Wait-list openings are at each trail head—Gordon River at the south end and Pachena Bay at the north end.

Broken Group Islands

Made up of more than 100 rocky islands and islets in **Barkley Sound,** the Broken Group Islands can only be reached by boat. Amidst this pristine archipelago, eagles, sea lions, and marine life abound, and tide pools and dozens of sandy cove beaches lure nature enthusiasts, photographers, and boating sightseers. Chartered boats, guided tours, and transport for campers and kayakers can be booked in Bamfield, Tofino, and Ucluelet, or, you can arrive via the MV *Lady Rose* (see "Exploring the Area," in "Heading West: Port Alberni & Bamfield," earlier in the chapter).

Only experienced boaters, canoeists, and kayakers should consider an expedition to this unit. Waters are studded with reefs, and visibility is often obscured by heavy fog. The weather in the channels that separate the islands can also be extremely variable. The most popular islands include Turtle and Effingham islands as well as those eight islands designated for camping: Gibralter, Hand, Turret, Dodd, Willis, Clark, Benson, and Gilbert islands. In July and August, you can expect to share these sites with many other campers, all seeking the authentic back-country wilderness experience. Other than pit toilets, there are no facilities. Bring your own water. Call the **Pacific Rim National Park** offices for details and reservations at (*C* **877/737-3783;** www.pccamping.ca.

Long Beach Unit

Located between Tofino and Ucluelet, the Long Beach Unit is the most accessible and most developed component of the park. Named for its 20km (12-mile) stretch of surf-swept sand, Long Beach offers outstanding beaches, surfing, and more. Open year-round, the area offers nine hiking trails, each between 1 and 3.5km (0.5–2.2 miles) long, and most of them are boardwalk-surfaced and wheelchair accessible. Star hikes include the 2.8-km (1.7-mile) round-trip **Willowbrae Trail,** just south of Tofino at the Ucluelet junction. It leads down some very steep stairs and ramps to either **Half Moon Bay** (the most romantic cove on the Long Beach stretch) or Florencia Bay. The partially board-walked **South Beach Trail** (about a 1.5km/0.9-mile round-trip) and the shorter **Schooner Beach Trail** both take you through rainforest before opening up onto sandy beaches. **Radar Hill,** formerly cellared for a radar installation during World War II, is the only elevated hike from which to see panoramas of Clayoquot Sound. It claims to be the wettest spot on Vancouver Island. ***Note:*** Storm action can wash trails out, or render them temporarily inaccessible, so it's always best to check with the **Wickaninnish Beach & Interpretive Centre** (*C* **250/726-4212**) at the south end of Long Beach. It has a marine interpretive center and provides information on park programs, activities, and events.

WHERE TO STAY
In Tofino/Clayoquot Sound

Cable Cove Inn ★   New owners have added an exotic Ayurvedic flair to this inn and the first Ayucare Spa Centre in North America—watch this name; these centers are slated to open in Vancouver, South Africa, England, and Holland by the end of 2009. Ayurveda

(Tips) Camping in Pacific Rim National Park

The only place you can camp on Long Beach is the forested bluff at **Green Point** (ⓒ **877/737-3783;** www.pccamping.ca), which has 20 walk-in campsites. Access down to the beach is quite steep. There's an indoor theater with nightly interpretive programs and a real sense of camaraderie among campers. This is a busy family spot in high season; if you're looking for quieter times, book in June or September. The campsite is open mid-March to mid-October; walk-in sites cost C$23. There are flush toilets, but no showers or hookups. Expect to be wait-listed for up to 2 days in July and August.

is an approach to health that has been practiced in India for 5,000 years. That said, Cable Cove is certainly no ashram, and you don't have to be a yogi to enjoy the inn's creature comforts, which still exude a West Coast ambiance. The seven suites, which feature comfortable queen-size beds, fireplaces, and decks with views, now include beautiful Indian silks, rugs, and upscale linens. The spa treatments are exceptional, as is the private dining experience, both for the food (which incorporates the Ayurvedic principles of eating for your body type), and for its location overlooking the cove. Dinner for two people is C$150 (three courses) or C$175 (five courses). There's a shared TV lounge with a fully stocked kitchen and telephone. Laundry facilities are also available. Cable Cove is located within a 5-minute walk of downtown Tofino.

201 Main St. (P.O. Box 339), Tofino, BC V0R 2Z0. ⓒ **800/663-6449** or 250/725-4236. Fax 250/725-2857. www.cablecoveinn.com. 7 units. Mid-June to Sept C$225–C$340 double; Apr to mid-June and Oct C$170–C$245 double; Nov–Mar C$150–C$225 double. Rates include breakfast. AE, MC, V. Pets not accepted. Children not accepted. **Amenities:** Lounge; private dining (by reservation); spa; sauna; washers and dryers; Wi-Fi. *In room:* Wi-Fi, hair dryer, Jacuzzi, no phone.

Clayoquot Wilderness Resort ★★★

The name says it all: splendid, luxurious isolation, in the heart of Clayoquot Sound, and reached either by floatplane or 25-minute boat ride out of Tofino. At night, the darkness is blacker than ebony, the stars brighter than diamonds, and the silence deliciously deafening. The resort's wilderness outposts are among the most unique destinations you will find. These luxurious camps are geared to tender-footed eco-adventurers, and give sleeping under canvas a new twist and a new name—"glamping" (glamorous camping). Fashioned after turn-of-the-20th-century Rockefeller safari campsites, accommodations are nestled in the trees and have opulently furnished, prospector-style tents raised on wooden platforms with antiques, handmade furniture, Persian rugs, four-poster beds topped with down duvets, and free-standing propane and wood stoves. The cuisine is spectacular, as is the wine list, from pancakes made with freshly picked blueberries in the morning to alder-smoked grilled salmon over wild greens, or four-peppercorn-crusted tenderloin medallions in the evening. Stays are sold only as multi-night packages. The resort has created a number of trails through the surrounding virgin forest, suitable for mountain biking and horseback riding. Other activities include a trip to Hot Springs Cove as well as kayaking, fishing, and wildlife-viewing excursions. Prices include a 3% sustainability fee, which also covers an environmental legacy program for habitat restoration and wildlife studies. Indeed, everything about this resort is as green as you will find, from innovative compostable plastics made from corn and potato to its own sustainable run-by-the-river hydropower generator. This is the place to visit if you're looking for cocktail-party bragging rights.

P.O. Box 728, Tofino, BC V0R 2Z0. ✆ **888/333-5405** or 250/725-2688. Fax 250/725-2689. www.wild retreat.com. 21 outpost tents. May–Sept 3- to 7-night stays C$4,750–C$11,000. Rates include 3 meals/day plus transport to and from Tofino. 3-, 4- and 7-night packages available. AE, MC, V. Parking in Tofino. Closed Nov–Feb. **Amenities:** Restaurant; lounge; spa; hot tubs; kayak rentals; free canoes; bike rental; sailing; whale-watching; fishing; hiking; horseback riding; library; Wi-Fi;. *In room:* Hair dryer, no phone.

Inn at Tough City ⟨Finds⟩

Take a close look and you'll see this inn for what it is—a recycled treasure, and one of the quirkiest small inns in downtown Tofino. Constructed with over 45,000 recycled bricks, refurbished hardwood floors, and original stained-glass windows from as far away as Scotland, the Inn at Tough City is a find. You've got to love the vintage collection of advertising signs and old tins. All guest rooms have their own color scheme, accented with stained glass and antique furniture. They also have decks or balconies with water views, though room nos. 3 and 6 have only peekaboo ones. The upstairs guest rooms have fireplaces. All have custom-made bed linens in soft, environment-friendly, unbleached cotton. The inn doesn't provide breakfast, but does have the only authentic sushi restaurant in town (see "Where to Dine," later in this chapter).

350 Main St. (P.O. Box 8), Tofino, BC V0R 2Z0. ✆ **250/725-2021.** Fax 250/725-2088. www.toughcity.com. 8 units. June–Sept C$169–C$199 double; Oct–Nov and Mar–May C$109–C$129 double. Closed Dec–Feb. AE, MC, V. **Amenities:** Restaurant; library-lounge. *In room:* TV, coffeemaker.

Long Beach Lodge Resort ★★

This upscale resort lies on the beach at Cox Bay, between Pacific Rim National Park and Clayoquot Sound. Set among towering trees and taking full advantage of the rugged coastline and sandy beach, the cedar-shingled lodge rivals the Wickaninnish Inn (reviewed below) for views and service that here rates two staff for every three guests. The welcoming Great Room—with its dramatic First Nations art, oversize granite fireplace, and deep armchairs—is an ideal spot to relax overlooking the bay and sample the chef's daily creations that feature fresh, organic ingredients for lunch and dinner, as well as shared plates of hors d'oeuvres. Accommodations include 41 beachfront lodge rooms with oversize beds, fireplaces, Jacuzzis or extra-deep-soaker bathtubs, and private balconies, as well as 20 two-bedroom cottages nestled in the rainforest. Surfers opt for the ground floor, beachfront rooms that literally put the rollers on their doorstep. Rain gear is provided to guests who want to venture forth into the storms. Rates include a buffet breakfast.

1441 Pacific Rim Hwy., Tofino, BC V0R 2Z0. ✆ **877/844-7873** or 250/725-2442. Fax 250/725-2402. www. longbeachlodgeresort.com. 61 units, cottages with hot tubs. Mid-Oct to mid-March C$169-C$259 double, C$279 cottage, C$569 Suite; mid-March to May C$199-C$299 double, C$329 cottage, C$569 suite; Jun to mid-Oct C$299-C$399 double, $479 cottage; penthouse $629 year-round. Extra person C$30. Children ages 6–15 C$15 extra. Pets accepted C$50. Rates include continental breakfast buffet. AE, MC, V **Amenities:** Restaurant; lounge; oceanfront health club. *In room:* Coffeemaker, hair dryer, fireplace.

Middle Beach Lodge

Set among tall hemlocks with a steep slope down to a kilometer of private beach, the rustic ambience of Middle Beach makes it less pretentious than some of the area's other resorts. Perhaps it's because much of the complex was built with recycled lumber, so it has a weathered appeal. There are various accommodations styles, including standard lodge rooms, suites, and self-contained cabins, one of which can sleep six. Of the entire complex, only two cabins are geared for families. Rooms are priced accordingly to what they offer: Some have no phones and great ocean views; others have TVs, balconies, and fireplaces, and still others have full kitchens and Jacuzzis. Room no. 26 is the most romantic with its king-size bed, kitchenette, and oceanfront location. The high-beamed restaurant and lounge overlook the ocean, serving up a menu of tasty standards such as salmon, steak, and pasta. Although it's open daily for breakfast and dinner during high season, open hours are sporadic in the winter. Some cabins close in winter.

400 MacKenzie Beach Rd., (PO Box 100), Tofino, BC V0R 2Z0. (C) **866/725-2900** or 250/725-2900. Fax 250/725-2901. www.middlebeach.com. 45 units, 19 cabins. Mid-June to Sept C$140–C$230 lodge rooms, C$165–C$450 suites and cabins; Oct to mid-June C$110–C$170 lodge rooms, C$200–C$375 suites and cabins. 2-night minimum stay. Spa packages and off-season discounts available. AE, MC, V. **Amenities:** Restaurant; lounge; exercise room; tour desk; coin-op. laundry; Wi-Fi. *In room:* TV/VCR/DVD (suites and cabins), kitchenette, fridge, coffeemaker, no phone.

Pacific Sands Resort ★★ This resort nudges against Pacific Rim National Park; white-sand beaches, islands, and old-growth rainforests are at your doorstep. In fact, the sound of the surf, although sometimes tumultuous, sets a tranquil, metronome-like quality for sleep. Accommodations range from one- and two-bedroom suites to oceanfront cottages, all with kitchens, fireplaces, balconies, and spectacular views. Some have Jacuzzis. The new two- and three-bedroom villas are especially spacious, with an open floorplan and West Coast modern decor including heated slate floors and deeper soaker tubs. They're especially suited for families or couples traveling together. Complimentary rain gear lets guests ignore the weather and ocean spray and get outside. That same weather, incidentally, makes Wi-Fi accessibility a bit hit-and-miss.

Cox Bay, Tofino, BC V0R 2Z0. (C) **800/565-2322** or 250/725-2322. Fax 250/725-3155. www.pacificsands. com. 77 units. July–Sept C$275–C$585; Oct–Jun C$175–C$560. Seasonal discounts available. AE, MC, V. **Amenities:** Bike rental; children's programs; concierge. *In room:* TV, dataport, Wi-Fi (some).

Wickaninnish Inn ★★★ Perched on a rocky promontory overlooking Chesterman Beach, between old-growth forest and the Pacific Ocean, this member of the renowned Relais & Châteaux network of hotels sets the standard by which other fine hoteliers seem to judge themselves. It describes itself as rustically elegant, which translates into handmade driftwood furniture, local artwork in every room alongside fireplaces, large-screen TVs, richly textured linens and furnishings, en suites with double soakers, and all with breathtaking views of the ocean. The corner suites have an additional wall of windows that seems to beckon the outside in. Adjacent to the original lodge is the **Wickaninnish on the Beach,** with 30 even more luxurious two-level guest suites and a health club.

In summer, the sprawling sands of Chesterman Beach are littered with sandcastles, tidal pools, and sun worshippers. In winter, it's quite a different story. As thundering waves, howling winds, and sheets of rain lash up against the inn's cedar siding, storm-watching becomes an art. Every guest room provides grandstand views through triple-glazed, floor-to-ceiling windows. The result is a surreal feeling of being enveloped by a storm in virtual silence, especially when snuggled up in front of the fire. Rain gear is provided for those brave souls who want to take on the elements first-hand. The **Ancient Cedars Spa** will mellow your mood, especially since every treatment begins with an aromatic footbath. The best treatment room is the new one out on the rocks. Cuisine is another one of the inn's draws. Reservations at the **Pointe Restaurant** are sought after, so be sure to make them when you book your room (see "Where to Dine," below).

Osprey Lane at Chesterman Beach (P.O. Box 250), Tofino, BC V0R 2Z0. (C) **800/333-4604** or 250/725-3300. Fax 250/725-3110. www.wickinn.com. 75 units. Mid-June to Sept C$480–C$1,500; Oct C$320–C$975; Nov to mid-June C$280–C$975. Rates may vary over holiday periods. Storm-watching, spa, and other packages available. AE, MC, V. **Amenities:** Restaurant; bar; coffee lounge; health club; spa; concierge; in-room massage; babysitting; nonsmoking facilities. *In room:* TV/DVD, dataport, Wi-Fi, minibar, coffeemaker, hair dryer, iron.

At press time, the Blackrock Oceanfront Resort was just opening its doors as Ucluelet's newest upscale destination. The West Coast–style 70-room lodge houses a fine-dining restaurant, spa, and lounge, while the 12 fully equipped cottages offer more self-sufficiency. Check out www.blackrockresort.com for information.

The Cabins at Terrace Beach   This cove-side hideaway was constructed to resemble a 1920s West Coast fishing village, but the sheltered cedar cabins feel more like overgrown adult treehouses, or even high-end camping. Furnishings are country chic, and all units are equipped with a kitchenette, deck, and BBQ. Boardwalks wind around the 350-year-old evergreens that lead to beachfront cottages, and the relatively calm waters of Terrace Beach, adjacent to the Wild Pacific Trail (accessible via a staircase), make this a good choice for young children. Cabin no. 2 can feel very romantic when the morning mist swirls around the hot tub. There's direct access to the beach, which, because of the waveless waters, is ideal for young tots.

1090 Peninsula Rd. (PO Box 315), Ucluelet, BC V0R 3A0. *C* **866/438-4373** or 250/726-2101. Fax 250/726-2100. www.thecabins.ca. July–Aug C$139–C$329 double; Sept–June C$139–C$179 double. Extra person C$20. Children 5 and under stay free. Pets accepted (C$20). **Amenities:** Hiking trails; beach. *In room:* Satellite TV, Wi-Fi, kitchen.

Canadian Princess Resort   This former hydrographic survey ship, moored in Ucluelet's central harbor and completely refurbished, sails to nowhere but offers no-nonsense, nautical-style accommodations. Small guest cabins, brightly decorated, offer basic bunk-style beds with washbasins; showers and bathroom facilities are shared. Standard, more comfortable onshore accommodations are also available. These guest rooms have two double beds and private bathrooms. Larger rooms sleep up to four in loft-style rooms. The vessel's dining and lounge areas are cozy and add to the seafaring atmosphere. Remember, this was once a working ship, which is a great part of its charm, and is probably why it seems to attract the fishing crowd. It's also a great find for families traveling on a budget.

1943 Peninsula Rd., Ucluelet Harbour, Ucluelet, BC V0R 3A0. *C* **800/663-7090** or 250/726-7771. Fax 250/726-7121. www.canadianprincess.com. 76 units. Mar to mid-Sept C$85–C$179 ship stateroom, C$145–C$345 on-shore room and loft. Extra person C$25. Salmon- and halibut-fishing packages available. AE, MC, V. Closed mid-Sept to Feb. **Amenities:** Restaurant; 2 lounges; tour desk; nature cruises. *In room:* A/C, TV in on-shore rooms, coffeemaker, hair dryer.

A Snug Harbour Inn ★   Set on an 26m (85-ft.) cliff overlooking the pounding Pacific, A Snug Harbour Inn is a romantic oasis that takes the credit for at least 85 wedding engagements. Each guest room is decorated a little differently: One has an Atlantic nautical theme, a three-level Lighthouse Suite boasts the best views, and the Sawadee tops the list for snuggly

---

Live Like a Local

If you plan to stay a while, **Tofino Vacation Rentals** (*C* **877/799-2779;** www.tofinovr.com) has all manner of suites and homes, from custom-built cedar houses on the beach to forest hideaway cottages. Some are pet friendly and include hot tubs, BBQ firepits, and gourmet kitchens. Others are more modest. Either way, there's usually something in their line-up to fit with prices ranging from C$200 to C$700 in high season, C$100 to C$450 in low season.

7

Camping in Tofino

Crystal Cove Beach Resort (Mackenzie Beach, Box 559, Tofino BC V0R 2Z0; *C* **250/725-4213;** www.crystalcove.cc) has 76 RV and tent campsites, all with fire pits and a picnic table. Flush toilets, free hot showers, and laundry facilities are in a clean, modern, Wi-Fi-wired building. Full and partial hookups, sewer and water outlets, and a sani-station are also available. There are also 34 private, modern log cabins with full kitchens, wood-burning fireplaces, decks with barbecues, and some with private hot tubs. Open year round. Sites are C$47, serviced C$55. Cabins range from C$290 to C$410 in high season. Off-season rates are available.

Bella Pacifica (Box 413, 400 MacKenzie Beach, Tofino, BC V0R 2Z0; *C* **250/725-3400;** www.bellapacifica.com) is another sought-after, year-round campsite offering 170 private sites nestled amid the trees, including a separate area for motor homes, and all with picnic tables, hook-ups, and outlets. The showers are coin-operated, so bring a supply of loonies. Book in October if you're hoping to secure one of the 18 virtually on-the-beach sites. Rates for these are C$48 in peak season, while the others range between C$38 and C$46 depending on site location. Rates drop by as much as 40% in winter.

For information on other campsites in the region, check out www.camping. bc.ca. Reservations can be made March to September at www.discovercamping. ca, or call *C* **800/689-9025** or 604/689-9025.

comfort. One suite was built for wheelchair accessibility, including a large, walk-in shower; and another is pet friendly. All have fireplaces, down duvets over queen- or king-size beds, double-jet bathtubs, and private decks boasting vast ocean views. For a nominal extra charge, you can order up items such as roses, champagne, and other gifts to add a special touch to your stay. There's a powerful telescope in the Great Room, through which you can watch sea lions on the rocks below, or at night, with no light pollution, enjoy some unparalleled stargazing. Outside, there's a trail of 75 steps down to the pebbly beach, appropriately called "Stairway from the Stars." It's worth the descent, but it's a bit of a hike back up—take it in the morning to whet your appetite for a terrific breakfast.

460 Marine Dr. (P.O. Box 367), Ucluelet, BC V0R 3A0. *C* **888/936-5222** or 250/726-2686. Fax 250/726-2685. www.awesomeview.com. 6 units. June–Sept C$270–C$355 double; Oct and Mar–May C$215–C$280 double; Nov–Feb C$190–C$225 double. MC, V. Pets accepted. **Amenities:** Lounge; Jacuzzi; Internet. *In room:* TV/DVD, Wi-Fi, hair dryer.

Tauca Lea Coast Resort ★   Overlooking the fishing boats, commercial trollers, and yachts moored in Ucluelet's inner harbor, Tauca Lea exudes a rustic, West Coast style. Its cathedral windows seem to beckon the outdoors in. The resort includes one- and two-bedroom suites, each solidly constructed and beautifully finished with a designer's eye for texture and detail. Furnishings include items such as leather La-Z-Boys in front of gas fireplaces, original artwork, kitchens with designer kitchenware, luxury linens, and all the amenities you would expect in a fine hotel. Some have two-person hot tubs on private decks. The Rainforest Spa and Boat Basin Restaurant (see "Where to Dine," below) have helped establish this resort as a sought-after romantic getaway.

1971 Harbour Dr., Ucluelet, BC V0R 3A0. ℭ **800/979-9303** or 250/726-4625. Fax 250/726-4663. www. taucalearesort.com. 32 units, some with hot tub. July–Aug C$319–C$349 1-bedroom, C$399–C$429 2-bedroom; Sept–Oct C$199–C$229 1-bedroom, C$299–319 2-bedroom; Nov–Mar C$179–C$209 1-bedroom, C$229–C$269 2-bedroom; Apr–June C$199–C$299 1-bedroom, C$299–C$319 2-bedroom. AE, MC, V. **Amenities:** Restaurant; lounge; spa; concierge; gift shop; coin laundry; Wi-Fi. *In room:* TV, CD player, kitchen, fridge, coffeemaker, hair dryer, iron.

WHERE TO DINE
In Tofino/Clayoquot Sound

Pointe Restaurant ★★★ WEST COAST If the 240-degree view of the Pacific Ocean pounding at your feet doesn't inspire, then the food and award-winning wine list certainly will. The menu is an imaginative showcase of fresh coastal food and seafood that's caught within a stone's throw of the inn. Chanterelles, boletus, angel wings, and pine mushrooms are brought in from neighboring forests. Gooseneck barnacles come off the rocks on the beach, and Indian Candy, made from salmon marinated and smoked for 6 days, comes from Tofino. Everything is exquisitely presented—a warm morel salad is perfectly combined with sweet corn and tempura oysters, and the prosciutto-wrapped rabbit saddle is extra flavorful for its aged sherry vinegar baste. A chef's six-course Tasting Menu showcases the best of the season for C$215 with wine pairings, C$115 without. And if the tempest outside is brewing over your meal, take note. The restaurant has special surround-sound to make it feel as if you're eating in the eye of a storm. Be sure to book a table well in advance, or at least when you book your room, or you might be disappointed.

At Wickaninnish Inn, Osprey Lane at Chesterman Beach. ℭ **800/333-4604** or 250/725-3100. www.wick inn.com. Reservations required. Main courses C$22–C$45. AE, MC, V. Daily 8am–9:30pm.

The Schooner on Second PACIFIC NORTHWEST Originally constructed as the hospital for the World War II RCAF Squadron Unit at Long Beach, it was towed to its present location when the war ended and has had various food incarnations, from coffee shop to crab shack, since. One of the former chefs, Morris, is even said to be its resident ghost. These days, however, the shack is the place for a romantic or special-occasion dinner. Menu items include appetizers (C$12/plate), primarily featuring seafood, such as tuna wontons and panko-crusted prawns, and entrees include beef tenderloin, a succulent rack of lamb, as well as a range of creatively prepared seafood, often with an ethnic touch, as in the West Coast Seafood Hot Pot—halibut, prawns, and scallops sautéed in a spicy red Thai-inspired curry-coconut cream and served with lime-leaf-scented basmati rice. If fish is your thing, go for the gusto with the Captain's Plate for Two (C$57), a tasty sharing platter of six or seven different fish dishes.

331 Campbell St. ℭ **250/725-3444.** Reservations recommended. Main courses C$24–C$38. MC, V. Daily 9am–3pm and 5–9:30pm.

Shelter ★ PACIFIC NORTHWEST Polished wood dominates the decor of this cozy spot, which also features a large stone fireplace. Although there's meat on the menu, fish is the house specialty, and it's done to perfection, whether seared albacore tuna, steamed mussels with caramelized onion and roasted garlic, or the yellow Thai seafood curry served with sticky rice steamed black in a banana leaf. Don't leave without at least trying the bouillabaisse (tasters are by request). It's the signature dish crammed with local fish, from sable and Chinook salmon to prawns, clams, and mussels that have simmered away in a fire-roasted tomato sauce. Fish aside, the Angus rib-eye with panko onion rings is pretty darn good, as is the best vegetarian dish on the menu: a char-grilled vegetable ratatouille. Most wines are award-winning whites from BC vineyards; nearly all are available by the glass.

601 Campbell St. ☏ **250/725-3353.** www.shelterrestaurant.com. Reservations recommended. Main courses lunch C$11–C$18; dinner C$13–C$32. MC, V. Daily 11am–10pm.

SoBo ECLECTIC   Chef-owner Lisa Ahier has a long pedigree of cooking at high-end lodges, but this is a far cry from froufrou cooking. SoBo is actually short for Sophisticated Bohemian, which describes the decor: lots of glass, high ceilings, a huge open kitchen, and a dining area filled with a hodgepodge of tables, chairs, and colorful art, as well as the imaginative cuisine. Because Ahier started in a tiny purple catering truck, many of her items then (and now) are hand-held eats such as "gringo" soft chicken tacos, crispy shrimp cakes, or a fish taco filled with local wild fish and topped with a fresh-fruit salsa. Items are priced tapas-style, so you can order one as a snack or three if you're starving. Now that she has the space, the menu is more expansive, and there's a deli counter for takeout with items like artisan pizzas, oysters encrusted with hemp seed, and frozen fish chowder to heat up later.

311 Neill St. ☏ **250/725-2341.** www.sobo.ca. Main courses C$9–C$28. MC, V. Daily 11am–5:30pm; Wed–Sun to 9pm.

Sushi Bar at Tough City ★ SUSHI   This restaurant has earned such a reputation for authenticity that it's grown from a small bar to the entire main floor of this popular B&B, and in warmer weather it even spills over onto the outdoor patio. The menu has all the traditional favorites: sushi rolls, tempura rolls, nigiri, and sashimi, as well as other Japanese dishes such as teriyaki salmon, chicken, and beef. If you're not a fan of sushi, but love crab, the Dungeness crab dinner (C$34) is one of the best, in part because it's so simply prepared—steamed and served cold with melted garlic butter and a fresh Caesar salad. In July and August, the bar opens for lunch as well as dinner.

350 Main St. (P.O. Box 8), Tofino, BC V0R 2Z0. ☏ **250/725-2021.** www.toughcity.com. Main courses C$10–C$24. AE, MC, V. Year-round daily 5:30–9pm; July–Aug 11:30am–9pm.

In Ucluelet

Boat Basin Lounge and Restaurant BISTRO   This marina-side bistro serves a seasonal West Coast menu that focuses on fish, free-range poultry, and local produce. One night this might be pan-roasted halibut with red curry, Arborio rice, and a papaya chutney, cedar-plank salmon with marinated artichoke hearts, or rare seared Albacore tuna with a sweet chili oyster sauce and coconut rice. The Alberta Black Angus filet is a menu staple, as is the selection of Agassiz specialty cheeses which, with the selection of BC wines, is a savory conclusion to any meal.

At Tauca Lea Resort, 1971 Harbour Dr. ☏ **800/979-9303** or 250/726-4625. www.taucalearesort.com. Main courses C$24–C$44. AE, MC, V. Daily 5:30–8:30pm.

Matterson House CANADIAN   From the outside, this tiny 1931 cottage is very nondescript, yet once inside you're in for a treat in terms of good food and warm, albeit often slow, service. By day, there are generous breakfasts and lunches of traditional favorites: burgers, pasta, salads, and homemade breads. By dusk, the menu turns to ocean and from-the-garden cuisine with filling standards such as prime rib, fancier items such as almond-crusted chicken with blackberry sauce, and excellent seafood dishes that include shrimp and scallop skewers and a tasty seafood chowder. The wine list features mostly BC labels, some of them special order. With only seven tables, plus an outside patio of another seven tables, reservations are recommended. While the food is consistently good, the service can be painfully slow. The restaurant opens daily year round, although in

Food on the Run

Three takeouts to note include **The Wildside** (1180 Pacific Rim Hwy; ℃ **250/725-9453**), tucked in a small cluster of buildings just off the highway on the way to Tofino where surfers tend to congregate. Don't be put off by the shack-like appearance: The pulled-pork sandwich is terrific and the fresh-from-the-ocean fish is served tempura-style. Next door is **The Tofitian,** a computer cafe with free Wi-Fi and the area's finest espresso (Lavazza). And in Tofino itself, the **Breakers** (430 Campbell St.; ℃ **250/725-2558;** www.breakersdeli.com) doles out tasty picnic supplies (Salt Spring Island goat cheese, Natural Pastures Pacific pepper verdelait, and the like) as well as whole-wheat pizzas. All take-out products are biodegradable and compostable to put your eco-conscience at ease.

winter call first because hours are determined by staff availability and what's happening in town. At time of printing, the place was up for sale—another reason to call first.

1682 Peninsula Rd. ℃ **250/726-2200.** Main courses C$18–C$26. MC, V. Daily 9am–9pm (call ahead to confirm).

Ukee Dogs (Finds ★★ CANADIAN

Operating out of a converted gas station and garage, there's a delicious informality about this tiny cafe where tables are within spitting distance of the open kitchen. Everything's made from scratch, and chef-owner Stephanie Deering chats to you over her hot stove about your order. You want onions? How about some cilantro? She gave up a long and lucrative career in fine dining to set up shop away from the rat race, so you can be assured of great dining taste with her no-frills dishes: Hearty bean chili and cheddar is so good that many of the fishermen have it for breakfast in addition to the various breakfast scramblers on offer. The vegetable curry pie is simmered in a creamy madreas sauce; and the hot dogs? Well, they're what made Ukee's a household name in these parts, so they're a have-to-have. Everything on the menu is C$5, and each meat item has a vegetarian counterpart.

1576 Imperial Lane. ℃ **250/726-2103.** www.uclueletvillagesquareshops.com. Main courses C$5. Cash only. Mon–Fri 8:30am–3:30pm; Sat 8:30am–3:30pm summer only; closed Sun.

The Wickaninnish Restaurant CANADIAN

Not to be confused with the restaurant at the Wickaninnish Inn up the road, this dining room sits right on, and above, one of the prettiest parts of Long Beach. There isn't a better spot to savor the area's expansive sands, either inside from behind humongous windows or on a heated oceanfront sun deck. Menu items can sometimes be overly ambitious, so if a lofty description takes your fancy, probe your waiter for an honest assessment. Lunches lean to excellent soups, sandwiches, crepes, and quiches; dinners include pasta, seafood, and standards such as New York steak. The crowd is a mix of upscale hikers and urban escapees (in other words, you don't see many gloriously muddy hiking boots—they've likely been changed in the car). This is one of *the* most romantic spots to view a West Coast sunset. *Note:* There's a regular shuttle that runs from the Canadian Princess Resort to the restaurant; if you're driving, be sure to ask your waiter for a complimentary parking pass.

Wickaninnish Interpretive Centre, Long Beach. ℃ **250/726-7706.** www.obmg.com. Reservations recommended. Main courses C$17–C$33. AE, MC, V. Daily Mid-Mar to mid-Sept 11:30am–9:30pm. Closed mid-Sep to mid-Mar.

Northern Vancouver Island

The differences between the north island and the south are profound. The farther north you drive, the wilder Vancouver Island becomes, and as urban sophistication falls to the wayside, you'll start to discover the diversity of the region. Fewer than 4% of the island's residents live in the northern part, with its vast forests of deep green, its crystal-clear rivers, and its inviting beaches. It's a paradise for eco-adventurers and nature photographers—a mecca for anyone looking for Canadian wilderness. Some communities, such as Kyoquot, are accessible only by chartered floatplane or boat, and to reach them you travel through country that is quintessential West Coast Canada. Travel inland is also an adventure. While the main road twists up and around the island's spine of coastal mountains (the weather can change on a single S-bend), off-the-beaten-track destinations are often reached via logging roads. If you drive these routes, remember to use caution. Logging is still a primary industry in this part of the world; logging trucks are numerous, and have the right of way.

Natural resources have long been the economic backbone of Vancouver Island,

and as those resources continue to diminish, towns are looking to alternative investments. In **Courtenay–Comox,** the fastest-growing region on the island, and home to the fish-happy **Campbell River,** resorts are springing up alongside entire retirement communities. Far-flung mining hamlets like **Zeballos,** which once made its fortune in gold, and **Holberg** are becoming bases for eco-adventurers, and picturesque places like **Telegraph Cove** are succumbing to 21st-century development. Despite these changes, you'll still come across communities, such as **Port McNeill** and **Port Hardy,** that are pretty rough-and-ready, as well as places like **Alert Bay,** whose isolation has protected its rich First Nations culture.

This great diversity is the region's primary appeal. If you're a culture buff, stay in Victoria. If you're traveling with very young children, again, stay south, unless you're heading for **Mount Washington** to ski, or to **Miracle Beach,** one of the province's most popular provincial parks. But if you're hankering to experience nature with no boundaries, you won't get much better than North Vancouver Island.

1 COURTENAY & THE COMOX VALLEY

If you drive 62km (39 miles) north of Parksville–Qualicum Beach on Hwy. 19, you'll come upon Vancouver Island's other set of twin towns, Courtenay–Comox. Unlike their neighbors to the south, Courtenay and Comox are refreshingly un-touristy, and so close together that you can hop from one to the other in a matter of minutes. Courtenay, with a population of 20,000, is a center of lumber milling on Vancouver Island, and basks in a wide agricultural valley, while its sister community, Comox, with a population of

12,000, lies on the peninsula just east of Comox Harbour. Originally known as Port Augusta, it was once the only harbor from which supply ships could reach mid-island communities such as Gold River.

Today, the Comox Valley is being discovered, almost gentrified, with its influx of families and retirees who are attracted to the region's rural ambience and urban amenities. The First Nations once called this region, K'Omoks, meaning "Land of Plenty," and for travelers—particularly outdoorsy types—it is certainly the gateway to plenty of wilderness adventure. The Beaufort Mountains, **Mount Washington Alpine Resort,** and **Strathcona Provincial Park** are within easy reach, and the promise of alpine lakes, glacial basins, and craggy peaks brings with it abundant opportunity to view wildlife, as well as to hike, ski, kayak, and much more. If you've time, spend a day or two touring **Denman and Hornby islands,** a 10-minute ferry trip from Buckley Bay, just north of Fanny Bay, best known for its famous oysters.

ESSENTIALS
Getting There
BY CAR   The driving distance from Victoria to Courtenay, along Hwy. 19, due north, is 220km (137 miles). From Nanaimo, the distance is 113km (70 miles). From Parksville, it is 73km (45 miles). Hwy. 19 becomes Cliffe Avenue as it enters Courtenay.

BY PLANE   **Air Canada Jazz** (✆ 888/247-2262; www.flyjazz.ca) and **Pacific Coastal Airlines** (✆ 800/663-2872; www.pacificcoastal.com) operate daily flights from Victoria, Port Hardy, and Campbell River to the **Comox Valley Regional Airport** (✆ 250/897-3123; www.comoxairport.com). **WestJet Airlines** (✆ 888/937-8538 or 800/538-5696; www.westjet.com) operates nonstop flights between Comox and Calgary. Small aircraft and floatplanes can land at the **Courtenay Airpark** (✆ 250/334-8545).

BY BUS   **Laidlaw Coach Lines** (✆ 250/385-4411) operates between Victoria and Port Hardy, with various stops along the way. **Greyhound Canada** (✆ 800/663-8390 or 604/482-8747; www.greyhound.ca) handles schedules and reservations. The one-way fare from Victoria to Courtenay is C$40 for adults. From Nanaimo to Courtenay, it's C$20 for adults. Fares for seniors are 10% less; fares for children 5 to 11 are 50% less. The trip from Victoria to Courtenay takes 4¹/₂ hours; from Nanaimo, it's 2 hours.

BY TRAIN   Courtenay is the termination point of the daily service offered by the **Malahat,** run by **VIA Rail** (✆ 800/561-8630; www.viarail.ca) between Victoria and Courtenay.

BY FERRY   **BC Ferries** (✆ 888/223-3779; www.bcferries.com) operates two daily crossings from **Powell River,** on the BC Sunshine Coast, to **Little River,** in Comox, a 10-minute drive from Courtenay. One-way fares are C$11 for adults, C$6 for children 5 to 11, C$38 for a standard-size vehicle. The crossing takes 1¹/₄ hours.

Visitor Information
The **Comox Valley Information Centre** is at 2040 Cliffe Ave., Courtenay, BC V9N 2L3 (✆ 888/357-4471 or 250/334-3234; www.discovercomoxvalley.com). If you'd like to find out more about the Comox Valley beforehand, you can contact the **Tourism Association of Vancouver Island,** Suite 203, 335 Wesley St., Nanaimo, BC V9R 2T5 (✆ 250/754-3500; www.islands.bc.ca).

NORTHERN VANCOUVER ISLAND

8

COURTENAY & THE COMOX VALLEY

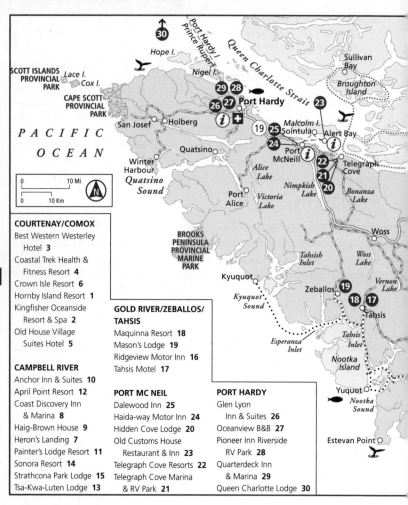

COURTENAY/COMOX
Best Western Westerley
  Hotel **3**
Coastal Trek Health &
  Fitness Resort **4**
Crown Isle Resort **6**
Hornby Island Resort **1**
Kingfisher Oceanside
  Resort & Spa **2**
Old House Village
  Suites Hotel **5**

CAMPBELL RIVER
Anchor Inn & Suites **10**
April Point Resort **12**
Coast Discovery Inn
  & Marina **8**
Haig-Brown House **9**
Heron's Landing **7**
Painter's Lodge Resort **11**
Sonora Resort **14**
Strathcona Park Lodge **15**
Tsa-Kwa-Luten Lodge **13**

**GOLD RIVER/ZEBALLOS/
TAHSIS**
Maquinna Resort **18**
Mason's Lodge **19**
Ridgeview Motor Inn **16**
Tahsis Motel **17**

PORT MC NEIL
Dalewood Inn **25**
Haida-way Motor Inn **24**
Hidden Cove Lodge **20**
Old Customs House
  Restaurant & Inn **23**
Telegraph Cove Resorts **22**
Telegraph Cove Marina
  & RV Park **21**

PORT HARDY
Glen Lyon
  Inn & Suites **26**
Oceanview B&B **27**
Pioneer Inn Riverside
  RV Park **28**
Quarterdeck Inn
  & Marina **29**
Queen Charlotte Lodge **30**

Getting Around
The Comox Valley Transit System (📞 250/339-5453; www.busonline.ca) operates local bus service in and between Courtenay, Comox, and Cumberland, a smaller community about 8km (5 miles) south of Courtenay. **United Cabs** (📞 250/339-7955) provides taxi service in these same communities.

EXPLORING THE AREA
Comox
The tallest building in **Comox** belongs to the Logger's Union, and bears testimony to the backbone of the region's economy. The center of town, however, belies that heritage. In

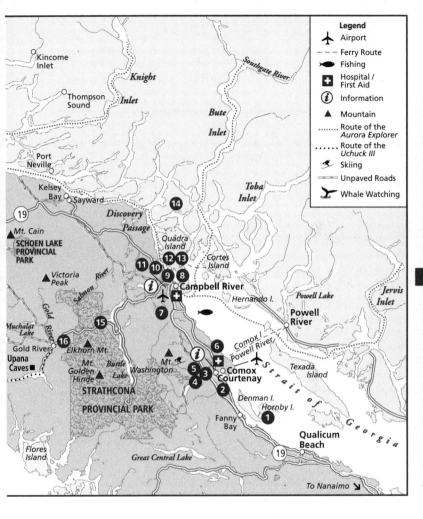

summer especially, the area bustles with activity, shops, galleries, tea cafes, and restaurants, including a hole-in-the-wall sushi bar. Even the Lorne Hotel, a hitherto rather forlorn institution since 1878, now has a happening pub. Be sure to stroll the very pretty, and landscaped, **harborside promenade,** where fishing boats are so plentiful, you can often buy fish or prawns straight from the vessel.

The Filberg Lodge and Park ★★   Once a private residence, the estate was first cleared in 1929 and today covers some 3.6 hectares (9 acres) of wooded and landscaped gardens. The handsome stone and timbered lodge rests on piles driven into an old salt marsh and Native shell midden (a refuse heap) and exudes old-world craftsmanship inside and out. Examples include hand-milled beams, a yew-tree handrail on the staircase, and a stone

Tips **Circle Pac Savings**

BC Ferries offers a special circle tour, enabling passengers to follow routes between the Mainland and Vancouver Island. You can choose to circle in any direction between Victoria, Nanaimo, and Comox on the island, across to Powell River, Horseshoe Bay, and Tsawwassen on the mainland. Whichever direction you choose, this special four-route travel package gives you up to 15% off regular, one-way fares.

fireplace featuring a Native petroglyph. Outside, the waterfront gardens are filled with rare and exotic trees, hundreds of rhododendrons, and numerous flower beds. There's even a four-figure totem pole. Filberg appeals to all ages, and if you're traveling with kids, be sure to visit the hands-on petting farm (open mid-June to mid-Aug). Take the morning or afternoon to explore Filberg; the teahouse serves lunch as well as traditional afternoon tea with cucumber sandwiches, scones, and Devonshire cream, so either way, you need not go hungry. Over the first weekend of August, the park is the site of the 4-day Filberg Festival (© **250/334-9242;** www.filbergfestival.com), an outdoor art exhibition showcasing the work of more than 150 of British Columbia's top craftspeople.

61 Filberg Rd., Comox. © **250/339-2715.** www.filberg.com. Admission by donation. May–Sept daily 8am–dusk. No pets.

Kitty Coleman Woodland Gardens　Named after a First Nations woman who set up residence in the area in the late 1800s, the gardens are a loving and extraordinary creation of one man, Bryan Zimmerman, without the help of heavy equipment that might have destroyed the land. These spectacular, half-wild gardens must be seen to be believed—for the 3,000 rhododendrons alone! There are 9.7 hectares (24 acres) to explore, so bring along shoes with good treads; the bark-mulch trails can be slippery.

6183 Whittaker Rd. (just north of Seal Bay Park), Courtenay. © **250/338-6901.** www.woodlandgardens. ca. Admission C$6 adults, C$2 children 5–12. Year-round daily 9am–dusk.

Courtenay

Courtenay's sexiest claim to fame is that it's the hometown of Kim Cattrall, from the TV show *Sex and the City*. And let's not forget jazz performer Diana Krall who also hails from here. But it just about stops there. Sure, Courtenay is a pleasant enough community, but it doesn't have a particular hub of activity, except for a few galleries and shops around 4th, 5th, and 6th streets, including the **Comox Valley Art Gallery,** 580 Duncan St. at 6th (© **250/338-6211**), opposite the library. There's also quite an enclave of local artists at the **Muir Gallery** (440 Anderton Ave.; © **250/334-2983,** as well as at the **Potter's Place** (180B 5th St.; © **250/334-4613**).

The **Kingfisher Oceanside Resort & Spa** and the **Crown Isle Resort** (see "Where to Stay," below) are doing their part to change all that, however. More than a place to stay, Crown Isle is an entire complex of lavish condominiums, restaurants, and lounges centered on an 18-hole links-style **championship golf course** that offers sweeping views of the Comox Glacier and Beaufort Mountains. The course is open year-round. From May to September, non-member green fees are C$90; from November to March, C$45; and in April and October, C$60. While you're there, be sure to see the **Classic Car Museum,** featuring a collection of predominantly '50s and '60s Chevrolets and Fords, some of which were previously owned by the likes of Sylvester Stallone and Mary Hart.

The Courtenay & District Museum and Palaeontology Centre ★ Housed in the town's old post office, the center holds a collection of First Nations masks and basketry, pioneer artifacts, and a 12m (39-ft.) cast skeleton of an elasmosaur, a crocodile-like Cretaceous-era reptile. Half-day tours are offered year-round, and run the gamut from exploring the paleontology lab to digging in the riverbed. A tropical sea once covered the Comox Valley, so there's a wealth of marine fossils to be found. Open year-round, admission is by donation. To make the most of the experience, a tour is the way to go. Great for kids.

207 4th St. ② **250/334-3611.** www.courtenaymuseum.ca. Admission by donation. Tours are C$25 adults, C$20 students and seniors, C$15 children under 12. May–Sept Mon–Sat 10am–5pm, Sun noon–4pm; winter hours Tues–Sat 10am–5pm.

Cumberland

Just 16km (10 miles) southwest of Courtenay, in the foothills of the Beaufort Mountains, the historic coal-mining town of **Cumberland** still stirs the imagination with pretty heritage homes, storefronts, and institutional buildings such as the rather imposing all-brick 1907 Customs & Post Office. Some buildings have found a new lease on life, which adds to the charm of this hamlet, with an Indian restaurant and a hostel geared to biking enthusiasts. (Cumberland hosts an annual 12-hour bike-race relay on its hilly and winding trails.) Founded by coal baron Robert Dunsmuir, and named after the famous English coal-mining district, Cumberland was once the second largest coal producer in North America. In 1912, one mine alone produced some 2,580 kilograms (5,688 lb.) of coal a day. Back then, the town's population was five times what it is today, made up of some 13,000 workers from around the world. Cumberland once claimed the largest Chinatown north of San Francisco. The mine was closed in 1966, but you can get a feel for Cumberland's story at the **Cumberland Museum & Archives,** 2680 Dunsmuir Ave. (② **250/336-2445;** www.cumberlandmuseum.ca).

Mount Washington Alpine Resort ★★

Drive north on Hwy. 19 and take exit 130 to the Mount Washington exit, about a 30-minute drive from Courtenay–Comox. Then it's an ear-popping climb to the base of the resort. (The road is in excellent condition.) Mount Washington is hardly a resort in the upscale, four-season, Whistler sense of the word, but you will find mountain bikers, alpine fly-fishing enthusiasts, and hikers adventuring through the landscape. Many trails, such as those leading off the 2km (1.2 mile) **Paradise Meadows Loop Trail,** connect to Strathcona Provincial Park (see below.) Take the scenic chairlift to the summit, and you'll find a number of easy bark-mulch, interpretive trails to explore. In winter, skiing is the mountain's raison d'être. With a 505m (1,657-ft.) vertical rise, and more than 60 groomed runs, most above 1,200m (3,937 ft.), Mount Washington's 1,600 acres of riding terrain boast the deepest snowfall in Canada – that's an average of 11m (35ft). All of them are accessed by six lifts, a tubing lift, and two beginners' tows.

As for other winter sports, there's a 0-Zone **snow-tubing park,** a 250m (820-ft.) **luge run,** and 30km (19 miles) of track-set **Nordic trails** connecting to Strathcona Provincial Park. To avoid crowds and lift lineups, plan to go on a weekday—the mountain is remarkably quiet. This is something that can never be said about Whistler. From December to March, day passes for skiing are C$60 for adults, C$48 for seniors and children

13 to 18, C$31 for children 7 to 12, free for children 6 and under. The Alpine and Raven Lodges have restaurants, rentals, and some shops, and there's enough accommodations units—be they condos, chalets, lodges, or hotels—for 4,000 overnight visitors. For details on lift passes, snow school programs, equipment, and condominium rentals, call the central information and reservations number, ✆ **888/231-1499** or 250/338-1386, or log on to www.mountwashington.ca. Another resource is www.tourismmount washington.com (✆ **250/338-0226**).

Strathcona Provincial Park ★★★

Located almost in the center of Vancouver Island, Strathcona Provincial Park is a rugged wilderness of more than 250,000 hectares (617,763 acres). In the summer it can be accessed via several moderately easy trails from Mount Washington Alpine Resort (see above), and year-round by driving to Campbell River on Hwy. 19 and taking the Hwy. 28 exit to Gold River.

Strathcona was British Columbia's first designated wilderness and recreation area (created in 1911), and is managed by the **Ministry of Environment, Lands, and Parks** (✆ **250/337-2400;** www.elp.gov.bc.ca/bcparks). The park brims with treasures: snow-capped mountain peaks, lakes set in amphitheaters of ice, valleys filled with pristine rain forest, alpine meadows painted with heather, as well as rivers and waterfalls—including Canada's tallest waterfall, **Della Falls,** at 440m (1,444 ft.). Wildlife is plentiful, and because of Vancouver Island's separation from the mainland, there are no chipmunks, porcupines, coyotes, or grizzly bears, and species such as Roosevelt elk, black-tailed deer, marmot, and wolf here are slightly smaller than their mainland cousins. Birds are also numerous, and include the chestnut-backed chickadee, red-breasted nuthatch, winter wren, ruffed grouse, and a limited number of unique Vancouver Island white-tailed ptarmigan.

But Strathcona's greatest treasures aren't exactly on display, so if you really want to explore this diverse park, you'll need to hike or backpack into the alpine wilderness. Getting to Della Falls, for example, requires a boat ride to reach the trail head and a multi-day hike that follows the old railway grade up the Drinkwater Valley.

In addition to Paradise Meadows (Mount Washington), **Forbidden Plateau** and **Buttle Lake** are good access points to the park, largely because they can be reached by car, and both have information centers. The Forbidden Plateau offers views to the horizon of glaciers, forests, and pastoral landscapes, and, starting at the former ski lodge, a fairly steep 4.8km (3-mile) trail up Mount Becher. The views of the valley and the Strait of Georgia make the effort worthwhile. At Buttle Lake, you'll find camping facilities (for reservations call Discover Camping, ✆ **800/689-9025**), a honey-hole for rainbow trout and Dolly Varden (a species of trout sometimes called bull trout or sea run dolly), and several trails. Three notable hikes are the easy 20-minute walk to Lady Falls, the 6.5km (4-mile) hike along Marble Meadows Trail, and the 3.2km (2-mile) Upper Myra Falls Trail through old-growth forests and past waterfalls.

Because of the diversity of this park, I suggest you check out the Strathcona Park Lodge (see "Where to Stay," below), if not to stay, at least to get the lowdown on their many programs, which are geared as much to wilderness neophytes as to experienced outdoor adventurers.

WHERE TO STAY

Best Western Westerley Hotel You can't miss it. The Westerley looks like an angular three-story greenhouse, right on Hwy. 19, the main route into Courtenay. Once you're past the uninviting glass facade, though, you'll find a comfortable spot to rest your road-weary bones. Guest rooms are clean, spacious, and comfortably furnished. The building is divided into two wings; the rear one is the better bet, offering rooms with balconies and views of the Courtenay River. The hotel has an indoor pool and health club as well as a casual restaurant, a pool lounge, and a lively sports pub, which is a lot more savory than some of the other drinking establishments you'll find down the street. Renovations are underway to expand the place, primarily in the conference area, but many of the rooms and public areas are also getting a facelift.

1590 Cliffe Ave., Courtenay, BC V9N 2K4. ✆ **800/668-7797** or 250/338-7741. Fax 250/338-5442. www.bestwestern.com. 108 units. C$144–C$169 regular and deluxe room; C$225 suite. Extra person C$10. Lower rates off season. Children 18 and under stay free in parent's room. AE, MC, V. Pets accepted. **Amenities:** Restaurant; sports pub; large heated indoor pool; health club and spa; limited room service; liquor store. *In room:* TV w/pay movies, dataport, Wi-Fi, minibar, coffeemaker, hair dryer, iron, fridge and microwave (C$10) upon request.

Coastal Trek Health & Fitness Resort   Getting here takes faith, mostly because even as you leave the paved road behind, you're still climbing. Nearing the summit of Forbidden Plateau, the views alone make the ascent worthwhile. The resort feels like a hybrid of a contemporary home and a modern motel. Guest rooms are comfortable though a bit on the small side, likely because they're not designed to be away-from-it-all personal retreats. That's left to the main area, with its magnificent post-and-beam construction that showcases a sunken great room with river-rock fireplace, a dining room that seats 12 at one long cypress wood table, and wall windows. Hiking is the resort's forte—backpacks, hiking poles, and non-toxic water bottles are part of the in-room amenities, and hikes are tailored to your ability and health goals, alongside fitness assessments and strength training (optional). The food, organic of course, puts to rest any notions of dull tofu and sprouts. Menus incorporate vegetables such as quinoa and Kohirabi, fruit-based butters, sugar substitutions, as well as black bean brownies and a chocolate beet cake that taste like their decadent cousins. In addition to room and board, 7-night packages include morning yoga classes, massages, a cooking class, daily guided hikes, and health-oriented evening programs/discussions.

8100 Forbidden Plateau Rd. (P.O. Box 3160), Courtenay, BC V9J 1L2. ✆ **250/897-8735.** Fax 866/860-8735. www.coastaltrekresort.com. 12 units. Apr–Oct C$3,595 for 7 nights. Lower rates available Feb–Mar. Closed Nov–Jan. MC, V. Free parking; complimentary airport shuttle. Children not accepted. Pets not accepted. **Amenities:** Spa; hot tub; steam room; yoga; hiking; fitness assessment. *In room:* Hair dryer, no phone.

Crown Isle Resort ★★★   This resort breathes golf at every turn, and little wonder. Its 72-par, Platinum-rated course is suitable for golfers at all levels, and is the centerpiece of the entire development. You don't have to be a member to play, and you don't have to be a golf nut to stay. The villas, which come in a variety of configurations, are lavish and are more like small town houses. Finishing touches include two-sided gas fireplaces with marble surrounds and deep soaker Jacuzzis, over which there's a starlit ceiling that twinkles from blue to yellow. Most have fully equipped kitchens; some have wet bars and separate dining areas. Another building offers equally sumptuous hotel-style rooms, though slightly set back from the fairway. All guests have access to the resort's fitness center in the upscale clubhouse. There's a cozy pub, and if you're a steak connoisseur, the Silverado Steak House (see "Where to Dine," below) is a must.

399 Clubhouse Dr., Courtenay, BC V9N 9G3. ✆ **888/338-8439** or 250/703-5050. Fax 250/703-5051. www.crownisle.com. 90 units. May–Sept C$159 standard, C$319 villa/loft; Oct and Apr C$129 standard,

C$199–C$259 villa/loft; Nov–Mar C$129 standard, C$169–C$219 villa/loft. Golf and ski packages available. Extra person C$25. Children 17 and under stay free in parent's room. AE, MC, V. Free parking. **Amenities:** Two restaurants; pub; golf course; health club; business center; limited room service; laundry service; same-day dry cleaning. *In room:* TV/DVD, dataport, some Wi-Fi, coffeemaker, hair dryer, Jacuzzi.

Kingfisher Oceanside Resort & Spa ★★

Located 7km (4¹/₃ miles) south of Courtenay, this adult-oriented resort still hints as to its Best Western origins: The rooms tend to be extra-large and sport balconies or patios with ocean views. The decor, however, is more like an upscale Holiday Inn, with pine furniture and brightly colored linens. All this, however, is set to change when the entire resort starts to reinvent itself in the lot next door, eventually to the demise of the existing complex. Construction is slated to start late 2009. Meanwhile, the beachfront suites, which come with kitchenettes and heated bathroom floors, are still your best bet and worth the extra money both for the extra comfort and the ability to do your own thing meal-wise. Most have Jacuzzis. The impressive spa is why most people come here. Facilities include a heated outdoor pool with shoulder-massaging waterfall, a cave steam-room and sauna, as well as a broad range of spa services (at an additional cost) such as thalassotherapy wraps, hot stone massages, Reiki, reflexology, and facials. There's also a small and elegant yoga studio with various drop-in stretch classes. A complimentary shuttle runs between the resort and downtown, and to the Comox Valley Regional Airport, as well as to Mount Washington Alpine Resort (see "Mount Washington Alpine Resort," above). The Kingfisher Oceanside Restaurant is one of the better places to dine in the area (see "Where to Dine," below).

4330 Island Hwy. S., Courtenay, BCV9N 9R9. ✆ **800/663-7929** or 250/338-1323. Fax 250/338-0058. www.kingfisherspa.com. 64 units. C$170 oceanview room; C$220–C$350 beachfront suite; C$455 deluxe suite. Low-season discounts; spa, ski and golf packages available. Extra person C$25. AE, DC, DISC, MC, V. **Amenities:** Restaurant; lounge; golf nearby; unlit outdoor tennis court; health club and spa; canoe and kayak rentals; activities desk; business center; 24-hr. room service; laundry service; dry cleaning; Wi-Fi. *In room:* TV (w/DVD in beachfront suites), dataport, coffeemaker, hair dryer.

Old House Village Suites & Hotel ★

There's nothing old about this boutique hotel, which exudes West Coast style with its timber frame, locally made furniture, stonework, windows, and natural hues. The 51-sq. m (550-sq.-ft.) one-bedroom suites include a king-size bed, and top-notch amenities such as a flatscreen HDTV, fireplace, and a queen-size sofa bed. There's also a full kitchen, replete with modern appliances and a washer/dryer. The two-level Penthouse Suite is more like a mini-townhome with a loft bedroom. It's very romantic and a perfect place for an away-from-it-all getaway.

1800 Riverside Ln., Courtenay, BC V9N 8C7. ✆ **888/703-0202** or 250/703-0202. Fax 250/703-0209. www.oldhousevillage.com. 36 units. May–Sept and Christmas C$179 suite, C$259 penthouse; Oct–Apr C$159 suite, C$199 penthouse. Golf, kayaking, and ski packages available. Extra person C$20. Children 15 and under stay free in parent's room. MC, V. Free parking. **Amenities:** Restaurant. *In room:* TV/DVD, Wi-Fi, coffeemaker, microwave, hair dryer, iron, laundry.

Strathcona Park Lodge & Outdoor Education Centre ★★

Perched on the shores of Upper Campbell Lake, just outside the park's eastern boundary, this privately owned lodge provides not only a comfortable place to stay, from lodge rooms and cabins to multi-bedroom chalet-type accommodations, but also a variety of opportunities for exploring the surrounding wilderness. Staying here has been described as a cross between Outward Bound and Club Med, with no Internet access. Everyone from hard-core outdoor types to parents with young children can find an educational and adventure program to fit their niche, experiencing activities such as sailing, wilderness survival, rock climbing, backcountry hiking, fishing, swimming, canoeing, and kayaking. Special packages are available, and guides and instructors can be hired by the hour. Unless you know the park well, or are comfortably at ease trekking through backcountry, the lodge is definitely worth checking out.

25 miles west of Campbell River on Hwy. 28. Mailing address: Box 2160, Campbell River, BC V9W 5C5. 📞 250/286-3122. Fax 250/286-6010. www.strathcona.bc.ca. 39 units. C$40–C$88 chalet double with shared bathroom; C$139–C$160 double with private bathroom; C$175–C$480 cabin. 2–3 night minimum stay in cabins. Adventure packages and off-season discounts available. MC, V. Amenities: Restaurant; exercise room; sauna; canoe and kayak rentals; children's programs; massage; babysitting; coin-op laundry. In room: No phone.

WHERE TO DINE

Atlas Cafe Bar ★ Ⓥalue INTERNATIONAL   From this small restaurant in downtown Courtenay, you can travel the world food-wise with large portions of Mexican quesadillas, Greek spanakopitas, Thai satays, and Italian-style sandwiches on focaccia, as well as a good selection of vegetarian dishes. Dinner adds more substantial dishes such as stir-fries, noodle creations, fish, and roast beef. The cafe is busy from the moment it opens—locals know where to come for breakfast, and it has specialty coffees that put Starbucks on the back burner. Weekends, breakfast is served until 2pm. Although the wine list is limited, the bar is making quite a name for itself on the martini circuit and is a great place to relax over a beer or non-alcoholic shake.

250 6th St., Courtenay. 📞 **250/338-9838.** www.comoxvalleyrestaurants.ca/atlas.htm. Reservations accepted for parties of 6 or more. Main courses lunch C$7–C$15; dinner C$15–C$25. MC, V. Mon 8:30am–3:30pm; Tues–Sat 8:30am–10pm; Sun 8:30am–9pm.

Avenue Bistro INTERNATIONAL   The owners of Atlas opened this contemporary eatery on the main drag in downtown Comox. The ambiance is Art Deco chic and a shade impersonal, but the food is excellent. A daily fresh sheet details the selections of the day: always char grilled steaks, a fish entree—hope for the fresh Pacific halibut with roasted carrot ginger coulis when you visit—and a vegetarian option. The takeout menu is extensive and includes everything from tiger prawn tempura and pork spring rolls with cilantro mango tamarind dip to creative pizzas, pastas, and a very good seafood coconut curry that gives an exotic punch to salmon, halibut, prawns, and mussels. Many takeout items are available in house. On Sunday nights, go for the house specialty: perfectly primed, prime rib.

2064 Comox Ave., Comox. 📞 **250/890-9200.** www.avenuebistro.ca. Reservations accepted for parties of 6 or more. Main courses lunch C$9–C$15; dinner C$15–C$27. MC, V. Tues–Thurs 11am–9pm; Sat–Sun 9am–10pm; closed Mon.

Black Fin Pub ★★ PUB/CANADIAN   The view is splendid, stretching from a log-strewn beach, across the water, and on to the distant Beaufort Mountains. The atmosphere is what you want in a stylish pub: dark wood trim complemented by deep blue upholstery with nautical accents. There's a sunken dining area and plenty of chairs against the bar, and the menu includes quality pub dishes like burgers, sandwiches, wraps, and fish and chips, as well as grazing options such as crab and shrimp cakes (they're really worth the trip), a spicy beef satay, and chicken wings.

132 Port Augusta St., Comox. 📞 **250/339-5030.** Reservations accepted for parties of 4 or more in early evening. Main courses C$10–C$23. AE, MC, V. Sun–Thurs 11am–10pm; Fri–Sat 11am–11pm.

Kingfisher Oceanside Restaurant SEAFOOD/CONTINENTAL   Although the food doesn't always match the hype of the lavish menu descriptions, it is good enough to make this one of the region's better eateries. And the waterfront views are terrific. Because of its proximity to the spa, the menu includes a number of low-fat, low-calorie options. The poached halibut jardinière with a salad of grilled fruit, roasted nuts, and crumbled Stilton cheese is one of the tastier choices. If lean cuisine's not your thing, there are steaks, schnitzels, and lamb dishes, as well as vegetarian choices such as porcini-mushroom homemade ravioli served with fresh tomato and chipotle-pepper coulis with a fresh asiago crisp. The restaurant is justifiably proud of its all-you-can-eat Sunday brunch and periodic gala seafood buffets. Both are local favorites, so book space in advance.

4330 Island Hwy. S., 7km (4½ miles) south of Courtenay. ℭ 250/338-1323. www.kingfisherspa.com. Reservations recommended. Main courses C$15–C$28. AE, DC, DISC, MC, V. Mon–Fri 7am–9pm; Sat–Sun 7am–10pm.

Martine's Bistro INTERNATIONAL   This heritage building has been a gathering place since 1886, first as a community hall and today as a contemporary restaurant with glinting hardwood floors, clean-lined furnishings, and a pretty garden patio overlooking some sculptures. The food runs the gamut from tapas-style sharing dishes to a delicious curried chicken fettuccini, flavored with sweet peppers and a mild mango curry sauce—not a combination you would think of as compatible, but it sure is. The menu also offers seafood, steaks, and chicken dishes; they're best when featured on the daily fresh sheet. The house specialties hint to the owner's Dutch heritage: Try the Bitter Ballen, Dutch meat croquettes which crunch and then melt in your mouth.

1754 Beaufort Ave., Comox. ℭ **250/339-1199.** www.martinesbistro.com. Reservations accepted. Main courses C$15–C$27. MC, V. Daily 5–10pm.

Silverado Steak House ★ FINE DINING   The atrium-style fine-dining restaurant specializes in AAA-grade steak from Alberta, and serves it up alongside some spectacular views of the Beaufort Mountains as well as the 18th hole. Big eaters can opt for the 20-oz. Delmonico rib steak chop, while for more modest appetites there's a 6-oz. filet mignon. Both are exceptionally good with either a red wine garlic or blue cheese cream demi. There's also a good selection of local seafood such as oysters from nearby Talbot Cove, trout, halibut, and salmon.

399 Clubhouse Dr., Courtenay. ℭ **888/338-8439** or 250/703-5000. Reservations recommended. Main courses C$20–C$35. AE, MC, V. Daily 5–10pm.

Tomato Tomato ★★ WEST COAST   Located in the Old House Village complex, this is a consistently good restaurant, with vestiges of the original house that add to its ambiance: rough-hewn timbers crossing the open ceiling, four fireplaces, and picturesque wooden windows inside, and flower-filled gardens edging the Courtenay River outside. The menu is typical West Coast cuisine, offering steak and local seafood. The grilled Sooke trout sounds ordinary, but the pine-nut butter makes it outstanding. There's a very good herb-crusted halibut with Thai red curry sauce that manages to complement, not overwhelm, the fish, and the rack of lamb with black currant is a popular choice. This is the place to celebrate family gatherings and romantic notions.

1760 Riverside Lane, Courtenay. ℭ **250/338-5406.** www.tomatotomato.ca. Reservations recommended. Lunch C$12; dinner C$22. AE, MC, V. Mon–Thurs 11:30am–9:30pm; Fri–Sun 11:30am–10pm.

Toscanos Trattoria ★★ ITALIAN   This casual, convivial, licensed bistro is filled with cheerful colors—oranges, yellows, and reds—and wonderfully aromatic smells. The menu includes huge panini, excellent pastas, and specialty entrees such as chicken breast filled with ricotta, sun-dried tomatoes, and spinach, and served in a basil sauce. Save room for Italian classics such as tiramisu, and the mmm, so delicious, Mario Gelato. Toscanos Trattoria is where the trendies on a budget dine.

140 Port Augusta, Comox. ℂ **250/890-7575.** www.toscanos.ca. Reservations required. Main courses C$14–C$25. MC, V. Mon–Sat 11am–2pm and 5–9pm.

---

2 HORNBY & DENMAN ISLANDS

A haven for aging flower children and Vietnam draft dodgers who stayed north of the 49th parallel after amnesty, Hornby and Denman islands are an inspiration. Their distinct bohemian charm is a throwback to 1960s creativity, and their beautiful landscapes have made them one of British Columbia's most popular beach vacation destinations. If you really want to appreciate the rural isolation of these islands, visit in low season; Hornby's year-round population of 1,000 swells to as many as 10,000 in summer.

GETTING THERE
To get there, canoe or kayak across the narrow channel, or hop onto the ferry at Buckley Bay, just north of Fanny Bay. To get to Hornby Island, you must first cross Denman. The dozen daily trips to each island take 10 minutes one-way, and each leg of the journey costs C$7.55 adult, C$3.80 child, and C$18 regular vehicle.

VISITOR INFORMATION
On Denman Island, the Denman General Store, 1069 Northwest Rd., Denman Island, BC V0R 1T0 (ℂ **250-335-2293**) acts as the Denman/Hornby Visitor Services. It offers a free island guide, information on the small one and two-bedroom B&Bs, as well as a brochure listing the *many* small arts and crafts galleries. You can also get information at www.denmanisland.com and www.hornbyisland.com.

GETTING AROUND
The islands are great for bicycling. Bring bikes on the ferry or contact **Denman Island Cycles & Repairs** (ℂ **250/335-1759**) for rentals; they can meet you at the ferry or wherever you may be staying.

EXPLORING THE ISLANDS
Denman
On Denman, beautiful sandstone and gravel shores are full of life: oysters, rock crabs, clams, eagles, and seabirds. There's good salmon fishing, particularly off the south end. Off the north shores, you can kayak across to **Sandy Island Provincial Marine Park,** a group of beautiful wooded islands with limited camping (ℂ **250/334-4600**). **Denman Hornby Canoes & Kayaks,** 4005 East Rd. (ℂ **250/335-0079;** www.denmanpaddling. ca), offers rentals (half-day C$45; full-day C$65) and custom-guided excursions ranging from 2½ hours (C$75) to a popular 4-hour trip (C$95) and a full-day excursion (C$115). These folks also offer a modest B&B, geared for paddlers. If nothing else, head for **Fillongley Provincial Park** on the east side of the island. It features an unspoiled sand and shell beach plus fabulous views of Texada Island, and the snow-capped mainland Coast Mountain range with a miles-long foreshore is edged by stands of old growth Douglas and Grand fir and red cedars. The trail is an easy half-hour circuit.

You need no other excuse to visit Hornby than **Tribune Bay Provincial Park.** Here, the sea has beaten the soft rock faces into dramatic cave and hoodoo formations. **Helliwell Bay Provincial Park** is worth exploring, both for the trails along the bluff and to see the thousands of nesting birds tucked into the side of the cliffs. Hornby's two claims to fame are as the only spot in Canada where you'll fine certain types of butterflies, including Flora Inlet, and being one of only two places in the world where divers can count on finding primitive deep-sea six-gill shark swimming in shallow waters.

WHERE TO STAY & DINE

Because of the islands' popularity, accommodations can be hard to come by, so even if you're sleeping under canvas, book at least 3 months in advance. There are also few places to eat. On Hornby, check out some of the tiny eateries at Ringside Market, the new Zocalo Market, or head for the **Thatch Pub,** 4305 Shingle Spit Rd. (© **250/335-0136**), open daily and offering casual pub fare. It's the only waterside watering hole on the island, not to mention the only place with ATM access and a liquor store, and is a popular local nightspot, with live music Friday and Saturday. Notice the tabletops; they represent the work of more than 20 local artists. Look further, and you'll notice imaginative art throughout. There's a tiny licensed bistro with very limited open hours at the **Denman Island Guest House** (© **250/335-2688**) in "downtown." The guesthouse, a 1912 heritage farmhouse, has a mix of accommodations with shared bathrooms as well as campsites. Rates range from C$15 to C$48 a night depending on where you hang your shingle.

Hornby Island Resort   Book months in advance if you want to get a spot at this popular waterfront resort, largely because it's the only show in town. The rustic cottage rooms are plainly furnished and come with small bathrooms and full kitchen; the campsites are fairly private, separated by roses and honeysuckle plants, and well-maintained. Each has a picnic table, a fire pit, and optional electrical plug-ins. Campground facilities include hot showers and laundry.

4305 Shingle Spit Rd. (next to the ferry terminal), Hornby Island, BC V0R 1Z0. © **250/335-0136.** Fax 250/335-9136. hornbyislandresort@hornbyisland.com. 2 units, 2 cottages, 10 campsites. C$110 double; C$35 campsite; C$1,100 weekly (only in summer) cabin, C$135 per night off-season cabin. MC, V **Amenities:** Restaurant; pub; tennis; laundry; boat moorage; Wi-Fi. *In-room:* TV.

3 CAMPBELL RIVER, GOLD RIVER & TAHSIS, NOOTKA & KYOQUOT SOUNDS

Once you hit mid-island, the entire topography starts to shift. Campbell River is the last major town you come across, and is the gateway to Vancouver Island's wilder nature. Head towards Gold River, and you start to see how important the island's inner waterways are to its economy. Go farther to Tahsis, Nootka, and Kyoquot Sounds, and you're in some of the most beautiful coastal waters in the world—the places where the Spanish and Captain Cook first explored, and that are now opening up to varied ecotourism activities.

Although you could take the fast inland highway, Hwy. 19, north from Courtenay for the 48km (30-mile) drive to Campbell River, the scenic and more leisurely route along Hwy. 19A, also called the **Oceanside Route,** is far more rewarding. Exit Hwy. 19 at **Miracle Beach,** and head north on Hwy. 19A. Follow the starfish signs past scenic coves and through small, picturesque communities, many of which have small galleries and art studios to browse through. Bring your camera and enjoy weaving along the water's edge. Check out **www.gonanaimo.com/nanaimo/oceanside-driving-tour.html** for details. Once in Campbell River, you'll be in a true North Island community with roots deep in lumber and fishing. The town center is marked by the high rigger *Big Mike,* a carved wooden lumberjack swinging from a harness at the top of a spar pole. There's also a new Torii Gate in Sequoia Park that was a celebratory gift from Ishikari, the city's twin sister in Japan. In Shinto tradition, the gate represents recognition of a special location or place. Although it looks somewhat anomalous, perhaps no more so than the reciprocal gift of a totem pole that now stands in Ishikari.

The renowned **Tyee Club** attracts fishing enthusiasts from around the world in their pursuit of landing excessively large Chinook salmon. Every year between July and September, the Campbell River, designated a British Columbia Heritage River, swells with both visitors and fish, as salmon pass through the mile-wide passage, known as the **Discovery Channel,** en route to spawning grounds in northerly rivers. The area has historically produced vast hauls of incredibly large fish; thus Campbell River has become known as the "Salmon Fishing Capital of the World."

But today, as salmon numbers diminish, catch-and-release programs are in force, and those leading fishing expeditions are billing them more as wildlife adventures in an attempt to diversify. Some local operators have already been successful in this regard. Day trips aboard the **MV *Uchuck III,*** from Gold River to the Tahsis, Nootka, and Kyoquot sounds, are great family fun, and mini cruises to Bute Inlet or Kingcome Inlet aboard the **MV *Aurora Explorer*** reveal parts of British Columbia many visitors never get to see.

Essentials
Getting There
BY CAR Driving distances up the center of Vancouver Island are fast and easy with the new inland highway (Hwy. 19) between Nanaimo and Campbell River. Campbell River is 264km (164 miles) north of Victoria (about 2½ hours' worth of driving); 153km (95 miles) north of Nanaimo (about 1½ hours); and 48km (30 miles) north of Courtenay (about half an hour).

BY PLANE Commercial airlines fly into the Campbell River and District Regional Airport (② 250/923-5012; www.crairport.ca). **Air Canada Jazz** (② 888/247-2262; www.flyjazz.ca), **Pacific Coastal Airlines** (② 800/663-2872; www.pacific-coastal.com), and **Central Mountain Air** (② 888/865-8585; www.flycma.com), operate daily scheduled flights from Vancouver, Calgary, and Victoria. Car-rental companies at the airport include **Budget** (② 800/668-9688 or 250/923-4283; www.budget.com) and **National Car & Alamo Car Rental** (② 888/387-4747 or 250/923-1234; www.nationalvictoria.com). Smaller carriers, such as **Coril Air** (② 888/287-8366 or 250/287-8371; www.corilair.com), provide harbor-to-harbor service between Campbell River and several small island communities. **Kenmore Air** (② 800/543-9595; www.kenmoreair.com) flies from Seattle Harbor on a seasonal basis.

BY BUS **Island Coach Lines,** operated by **Laidlaw Coach Lines** (© 800/318-0818 or 250/287-7151; www.victoriatours.com), runs daily service from Victoria to Port Hardy, stopping in Nanaimo, Campbell River, and other towns along the way. **Greyhound Canada** (© 800/661-8747; www.greyhound.ca) handles reservations. The one-way fare from Victoria to Campbell River is C$51 for adults. From Nanaimo to Campbell River, it's C$26 for adults. Fares for seniors are 10% less; fares for children 5 to 11 are 50% less. The trip from Victoria takes 5½ hours, while the trip from Nanaimo takes 3½ hours.

Visitor Information

The **Campbell River Visitor Information Centre** is located at 1235 Shoppers Row (P.O. Box 44), Campbell River, BC V9W 5B6 (© 866/830-1113 or 250/830-0411; www.campbellriver.travel or www.northcentralisland.com).

Getting Around

In Campbell River itself, **Campbell River Airporter & Taxi Service** (© 250/286-3000) offers door-to-door service anywhere. As well, **Campbell River Transit** (© 250/287-7433) operates regular bus service.

Fabulous Fishing

Campbell River is an excellent home base for numerous sport-fishing excursions, and there are several quality outfitters and charter-boat companies. These include **Coastal Island Fishing Adventures,** 663 Glenalan Rd. (© 888/225-9776 or 250/923-5831; www.coastalislandfishing.com). Rates are from C$110 an hour (not per person), inclusive of gear and tackle and your choice of a Grady White or Trophy vessel, or a 17-foot open Boston Whaler at C$75 per hour. **Sea Beyond Adventures,** 526 Thulin St. (© 250/287-4497) charges C$120 per hour for a minimum of 5 hours in a covered 24-foot Grady White, C$600 per day for freshwater fishing, and if you're looking for a Tyee rower, they'll do that too, at C$500.

Virtually every hotel and inn has a recommendation or package to do with fishing, so ask when you make your reservation, and the Info Centre has a comprehensive directory to fishing guides. As the largest outdoor store on Vancouver Island, **River Sportsmen,** 2115 Island Hwy. (© 800/663-7117 or 250/286-1017), is an excellent one-stop resource for the latest fishing information, as well as a huge selection of outdoor, camping, and fishing gear.

Charter companies will handle licensing requirements, but if you decide to fish independently, **nonresident fishing licenses** are available at outdoor recreation stores throughout Campbell River, including **Painter's Lodge Holiday & Fishing Resort,** where you can also watch all the action from beautiful decks (see "Where to Stay," below). Saltwater licenses cost C$14 per day; C$26 for 3 days and C$39 for 5 days. Freshwater licenses cost C$21 per day or C$53 for 8 days. Fees are reduced for BC and Canada residents.

If private charters are still your preference, be aware that most are geared for fishing. That said, **Rippingale's Fishing,** 2330 Steelhead Rd., Campbell River (© 800/988-8242 or 250/286-7290; www.rippingalesfishing.com), offers all-inclusive 3-night packages ranging from C$1,700 per person.

Where to Stay

Anchor Inn & Suites (Kids) If you're looking for the extraordinary, the inn's five themed suites will satiate the most whimsical dreams with decor that runs from exotic

Cruising the Queen Charlotte Strait

A rather unique option exists if you want to explore the island's coastal communities. Book a trip aboard the MV *Aurora Explorer*, a 135-foot landing craft that plies the western waterways on 5-day excursions to the remote inlets of the Queen Charlotte Strait. The MV *Aurora Explorer* is the only overnight passenger-freight vessel of its kind, sailing on an itinerary that is set by the tidal currents and the cargo she carries on her open deck. This might include supplies for solitary island retreats, refrigerators for First Nations villages, heavy equipment for a logging outpost, or mail and newspapers for a floating post office.

Passenger quarters, housed just below the main lounge and galley, sleep 12 in cramped but hospitable bunk-style cabins. The crew is friendly, and food is hearty and constant, with a daily supply of fresh-baked cookies and bread. Most passengers are active retirees or 40-something soft adventurers who come from all walks of life, so entertainment relies on conversation, a good book, the awesome scenery, unexpected wildlife, and being part of a working vessel in action, watching the crew on the deck below hoist that winch and tote that bale—sometimes at 4am. Usually, the schedule includes stops at heritage sites, abandoned villages, or even a pebbly beach for an impromptu BBQ (if trolling for supper has proved successful). So in addition to a seafaring adventure, there are opportunities for shore explorations.

From May to mid-September, all-inclusive fares start at C$2,225 a person; from mid-September through October and from the end of March through April, all-inclusive fares are C$1,690 to C$1,950. The MV *Aurora Explorer* does not sail November through February. For information, contact Marine Link Tours, P.O. Box 451, Campbell River, BC V9W 5C1 (© **250/286-3347;** www.marinelinktours.com).

Arabian and wild African to an Arctic-inspired room with igloo-style bed canopy. The English is twee with its carriage bed; the Western is great for kids, as they have bunk beds hidden in a "jail cell." More standard rooms are available, each sporting ocean views and comfortably furnished with a choice of queen or king-size beds. The restaurant serves all three meals, and in the evening adds a sushi dimension to tried-and-true regular fare of pasta, chicken, and steak.

261 Island Hwy., Campbell River, BC V9W 2B3. © **800/663-7227** or 250/286-1131. Fax 250/287-4055. www.anchorinn.ca. 76 units. C$139 double; C$249–C$289 theme-room double. Extra person C$10. Theme, honeymoon, golf, and fishing packages available. AE, MC, V. Free parking. **Amenities:** Restaurant; lounge; indoor pool; golf course nearby; exercise room; Jacuzzi; business center; coin-op laundry; laundry service; dry cleaning. *In room:* TV, Wi-Fi, fridge, coffeemaker, hair dryer, iron.

Coast Discovery Inn & Marina Adjacent to a busy shopping plaza right on the main drag, this is the only deluxe hotel you'll find downtown. As you might expect, it's a bit noisy by day, but since nothing much happens in Campbell River post-10pm, the location doesn't affect a quiet night's sleep. Guest rooms and suites are nondescript, though roomy enough and comfortable. All guest rooms have views of the harbor, and suites have welcome extras like Jacuzzis. The marina can accommodate 70 yachts of up to 150 feet, as well as smaller pleasure crafts. Moorage can be arranged through the marina. Guided fishing tours are also available. There's a restaurant, and a pub that features live evening entertainment Thursday through Saturday.

975 Shoppers Row, Campbell River, BC V9W 2C4. (© **800/663-1144** or 250/287-7155. Fax 250/287-2213. www.coasthotels.com. 90 units. May–Sept C$138 standard, C$154 superior, C$174 suite; Oct–Apr C$119 standard, C$134 superior, C$156 suite. Extra person C$10. MC, V. Free parking. Pets accepted (C$20). **Amenities:** Restaurant; lounge; golf course nearby; exercise room; Jacuzzi; 24-hr. room service; same-day dry cleaning; Internet. *In room:* AC, TV w/pay movies, Wi-Fi, minibar, coffeemaker, hair dryer, iron.

Haig-Brown House   Prolific writer, avid outdoorsman, and respected judge, Roderick Haig-Brown was also one of British Columbia's most spirited conservationists (check out www.haigbrowninstitute.org). It was largely because of his efforts that the Fraser River, which runs down through the BC interior to Vancouver, was never dammed. From his 1923 farmhouse, set amidst 8 hectares (20 acres) of gardens beside the Campbell River, he wrote ardently about fly-fishing, resource management, and preserving BC's natural environment. Fully restored as a BC Heritage Property, Haig-Brown's home is a delightful B&B where you can enjoy big country breakfasts while looking out over the orchard and garden to the river. For many anglers, staying here is like a pilgrimage of sorts. Guest rooms are decorated with comfy furnishings, although nothing too palatial. Guests share bathroom facilities.

2250 Campbell River Rd., Campbell River, BC V9W 4N7. (© **250/286-6646.** 3 units. May to late Oct C$80–C$100 double. Extra person C$20. MC, V. Closed in winter. Young children not accepted. **Amenities:** Lounge. *In room:* No phone.

Heron's Landing (Finds)   This lovely Bavarian-style hotel, formerly known as the Bachmair, has been refurbished and updated to create a European boutique ambience. All rooms and one-bedroom suites, while standardized in terms of amenities, are decorated with tasteful antiques, hardwood floors, oriental rugs, coordinated linens, and drapes. Many have cozy living areas and full kitchens, making Heron's Landing a good choice for longer stays. Guests have access to the restaurant, pub, and other facilities across the street at the Best Western Austrian Chalet Village ((© **800/667-7207** or 250/923-4231), a first-class second choice if Heron's Landing is full.

(Finds)   **Camping**

Miracle Beach Provincial Park ((© **250/954-4600**) is one of BC's best parks. Native legend speaks to a supernatural stranger who appeared on the beach and miraculously transformed a Native princess into Mitlenatch Island. True or not, the beach itself is appropriately named, with countless tidal pools; warm sand; and soft, undulating waves. Add to this roomy campsites beneath tall, sun-dappled trees; forested trails down to the beach; hot showers; and playgrounds, and you've got the makings of a great family camping holiday. A seasonal visitor center has nature displays and park interpreters. For reservations, call Discover Camping (© **800/689-9025** or 604/689-9025; www.discovercamping.ca.

492 South Island Hwy., Campbell River, BC V9W 1A5. ☏ **888/923-2849** or 250/923-2848. Fax 250/923-2849. www.heronslandinghotel.com. 30 units. C$139 standard; C$159 1-bedroom; C$300–C$500 penthouse. AE, MC, V. Indoor parking. Small pets accepted C$25. **Amenities:** Restaurant; bar next door; golf course nearby; coin-op washers and dryers. *In room:* TV, dataport, Wi-Fi, kitchen, fridge, coffeemaker, hair dryer, iron.

Painter's Lodge Holiday & Fishing Resort ★★   An international favorite of avid fishermen and celebrities, Painter's Lodge has welcomed the likes of Bob Hope, Julie Andrews, Goldie Hawn, and the Prince of Luxembourg. Its location overlooking Discovery Passage is awesome, and its rustic grandeur has a terrific West Coast ambience, with comfortable lounges, large decks, and spacious guest rooms and suites decorated in natural wood and outdoorsy colors. Wrapped in windows, the lodge's restaurant, **Legends,** boasts a view of the Passage from every table (see "Where to Dine," below). One of the neatest dining experiences is to take the speedboat trip (10 minutes in each direction) over to **April Point Resort & Spa on Quadra Island** (see "Where to Stay," "Quadra Island," later in this chapter) for a pre-dinner martini at their sushi bar before returning to Legends for the catch of the day. The trip is included in hotel rates.

1625 MacDonald Rd. (P.O. Box 460, Dept 2), Campbell River, BC V9W 4S5. ☏ **800/663-7090** or 250/286-1102. Fax 250/286-0158. www.painterslodge.com. 94 units. Apr–Oct C$175–C$449 double. Extra person C$20. AE, DC, MC, V. Closed mid-Oct to early Apr. **Amenities:** Restaurant; pub; lounge; large heated outdoor pool; golf course nearby; 2 outdoor tennis courts; health club; 2 Jacuzzis; children's center; activities desk; babysitting; guided salmon fishing; whale-watching; wildlife tours. *In room:* TV, Wi-Fi, coffeemaker, hair dryer.

Sonora Resort ★★★ Finds   Once known only as an upscale fishing lodge, Sonora Resort has undergone a multi-million-dollar uplift to become one of the region's most sought-after retreats, and every season it adds another amenity, be it a spa, new grizzly bear tours, or a lodge. Fishing is still a primary activity—the resort has a fleet of well-equipped Grady White boats—but with an indoor tennis court, 12-seat movie theater, virtual golf, a luxurious spa, hiking trails, and zodiac eco-tours, Sonora has high-end appeal. Lodges offer a variety of differently themed accommodations from luxurious multi-roomed cottages to hotel-like suites and guest rooms. Bedding is plush, bathrooms feature quality amenities, and furnishings are warm and inviting. The all-inclusive rates cover use of all resort facilities, all meals, and even alcohol. Spa treatments, fishing trips, and tours are extra, as are its private transfers to the island. Sonora can provide a boat shuttle from Campbell River, as well as direct flights from Vancouver and Seattle via its private, state-of-the-art Agusta Bell helicopters. Kenmore Air and SeaAir Seaplanes can also get you there from Seattle and Vancouver respectively. Kids are welcome. *Tip:* Be sure to be dockside when the boats return after a day's fishing; the discards after cleaning the fish attract a gathering of harbor seals all playing and vying for these easy-to-get delicacies.

Sonora Resort, Sonora Island. Mailing address: 105–5360 Airport Rd. S., Richmond, BC V7B 1B4. ☏ **888/576-6672** or 604/233-0460. Fax 604/233-0465. www.sonoraresort.com. 87 units. July to mid–Sept C$825 per couple per day, C$525 children ages 5–19 or C$350 when sharing parent's room; May–June and mid-Sept to late Oct C$575–C$650 per couple per day, C$356–C$412 children ages 5–19 or C$237–C$275 when sharing parent's room. Closed Nov–Apr. **Amenities:** Restaurant; outdoor pool; golf nearby; tennis; gym; spa; Jacuzzi; sauna; kayaks; game room; movie theater; concierge; 24-hr. room service; laundry; yoga/pilates; fishing; hiking; fly-fishing pond; eco-tours. *In room:* A/C, TV/DVD, stocked bar fridge.

Baan Thai THAI CUISINE   It's so refreshing to find a great ethnic eatery away from the big city lights, and this one is as good as it gets. In fact, the menu is so popular it hasn't changed much over the years. You can always judge a quality Thai restaurant by its pad thai, and this one is extremely flavorful, as are the curries. If your palette isn't up for the fire of Thai spices, all dishes can be modified to suit. The 40-seat saffron-colored restaurant is located over a storefront on Shoppers Row (Campbell River's main drag). The entrance is easy to miss, but let the aromatic smells be your guide. Tables are on the small side, but close quarters simply add to the intimate atmosphere of this eatery. There's also a rooftop patio.

1090B Shoppers Row. ✆ **250/286-4853.** Reservations recommended. Main courses C$12–C$15. MC, V. Mon–Fri 11:30am–2pm and 5–9pm; Sat 5–9pm; closed Sun and Mon lunch.

Fusilli Grill ITALIAN FUSION   Chances are that if you're at any catered event around town, these folks are the cooks behind the scenes; yet their 56-seat restaurant is so unassuming, at first glance you would have a hard time believing them capable of such fare. But it is the best Italian food in town, in large part because all its pastas, breads, and dressings are made in-house, from scratch. Even when they tackle another ethnic cuisine, noodles are usually somewhere on the plate. The Vietnamese-style prawns, chorizo, and scallions with chile, ginger, and fennel is a delicious example, as is the shrimp and scallop stirfry. The takeout menus are great value: A three-course pasta lunch is C$8.50; dinner is C$10.

220 Dogwood St. ✆ **250/830-0090.** www.fusilligrill.bc.ca. Reservations recommended. Main courses C$7–C$12 lunch; C$12–C$28 dinner. DC, MC, V. Tues–Fri 11am–9:30pm; Sat–Mon 4:30–9pm.

Harbour Grill ★★ STEAK & SEAFOOD   You wouldn't expect to find the best restaurant in town at a shopping mall, but that's exactly where Harbour Grill set up shop. Thankfully, the restaurant faces the waterside Discovery Harbour Marina, rather that a hoard of retail outlets, so the mall experience doesn't touch on the dining experience one iota—except for always being able to find a parking spot! Grab a window seat and you're likely to see cruise ships pass by on their way to the Inside Passage. Food-wise, Harbour Grill is classic fine dining with crisp white linens, attentive staff, and traditional French-influenced dishes such as veal Oscar and duck a l'orange. Steaks (Alberta grain-fed AAA beef only) are the house specialty: Peppered, bearnaised, *la Wellington*—you name it— and then there's its gi-normous Chateaubriand, done to perfection. The wine list features many VQA wines from BC as well as a selection from France, Australia, and California.

In the Discovery Harbour Centre, 112–1334 Island Hwy. ✆ **250/287-4143.** www.harbourgrill.com. Reservations recommended. Main courses C$27–C$38. AE, DC, MC, V. Daily 5:30–10pm.

Legends Dining Room ★ WESTCOAST/CONTINENTAL   Located at Painter's Lodge, this restaurant's only open in season, which is a shame. Floor-to-ceiling windows afford terrific views of the comings and goings across Discovery Passage and an intimate fine-dining area. The menu is varied, and, not surprisingly, includes many fish and seafood specialties. This is, after all, a fishing lodge. The perennial favorite? The crab and salmon cakes, with chipotle garlic aioli and sweetcorn vinaigrette. You can't go wrong with the halibut, which always has a different twist, whether it's with purple mustard or sautéed tandoori-spiced almonds. If you've just come off the water and are looking for something more casual, the Tyee Pub is an informal option with an oversize deck offering ringside seats to the water. ***Note:*** The restaurant often opens at 5am to get fishing enthusiasts off to a good start.

Riptide Marine Pub & Grill PUB/WEST COAST   If you're exploring the Discovery Harbour Shopping Plaza, this is a great pit stop for lunch, snacks, and dinner, or just a drink over appies. There's nothing unexpected here; traditional burgers, salads, and pizza go alongside more substantial meals like rack of lamb, filet mignon, salmon, and even lobster tail—an item that seems a bit ambitious for this style of eatery. But its smart-casual style, and its location next to the bustling marina, attracts boaters, walkers, and folks in transit to another island via water taxi or seaplane. Showers, laundry facilities, and a liquor store are part of the complex.

Discovering Harbour Shopping Plaza, 1340 Island Hwy. ℭ **250/830-0044.** Main courses C$17–C$23. AE, MC, V. Tues–Sat 11am–1am; Sun–Mon 11am–midnight.

GOLD RIVER

The traditional territory of the Mowachaht and Muchalaht peoples, it wasn't until the 1860s, when the Chinese started pulling gold from the river, that Gold River started to find its way onto maps and into public awareness. Even then, when the gold ran out, it would take almost 100 years for lumberjacks to arrive and start harvesting the forested hills. When a pulp mill opened here in 1965, **Gold River** was literally built out of the wilderness—a British Columbia "instant community," whose existence was predicated on forestry and economic need. Gold River was Canada's first all-electric town and the first to have underground wiring. Since the pulp mill closed in 1998, however, Gold River has been forced to reinvent itself in order to survive. Looking to its natural resources once again, the community now is creating an ecotourism industry that includes salt-water and fresh-water fishing and the opportunities that abound in the surrounding wilderness. If you're just passing through, at least try a hike on the **Peppercorn Trail;** it's an easy, well-groomed path that takes about 40 minutes and follows Gold and Heber rivers. Watch for whitewater kayakers taking on the eddys.

Essentials
Getting There
Aside from Tofino and Ucluelet (see chapter 7), Gold River is the only community on Vancouver Island's west coast reachable by a well-maintained paved road. It's 92km (57 miles) west of Campbell River along **Hwy. 28;** driving there takes about 1½ hours. You pass through spectacular **Strathcona Provincial Park** and on to the remote **Muchalaht Inlet.**

Visitor Information
For more information and maps on Gold River and the surrounding area, visit the **Gold River Visitor Information Centre** at 499 Muchalat Dr., Gold River, BC V0P 1G0 (ℭ **250/283-2418** [mid-May to Labor Day] or 250/283-2202 [Labor Day to mid-May]; www.goldriverbc.ca).

Exploring Gold River
Sport fishing, rugged scenery, and abundant wildlife have always been the region's trademarks, and since the pulp mill closed in 1998, these natural attractions are becoming the center of a tourist-based local economy. One of the area's largest and most reliable fishing outfitters, particularly for saltwater salmon, halibut, and cod, is **Nootka Sound Sports**

Fishing Charters (✆ 877/283-7194 or 250/338-7679; www.nootkasoundfish.com). Trips start at C$80 per hour for up to two people; 5-hour minimum. Additional passengers incur a nominal extra charge.

If fishing's not your thing, there's kayaking, hiking, and wildlife viewing, as well as spelunking in the **Upana Caves**, 27km (17 miles) northwest of Gold River. A well-marked trail connects the five caves, which include the two-chambered Main Cave with a waterfall at the end of one passage, the marble-smooth Resurgence Cave, with its toothy outcrops, and the spiraling Corner Cave. There are a number of modest restaurants, B&Bs, and motels, which makes Gold River a good base from which to explore places like **Nootka Sound,** especially if you opt to experience the *Uchuck III,* a working passenger and freight vessel offering scenic tours (see below). Local helicopters (Vancouver Island Helicopters, ✆ **250/283-7616**) and floatplanes (Air Nootka, ✆ **250/283-2255**) provide the closest air access to popular Hot Springs Cove.

Where to Stay & Dine
Ridgeview Motor Inn   Clean, simply furnished, and comfortable, this motor inn is pretty standard fare, and while it may not win any awards for style, the folks who run it are friendly and knowledgeable about the area. This is the first choice for most visitors, especially fishing enthusiasts; the inn has a fish-cleaning station. Rates include continental breakfast and some rooms have microwaves, kitchenettes, and valley views. The Ridge Neighbourhood pub/restaurant (✆ **250/283-2461**) is next door.

395 Donner Court, Gold River, BC V0P 1G0. ✆ **800/989-3393** or 250/283-2277. Fax 250/283-7611. www. ridgeview-inn.com. 44 units. C$99–C$109 standard; C$135 suite. Extra person C$10. AE, MC. **Amenities:** Dining area; golf nearby; activity desk. *In room:* TV, fridge, microwave (in some), coffeemaker.

TAHSIS, NOOTKA & KYOQUOT SOUNDS
If you decide to venture farther west from Gold River, you'll explore the coastal communities in and around **Tahsis, Nootka, and Kyoquot sounds**—some of the most beautiful coastal scenery in the world. Kyoquot is the ancestral home of the Mowachaht/Muchalaht people of the Nuu-chah-nulth (formerly Nootka) nation. A little farther along, the almost uninhabited First Nations village of historic Yuquot (Friendly Cove) is where British explorer Captain James Cook first came ashore in 1778, making this area, in effect, the birthplace of British Columbia.

Tahsis is the only community that's accessible by a well-maintained gravel road, affectionately dubbed the Tree to Sea Drive. Take this road to the Upana Caves that lie just before Bull Lake Summit. As you near Tahsis, you'll find the Leiner River Bouldering Trail, a short loop trail along the narrow valley of Leiner River, as well as a longer (4-hr.) trail to The Lookout over Tahsis Inlet. Typical of those in rugged coastal communities, most visitor services are geared to wilderness tourism. Hiking the rainforests and coastline is big business here, as are fishing and wildlife viewing.

Essentials
Getting There
Although Tahsis can also be reached by gravel road, the best way to visit Tahsis, or explore Nootka and Kyoquot sounds, is aboard the *Uchuck III* (see below) or via seaplane (Air Nootka, ✆ **250/283-2255**). Both operate out of Gold River.

Visitor Information

For maps and information, contact Gold River Information Centre (499 Muchalat Dr., Gold River, BC V0P 1G0; ☎ **250/283-2418** [mid-May to Labor Day] or 250/283-2202 [Labor Day to mid-May]; www.goldriverbc.ca), or the **Tahsis Chamber of Commerce** (36 Rugged Mountain Rd., Box 278, Tahsis, BC V0P 1X0; ☎ **250/934-6425**).

Exploring The Area

Uchuck III ★★★   Exploring this coastline aboard the workboat MV *Uchuck III* is not only a treat for the whole family, but good value for the money. It's a much more cost-effective option than chartering a private boat, and you'll see, hear, taste, and smell more along the way than you will in the more "sanitized" environment of a private vessel. A converted World War II minesweeper, the MV *Uchuck III* sails year-round on day-long and overnight stays. Depending on the day and time of year, your destination might be **Tahsis, Zeballos, Kyoquot,** or **Yuquot** (Friendly Cove). As the workhorse of the sounds, and the lifeline of many of these isolated communities, the MV *Uchuck III* also puts in at remote logging camps and fishing ports, picking up passengers and offloading anything from stoves to Oh Henry! bars.

Nootka Sound Services, Gold River. ☎ **250/283-2325**. www.mvuchuck.com. Year-round day-trip rates are C$70 for adults, C$65 seniors, C$35 children 7–12, free for children 6 and under; overnight trip rates C$240–$335 adults, C$90–C$145 children 7–12, free for children 6 and under. There are no seniors' rates on overnight trips.

Where to Stay & Dine

Most of the lodges in Nootka Sound have a definite fishing bent, either floating in protected coves, operating as part home/part one- and two-bedroom inns, or as small executive-style homes for high rollers. Many close in winter.

Maquinna Resort   Located next door to the Maquinna Mall, this resort offers the conveniences of a tackle and bait store, postal services, a small gallery, and a bakery. It also offers well-maintained, quality hotel rooms, well furnished with comfortable beds, as well as a selection of self-catering one- and two-bedroom condos. The hotel corner rooms are the most spacious and have great ocean views. The resort has a lively pub (☎ 250/934-5522), and a licensed bistro-style restaurant serving seafood dishes, steaks, chicken, pasta, and burgers. **Nootka Sound Charters** (☎ 250/934-5558) operates fishing trips out of here. Divers, however, need to head over to **Tahtsa Dive Charters** (☎ 866/934-6365 or 250/934-6365), now based on Wharf Street.

1400 S. Maquinna Dr. (Box 400), Tahsis, BC V0P 1X0. [tel **250/934-6367**. Fax 250/934-7884. www. maquinnaresort.com. 24 units. May to end Oct C$115–C$135 standard room, C$250 condo w/kitchen. MC, V. Free parking. **Amenities:** Restaurant; pub; laundry; marina; Wi-Fi. *In room:* TV, no phone.

Tahsis Motel   Very basic but at least clean, this motel is up to date and provides creature comforts that will probably feel luxurious after a day on the water or trekking through rainforest. The Millhouse Café serves breakfast, lunch, and dinner—the burgers and pizzas are safe bets. They're also available in the Spar Tree Pub. Bag lunches are provided by request.

187 Head Bay Rd., Tahsis, BC V0P 1X0. ☎ **250/934-6318**. Fax 250/934-7808. www.cablerocket. com/~tahsismotel. 11 units. C$80 double. Extra person C$20. MC, V. Pets C$5. **Amenities:** Pub/restaurant; liquor store; convenience store; high-speed Internet. *In room:* TV, no phone.

(Moments) Nootka Trail

Hugging the west coast of Nootka Island, the Nootka Trail is world-famous for its wilderness hiking experience featuring long beaches, secluded bays, and spectacular headlands jutting into the Pacific Ocean. Unlike its tough cousin, the West Coast Trail (see chapter 7), this is a relatively easy hike that never rises more than 50m (164 ft.) above sea level. Along the way, you're likely to see whales and old native middens. Hikers can take a water taxi to either trail head (Louie Bay or Friendly Cove) from Tahsis or can arrive by floatplane from Gold River. Purchasing a tide guide before your trip is mandatory, as you can use low tides to follow the beach flats. Most people take 4 days or longer to complete the hike.

4 QUADRA & CORTES ISLANDS

Affectionately called the Discovery Islands, Quadra and Cortes islands march to the beat of a different drummer. Both are richly pastoral with stretches of sandy beaches to explore and meandering roads that lead to hidden coves, artist studios, and sudden dead-ends that may or may not have an overgrown path to the beach. Quadra is more mainstream, probably because of its proximity to Campbell River, while Cortes is a haven for those walking the talk of living a holistic, alternative lifestyle.

ESSENTIALS
Getting There

The islands are accessible only by water. To reach Cortes by public transit, you'll need to cross to Quadra Island.

BC Ferries (© **250-386-3431**) operates year-round between these islands with 18 sailings from Campbell River and Quadra Island. The crossing takes 10 minutes and costs C$7.55 adult, C$3.80 child, and C$19 standard-size vehicle. To get to Cortes Island, you need to travel to Quadra Island for the connector to Cortes. There are half a dozen daily trips both ways between Quadra and Cortes islands. This crossing takes 45 minutes and costs C$8.70 adult, C$4.35 child, and C$22 standard vehicle. All fares are round-trip. *Note:* The Ship's crew collects fares, so either pay via credit card for a through fare from Campbell River to Cortes Island, or have enough cash on you to bunny-hop from Quadra Island to Cortes Island.

Visitor Information

There is no visitor center on Quadra, though you can check out www.quadraisland.ca, or the **Campbell River Visitor Information Centre** (© **866/830-1113** or 250/830-1113).

EXPLORING THE ISLANDS
Quadra Island

Touring Quadra Island by car, bike, or scooter (rent the latter from April Point Resort & Spa) is a delight, with plenty of stop-off points at parks and beaches to enjoy. There

Nuyumbalees Cultural Centre

This museum is one of the few places where you can explore the area's Native heritage. On display is one of the world's best collections of potlatch artifacts, ceremonial masks, and tribal costumes, once used by the Cape Mudge Band. Behind the museum is K'Ik'Ik G'Illas, or "The House of Eagles," a longhouse-like structure used to teach carving, dancing, and other traditional skills. There's also an opportunity to make petroglyph rubbings from fiberglass castings of ancient stone carvings. 34 WeiWai Road, Cape Mudge Village. Quathiaski Cove. ✆ **250/ 285-3733.** www.nuyumbalees.com.

are over 20 studio locations to visit potters, carvers, painters, and sculptors; visit www.quadraislandarts.com for more information. One of the most rewarding destinations is the Nuyumbalees Cultural Centre, formerly the **Kwagiulth Museum and Cultural Centre**—if it's open. Located in Cape Mudge Village, the museum drifts from one season to the other—sometimes opening at odd hours, sometimes not at all. Islanders will have the latest scoop.

Cortes Island

Located at the entrance to Desolation Sound, one of BC's most celebrated cruising areas, Cortes Island (www.cortesisland.com) is a beautiful wilderness hideaway. It is a lovely island to wander through, with breathtaking vignettes: Gorge Harbour Marina, Von Donop Provincial Marine Park, Squirrel Cove with an anchorage facing Desolation Sound, and 100-hectare (247-acre) Manson's Landing Provincial Marine Park. Here's where you find excellent sandy beaches—the park (as well as Smelt Bay and Squirrel Cove) is one of the few places where you can collect shellfish legally. An easy 15-minute walk south from the government float at Manson's Landing leads to Hague Lake, which has a 1km (0.6-mile) perimeter trail to the sandspit. Watch your step, it's steep in places. Most walks around Cortes aren't this formal; so if you decide to explore, say, the wilderness of Von Donop Provincial Marine Park, you would do well to create your own marking system. Just be sure to retrieve them all—islanders don't take kindly to eco-unfriendly practices.

WHERE TO STAY & DINE

Quadra Island

April Point Resort & Spa The sister resort to Painter's Lodge, April Point caters to a more eco-oriented crowd with its kayak, bike, and scooter rentals, as well as its Aveda concept spa at the water's edge. Accommodations range from deluxe suites with Jacuzzi tubs to comfortable 1- to 4-bedroom "'woodsy' cabins," all of which have ocean views and decks. The spacious restaurant has floor-to-ceiling windows with views, and serves quality West Coast cuisine from early morning breakfast to fine dining at night, but the sushi bar sometimes steals the show, especially as a prelude to dinner. A free water taxi shuttles guests between April Point and Painter's Lodge.

900 April Point Rd., Quadra Island, (Box 248), Campbell River, BC V9W 4Z9. ✆ **800/663-7090** or 250/285-2222. www.aprilpoint.com. 56 units, some w/Jacuzzi. C$155–C$426 double. Extra person C$20. Closed mid-Oct to early Apr. AE, DC, MC, V. **Amenities:** Restaurant; sushi bar; lounge; spa; bike, scooter, and kayak rentals; tour/activities desk; babysitting; laundry service. *In room:* TV, Wi-Fi, coffeemaker, hair dryer.

Tracking the Wild Side

As you travel through the northern regions of Vancouver Island, the richness of the aboriginal heritage becomes evident. Two outfitters, both owned and operated by different First Nations peoples, offer wildlife and bear tours of their traditional territories, alongside stories, history, and cultural insights. **Aboriginal Journeys** (398–1434 Island Hwy., Campbell River; ✆ **888/455-8101** or 250/850-1101; www.aboriginaljourneys.com) operates wildlife viewing and adventure tours within the traditional territory of the Laichwiltach peoples. This extends from Cape Mudge to the mouth of Bute Inlet, to Smith Inlet and around northern Vancouver Island. Tours include whale-watching, grizzly- and black-bear viewing, and other wildlife sightings from a 24-foot Zodiac or a 55-foot classic wooden fishing vessel. **Homalco Wildlife Tours** (1218 Bute Crescent, Campbell River; ✆ **866/234-2327** or 250/923-0758; www.bearsof bute.com), operated by the Homalco First Nations people, offer tours aboard the 32-foot M.V. *Chinook Spirit* to the Orford River, one of the last pristine watersheds in Bute Inlet and home to the largest concentration of grizzly bears in British Columbia. With both companies, prices and tour length varies depending on the tour and destination selected. For example, a 4-hour marine tour is C$129 per person; an 8-hour grizzly-bear tour is C$320 per person.

Tsa-Kwa-Luten Lodge & RV Park   This establishment is owned and operated by the Laichwiltach (the Cape Mudge Band); you can enjoy the Native experience with a luxurious twist (hence the Canada Select four-star rating). This modern resort resembles a native Big House, offering lodge suites, waterfront cabins, and two four-bedroom guest houses, as well as an excellent (primarily) seafood restaurant that often stages Native dancing; reservations are recommended. All rooms have an ocean view and either a balcony or patio; decor is contemporary with earth tones coordinating floors, bedspreads, and walls. Tsa-Kwa-Luten translates as "gathering place" in the Kwak'wala language of the Laichwiltach people, and is located on the site of the band's original village. There are also 13 RV sites with full hookups.

1 Lighthouse Rd. (Box 460), Quathiaski Cove, Quadra Island, BC V0P 1N0. ✆ 800/665-7745 or 250/598-3366. Fax 250/285-2532. www.capemudgeresort.com. 35 units. C$95–C$140 lodge suite, C$145–C$180 cottage, C$119–C$379 guest house; RV C$30 oceanview, C$35 beachfront. Children under 12 stay free. Meal plans available. AE, DC, MC, V. Free parking. Closed mid-Oct to early April. Small pets allowed in RV sites. **Amenities**: Restaurant; lounge; lit tennis courts nearby; exercise room; Jacuzzi; sauna; free bikes; massage; laundry service; Wi-Fi. *In room*: Phone; coffeemaker, hair dryer, iron, bathrobe and umbrella upon request.

Cortes Island

Cortes is small, so it's a good idea to reserve accommodations. The New Age set tend to head for **Hollyhock** (Box 127, Manson's Landing, Cortes Island, V0P 1K0; ✆ **800/933-6339;** www.hollyhock.ca), a holistic and spiritual retreat center. The back-to-the-wilderness, kayaking crowd favor **T'ai Li Lodge** (Box 16, Cortes Bay, Cortes Island, V0P 2K0; ✆ **800/939-6644** or 250/935-6711; www.taililodge.com) staying either in the recently refurbished upscale lodge, or opting for the beachfront Arbutus Point campsite that now has simple amenities such as a solar hot shower and fridge access. **Cortes Island Vacation Rentals** (© 800/939-6644 or 250/935-6711) has access to several privately owned beach cabins and family homes with rates from C$500 to C$1,500 a week.

5 EN ROUTE TO PORT HARDY

Trees, trees, and more trees line either side of Hwy. 19 heading north from Campbell River. The communities along this stretch still have mine- and timber-based economies, and every now and then, the stands of trees break to reveal mountainsides scalded by machinery or fields of blackened stumps, left to rot before replanting. The destinations that follow are listed geographically, heading north from Campbell River along Hwy. 19.

While logging is still the mainstay for communities such as **Port McNeill,** much to the chagrin of environmentalist activists, smaller hamlets such as **Holberg, Woss, Zeballos,** and picturesque **Telegraph Cove** seem to co-exist with their lumber-industry environment more peacefully. As a result, they have developed distinct personalities, whether from the Finnish influence still holding court in **Sointula,** or the richness of First Nations culture in **Alert Bay.**

ESSENTIALS
Getting There
BY CAR Although the road north is a well-maintained two-lane highway, this is the only drivable route, and it's used by logging trucks as well as local traffic. Getting stuck behind one of these lumbering vehicles can slow you down, since they aren't always easy to pass. Give yourself extra time, and avoid frustration by taking detours. In summer, the road gets particularly busy with ferry travelers heading to and from Port Hardy. The distance from Campbell River to Port Hardy is 238km (148 miles), which could take up to 3½ hours to drive. From Nanaimo to Port Hardy it's 391km (243 miles)—allow at least 5 hours. For the long haul from Victoria to Port Hardy, it's a whopping 502km (312 miles). For this killer road trip, set aside 7 hours.

BY PLANE **Air Canada Jazz** (© 888/247-2262; www.flyjazz.ca) operates daily flights among Vancouver, Victoria, Port Hardy, Comox, and Campbell River, as does **Pacific Coastal Airlines** (© 800/663-2872; www.pacific-coastal.com). **Kenmore Air** (© 800/543-9595 or 425/486-1257; www.kenmoreair.com) flies from Seattle Harbor to Port Hardy, Port McNeill, and Quadra Island.

BY BUS **Island Coach Lines,** operated by **Laidlaw Coach Lines** (© 800/318-0818 or 250/385-4411; www.victoriatours.com), runs daily service from Victoria to Port Hardy, stopping in Campbell River. The one-way fare from Victoria to Port Hardy is C$82 for adults (be aware it's a 5:45am departure). From Nanaimo to Port Hardy, it's C$64 for adults. Fares for seniors are 10% less; fares for children 5 to 11 are 50% less. The trip from Victoria to Port Hardy is just under 10 hours. From Nanaimo to Port Hardy, it's approximately 7 hours. You can save a couple of dollars by traveling midweek; contact **Greyhound Canada** (© 800/661-8747; www.greyhound.ca) for reservations.

BY FERRY **BC Ferries** (© 888/223-3779; www.bcferries.com) operates nine crossings daily between Port McNeill and the community of **Alert Bay,** on Cormorant Island,

and between Port McNeill and **Sointula,** on Malcolm Island. Round-trip fares are C$8.70 for adults, C$4.35 for children 5 to 11. Passenger vehicles are C$22. Crossing time is 45 minutes. BC Ferries also operates service between Port Hardy and Prince Rupert, a 15-hour journey via the famed **Inside Passage.** One-way day sailing fares are C$141 adult, C$84 senior, C$78 for children 5 to 11. Passenger vehicles are C$334. Overnight and off-season rates are also available.

Visitor Information

There are visitor information centers in several of the communities along the route to Port Hardy, such as **Port McNeill Visitor Information** at 351 Shelley Crescent (P.O. Box 129), Port McNeill, BC V0N 2R0 (① **250/956-3131;** www.portmcneill.net) and **Alert Bay Visitor Information** at 116 Fir St., Alert Bay, BC V0N 1A0 (① **250/974-5024;** www.alertbay.net). Once in Port Hardy, head to the **Port Hardy Visitor Information Centre,** 7250 Market St. (P.O. Box 249), Port Hardy, BC V0N 2P0 (① **250/949-7622;** www.ph-chamber.bc.ca). Open daily during normal office hours, these folks also provide an **accommodations reservations service** for Port Hardy and Prince Rupert (for those going to Prince Rupert with BC Ferries). For more information on the north region of Vancouver Island, contact **Vancouver Island North Visitors' Association** (① **800/903-6606** or 250/949-9094; www.tourismni.com/vinva).

ZEBALLOS

Located 191km (119 miles) north of Campbell River, at the end of a 40km (25-mile) gravel road off Hwy. 19, historic **Zeballos** once produced more than C$13 million worth of gold. Tailings from the mines were used to build up the roads and led to a local legend that the streets were literally "paved with gold." But when Zeballos lost its Midas touch, logging, fish farming, and tourism became its mainstays. Although still fairly rough and ready, some of the false-fronted historic gold rush buildings have been spruced up, including the old hospital downtown and the old Privateer gold mine a few minutes up the Zeballos River. Today, this pretty village is also the jumping-off point to an eco-adventurer's dream—everything from kayaking and fishing to diving. Recreational cavers and experienced spelunkers will head to **Little Hustan Caves** for its sinkholes, canyons, and fast-moving river that disappears and reappears in the rock formations. Hikers will find any number of trails including the old logging road down to Little Zeballos and a fairly strenuous climb up Sugarloaf Mountain for amazing views of Little Espinoza Inlet. If you decide to check in with a local outfitter, be sure to ask about the tidal fall change on this inlet. You need a boat to get up close to the swirling waters, and an experienced hand at the wheel.

Zeballos Village Museum (① **250/761-4070** May–Sept; 250/761-4229 Sept–Apr) doubles as a **Visitors Information Centre** and is your best bet for arranging excursions, since many outfitters are seasonal or seemingly come and go with the tide. The center can also help you reserve accommodations and campsites, both of which are fairly limited, or one of the 30 RV sites. The museum part of the center is filled with old mining equipment and photos of 'old' Zeballos, and is a good starting point to learn about this community that's survived a history of hard knocks, including a tsunami in 1964.

Where to Stay & Dine

Mason's Lodge Built in 1936, during the height of the gold rush, owners Daniel O'Connor and Cristina Lepore have done a good job in maintaining its heritage ambience while providing creature comforts. Rooms are bright with touches of cedar paneling, and spacious enough to have sitting areas, although the public lounge has nice leather bound chairs to sink into. All rooms have views of the Zeballos River and mountains. All have private baths; some have kitchenettes. **The Blue Heron Restaurant** offers hearty breakfasts (this meal is not included in the room rate), first-rate boxed lunches, local oysters, excellent cappuccinos, and a dinner selection that changes frequently depending on the catch and the season. True to the multitasking nature of those on the Zeballos tourism scene, you'll find kayak rentals, fishing charters, and water taxi services here.

203 Pandora Ave. (P.O. Box 10), Zeballos, BC V0P 2A0. ☎ **866/222-2235** or 250/761-4044. www.masons lodge.zeballos.bc.ca. 13 units. C$85–C$130 double. Extra person C$20. Children under 12 stay free in parent's room. AE, MC, V. Free parking. **Amenities:** Restaurant; lounge. *In room:* Satellite TV, Wi-Fi, fridge, hair dryer.

TELEGRAPH COVE

A highlight of your trip north must be Telegraph Cove, a picture-perfect village located 239km (149 miles) north of Campbell River. Overlooking Johnstone Strait, it epitomizes the West Coast, and is one of the few remaining **elevated-boardwalk villages** on Vancouver Island. This historic community got its start in 1912 as a one-room telegraph station that marked the end of a cable, strung tree to tree, all the way from Victoria. When messages were received, the operator hopped into a boat and rowed to the community of **Alert Bay,** on Cormorant Island, to deliver the news. Part of the cove's charm is that many of the original buildings still stand, including the telegraph station, an army mess hall, picturesque residences, and cozy cabins perched on stilts over the water's edge and joined by boardwalks. Walk to the end and you'll find the **Johnstone Strait Whale Interpretive Centre,** dubbed the Bones Project, where they are piecing together the skeleton of a fin whale. You'll also find hands-on displays of the numerous species of marine life populating the area. Across from here, however, is a busy and evolving marina where an expanse of asphalt caters to RVs, and roads lead to expensive cliff-hanging lots and even more expensive homes. The good news is that the road to Telegraph Cove is now entirely blacktopped; the bad news is that development is marginalizing something that is still clinging on to "quaint."

Outdoor Activities

Because of its proximity to Robson Bight Ecological Reserve, whale-watching is big business, though any trip along Johnstone Strait will include sightings of dolphins, seals, porpoises, and eagles. At the end of the boardwalk lies **Stubbs Island Charters** (☎ **800/665-3066** or 250/928-3185; www.stubbs-island.com), BC's first orca- and wildlife-watching company. The 60-foot boats are equipped with hydrophones so you can listen to the whales' underwater conversations. The 3½-hour cruises run May through late October and cost C$89 for adults. Choose either the first or last departure of the day (9am or 5:30pm) and you'll save C$10.

For those who want to stay on land, **Tide Rip Tours,** 28 Boardwalk (☎ **888/643-9319** or 250/339-5320; www.tiderip.com), runs various wildlife-viewing excursions, including seeking out grizzly bears (from C$250).

For kayak rentals and guided multi-day kayaking trips into Telegraph Cove and Johnstone Strait, contact **Telegraph Cove Sea Kayaking** (☎ **888/756-0099** or 250/756-0094; www.tckayaks.com). Rentals are C$50 a day, single; C$75 double. A 3-day trip runs C$650 per person, and includes all camping gear. **Discovery Expeditions** is the company's more adventurous arm, and focuses on 4- to 6-day trips, using Sophia Island (across from Robson Bight) as a base camp. A 4-day trip is C$899 per person; a 6-day adventure is C$1,395 per person.

Where to Stay & Dine

Hidden Cove Lodge   Located 6.5km (4 miles) from Telegraph Cove, this 557-sq.-m (6,000-sq.-ft.) retreat lodge was once only accessible by water. It exudes an easy-going, West Coast charm, with cedar beams throughout, floor-to-ceiling windows to take advantage of the terrific waterfront views, and comfortable furnishings. There are eight lodge rooms, and three private self-contained cottages. All accommodations are clean and simply decorated; children are welcome in the cottages only. The licensed dining room, which serves quality international dishes, is open to non-guests by reservation only. Numerous eco-tours, including heli-fishing, can be arranged.

Lewis Point, 1 Hidden Cove Rd., Telegraph Cove, BC V0N 2R0. ©/fax **250/956-3916.** www.bcbbonly. com/1263.php. 8 units with private bathroom, 3 cottages. C$99–C$155 lodge double; C$199 1-bedroom cottage; C$299 2-bedroom cottage. Extra person C$25. Lodge rates include full breakfast. 2-night minimum stay. Off-season rates available. MC, V. Free parking and moorage for boaters. No pets. **Amenities:** Restaurant; golf course nearby; Jacuzzi; in-room massage; babysitting; coin-op laundry. In room: No phone.

Telegraph Cove Marina & RV Park   The "old" Telegraph Cove still holds its charm of antiquity; the same can't be said of the cove's other side, which is dominated by a 48-space full-hookup RV park. It's part of a larger development program that includes cliff-clinging real estate lots for sale, a 130-slip marina (currently under expansion), and Dockside 29, a hotel offering a comparatively luxurious alternative to the 1930s-style structures across the water. Open year-round, the over-the-water rooms and suites are well furnished, clean, and bright, with hardwood floors, small kitchens, and "perfect reception" satellite TV.

Box 2–8, Telegraph Cove, BC V0N 3J0. © **877/835-2683** or 250/928-3161. Fax 250/928-3162. www. telegraphcove.ca. 29 units, 48 RV sites. C$130–C$160 double. Off-season rates available. RV sites C$35 per day. Marina C$12–C$20 per day. Boat/kayak launch access C$7 per day. MC, V. **Amenities:** Marina; coin-op laundry; Wi-Fi. In room: TV, kitchen.

Telegraph Cove Resorts   The accommodations here are refurbished, self-contained homes from the 1920s and 1930s, and include everything from a converted floating hospital on the boardwalk to a fisherman's cottage. Each has a story to share, and upgrades in decor have managed to combine simplicity with heritage charm. Some homes are cozy enough for two, while others sleep four, six and even up to nine people. Wastell Manor, a two-level family home built in 1929, is a bit fancier. Because the manor is perched on a bluff, it offers exceptional views of the cove. Some 120 campsites are set back from the village, among the trees; all have water hookups; some also have electrical access; some have full hookups. Telegraph Cove Resorts also run the Old Saltery Pub (a converted saltery) and the **Killer Whale Café** (© **250/928-3155**). Both are good eateries, which is fortunate as they really are the only shows in town.

Box 1, Telegraph Cove, BC V0N 3J0. © **800/200-HOOK** [4665] or 250/928-3131. Fax 250/928-3105. www. telegraphcoveresort.com. 24 units. Jun–Sept C$99–C$290 cabins/suites. Extra person C$10. C$23–C$28 campsites. Lower rates May and October. Packages available. MC, V. Closed mid-Oct to Apr. Pets allowed in some cabins for C$5 per night. **Amenities:** Restaurant; pub; kayak rentals; coin-op laundry. In room: Coffeemaker, no phone.

Robson Bight Ecological Reserve, near Telegraph Cove, provides some of the most fascinating whale-watching in the province. Orcas regularly beach themselves in the shallow waters of the Bight's pebbly beaches to rub their stomachs free of barnacles. Boaters, including kayakers and tour operators, are not allowed to enter the reserve, but can visit nearby areas. Whale fans anywhere within 15km (9⅓ miles) of the Bight can tune in to CJKW 88.5 to hear the orcas sing.

PORT MCNEILL, ALERT BAY & SOINTULA

From Telegraph Cove, it's approximately 40km (25 miles) to **Port McNeill,** a hard-working, hard-edged township founded on logging and fishing. To wit, one of the main attractions is a record-breaking, 500-year-old burl (a dome-shaped tree growth) that weighs in at 21,772 kilograms (24 tons), making it the world's largest, and an old steam donkey engine, circa 1938.

Besides those dubious attractions, Port McNeill offers visitors the chance to embark upon whale-watching expeditions. **Mackay Whale Watching,** Port McNeill (*©* **877/663-6277** or 250/956-9865; www.whaletime.com), which uses 55-foot aluminum vessels, has been around for more than 25 years and was instrumental in helping to establish the Robson Bight whale reserve nearby. Tours run about 4½ hours, cost C$95 per person, and include a light lunch. **Sea Orca Whale Watching,** Government Dock, Alert Bay (*©* **800/668-6722** or 250/974-5225; www.seaorca.com) offers 5- to 8-hour sail-with-the-whales excursions aboard S.V. *Tuan,* a 40-foot craft, for C$95 to C$180 per adult.

From Port McNeill, BC Ferries runs nine daily crossings to the 1,800-strong community of **Alert Bay** on Cormorant Island or to **Sointula** on Malcolm Island. Round-trip fares are C$8.70 for adults, C$4.35 for children 5 to 11. The crossing time is 45 minutes. Alternatively, North Island Air (*©* **250/956-2020**) runs charters and daily scenic flights out of Port McNeill. Prices vary according to destination and time in the air.

A Kwagiulth tribal village for thousands of years, Alert Bay exudes its rich, cultural heritage, and is most proud of the 53m (174-ft.) cedar totem pole featuring 22 hand-carved figures of bears, orcas, and ravens. It stands outside the Big House at the top of the hill. The modern building is modeled after a Kwakwaka'wakw Big House, and in July and August hosts performances by 'Na'Nakwala dancers, usually Wednesday through Saturday. The cost is C$15 for adults and C$6 for children under 12. Near the ferry dock at Alert Bay, at the **U'Mista Cultural Centre** (*©* **250/974-5403;** www.umista.org), you'll find an extraordinary collection of carved-wood ceremonial masks, cedar baskets, copper jewelry, and other potlatch artifacts that were confiscated by the Canadian government in 1922, and repatriated in 1980. Although the displays are self-explanatory, try to take a guided tour to really appreciate the stories and folklore that the exhibits represent. Admission is C$5 for adults, C$4 for seniors and students, and C$1 for children 12 and under. The museum is open in summer daily 9am to 5:30pm, and in winter Monday through Friday 9am to 5pm.

At the other end of town—about a 15-minute stroll along the waterfront—is the ancient 'Namgis burial ground. It's sacred territory, so don't step over the wall to take photos of the many colorful and unusual totem poles. En route, keep an eye open for the **Anglican Church,** with a graveyard which reflects the arrival of Scottish immigrants into the area at the turn of the 20th century. Erected in 1881, the church's stained-glass windows are an interesting blend of Native Kwagiulth and Scottish design motifs. Also, check out the Ecological Park, a natural wonder that resembles the Florida Everglades without the alligators. An extensive system of trails for hiking and mountain biking crisscross the island. Maps are available at the information center.

Founded by Finnish settlers in 1901, the community of **Sointula,** on Malcolm Island, was to be a Utopian society, "a place of harmony." Although the concept collapsed, you can still feel the peaceful atmosphere of that dream. Finnish was the island's principal language until as recently as 30 years ago. But today, less than half of the 1,000-strong population is Finn. Sointula is a charming fishing village. There's a local gallery, store, and the **Sointula Museum** (✆ 250/973-6683) 4 blocks left of the ferry terminal, which tells the Finnish story. The Museum shares space with the library, both in the old Superior School building. Six kilometers of gravel road takes you to **Bere Point Regional Park,** a known killer-whale rubbing beach over which there's a viewing platform. The park offers two hiking trails of note: The 3.2km (2-mile) Matejeo Heritage Trail is a short walk from the ferry terminal and takes you through bogs, forest, and beside pretty lakes; the 2.5km (1.6-mile) Beautiful Bay Trail is more challenging. It starts at Bere Point and follows the bay to Malcolm Point.

Where to Stay & Dine

Although tourists visit for the fishing, First Nations culture, and outdoor pursuits, Port McNeill, Alert Bay, and Sointula aren't geared for visitors. Accommodations are basic, and restaurants cater to local tastes with burgers, fish and chips, and pasta.

In Port McNeill, **Haida-Way Motor Inn** (1817 Campbell Way; ✆ 800/956-3373 or 250/956-3373; www.pmhotels.com) and **Dalewood Inn** (1703 Broughton Blvd.; ✆ 877/956-3304 or 250/956-3304; www.dalewoodinn.com) are two motels with decent rooms as well as on-site pubs and restaurants that add good (but nothing to write home about) steaks and chicken dishes to their dinner menu. Both inns have comparable rates, ranging from C$90 to C$119.

In Alert Bay, try the **Old Customs House Restaurant & Inn,** (119 Fir St. Alert Bay, BC V0N 1A0; ✆ 250/974-2282), a 1918 historic building that has three rooms, kitchen facilities, and a great deck overlooking Johnstone Strait. **Alert Bay Lodge** (549 Fir St., Alert Bay, BC V0N 1A0; ✆ 800/255-5057 or 250/974-2026; www.alertbay lodge.com) is more upscale and certainly roomier, in large part because it was once the United Church for Alert Bay. The great room and library features high, arched cedar beams; the cedar adds a warmth to its five simply furnished guest rooms—that means no TVs or radios. Rates range from C$55 to C$145 per person.

On Malcolm Island, **Sund's Lodge,** 445 Kaleva Rd., Box 10, Sointula, BC V0N 3E0 (✆ 800/991-SUND [7863] or 250/902-1400 Oct–May; 250/973-6381 June–Sept; www.sundslodge.com) is a fully inclusive "adventure or do nothing" luxury resort located on 16 hectares (40 acres) of unspoiled wilderness on Blackfish Sound. Open mid-June until the end of September, the family-run, luxury lodge accommodates up to 20 guests in cabins furnished with overstuffed log chairs and cozy beds with thick down comforters. Food is equally inviting, with an emphasis on local fare with spicy marinades,

Kayaking Adventures with a Twist

Paddling softly through some of the hundreds of islands in the Broughton Inlet must be one of the most magical kayaking experiences available, especially when eagles, sea lions, and whales join in the fun. Your "base camp" is a beautifully restored heritage vessel called **MV Columbia III** that, 50 years ago, served as a missionary, hospital, and overall life-line vessel to BC's coastal communities. Today, outfitted with half a dozen quality kayaks, the ship travels between different dropoff and pickup paddling points that you could never hope to reach from an on-shore origin. Passenger accommodations comprise five tiny staterooms with extremely comfortable, queen-size bunk beds, a cozy lounge/dining area, and a sheltered deck.

The Campbell family, who own and operate this venture, has pooled its talents to provide expert naturalist and guiding tips, scrumptious food, and informal hospitality that might include an impromptu recital of Irish music after dinner. Passengers range from older teenagers to active retirees, and schedules often include shore stops to explore First Nations communities, a hike through the rain forest, or a beachside picnic of just-caught crab. If ever you get paddle weary, the ship's zodiac will quickly take you back to the boat. The *Columbia* runs out of Port McNeil June through September; all-inclusive 4- and 7-day trips are C$1,900 to C$3,000 per person.

Mothership Adventures, Heriot Bay. *C* **888/833-8887** or 250/202-3229. www.mothershipadventures.com.

homemade sauces, and fresh herbs. A 3-night/4-day stay starts at C$2,400 per person inclusive of accommodations, meals, guided fishing, hiking, and kayaking. As a seaside campground, Bere Point Park is more affordable, with 11 unserviced sites on the waterfront (great for kayakers) plus 11 more sites up the hill in full sun. Here's where to find the trail head for Beautiful Bay Trail and a whale-watching platform.

6 PORT HARDY & CAPE SCOTT PROVINCIAL PARK ★★★

Port Hardy is 44km (27 miles) north of Port McNeill and the final stop on Island Highway. Many visitors, however, come via ferry, en route either to or from **Prince Rupert.** Port Hardy is also the departure point for the Discovery Coast Passage trip to the First Nations communities of Bella Bella, Shearwater, Ocean Falls, and Klemtu, among others. In summer, this tiny town gets so busy with ferry travelers that decent accommodations get full fast, leaving a motley assortment of tired motels to choose from.

Until recently, the town's prosperity was fueled by forestry, mining, and commercial fishing, but the refurbished seaside promenade, and the fresh coat of paint here and there, are evidence of Port Hardy's efforts to diversify its economic base through tourism.

Is this why the timbered **Port Hardy Visitor Information Centre,** 7250 Market St. (P.O. Box 294), Port Hardy, BC V0N 2P0 (✆ **250/949-7622**), is the nicest building downtown? If you have an hour to spare, drop into the **Port Hardy Museum,** 7110 Market St. (✆ **250/949-8143**), which has some interesting relics from early Danish settlers, plus a collection of stone tools, found nearby, which date from about 8,000 BC.

When you make it to **Port Hardy,** you may feel like you've reached the edge of the world, but in fact, Port Hardy is the jumping-off point for exhilarating, year-round outdoor activities, such as hiking in **Cape Scott Provincial Park** (see below), fishing, kayaking, and diving, as well as to several very remote, very exclusive fishing lodges farther north. **North Island Daytrippers** (✆ **800/956-2411** or 250/956-2411; www. islanddaytrippers.com) is a good option for hikers who would rather not go it alone in these wilderness areas. Based in Port McNeill, these savvy guides offer year-round half-day and full-day hikes to San Josef Bay and Ronning Gardens, Raft Cove, and many of the beaches and coves in between. Fees include lunch and start at C$150 per person for a full day and decrease according to the number of people in the party.

OUTDOOR ACTIVITIES

The northern region epitomizes Vancouver Island's wildest (and wettest) coastal country. Although a lot of it can be enjoyed by visitors who just want a look-see, you'll learn that the deeper you explore, the greater the rewards. But to do that, be sure that you go with an experienced outfitter or that you are completely at ease when left to your own devices in the great outdoors.

DIVING   Water clarity and tidal action have made this one of the best dive locations in the world. There are more than two dozen outfitters in the area, some of which will provide fully equipped dive boats. A good resource is **North Island Dive & Charters,** 8665 Hastings St. (✆ **250/949-2664;** www.northislanddiver.com), a full-service dive store that also offers rentals and instruction. Pricing varies depending on the type of dive you're looking for, and whether or not equipment is required, but as a guideline, a two-tank dive involving about 6 hours on the water is C$150 per person, usually with a three-diver minimum.

FISHING   Fishing nirvana awaits, as do several of the local outfitters. Charter trips and self-skippered boat rentals abound. **Catala Charters** (✆ **800/515-5511** or 250/949-7560; www.catalacharters.net) offers guided fishing trips, as well as diving charters, and **Codfather Charters** (✆ **250/949-6696;** www.codfathercharters.com) offers year-round fishing as well as accommodations in a waterfront lodge. If you just want to rent a boat, contact **Hardy Bay Boat Rental,** Quarterdeck Marina, 6555 Hardy Bay Rd. (✆ **250/ 949-7048;** www.hardybayfishing.com). Rates start at C$25 per hour and C$200 per day.

Port Hardy is the gateway for trips to remote fishing camps, many of which cater to the heavy wallet brigade with upscale exclusivity. These include **King Pacific Lodge** (www.kingpacificlodge.com), and **Nimmo Bay Resort** (www.nimmobay.com), where access is by floatplane or boat, and all-inclusive prices start at about C$5,000 for 3 nights.

Duval Point Lodge (✆ **250/949-6667;** www.duvalpointlodge.com) is an affordable alternative where you can do your own thing without frou-frou frills. Located 8km (5 miles) north of Port Hardy (accessed by boat), the lodge has both a floating lodge and land-based log cabins, all of which share a full kitchen (guests do their own cooking) and living area. Some rooms share bathrooms too. Open May through October, the outfitter provides fishing tackle, bait, and boat for multi-day packages that start from C$945 per person for 3 nights; and less (from C$525) if you bring your own boat. All guests can use the lodge's kayaks at no extra charge.

The **Ocean Explorer** (℡ 877/346-9378) takes the best of a resort and puts it at sea, exploring the Inside Passage and fjordic inlets. This 110-foot luxury boat is the only fishing experience of its kind, offering nine private staterooms, lounge, a state-of-the-art galley (aka gourmet meals) and a deck-top hot tub. It guarantees your catch or promises your next trip for free. Three-night packages are priced at C$2,995, including roundtrip airfare from Vancouver International Airport, all meals, accommodations, fishing gear, and Cuban cigars.

HIKING   Heavy rainfalls (nearly 500cm/197 in. per year) and violent windstorms predominate in this wild landscape, turning hiking trails into muddy quagmires. But if you thrive on doing things off the beaten track, these trails deliver. The easiest and most popular hike is the 2.5km (1.6-mile) **San Josef Bay Trail,** a fairly easy walk through marshy ferns, skunk cabbage, and along the San Josef River to San Josef Bay, where there's an expanse of sandy beach and the ruins of a Danish settlement.

More experienced and well-equipped hikers can opt for the challenging 24km (15-mile) **Cape Scott Trail.** This grueling trek starts in mud, but once you're on your way, the scenery is pure wilderness: ocean bay beauty, weathered grass, high-rise canopies of Sitka spruce, and vast stretches of natural beach. Stops along the way include **Eric Lake,** an ideal spot for fishing and warm-water swimming, and **Hansen Lagoon,** once a Danish settlement, and now a stopping place for Canada geese and a variety of waterfowl traveling the Pacific Flyway. Allow 3 days of heavy hiking, and a good week if you want to explore all the offshoot trails. One suggestion is the just-opened **North Coast Trail** (approximately 44km/27 miles) that ends up at Shushartie Bay. You can catch a land shuttle from Port Hardy to the trail head (℡ **250/949-6888;** www.northcoasttrail shuttle.com) for C$65 and then organize a water taxi return. Unlike the West Coast Trail (p. 164) hiking reservations aren't required for Cape Scott; however, be sure to book ahead if you require transport.

Other than Eric Lake, where there are 11 designated camp pads, camping is unrestricted. You'll find food caches and pit toilets here and at Guise Bay, Nels Bight, San Josef, and Nissen Bight. There's an honor-system backcountry fee (C$6 per person) for overnight camping operative May to September. Self-registration vaults are located at the San Josef River boat launch and trail head. South of Cape Scott lies Raft Cove Provincial Park, 405 hectares (1,001 acres) of rugged wilderness and wind-swept beaches that make for a good full day's excursion or longer. Campers will find the cove extremely exposed to the Pacific, so even in summer you can expect temperamental weather systems to dampen your canvas, so prepare accordingly. Access to the park by road is on Ronning Main, off the Cape Scott road out of Holberg. Experienced sea kayakers paddle to Raft Cove down the San Josef River and out to the Pacific through San Josef Bay.

KAYAKING   The shores of Hardy Bay are scattered with coves, inlets, and islands to explore and stop along the way. The major islands are Deer, Peel, Cattle, Round, and Shell islands, all of which you can make into a leisurely day trip or single over-nighter. **Odyssey Kayaking** (℡ **888/792-3366** or 250/902-0565; www.odysseykayaking.com) offers day-long guided paddles from C$99 per person as well as longer, customized trips. Kayak rentals are from C$45 per day.

Clinging to the northwest tip of Vancouver Island, Cape Scott Provincial Park is 21,840 hectares (53,968 acres) of untamed raincoast wilderness, where the wild Pacific Ocean pounds wide, windswept beaches and crashes against rocky headlands. In the late 1890s, enterprising Danish colonists from the American Midwest carved the tortuous route to Cape Scott itself out of the tangled bush. They hoped to build a community there. But the land was too isolated and the weather too inhospitable to let the settlement grow. Today, their wagon roads are now hiking trails, and heritage markers along the way point out the remains of their endeavors: tumbledown cabins, sun-bleached driftwood fence posts, a dilapidated cougar trap, and cedar planked "corduroy roads."

Getting there is a 2-hour, 67km (42-mile) drive west from Port Hardy down a heavily used gravel logging road toward the tiny town of **Holberg,** a good place to break the journey, especially if you stop in at the **Scarlet Ibis Pub** (© **250/288-3386**). On the outskirts of Holberg, you'll find **Ronning Gardens.** Established in 1910 by Bernt Ronning, a Norwegian settler, the gardens are an extraordinary anomaly of exotic trees and plants from all over the world, including a pair of enormous Chilean Araucario araucana—also known as monkey-puzzle trees. These were grown from seedlings, male and female, and have been the starting point of several hundred of the monkey puzzle trees in North America.

Then continue on until the Cape Scott parking lot, where you'll find the trail heads to the rugged 24km (15-mile) **Cape Scott Trail** with its stunning coastal scenery and some 30km (19 miles) of sandy beach. There's also a more accessible, 45-minute, 2.5km (1.6-mile) hike that leads to scenic San Josef Bay.

WHERE TO STAY

Cluxewe Resort   Owned and operated by the Kwakiutl Band, this year-round resort has undergone considerable upgrades, and now includes 12 waterfront cottages and a number of RV and tent sites, most either on or near the beach or estuary—Cluxewe means "changing river mouth." Fully stocked cottages are clean and simply furnished with a BBQ deck, Wi-Fi, and satellite TV; kids will enjoy climbing the ladder to the loft room in cabins 6 and 7. There's a massive wood supply on site, and a decent guest laundry, washroom/shower facility for campers (both tenters and RVers); a small cafe serving burgers, soup, and sandwiches; a boat/kayak launch—fisherman gravitate towards the estuary waters; and there is a new trail system that's fun to explore, especially since there's a wildlife refuge next door. The beach is pebbly and the waters safe.

Hwy 19 (P.O. Box 245), Port McNeil, BC V0N 2R0. © **250/949-0378**. www.cluxewe.com. 12 cabins. 147 campsites. May to mid-Oct C$125–C$165 cabin; campsites C$19 (unserviced) to C$25 (full hook-ups). Winter rates up to 40% less. AE, MC, V. Pets accepted (C$10; cottages). **Amenities:** Restaurant; laundry facility; grocery store; trail system; boat launch; Wi-Fi. *In room:* TV, Wi-Fi, fridge, coffeemaker.

Glen Lyon Inn & Suites ★★   Once you make it past the rather daunting stuffed eagle showcased in the lobby, you'll find a clean, modern motel. All rooms have an ocean view, decent furnishings and come in a mix of configurations to match your needs, whether it's a family suite with bunk beds for the kids, an executive-style room, or the honeymoon suite, with Jacuzzi and wet bar. The balconies on the third floor are great for eagle-spotting. The family-style restaurant is bright and welcoming (see "Where to Dine," below) and the Glen Lyon pub opens for lunch and is a popular spot until last orders at around midnight. The staff have a terrific "anything we can do?" helpful attitude.

Fun Facts   Why No Grizzly Bears?

According to native legend, there were once many grizzlies and black bears on the Mainland that longed to live on Vancouver Island, but it was too far for them to swim. Finally the Great Spirit announced that if the bears could make the distance in one mighty leap, they might stay there. The catch, however, was that they weren't to get as much as one claw wet or they would turn to stone. It is said that the mountains and valleys on the mainland were created by the bears digging in for a run at the Island, yet still many black bears tried and failed, as the boulders strewn along the island's shoreline attest. One day, after watching many of his black bear relatives make the jump, a king-sized grizzly boasted he could jump the distance. He went miles back into the mainland to make the mighty leap. Alas, the tide was in, and he landed in the shallow tide, near Campbell River, and was instantly turned to stone. And there he stands today as The Big Rock.

6435 Hardy Bay Rd. (P.O. Box 103), Port Hardy, BC V0N 2P0. ✆ **877/949-7115** or 250/949-7115. Fax 250/949-7415. www.glenlyoninn.com. 44 units. May to mid-Oct C$110–C$160 double, C$145–C$195 suite; mid-Oct to Apr C$62–C$69 double, C$95–C$125 suite. AE, MC, V. Small pets accepted (C$10). **Amenities:** Restaurant; pub; exercise room; laundry service. *In room:* TV, dataport, Wi-Fi, fridge, coffeemaker, hair dryer.

Oceanview B&B ★★   Although it has rather a grandiose exterior, this lovely home extends a warm welcome to weary travelers. Guest rooms are spacious—they have small sitting areas—and quaintly decorated, with brass or wrought-iron beds. All have a private ensuite bathroom. Thoughtful touches such as fresh-cut flowers, pillow chocolates, and a plate of homemade cookies greet you in your room—baking is this inn's forte. A generous, hot breakfast is served up in a bright and spacious kitchen. The comfortable sitting room offers various reading materials, a piano, and a fireplace, and is a perfect spot to enjoy afternoon tea. The house has wonderful views of Hardy Bay and the snow-covered mountains on the mainland. An unexpected bonus is free parking for guests who wish to leave their vehicles while they take the ferry to Prince Rupert or to Discovery Passage.

7735 Cedar Place (P.O. Box 183), Port Hardy, BC V0N 2P0. ✆/fax **250/949-8302.** www.island.net/~oceanvue. 3 units. C$105–C$120 double. Rates include breakfast. Extra person C$15. MC, V. Free parking. **Amenities:** Lounge, Wi-Fi. *In room:* TV, hair dryer, no phone.

Pioneer Inn Riverside RV Park   Located in a park-like setting of the Quatse River, the inn is located only minutes away from the ferry terminal, and is a great choice for travelers taking the Inside Passage cruise to Prince Rupert. Rooms aren't fancy, but they're bright, clean, and some contain kitchens. One room is wheelchair-accessible. The RV park is one of the nicest in the area, though be prepared to use patient communication skills, since some of the Asian on-site staff are still grappling with the finer points of the English language. Rates include full electrical, sewer, and water hookups; cable TV and telephone are extra.

4965 Byng Rd., Box 699, Port Hardy, BC V0N 2P0. ✆ **800/663-8744** or 250/949-7271. Fax 250/949-7334. 36 units. Mid-May to mid-Oct C$95–C$125; mid-Oct to mid-May C$46–C$70. 25 RV sites C$120 per vehicle, per week.. AE, MC, V. Free parking. Pets allowed (C$10). **Amenities:** Restaurant; coffee shop; golf course nearby; playground; miniature golf; coin-op laundry. *In room:* TV, kitchen, coffeemaker.

Quarterdeck Inn & Marina Resort ★★   A smart, if generic-looking hotel. Peppermint-green corridors (a favorite color of many Port Hardy buildings—must be something to do with the perpetual grey weather) lead to spacious, pastel-colored rooms, with comfortable beds, quality furniture, and ocean views from every window. Some have kitchenettes and DVD players. The hotel is surrounded by a working boatyard and marina, so there's always something to see. The friendly staff can arrange a variety of outdoor activities such as charter fishing, whale-watching, and kayaking, as well as water taxis to Cape Scott.

6555 Hardy Bay Rd. (P.O. Box 910), Port Hardy, BC V0N 2P0. (*) **877/902-0459** or 250/902-0455. Fax 250/902-0454. www.quarterdeckresort.net. 40 units. May–Sept C$125–C$145; Oct–Apr C$89–C$99. Rates include continental breakfast. AE, DC, DISC, MC, V. Free parking. Small pets allowed for C$10. **Amenities:** Restaurant; pub; golf course nearby; gym; Jacuzzi; tour/activities desk; in-room massage; coin-op laundry; Wi-Fi. *In room:* TV, DVD, kitchenette, coffeemaker, hair dryer.

WHERE TO DINE

Glen Lyon Restaurant CANADIAN   Bright and airy, the restaurant bustles with activity from breakfast in the early morning through to dinner. The extensive menu covers all bases, with great salads and burgers by day and dishes such as barbecued ribs, steak, and a very good seafood platter by night, though the fancier dishes can be a bit hit-and-miss. Best to stick to the basics. Families are especially welcome (kids' portions are available) and all the desserts, whether apple crumble or the surprisingly good tiramisu, are homemade.

6435 Hardy Bay Rd. (*) **250/949-7115.** www.glenlyoninn.com. Main courses C$7–C$23. AE, MC, V. Daily 6:30am–9pm.

IV's Quarterdeck Pub PUB/CANADIAN   This nautical-style pub-restaurant, situated on the marina, serves great fresh halibut and chips, sandwiches, burgers, and other traditional pub fare, as well as standards like steaks and chicken. It's really the only decent eatery in town with evening specials and to-go items, making it a local favorite for both working fisherman and visitors. That, and the variety of beer on tap!

6555 Hardy Bay Rd. (*) **250/949-6922.** www.quarterdeckresort.net. Main courses C$7–C$20. AE, MC, V. Daily 11am–midnight.

> (**Fun Facts**)   **Oyster Eden**
>
> Fanny Bay oysters are served in restaurants from New York to Manila to Beijing. Tasting a little like a cucumber, with a fruity finish, nearly 8.5 million of the mollusks are hauled from the Fanny Bay waters in an average year. Unlike the surrounding farmed salmon, oyster farms are considered environmentally helpful, since they attract and sustain other sealife and birds.

The Gulf Islands

Snuggled between Vancouver Island and the mainland, the Gulf Islands are pastoral havens. Their protected waterways provide some of the finest cruising in the world, and their semi-Mediterranean climate is enviable, even by West Coast standards. Add to this sweeping scenes of woods and water, pebble and shell beaches, and placid lakes stocked with bass and rainbow trout ideal for fly-fishing, and you can understand why the Gulf Islands have been described as "fragments of paradise."

The raggedly beautiful archipelago, the northern extension of Washington's San Juan Islands, is made up of more than 200 islands. Although most are small, uninhabited, and accessible only by private boat, the five larger islands, off the southeastern tip of Vancouver Island—Salt Spring Island, the Pender Islands, Galiano, Mayne, and Saturna islands—are home to about 15,000 permanent residents and are served by a regularly scheduled ferry service.

From the beginning, the islands have attracted a diversity of individuals: writers and artists, poets and cooks, ecologists, and escapists. So, far from being an unsophisticated backwater, the region offers the visitor first-class restaurants, as well as heritage B&Bs, galleries, farmhouses, and artisans' studios. In recent years, relocated urbanites have started to gentrify the islands, resulting in an uneasy mix with the existing counterculture. Land values have skyrocketed, and petty crime is on the rise. Only the self-governing Islands Trust holds development in check, although there's creeping evidence that even this influential, tree-hugging group is beginning to lose its grip. Gentrification is happening. One example of the fallout

from this concerns the islands' water supply. As more and more city folk migrate to the islands (prompting a population increase of almost 30% in the past decade), resources must stretch to accommodate their city habits. With the onslaught of multi-bathroom homes, dishwashers, and Jacuzzis, fresh water has become a precious commodity. Today, homesteaders must dig twice as deep for water as they did 20 years ago. Boiling and filtering is becoming a way of life, and summer often means water shortages.

That said, the Gulf Islands are still a heavenly place to hike, kayak, and canoe, or simply enjoy a glass of wine from the deck of a cottage. Families usually resort to the latter because many of the islands' inns and B&Bs are geared to adults. When a hotel welcomes children, this information is included in the review in this guide. Refer to the "Where to Stay" sections for individual islands. The islands may lack many urban amenities such as ATMs and laundromats, but they do have a wealth of quirky features that will make your visit memorable. One example is the "honesty stands" that dot the roadsides. You drop your money in the box provided, and walk away with honey, flowers, veggies, jams, and whatever else local folk have for sale. Deer are another feature. With no natural predators on the islands, they are free to roam roads, gardens, and forests, so be sure to drive carefully, especially at night.

Of all the islands, Salt Spring is the most dynamic, and the easiest to get to from Vancouver Island, especially if you have only a day to spare. Once on a Gulf Island, it is easy to hop to another, arriving in the early morning and departing late afternoon. You're best to incorporate at least one night on each island—it's the only way to experience the very different personality of each, although you might be tempted to stay far longer. After all, they are fragments of paradise.

1 ESSENTIALS

GETTING THERE

BY PLANE Seaplanes crisscross the skies above the Gulf Islands at regular intervals, between Vancouver Island, Vancouver on the mainland, and Seattle. **Seair Seaplanes** (© **800/447-3247** or 604/273-8900; www.seairseaplanes.com) and **Harbour Air** (© **800/665-0212** or 604/274-1277; www.harbour-air.com) offer daily flights. One-way fares average C$95. **Kenmore Air** (© **877/359-5366** or 425/486-1257; www.kenmoreair.com) flies from Seattle May through September. One-way fares are US$294 each way with no round-trip discounts. Prices are fluctuating, however, with fuel surcharges. There are no areas on the islands that accommodate commercial flights, although some islands have small, grassy airstrips for private aircraft.

BY FERRY Juggling your schedule with ferry departures is an art that requires patience, if not a master's degree in reading timetables. **BC Ferries** (© **888/223-3779** or 250/386-3431; www.bcferries.com) provides good basic service to the Gulf Islands, with at least two sailings a day from **Tsawwassen,** a 22km (14-mile) drive south of Vancouver on the mainland, and from **Swartz Bay,** 32km (20 miles) north of Victoria on Vancouver Island. Ferries also run frequently between islands. Schedules are available from **BC Ferries.** One-way fares from Tsawwassen to the Gulf Islands average C$14 per person; C$52 for a standard-size vehicle. One-way fares from Swartz Bay to the islands average C$9.50 per person; C$32 for a standard-size vehicle. Return fares to Tsawwassen are less, and vary according to which island you are returning from. Return fares to Swartz Bay are free. Inter-island trips average C$5 per person; C$11 for a standard-size vehicle.

Note: Ferry travel can be costly if you're taking a vehicle, and long boarding waits are not uncommon. Ticket prices vary seasonally; mid-week travel is slightly less expensive than that on weekends and holidays, when reservations are essential. During these peak periods, book at least 3 weeks in advance to avoid disappointment. Reservations can be made with BC Ferries by phone or online. **Washington State Ferries** (© **800/843-3779** in Washington, 888/808-7977 in Canada, or 206/464-6400; www.wsdot.wa.gov/ferries) provides daily service from **Anacortes to Sidney,** a short distance from Swartz Bay (see "The Saanich Peninsula" in chapter 6). From Swartz Bay, you can transfer to a BC Ferries ferry to the Gulf Islands. There is only one Anacortes–Sidney crossing daily; two in summer, during which vehicle reservations are strongly recommended. Reservations must be made by 5:30pm the day prior to travel. From May to early October, one-way fares are C$16 for adults, C$8.90 for seniors, C$12 for children 6 to 18, and C$59 for a standard-size vehicle and driver. From mid-October to April, fares remain the same for adults, seniors, and children, but drop to C$48 for a standard-size vehicle and driver. Crossing time is 3 hours.

A local **inter-island water taxi** (© **250/537-2510;** www.saltspring.com/watertaxi) operates June through August on Saturdays. When school is in session, September through June, it operates as a weekday school boat, and adults often hitch a ride for day excursions. The one-way fare between any two points is C$15 per person. Round trips are C$25. People often transport kayaks for C$5. Transporting bicycles is free.

Services operate through the local chamber of commerce or general store on individual islands (see "Essentials," throughout the chapter, for the island in question). You can also check out **www.gulfislands.net** for general information. Tourism Vancouver Island (*℗* **250/754-3500;** www.islands.bc.ca) is another good resource. Not all islands have public campgrounds, and moorage facilities for pleasure craft vary in size and amenities considerably.

2 SALT SPRING ISLAND

Named for the briny springs on the island, Salt Spring Island is the largest and most accessible of the Gulf Islands. Lying just north of Vancouver Island's Swartz Bay, this thriving community is made up of almost 10,500 commuters, retirees, farmers, and artistic free-spirits. You'll come across a number of home-based entrepreneurs: everything from potters and weavers to llama farms and cheese-makers! And make no mistake, Salt Spring is filled with characters whether dreadlocked or salt-and-peppered, who are as likely to hold a PhD in comparative literature as to be a self-professed expert in UFO technology. Much of the island is considered sacred by the local Coast Salish people. Mount Tuam, the site of a Buddhist Retreat Centre, contains quartz crystal that purportedly infuses those who visit with calm and well-being.

Salt Spring has two golf courses, a small movie theater that substitutes ads and trailers with slides of local people and places, an ice rink, lots of restaurants, and a scattering of hotly debated condominium developments, mostly in the **Ganges** area. Tour Salt Spring's pastoral landscape and you'll quickly see why sheep are Salt Spring's insignia—they're everywhere. You'll also discover any number of lakes (many are good fishing spots) and hiking trails, such as those in **Mount Maxwell Provincial Park,** which includes a 1.5km (0.9-mile) trek up to **Baynes Peak.** Rising 595m (1,952 ft.), it is the third highest mountain on the Gulf Islands. You can drive to the trail head, but go easy; the paved road becomes a narrow, gravel surface that's too rough for RVs to negotiate.

ESSENTIALS
Getting There
BC Ferries sails to **Fulford Harbour,** in the southern part of Salt Spring, or **Long Harbour,** toward the north. Seaplanes land in **Ganges Harbour,** in the center of the island. See "Getting There," above, for information about fares and schedules.

If you're arriving via ferry to Fulford Harbour, look out for **St. Paul's Church** (best seen from the water). Founded by a Roman Catholic missionary in 1878, this picturesque tiny stone church was built by immigrants from Hawaii who worked for the Hudson's Bay Company, descendants of whom still live on the island.

Visitor Information
Head to the **Salt Spring Island Chamber of Commerce,** 121 Lower Ganges Rd., Salt Spring Island, BC V8K 2T1 (*℗* **866/216-2936** or 250/537-5252; www.saltspring tourism.com), in the village of Ganges. Open daily, year-round, from 11am to 3pm (9am–5pm in July and Aug).

Legend

⚓ Beach

- - - Ferry Route

🐟 Fishing

ⓘ Information

▲ Mountain

🍷 Winery

Reid Island

Alcala Point

DIONISIO POINT PROVINCIAL PARK

Hall I.

Norway I.

Secretary Islands

Devina Dr.

Porlier Pass Rd.

Bodega Beach Dr.

27

Bodega Ridge

Vineyard Way

GALIANO

Houston Passage

Wallace Island

Retreat Cove

Porlier Pass Road

ISLAND

Tent Island

Sunset

1

North N. Beach Rd.

2

N. End Rd.

Fernwood

3

Walker's Hook Rd.

Strait of Georgia

Trincomali Channel

Wise I.

Charles I.

26

Parminter Point

Saint Mary Lake

Stark Rd.

Channel Ridge

Vesuvius Bay

Vesuvius

Vesuvius Bay Rd.

Bullock Lake

Robinson Rd.

Mansell Rd.

Long Harbour Rd.

Long Harbour

Sturdies Bay Rd.

Montague Rd.

Parker Island

Montague Harbour

25

Georgeson Bay Rd.

Morgan Bluff Rd.

24

BLUFFS PARK

Mt. Galiano ▲

Georgeson Bay

Vesuvius Bay / Crofton

Stuart Channel

Maple Mt.

4

ⓘ 5

Ganges

Ganges Rd.

Ganges Harbour

SISTER ISLANDS

Julia I.

Captain Passage

Tsawwassen

Village Bay

MAPLE MOUNTAIN PARK

Maple Mt. ▲

Sansom Narrows

Cranberry Rd.

6

Fulford-Ganges Rd.

Beddis Rd.

Prevost Island

Maple Bay

Maxwell Lake

Maxwell Rd.

Blackburn Lake

7

SALT

Cusheon-Stewart Lake

8

Maple Bay

Mt. MAXWELL PROVINCIAL PARK

Fulford-Ganges Rd.

SPRING

Stowell Lake

Beaver Pt. Rd.

Weston Lake

RUCKLE PROVINCIAL PARK

Vancouver Island

Burgoyne Bay

Fulford-Ganges Rd.

Fulford Harbour

Isabella Pt. Rd.

Beaver Pt. Road

Mt. Sulivan ▲

Mt. Bruce ▲

ISLAND

Fulford Harbour

Cowichan Bay

Cowichan Bay

Separation Point

Musgrave Rd.

Mt. Tuam ▲

ECOLOGICAL RESERVE

16

Swartz Bay

Swartz Bay / Tsawwassen

Satellite Channel

Piers Island

PRINCESS MARGARET PROVINCIAL MARINE PARK

Portland Island

SALT SPRING ISLAND

Anne's Oceanfront
  Hideaway B&B **1**
Cloud 9 **2**
Cusheon Lake Resort **8**
Hastings House **5**
Monivea B&B **6**
Salt Springs Spa Resort **3**
Sky Valley Inn **7**
Wisteria Guest House **4**

THE PENDER ISLANDS

Inn on Pender Island **10**
Oceanside Inn **9**
Poets Cove Resort **12**
Shangri-La Oceanfront B&B **11**

SATURNA ISLAND

Breezy Bay B&B **13**
Lyall Habour B&B **15**
Saturna Lodge & Restaurant **14**

MAYNE ISLAND

Blue Vista Resort **18**
Mayne Island Eco Camping **19**
Oceanwood Country Inn **16**
Sage Cottage **17**

GALIANO ISLAND

Bellhouse Inn **21**
Bodega Ridge Resort **27**
Cliff Pagoda B&B **25**
Driftwood Village Resort **20**
Galiano Inn & Spa **22**
Rocky Ridge B&B **26**
Whaler Bay Lodge **23**
Woodstone Country Inn **24**

Bellhouse
Provincial
Park
23
22
21
20
19
Georgina
Point
Lighthouse
Oyster
Bay
Tsawwassen
Waugh Rd.
Active
Miners
Bay

MAYNE
MT. PARKE
PARK
ISLAND
Mariners Way
East West Rd.
16
Dinner Bay
Campbell Bay
Wilkes Rd.
Fernhill Rd.
Bennett
Bay
18
17
Curlew I.
Horton
Bay

Strait
of
Georgia

Navy Channel
Piggott
Bay
Port
Washington
9
Swartz Bay / Tsawwassen
Port Washington Rd.
Hope
Bay
Amies Rd.
Otter Bay
S. Otter Bay
Bedwell
Harbour
Road
NORTH PENDER
ISLAND
Morning Bay
Winery
10
Medicine
Beach
Magic
Lake
Pirates
BEAUMONT
MARINE
P.P.
Bedwell Harbour
11
Browning Harbour
MT. NORMAN
REGIONAL
PARK
Canal Rd.
Spalding Rd.
SOUTH
PENDER
ISLAND
12
Samuel
Island
Veruna Bay
WINTER COVE
PROVINCIAL
MARINE
PARK
Lyall Harbour
Saturna Pt. East Point Rd.
Saturna
Island
Vineyards
15
14
Harris Rd.
SATURNA ISLAND
ECOLOGICAL
RESERVE
13
Breezy
Bay
Warburton
Pike
East Point Rd.
Russell Reef

Tumbo Island
Tumbo Channel
Tumbo Channel Rd.
Cliffside Rd.
East Point
Regional
Park
Narvaez Bay Rd.

Swanson Channel
Brookes Pt.
Boundary Pass

Moresby
Island

0		2 mi
0		2 km

Collect Island Dollars

Although they're not worth a pinch of salt off the island, Salt Spring Island Dollars are a valued commodity when you're there. They are accepted by most island businesses, some of which have bills on hand to give as change, or they can be purchased dollar-for-dollar at the tourist Information Centre in Ganges. The goal of the local currency is to raise funds for worthwhile community projects while promoting local commerce and good will. Art featured on the back of limited editions of the notes helps to make them collectible after the 2-year expiry date. Legally considered gift certificates, the Salt Spring Island Dollar is Canada's only local legal-tender currency in circulation.

Getting Around

Silver Shadow Taxi (© 250/537-3030) services the island. If you want to rent a car, **Salt Spring Marine Rentals** (© **250/537-5464** or 250/537-3122) in downtown Ganges can set you up with a mid-range vehicle for about C$60 a day. This company also rents scooters for C$50 per hour or C$70 for 24 hours. **Salt Spring Adventure Co.,** at Salt Spring Marina, 7-126 Upper Ganges Rd. (© **877/537-2764** or 250/537-2764; www.saltspring adventures.com), rents both bikes (C$25 per day) and kayaks (C$55–C$85 per day), and will deliver them to anywhere on Salt Spring Island for a nominal charge. Although there are no boat rentals available anywhere on the island, **Salt Spring Marina** at Harbour's End (124 Upper Ganges Rd.; © **800/334-6629** or 250/537-5810) does offer fishing charters. Costs start at C$450 for 4 hours for two people.

EXPLORING SALT SPRING ISLAND
Ganges

The bustling seaside village of **Ganges ★★★** belies the notion that the Gulf Islands are sleepy hideaways. The sheer number of realtors is a gauge of Salt Spring's "love-at-first-sight" appeal. Historic buildings and bright new commercial structures harbor banks and shopping malls, liquor stores, cafes, bakeries, and a busy marina. In this cultural center of the island, you'll also find several quality galleries of locally crafted goods. In spring, this showcase expands into **Artcraft,** an exhibition of more than 250 Gulf Island artisans. Housed at Mahon Hall, Artcraft runs May through September daily from 10am to 5pm (© **250/537-0899**). A **Studio Tour** (www.saltspringstudiotour.com) explores all manner of studios scattered among nooks and crannies on the island, letting you chat with the artists, view their work, and watch them create. Although officially tour season is from mid-May to the end of September, many spots are open year-round. Keep a lookout for the blue "sheep" signs for participating studios. Be warned, it can take about a week to visit them all!

Salt Spring's Saturday **farmers' market,** held in Centennial Park in the heart of Ganges, is another summer must-see. This weekly gathering is a glorious melee of islanders and visitors, dogs and children, craftspeople, food vendors, jugglers, and musicians. Everything for sale must be handmade or homegrown, so it's as much a feast for the eyes as for the stomach. If you're looking to snatch up some of the freshly baked goods, be sure to arrive before 10am, as they're often sold out within an hour or so of opening.

Otherwise, be prepared to stroll through the crowds, right up until late afternoon, when fresh-produce vendors, having sold their lot, start to drift away. And be prepared to find a few items that are unexpected, whether it's an alpaca throw, hand-painted Wellington boots, a pottery apple-baker, or whimsical jewelry. It's *the* place to shop if you're heading out for a weekend picnic or sail. Go to **www.saltspringmarket.com** for more information.

As good as it is, the farmers' market pales in comparison to the **Salt Spring Island Fall Fair,** an annual weekend event held toward the end of September at the Farmers' Institute Fairgrounds (351 Rainbow Rd.). Filled with all the sights, sounds, tastes, and smells of a good old-fashioned country fair, it showcases award-winning livestock and home-baked pies, alongside rides and classic games like balloon darts. The sheepdog trials are superb, with hardworking collies maneuvering bundles of sheep from one corner of the field to another, all to the command of a whistle. A shuttle runs from Ganges to the fairgrounds; call © **250/537-2484** for fair information.

Ruckle Provincial Park ★★

This 433-hectare (1,070-acre) park starts out along 8km (5 miles) of shoreline around **Beaver Point** and sweeps up to an expanse of open and grassy meadow. Once owned by the Ruckle family, Irish immigrants in the late 1800s, part of the park is still operated as a sheep farm by the Ruckle family. Several of the original buildings, including a barn and an old residence, still stand. Ruckle Park is by far the easiest hiking ground on Salt Spring Island, offering more than 15km (9¹/₃ miles) of trails, the favorite being a shoreline trail than runs 4,400m (14,436 ft.) from the heritage farm area right through to Yeo Point. Another trail, about the same distance but with some hills to climb, leaves from the park headquarters and heads inland in a loop around Merganser Pond. Trail maps are available at the park's visitor center. Be sure to remember your binoculars so that you can enjoy the abundance of wildlife. You're also likely to see scuba divers in the waters off Ruckle Park, where castle-like underwater caves and a profusion of marine life create intriguing dives.

The park has 75 walk-in campsites with fire pits (firewood is provided in the summer), 8 RV sites without hook-ups, plus some group sites, a picnic area, a large kitchen shelter, drinking water, several pit toilets, and a security patrol for the entire camping area. The park attracts eco-adventurers and families alike, though for young children you would be better off heading for **Cusheon Lake.** Ruckle Park has no designated swimming and playground areas, and no interpretive programs. From mid-March to October, a camping fee of C$15 per night applies, and you must reserve your campsite in advance. Camping is free from November to mid-March, on a first-come, first-served basis. No firewood is supplied November through mid-March. Call (© **877/559-2115** or 250/539-2115) for local reservations and information, or log on to www.discovercamping.ca.

Vesuvius

Located at the western edge of Salt Spring Island, the village, which consists of old seaside cottages knitted together by winding lanes, was named for its wonderful sunsets, made all the more dramatic by the clouds of smoke that spew forth across the Stuart Channel, from a pulp mill in Crofton on Vancouver Island. Unfortunately, this artistry also carries an off-putting pulpy odor, though that's not putting off a remake of the area. It started with the closure of one of the island's time-honored watering holes, the Vesuvius Inn, rumored to be morphing into a jazz bar, and continues with the development of the

Palatable Diversions

Treats for your taste buds, here are some of Salt Springs' top culinary diversions:

- **Big Foot Organic Herb Farm** (104 Eagle Ridge Dr.; © 250/537-4466): Unusual varieties of fresh and dried herbs along with salsas, jams, jellies, chutney, flavored vinegars, honeys, and mustards.
- **Salt Spring Cheese Company** (285 Reynolds Rd.; © 250/653-2300) and **Moonstruck Organic Cheese** (1306 Beddis Rd.; © 250/537-4987; www. moonstruckcheese.com): Artisan goat cheeses and a gourmet selection of blues, savory, and ash-ripened Camembert cheeses.
- **Salt Spring Vineyards & Winery** (151 Lee Rd.; © 250/653-9463; www. saltspringvineyards.com), and Garry **Oaks Vineyard** (1880 Fulford-Ganges Rd.; © 250/653-4687; www.garryoakswine.com): Cottage wineries lying side by side, with wine tasting and retail sales of Pinot Gris, Pinot Noir, Blackberry port, and Gewürztraminer. The Oaks even offers a labyrinth to walk.
- **Sacred Mountain Lavender Farm** (401 Musgrave Rd.; © 250/653-2315; www.sacredmountainlavender.com): A "boutique" lavender farm that grows more than 60 varieties of the plant, from which are made specialty and custom-made products from lavender salts and scrubs to lavender coffee and chocolates.
- **Gulf Islands Brewery** (270 Furness Rd.; © 250/653-2383; www.gulfislands brewery.com): Producer of golden ales and an Irish-style extra stout; it's the only brewery in the Gulf Islands.

And for those who would rather not go it alone, **Island Gourmet Safaris** (© 250/537-4118; www.islandgourmetsafaris.com) hosts year-round tours to discover Salt Spring through its art and cuisine. Tours are 6 hours long and start at C$500 for one to four people, including lunch, which features only Salt Spring Island produce.

Vesuvius Villas, an upscale vacation condominium complex. **BC Ferries** (© 888/223-3777 or 250/386-3432; www.bcferries.com) runs a regular service—almost every hour—across the Stuart Channel to Crofton. Return fares are C$9 for adults, C$4.50 for children, and C$29 for a standard-size vehicle. The crossing takes 20 minutes.

WHERE TO STAY

Anne's Oceanfront Hideaway B&B   This oceanfront inn offers cozy lounges (one a library with a TV/DVD/VCR, the other with a coffee/cookie counter) and comfortable furnishings. A central staircase leads upstairs to guest rooms that are well appointed and individually decorated, and include a fireplace. Decor ranges from French country styling to Queen Anne elegance and tends to appeal to the older crowd on a romantic getaway. Situated on the edge of a cliff, Anne's provides sweeping views of the island and sea. Thoughtful touches include free soft drinks in the guest-room fridge upon arrival, slippers and robe for when you want to head outside to the Jacuzzi, and evening turndown

service. An elevator makes the four upstairs guest rooms wheelchair accessible, as well as **219**
the lower level, where, with advance notice, you can enjoy an aromatherapy massage.
Four-course breakfasts are elegantly served and include items such as a salmon scramble
wrap, a portobello Benedict, and an artichoke and pimento frittata. The inn prides itself
on being completely free of allergens, if indeed such a thing is possible.

168 Simson Rd., Salt Spring Island, BC V8K 1E2. © **888/474-2663** or 250/537-0851. Fax 250/537-0861.
www.annesoceanfront.com. 4 units. May–Sept C$210–C$275; Oct–Apr C$195–C$225. Rates include
breakfast. AE, MC, V. Pets not accepted. Children not accepted. **Amenities:** Lounges; Jacuzzi; massage;
Wi-Fi. *In room:* Fridge, hair dryer, no phone.

Cloud 9 ★★   Perched atop one of Salt Spring Island's highest hills, Cloud 9 lives up
to its name, with unobstructed 180-degree views of the ocean and neighboring islands.
With vaulted ceilings, scores of large windows, and more than 46 sq. m (495 sq. ft.) of
decks, the views are spectacular. And that's just the main house. Two guest suites, the
Celeste and Orion, are in a similar, but separate, cedar-sided building, and there's a self-
contained craftsman coach house that's ideal for longer stays. In the main house, all guest
rooms have private entrances with French doors, spacious patios, and enough pampering
touches to encourage cocooning and romance. Of special note are the individually controlled heated floors, fireplaces, down duvets and pillows, satellite TV, and genuine Persian rugs that complement the overall modern West Coast decor. Enormous bathrooms
have deep double-soaker or jetted bathtubs. You even get two pairs of slippers: one for
inside, the other for outside (to get to the cliff-side Jacuzzi), as well as a pair of binoculars.
If you choose to have breakfast in your suite, it's included in the rate. If you choose the
more formal option of dining in the main house, there's a surcharge of C$20. The first
is a very good continental breakfast; the latter includes a hot selection.

238 Sun Eagle Dr., Salt Spring Island, BC V8K 1E5. © **877/722-8233** or 250/537-2776. Fax 250/537-2776.
www.cloud9oceanview.com. 3 units. Mid-Jun to Sept C$180–C$200; Oct and May to mid-June C$155–
C$175; Nov–Apr C$135–C$155. Extra person C$50. MC, V. Pets accepted with prior approval. Children 12
and under not accepted. **Amenities:** 2 lounges; Jacuzzi; bike rentals; laundry service. *In room:* TV/VCR,
dataport, Wi-Fi, hair dryer.

Cusheon Lake Resort (Kids)   With its location right on the shores of Cusheon Lake,
this great family-oriented resort has a holiday camp feel. The one- and two-bedroom log
cabins and A-frame chalets are spotlessly clean and furnished in a no-nonsense style that
suits families and people who want a self-catering, un-froufrou getaway. The kitchen is
well stocked with all the essentials, including coffee filters. Beach towels are also part of
the deal because there's so much to do in and around the lake: canoeing, swimming,
rowing, picnicking, and lawn games. Although there's generally a 2- or 3-night minimum
stay, if there's an opening, they'll accept 1-night stands!

171 Natalie Lane, Salt Spring Island, BC V8K 2C6. © **250/537-9629.** www.cusheonlake.com. 16 units.
Mid-May to mid-Oct C$148–C$222; mid-Oct to mid-May C$115–C$180. Additional person C$20. 2-night
minimum stay; 3-night minimum July and Aug. Weekly rates available. MC, V. Pets not accepted (kennel
nearby). **Amenities:** Lake swimming; outdoor hot tub; canoes; rowboats; picnic tables; BBQ; Wi-Fi. *In
room:* Kitchen, fridge, coffeemaker, microwave, fireplace (some), no phone.

Hastings House ★★★   A member of the exclusive Small Luxury Hotels of the
World, this upscale inn lies an olive pit's throw from the village of Ganges, in a magnificent garden and orchard overlooking Ganges Harbour. First a Hudson's Bay Company
trading post, and then a farm, the homestead was bought in the 1930s by Barbara Wedg-
wood, the British pottery heiress, who turned the site into a replica of a 16th-century
Sussex estate (all the while driving around Salt Spring's country roads in a Rolls-Royce).

Since then, the Tudor-style manor house, farmhouse, barn, and trading post have been renovated into cottages and suites, each charged with character and filled with original art and antiques, and all the modern luxuries of a first-class hotel (including bathrooms large enough for deep soaking tubs), save for TVs and DVD players, which are provided only on request. An inviting, two-room spa includes luxuries such as a steam shower and heated floors; in 2009, a sculpture garden was added, which includes a 1.5km (0.9-mile) trail of forest paths past intriguing onsite installations and art. The restaurant is equally impressive (see "Where to Dine," below). Reserve 6 months in advance for summer visits. Rates include a morning hamper (a lavish continental breakfast); if you're still hungry, breakfast is offered at a la carte prices. One of the neatest add-on packages offered is to catch your own Dungeness crab in one of the hotel's crab traps. If you want to learn how to clean and prepare crabs yourself, the chef will show you how, or you can just have him create a crab specialty for you to enjoy.

160 Upper Ganges Rd., Ganges, Salt Spring Island, BC V8K 2S8. © **800/661-9255** or 250/537-2362. Fax 250/537-5333. www.hastingshouse.com. 18 units. June–Sept C$360–C$910; mid-Mar to May and Oct to mid-Nov C$295–C$800. Rates include wake-up hamper and afternoon tea. Extra person C$85. AE, DC, MC, V. Closed mid-Nov to mid-Mar. Children 16 and under not accepted. **Amenities:** Restaurant; lounge with honor bar and Wi-Fi; spa. *In room:* No phone.

Monivea B&B **Finds** Owner John French claims, with some justification, to be the son of James Bond, or at least the next best thing. The story goes that Ian Fleming was friends with his father, a world-traveled British spy, and apparently parlayed dad's dashing ways into the 007 character. There's nothing furtive about Monivea, however. Located within an easy walk of Ganges, this beautifully furnished inn offers three self-contained artisan suites, each with private entrance, en suite, and decor that's a comfortable mix of antiques, heritage quilts, and local art. Locally, the inn is know as the Starry Night Artisan Gallery. The garden is stunning with ponds and fountains; it can be enjoyed from the main deck, which also offers peekaboo ocean views, or the conservatory where breakfast is served (if the weather's good, breakfast is especially intimate on one of the garden's private patios). The inn uses only organic produce and even has its own laying hens for fresh eggs.

420 Fulford Ganges Rd., Salt Spring Island, BC V8K 2K1. © **888/537-5856** or 250/537-5856. Fax 250/537-5856. www.moniveasaltspring.com. 3 units. Apr–Sep C$159–C$169; Oct–Mar C$111–C$133. Extra person C$35. 2-night minimum stay. Rates include breakfast. MC, V. Pets not accepted. Children sometimes accepted. **Amenities:** Lounge; Wi-Fi. *In room:* TV, no phone.

Salt Springs Spa Resort This spa resort is the only spot where the island's salty spring waters can be enjoyed. The day spa offers a variety of facials, body wraps, and massages, as well as some exotic Ayurvedic therapies and yoga sessions. Even if the spa isn't your thing, Salt Springs is a great getaway; choose from several one-, two-, and three-bedroom A-frame chalets. A handful are in the forest, but most sport an ocean view, looking across Trincomali Channel to Wallace Island, a marine park. All chalets have full kitchen; wood-burning fireplaces (including complimentary supplies of firewood); wide porches with BBQs; and an oversize, two-person mineral tub in addition to a regular bathtub. Clamming gear and crab traps are available for those wanting to try their luck on the beach across the road.

1460 North Beach Rd., Salt Spring Island, BC V8K 1J4. © **800/665-0039** or 250/537-4111. Fax 250/537-2939. www.saltspringspa.com. 13 chalets. Late June to Aug C$199–C$299; Mar to late June and Sept–Oct C$135–C$219; Nov–Feb C$109–C$199. Extra person C$20. 2-night minimum stay in summer. Weekly rates and packages available. AE, MC, V. Free parking. Pets not accepted. Children not accepted. **Amenities:** Badminton court; spa; free bikes and rowboats; game room; coin-op washer and dryer; Wi-Fi. *In room:* Kitchen, fridge, coffeemaker, microwave, hair dryer, fireplace, no phone.

Sky Valley Inn (Finds)   With a touch of Provence in every renovated corner, Sky Valley is more like an old French country retreat nestled on 4.5 hectares (11 acres), with outstanding views to neighboring islands. Each of the three guest rooms is distinctly decorated with hardwood floors, French toile wallpaper, and wainscoting. The king- and queen-size down-feather mattresses are topped with down duvets and crisp white linens for a luxurious feel. Each room has a private entrance; the Garden Room is completely separate from the main house. Amenities even include hand-crafted, homemade soap. Gourmet breakfasts are served in an open French-style country kitchen and will likely include cheese blintz crepes, a frittata or soufflé, as well as lavender scones and peach and lavender jams that have won first prizes in the Salt Spring Island Fall Fair.

421 Sky Valley Rd., Salt Spring Island, BC V8K 2C3. ✆ 866/537-1028 or 250/537-9800. www.skyvalleyinn. com. 3 units. C$170–C$220 year-round. 2-night minimum stay in summer. MC, V. Pets not accepted. Children not accepted. **Amenities:** Lounge with TV/DVD; outdoor swimming pool; Wi-Fi. *In room:* No phone.

Wisteria Guest House ★   Located within a 10-minute stroll of Ganges, this charming inn is so full of color and character, it's hard to believe that it was once a nursing home. Its renaissance has certainly created something for everyone. The main guest house has six vibrantly decorated rooms: two with en suites, and four that share two bathrooms, making them a good choice for friends and family traveling together. The two studios are the most romantic. Each has a private entrance, French doors leading onto a sunny patio, and a well-equipped kitchenette. One has a king, the other a queen-size bed. If you want to be totally independent and able to prepare your own meals, the private cottage, with twin beds, has a fully equipped kitchen, cable TV, and private patio. In winter, only a cold breakfast is served, though that might not be the drawback it sounds. One of the owners was a pastry chef at the Westin New York, so breakfast is still a pretty lavish affair of home-made Swiss-style muesli and almond croissants. In summer, you can enjoy additional items such as savory egg strudels, bramble crumbles, or baked eggs.

268 Park Dr., Salt Spring Island, BC V8K 2S1. ✆ 250/537-5899. Fax 250/537-5644. www.wisteriaguest house.com. 9 units. Mid-May to mid-Oct C$159–C$169, C$119–C$139 with shared bath; mid-Oct to Feb C$119–C$129, C$99–C$109 with shared bath; Mar to mid-May C$139–C$149, C$109–C$149 with shared bath. Extra person C$10–C$15. Pets accepted. AE, MC, V. **Amenities:** Common room w/TV and fireplace. *In room:* No phone.

WHERE TO DINE

Auntie Pesto's Café ECLECTIC WEST COAST   With a lovely view of Ganges Harbour and a waterfront patio, this tiny eatery is busy all day long, whether because of its hearty soups and over-stuffed sandwiches on fresh-baked breads, or its excellent pasta dishes (including wheat-free) that come with a choice of toppings such as marinated tofu, prawns, meatballs, and homemade sauces. The dinner menu features steak and seafood specials that may include Thai-prawn stir-fry or grilled halibut with salsa topping. The latter is homemade using whatever is in season.

2104–115 Fulford-Ganges Rd., Grace Point Sq. ✆ 250/537-4181. www.auntiepestos.com. Reservations recommended (and only accepted) for dinner July–Aug. Main courses C$8–C$12 lunch; C$10–C$20 dinner. MC, V. Daily 8am–9pm.

Hastings House ★★ PACIFIC NORTHWEST   Impeccable cuisine, attentive service, and a gracious setting have helped make Hastings House one of the most sought-after destination restaurants—and inns—in the Pacific Northwest (see "Where to Stay," above). In addition to a la carte selections, there's a superb, multi-course menu that changes daily; many of the ingredients come from the estate's gardens and orchards. Dinner can be a sophisticated, evening-long affair with an excellent wine list. The choice of entrees nearly always features Salt Spring lamb, the house specialty (try it grilled with rosemary spaetzle and a grainy mustard jus), local salmon (perhaps a paprika-crusted white spring), as well as such selections as an excellent duck breast with wild mushroom risotto and port wine jus. In warm weather, the best tables are on the veranda overlooking the gardens and harbor.

160 Upper Ganges Rd. (℗ **250/537-2362.** Reservations required. 4-course prix fixe dinner C$95; entrees C$12–C$48. AE, DC, MC, V. Mid-Mar to mid-Nov daily 6–10pm. Closed mid-Nov to mid-Mar.

House Piccolo ★ SCANDINAVIAN CONTINENTAL   This small blue-and-white heritage farmhouse-turned-restaurant is wonderfully intimate. Two-person tables are scattered through two connecting country-style dining rooms accented with copper kettles set high on shelves. Everything on the Scandinavian-style menu is enticing, particularly the fresh bread, broiled prawn and sea-scallop brochettes, and weiner schnitzel. You might even want to open your wallet up for the caviar (at C$125 per oz.) and buckwheat blinis—they're that good. Save room for homemade ice cream or the signature chocolate terrine. House Piccolo is a member of Chaine des Rôtisseurs, an international gastronomic society dedicated to the promotion of fine dining around the world.

108 Hereford Ave. (℗ **250/537-1844.** www.housepiccolo.com. Reservations recommended July–Sept. Main courses C$27–C$38. AE, DC, MC, V. May–Sept daily 5–10pm; Oct–Apr daily 5–8pm.

Moby's Marine Pub PUB FARE   This is a contemporary multilevel marine pub with big beams, wood floors, and great views of Ganges Harbour from cathedral-size windows. It's a local favorite, especially on live entertainment nights when an eclectic mix of R&B, folk, jazz, and rock takes the stage. If it's a local headliner, such as Valdy, performing, get there early to grab a table. Rocker Randy Bachman, of The Guess Who and Bachman-Turner-Overdrive fame, is one of the island's favorite sons, and makes an occasional appearance. The menu includes burgers and fajitas alongside savory entrees like Caribbean fish pot (to die for) and Louisiana lamb curry. Jazz on Sunday nights is a dinner tradition. Ten beers are on tap. Moby's deck hangs over the water, within inches of bullwhip kelp and minnows. It's a great place to catch some summer rays over a cold one.

124 Upper Ganges Rd. (℗ **250/537-5559.** Main courses C$8–C$19. MC, V. Sun–Thurs 10am–midnight; Fri–Sat 10am–1am.

Raven Street Market Café Pizza   The thin-crust, wood-fired pizzas here are among the best and most creative you'll find anywhere. Made in the traditional Neapolitan way, they include combinations such as roasted pepper chicken, basil, cilantro, and fresh tomatoes; herbed lamb and artichoke pesto; and "the Canadianne": real back bacon, chorizo sausage (or substitute with crab meat), mushroom, white mozzarella, black olives, and green pepper. Other dishes include a delicious seafood and sausage gumbo; a spicy, very good curried chicken mulligatawny; as well as focaccia sandwiches, burgers, and salads. Love the kids menu too, because it's uncluttered: simple cheese pizza, chicken strips, and a 4-ounce cheeseburger. This is a grocery and deli market as much as it is an eatery, which makes the atmosphere convivial and a tad busy; so the waitstaff may not be as attentive as you might like.

321 Fernwood Rd. (℗ **250/537-2273.** www.ravenstreet.ca. Main courses C$10–C$17. Mon noon–5pm; Tues–Sun 9am–8pm.

Tree House Cafe CAFE   Set in the heart of Ganges, this 12-seat cafe spills over onto a larger patio that stakes its claim around and beneath a sprawling old plum tree. In summer, the place is jammed, in part because of the folksy musical entertainment, but also because of the great food that includes everything from Thai peanut tofu and vegetarian chili to burgers and BLTs. The organic Salt Spring coffee sidelines Starbucks.

106 Purvis Lane, Ganges ℭ **250/537-5379.** Main courses C$5–C$7. MC, V. Oct–May daily 8am–3pm; June–Sept daily 8am–11pm.

---

3 THE PENDER ISLANDS

Known for their secluded coves, beautiful beaches, and islets, the Penders are a tranquil escape, and a boater's nirvana. With a population of barely 2,000, they remain small enough that, as one resident says, "The sight of another human being still conjures up a smile!"

The Penders are actually two islands, linked by a short wooden bridge that spans a canal between **Bedwell and Browning harbors.** Until 1903, when the canal was dug, island pioneers were forced to haul their boats laboriously over a wide neck of land known as "Indian Portant." Centuries before, the Coast Salish, a local First Nations group, used to set up seasonal camps in the area, and several shell middens (refuse heaps), some dating from 4500 B.C., have revealed thousands of artifacts, including carved spoons and lip ornaments. With several parks, picnic areas, and overnight camping facilities, the Penders are threaded with meandering, illogical roads that are a delight to tour by car or bicycle. The Penders have more public beach access points for their size than any other Gulf Island—37 in all, which add to the idyllic setting, as do picturesque cottages, orchards, and a dozen or so artisans' home galleries. The 9-hole golf course is a pleasant diversion, as is the golf Frisbee–throwing park, where the "tees" are metal poles tucked in between trees. The real trick is to keep your Frisbee from ricocheting off the trees on its flight to the target.

ESSENTIALS
Getting There
BC Ferries sails to **Otter Bay,** on the northwest side of North Pender Island. Pleasure boats can dock at **Bedwell Harbour,** on the southern cove where North and South Pender meet. See "Getting There," at the beginning of the chapter, for information on ferry fares and schedules.

Visitor Information
There is no formal visitor information center on Pender Island, although you can pick up brochures at the "mall," **The Driftwood Centre** (4605 Bedwell Harbour Rd.; ℭ **250/629-6555**). Or contact the **Pender Island Chamber of Commerce** (ℭ **866/ 468-7924;** www.penderislandchamber.com).

Getting Around
Pender Island Cab Company (ℭ **250/629-2222;** www.penderislandcab.com) provides service to various points around the islands. Bike and scooter rentals are available in season at **Otter Bay Marina** (ℭ **250/629-3579**) at a daily rate of C$25 and C$85 respectively. Hourly rentals are C$8 for bikes and C$25 for scooters.

North Pender

The larger of the two islands, **North Pender** is more populated and more developed than its southerly neighbor. Surprisingly, there's no real town center in the traditional sense on North Pender, so the modern **Driftwood Centre** (4605 Bedwell Harbour Rd., near Razor Point Rd.) in the center of the island, is the nucleus of island life. Here's where to stock up on groceries, gift items, and indulge in your sweet tooth at the must-visit gourmet Pender Island Bakery. The **Saturday Market** (May–Oct, 9:30am–12:30pm) is a fine place for mixing with the locals, sampling island-grown produce, and browsing through artisan stalls. Continue on along Razor Point Road toward Browning Harbour and you'll find one of the island's newer additions: **Morning Bay Vineyard,** 6621 Harbour Hill Dr. (📞 **250/629-8352;** www.morningbay.ca). Overlooking Plumber Sound and with a main building designed to look like a barn, it features 20 terraces that climb up the south side of Mount Menzies. In 2007, the vineyard delivered its first estate wines: Pinot Noir, Pinot Gris, Maréchal Foch, and Schonberger. Its Gewürztraminer-Riesling (the first vintage) has since won a silver medal in the 2008 All-Canadian Wine Championships, and its Reserve Merlot was awarded a bronze medal at the prestigious New York–based Finger Lakes competition. Tastings are Wednesday through Saturday, 10am to 5pm.

Away from the Driftwood, most activity happens around **Otter Bay,** where the ferries arrive, and **Port Browning.** At **Port Washington,** northwest of Otter Bay, you'll find orchards and charming old cottages reminiscent of a turn-of-the-20th-century coastal village. Check out **Pender Island Kayak Adventures** at the Otter Bay Marina (📞 **250/ 629-6939;** www.kayakpenderisland.com) for kayak rentals and guided kayaking tours and lessons in and around island coves and to neighboring Mayne and Saturna islands. Everyone from beginners to advanced kayakers are welcome. Two-hour guided tours are C$45 for adults, C$30 for children 11 and under; 3-hour tours are C$55 per person; and all-day paddles are C$100. *Tip:* Mondays are geared for family outings: Pay for your first child and the second paddles for half price. **Port Browning Marina,** 4605 Oak Rd. (📞 **250/629-3493**), on the northern cove where North and South Pender meet, is an inviting "watering hole," with First Nations decor, including a totem pole. This marina is cheerfully downscale from Bedwell Harbour on the other side of the narrow neck of land that separates the two islands, where Poets Cove Resort has made its mark. (see "Where to Stay," below). North Pender parks include **Medicine Beach,** one of the last wetlands in the Gulf Islands, and home to many native plants once used for food and medicine. The beach is within walking distance of **Prior Centennial Provincial Park,** a forest of cedar, maple, fir, and alder trees. Located 6km (3³/₄ miles) from the ferry terminal, Prior Centennial can also be reached off Canal Road. **Roesland** is a 230-hectare (568-acre) park that includes a headland, Roe Lake, a freshwater lake, beaches, and lots of forest. The site was once a summer cottage resort, and has an original farmhouse dating back to 1908 that now serves as a tiny museum. Take the trail past the Davidson home to the headland to see the rotting remains of a 220-year-old **Indian canoe** that lies 6km (3³/₄ miles) from the Otter Bay ferry terminal off Canal Road.

South Pender

This remote part of the island has always attracted independent, sometimes eccentric, fun-loving spirits who don't mind the isolation. Although the only services to be found are at the **Poets Cove Marina,** 9801 Spalding Rd. (📞 **250/629-3212**), there are lots of beaches, parks, and trails to enjoy. Hikers should head for **Mount Norman Regional**

(Fun Facts) Nature Preserved

Established in 2003, the Gulf Islands National Park Reserve now safeguards park lands and waters spread out over more than 15 islands and numerous smaller islets and reefs. Some are unforested and highly valued as marine mammal haulouts (for seals and sea lions) and nesting sites for black oyster-catcher, glaucous-winged gulls, and pigeon guillemot. Other areas are penin-sulas of old-growth, arbutus, and Garry oak forests.

Park (www.britishcolumbia.com/parks). At 244m (801 ft.), Mount Norman is the highest point on the Penders.

The gravel access road up to Mount Norman is uninteresting, but the 1km (0.6-mile) hike to the summit is well worth the effort. It starts at the Ainslie Point Road trail head, and as the trail begins to climb, the landscape changes from wetlands to forests of Douglas fir and western red cedar and ends with lichen-covered bedrock up top, where the panoramas are stunning. From Mount Norman Regional Park, you can access **Beaumont Marine Provincial Park**, without a doubt the prettiest marine park in the Gulf Islands, its picturesque coastal wilderness seemingly tamed by gentle waters, moss-covered rocks, and grassy verges. It's now a part of the Gulf Islands National Park Reserve (© 250/654-4000; www.pc.gc.ca/pn-np/bc/gulf), and is a moderate, 40-minute hike from Mount Norman.

Unlike the limited facilities of most of these parks, nearby Prior Centennial (also a part of the Reserve) includes 17 vehicle/tent sites, pit toilets, water, fire pits, and picnic tables. Call © 800/689-9025 for reservations. Sites are C$14 per night. Another favorite recreation area, **Brookes Point,** is one of the last undeveloped headlands in the Gulf Islands. The coastal bluff is ecologically important as it hosts rare types of native grass and more than 100 bird species, some of which are endangered. Large pods of **killer whales** sometimes swim right under the point in the nearby kelp beds, as do mink, seal, otter, and Dall's porpoises. Tidal pools contain abalone, sea anemones, and coral. If you have good shoes, the walk along the shoreline from here to Gowlland Point is captivating.

WHERE TO STAY

Inn on Pender Island ★ (Value) Situated next to Prior Centennial Provincial Park, this unpretentious inn offers a choice of nine motel-style lodge rooms or three studio log cabins, many with ocean views and some with private Jacuzzis. Lodge rooms are clean and spacious; cabins have fireplaces and deck swings. Children and pets are welcome. **Memories at the Inn** is a fully licensed restaurant, and although the decor's a bit plain, it's a popular choice for affordable dining. The homemade pizza is exceptionally good.

4709 Canal Rd. (P.O. Box 72), Pender Island, BC V0N 2M0. © 800/550-0172 or 250/629-3353. Fax 250/629-3167. www.innonpender.com. 12 units. May–Sept C$79–C$99 lodge room, C$149 cabin; Oct–Apr C$69–C$89 lodge room, C$139 cabin. MC, V. Small pets accepted. **Amenities:** Restaurant; Jacuzzi. *In room:* TV/VCR, fridge, coffeemaker.

Oceanside Inn ★ You can't beat the location: minutes from the ferry terminal and nestled amid arbutus trees on a secluded oceanfront. The name of each room describes its best attribute: Ocean View, with its modern, chocolate-toned decor; Garden View, with country wicker furniture; and the largest and most romantic suite, the Channel View, from which you can see Mt. Baker in Washington State. Also, the Ocean and Garden View rooms are the only two with fireplaces, though all rooms have private decks and outdoor hot tubs. Rates include a breakfast such as eggs Benedict, orange French toast, or seafood omelet alongside fresh fruit and home-baked scones.

4230 Armadale Rd. (P.O. Box 50), Pender Island, BC V0N 2M0. (②) **800/601-3284** or 250/629-6691. www.penderisland.com. 3 units. C$159–C$239 double. Closed mid-Oct to early Apr. V only. Children not accepted. **Amenities:** Lounge; private hot tub; tour/activities information; in-room massage; beach access from property; Internet. *In room:* TV, Wi-Fi, fridge, hair dryer, iron, no phone.

Poets Cove Resort & Spa ★★ (Kids)   This seaside resort is one of the most upscale, year-round destinations in the Gulf Islands, offering so much to do that you never have to leave the resort. Accommodations range from 22 modern lodge rooms (they all face west to catch terrific sunsets) to deluxe two- and three-bedroom cottages (best for romantic getaways) and spacious and family-oriented villas complete with kitchens, dining rooms, living rooms with fireplaces, balconies, and BBQs. Most have private hot tubs. Children's programs and a 110-slip marina make it a popular spot for families and boaters. The bright, airy Aurora Restaurant (see "Where to Dine" below) features French-influenced fine dining, and Syrens Lounge & Bistro offers casual dining inside or on the enormous deck. The menu includes kid-friendly burgers and pint portions of other selections for smaller appetites. If you're staying in a cottage or villa, you can order items from the "raw menu" to barbecue yourself. The Susurrus Spa is a destination unto itself, with six large treatment rooms, a steam cave, and oceanfront Jacuzzi.

Tip: The "Poets Cruises" is an excellent 3-hour island hop and eco-adventure (C$109) with different itineraries that include stopovers at historic Hope Bay on North Pender, the vineyard on Saturna Island, and places to spot wildlife in the area.

9801 Spalding Rd., South Pender Island, BC V0N 2M3. (②) **888/512-7638** or 250/629-2100. Fax 250/629-2105. www.poetscove.com. 22 rooms, 15 cottages, 9 villas. C$239–C$299 lodge room; C$489–C$699 cottage; C$399–C$569 villa. Children 17 and under stay free in parent's room. AE, MC, V. **Amenities:** Restaurant; pub; large heated outdoor pool; 2 outdoor tennis courts; spa; extensive watersports rentals; children's programs; activity center; marina; Wi-Fi. *In-room:* TV/DVD, dataport, Wi-Fi, fridge, coffeemaker, hair dryer.

Shangri-La Oceanfront B&B   Perched on Pender's Oaks Bluff with 4 hectares (10 acres) of wilderness at its feet, this sprawling house is the only B&B on the island with 360-degree views and 511 sq. m (5,500 sq. ft.) of wraparound balconies from which to drink it all in: a panorama that stretches across Swanson Channel to Washington State's Mount Baker and the Olympic Range to the coastal mountains on the mainland. Staying here is like nesting in your own deluxe aerie, complete with private deck and Jacuzzi. Guest rooms have fireplaces, hot tubs, covered decks with furnishings of pale earth tones, and muted floral fabrics. Beds include down duvets, and queen-size mattresses have foam toppers for extra comfort. The Lost in Space Suite even has glow-in-the-dark planetary murals, and, because of its extra size and amenities such as a BBQ, microwave, and private hot tub, it's good for longer stays. A range of in-room spa services is available, from massage to Reiki.

5909 Pirate's Rd., Pender Island, BC V0N 2M2. (②) **877/629-2800** or 250/629-3808. Fax 250/629-3018. www.penderislandshangrila.com. 3 units. May to mid-Sept C$215–C$235; mid-Sept to early Jan C$145–C$175; mid-Jan to Apr C$140–C$165. Extra person C$35. Rates include full breakfast. AE, MC, V. Pets accepted (C$20). **Amenities:** Jacuzzi; complimentary bikes; game room; massage. *In room:* TV, fridge, coffeemaker, no phone.

Aurora ★ PACIFIC NORTHWEST   By far the most sophisticated dining room you'll find anywhere on the Penders, Aurora serves food to match the great marine views. There's a French influence to the menu items, which lean to local produce. Standouts include the Salt Spring goat-cheese tart and herb salad, an herb-crusted Pacific salmon (the catch of the day is always a good choice), and Pender Island lamb. For dessert, try the excellent crème brûlée or choose the cheese plate; it's an excellent sampling of local artisan creations. The restaurant is a romantic spot, whether you sit by the huge stone fireplace that dominates one wall or beside the floor-to-ceiling windows. If you're an oenophile, you'll probably prefer a table near the wall of wine bottles—the wine list is extensive.

In Poets Cove Resort & Spa, 9801 Spalding Rd. ✆ **250/629-2100.** Reservations recommended. Main courses C$24–C$35. AE, MC, V. Daily 5:30–10pm.

Hope Bay Café ★ ⓕ (Finds) NEW CANADIAN   At first blush, you wouldn't expect this casual, light-filled bistro to have such a gourmet attitude to food. But you're in for a treat. It's the only on-the-water restaurant on the island, and virtually every table has a view of the ocean only feet away. Everything is prepared in an open kitchen, which adds to the bustle. It starts in the morning as a coffee-and-scones place, and at lunch serves excellent fish and chips, burgers and quesadillas, and soups and salads. Dinners feature nourishing, substantial meals such as a hearty bouillabaisse, and a pork tenderloin crusted with hazelnuts and served with garlic mashed potatoes. The wine list has about 20 red and white selections, including some from the local Pender winery, Morning Bay. Hot breakfasts and brunch are served only on Sundays. The deck is a favorite spot for alfresco dining.

4301 Bedwell Harbour Rd. ✆ **250/629-6668.** Reservations recommended in summer. Main courses C$15–C$22. MC, V. Sept–June Wed–Sun 9am–8pm; July–Aug daily 9am–10pm.

Pistou Grill Casual Bistro ★ BISTRO   It's nearly always the first recommendation you'll hear from any local, and even though the service can be brusque (there's a definite French attitude here), the food is consistently good, and the place is always busy. The chef-owner has cooked for presidents, prime ministers, four-star generals, and many celebrities, so it's no surprise that his cuisine exudes flair and creativity. Try the broiled garlic prawns with sweet potato puree and mango fresh coriander coulis, the butternut squash and wild mushroom moussaka with smoked red pepper sauce, or the hearty slow-cooked organic buffalo short ribs. All the made-from-scratch soups are excellent.

Driftwood Centre, 4605 Bedwell Harbour Rd. ✆ **250/629-3131.** Dinner reservations required. Main courses C$6–C$10 lunch; C$18–C$25 dinner. MC, V. Tues–Sun 11:30am–2:30pm and 5:30–8pm.

4 GALIANO ISLAND

Galiano Island is a magnet for outdoor enthusiasts. It's a long, skinny island that stretches more than 26km (16 miles) from top to bottom, and is no more than 2km (1¹⁄₂ miles) across. Two harbors and several parks provide abundant opportunity to hike, camp, fish, boat, and bird-watch—activities that have, in fact, been hard won. Logging was once Galiano's biggest industry, and when clearcutting almost destroyed the wilderness, the community rallied, purchasing key tracts of land that have now returned to wilderness. Remnants of lumber operations are still evident in parts, including a shoreline strewn with salt-laden, sun-bleached logs. In spite of their activism, the folks on Galiano are actually very laid-back. It's as if they've not quite outgrown their obsession with growing marijuana back in the '70s. For boomers, this may be strangely comforting.

Most of the 1,100 or so permanent residents live on the southern part of the island, close to **Sturdies Bay,** which, for all intents and purposes, is the island's downtown. So it's here that you'll find most of the accommodations, restaurants, and stores, as well as in the surrounding areas of **Georgeson Bay, Montague Harbour,** and **Spotlight Cove.** North Galiano is much wilder, and although there are pockets of housing, the country is dense with cedar and fir trees, maple and alder stands.

ESSENTIALS
Getting There

BC Ferries sails to **Sturdies Bay** on the southern tip of the island. Boaters and float-planes dock at **Montague Harbour,** on the west coast, about a 20-minute drive from Sturdies Bay.

Visitor Information

Contact the **Galiano Chamber of Commerce,** 2590 Sturdies Bay Rd. (P.O. Box 73), Galiano Island, BC V0N 1P0 (✆ **250/539-2233;** www.galianoisland.com). Open in July and August daily from 9am to 5pm and September to June on occasional weekends from 9am to 5pm.

Getting Around

Taxi Galiano (✆ **250/539-0202**) provides year-round land-based taxi service, and the **Gulf Islands Water Taxi** (✆ **250/537-2510**) runs a service between Galiano, Mayne, and Salt Spring islands. You can also rent boats and mopeds from **Galiano Adventures,** at Montague Harbour (✆ **250/539-3443**), and bicycles from **Galiano Bicycle,** 36 Burrill Rd., Sturdies Bay (✆ **250/539-9906**). Mopeds are available from May to September and cost C$20 per hour. Bike rentals are C$35 for a 24-hour period.

EXPLORING GALIANO ISLAND

In and around **Sturdies Bay,** you'll find picturesque B&Bs, a few galleries, and a handful of shops. Nearby, **Bellhouse Provincial Park** is one of prettiest spots on the island, with a rocky, moss-covered peninsula, sculpted sandstone, and magnificent groves of copper-red arbutus trees. Situated at the entrance to **Active Pass,** it's an ideal place to picnic and to linger for an hour or two, watching the myriad kinds of wildlife. Tides run up to 5 knots here, and the shoreline drops sharply into deep water, making it an excellent point to spin-cast for salmon.

Galiano Bluffs Park, another favorite area, is also at the entrance to Active Pass but sits 120m (394 ft.) above it. The views from the bluffs deserve rave reviews. Watch BC Ferries' largest ships rumble past, and grab your binoculars to see eagles catching the updrafts, as well as seals, sea lions, and other marine life. Seasonal wildflowers are an equal delight. Go easy on the approach road; it has some serious potholes. **Montague Harbour Marina** (✆ **250/539-5733**) is a fun place to visit, if only to yacht-watch or grab a light meal in the marina restaurant. While there, check out **Galiano Island Kayaking** (✆ **250/539-2442;** www.seakayak.ca). The 3-hour rentals range from C$28 to C$40 a person, depending on the kayak; full-day paddles are from C$50 to C$70 a person. You can also rent canoes. **Gulf Island Safaris** (✆ **888/656-9878**) runs wildlife and whale-watching tours that get you up close with marine life aboard rubber Zodiac boats, with pre-arranged pick ups from Galiano.

One of the Gulf Islands' most popular provincial parks, Montague Harbour is a great place from which to watch giant American yachts arriving, and chattering kingfishers diving for salmon. Swim and beachcomb to your heart's content along gorgeous shell and gravel beaches, enjoy a picnic on the bluff, and search through shell middens dating back 3,000 years. The protected waters are perfect for beginner rowers, and hiking trails include an easy 3km (2-mile) forest and beach walk that loops around Gray Peninsula, originally inhabited by First Nations peoples. Along the northwest edge of the peninsula are spectacular rippled rock ledges as well as white shell beaches, and along the southern shore are two caves that can be reached by foot at low tide, or by boat.

If you want to stay awhile, the park has two year-round campgrounds: one with 15 walk-in sites for boaters and cyclists, another with 25 drive-in sites for motorists. *Note:* There are no RV hookups. There's a boat ramp, 35 mooring buoys, and a store. Free interpretive talks are offered during July and August. Check the **Nature House** for schedules. Buoys are C$10 per vessel; campsites are C$17 each. Call **Discover Camping** at ✆ **800/689-9025** or 250/391-2300 for information and reservations, or go online to www.discovercamping.ca. For a more rustic camping experience, head up to the northern tip of Galiano, where you'll find Dionisio Point Provincial Park. Sitting at the entrance to Porlier Pass, it is accessed only by water. Be sure to approach it at slack tide, as the currents can be unruly. There are 30 first-come, first-served walk-in campsites. Even if you're not overnighting here, the park's beaches are strewn with shell middens to comb, making them a good pit stop for day-tripping kayakers.

WHERE TO STAY

Bellhouse Inn ★★   Built in the 1880s, this scenic waterfront farmhouse is surrounded by meadows, grazing sheep, and orchards. Views of Active Pass are up close and personal, whether you're playing croquet on the lawn, lazing on the sandy beach, or sprawling in a hammock. Guest rooms are small and decorated with hardwood floors, wicker furniture, and quilted country-style bedspreads. Rooms have lovely bathrooms and private balconies. Thankfully, the main lounge is large and extremely comfortable (think sink-into sofas and deep chairs). The owners will arrange an in-room massage, just in case lazing around hasn't worked out all the muscle knots. This inn even provides guests with hot water bottles—not because the rooms are cold, but because the owners

---

ⓕFinds   Stoneworld Studio

Located above the Bodega Ridge Resort, Stoneworld (✆ **250/539-3262;** www.cedarplace.com/stoneworld) is an extraordinary indoor/outdoor gallery of engineering art, both for the seven-sided building itself and for the sculptures it contains. Ex-forestry engineer Steve Ocsko started stone sculpting in his sixties and has since created work of museum quality. Some are figures that spin on their weight or glisten with natural ores; others are iconic henges that are thrust deeply into the ground and, in the early morning mist, take on an ethereal quality. Even more remarkable is that even though Ocsko lost three fingers on his right hand many years ago, it hasn't impeded his ability to become a master sculptor. To find other island artists, pick up a Galiano Art Guide.

are English and therefore have a natural predisposition to these homey comforts. In summer you'll probably spend most of your time on the expansive decks, unless you're tempted to go sailing; the owners also charter a 43-foot yacht.

29 Farmhouse Rd. (P.O. Box 16), Site 4, Galiano Island, BC V0N 1P0. ✆ **800/970-7464** or 250/539-5667. Fax 250/539-5316. www.bellhouseinn.com. 3 units. June–Sept C$135–C$195; Oct–May C$85–C$135. 2-night minimum stay in cabins. Rates include full breakfast. MC, V. Children not accepted. **Amenities:** Lounge; in-room massage; library. *In room:* Hair dryer, no phone.

Bodega Ridge Resort ★ (Kids) (Value)   Located near Spanish Hills, at the island's northern end, this hilltop resort and sheep farm is a rambling collection of hand-hewn cottages, offering majestic views and basic comforts. The immaculate two-level log chalets are simply decorated and have full kitchens, making them ideal for families, while no. 7, the only single-level building, is a cozy hideaway for romantics. They feature stained-glass doors and tasteful wood furnishings. Kiwi and grape vines clamber over the main farmhouse, and landscaped gardens are sprinkled with Celtic standing stones, ponds, and kilometers of hiking trails. The resort offers mountain bike rentals and exclusive guided tours through the network of private trails.

120 Manastee Rd. (P.O. Box 115), Galiano Island, BC V0N 1P0. ✆ **250/539-2677.** Fax 250/539-2677. www. bodegaridge.com. 7 units. Apr to mid-Oct C$125–C$150; mid-Oct to Mar C$125. Extra person C$25. MC, V. Pets accepted (C$15). **Amenities:** Lounge; mountain bike rentals; Wi-Fi. *In room:* Kitchen, BBQ, no phone; TV/DVD upon request.

Cliff Pagoda   The purpose-built B&B looks like a pagoda, and sets the tone for the whimsical decor you'll find inside. The multicultural theme of this B&B is immediately apparent with its pagoda-style architecture. Every bedroom features colorful fabrics from India, local art, canopied beds, and spectacular views over Montague Harbour. The Maharaja Suite has a bathtub set into the rock and is the most opulent, although the Meditation Room is hard to beat—perched at the top of the Pagoda, it feels more like an exotic tree house with a private deck. The folks here are very laid-back, so if you're a Type-A personality, the slower rhythm might drive you nuts.

2851 Montague Rd., Galiano Island, BC V0N 1P0. ✆ **250/539-2260.** http://galiano.gulfislands.com/ cliff_pagoda. 5 units. C$75–C$125 double, year-round. Extra person C$45. Rates include continental breakfast. MC, V. **Amenities:** Lounge; hot tub; sauna; meditation garden. *In room:* Private patio or deck, no phone.

Driftwood Village Resort ★ (Kids) (Value)   Set in a delightful garden filled with fruit trees, the Driftwood Village Resort epitomizes Galiano's easy-going attitude, making for the ideal setting for relaxed, stress-free family vacations. Each of the studio, one-, and two-bedroom cottages is charming, cozy, and decorated with original artwork. While various bed-linen combinations give each cabin a different feel, all have oceanfront views, private bathrooms, well-equipped kitchens, and private decks with barbecues. All but one of the cottages have wood-burning fireplaces. There's a Jacuzzi in the center of the garden—a great spot from which to stargaze or watch deer meandering by. A footpath leads down to a sandy beach on Matthews Point, one of Galiano's many bird-watching spots. The "Ocean" cottages, which come with skylights and a private Jacuzzi, are especially nice.

205 Bluff Rd. E., Galiano Island, BC V0N 1P0. ✆ **888/240-1466** or 250/539-5457. www.driftwoodcottages. com. 10 units. Mid-June to mid-Sept C$129–C$165; mid-Sept to mid-June C$85–C$135. Extra person C$10–C$20. Children 12 and under stay free in parent's cottage. MC, V. Pets accepted (C$10). **Amenities:** Jacuzzi; free ferry pickup/dropoff; massage. *In room:* TV or TV/DVD, kitchen, no phone.

Galiano Inn & Spa ★★★ A sophisticated boutique destination spa resort, here every room is its own tranquil, eco-conscious retreat. Rooms are invitingly uncluttered with open-beam ceilings and decor that includes chocolate-brown cork floors and a ledge-rock wood-burning fireplace that conceals a plasma TV/DVD player. At a push of a button, a hidden table emerges from the cherry-wood wall for intimate, in-suite dining. A push of another button reveals a massage table for in-room spa services. All beds have silk stuffed duvets (versus allergenic down duvets). All rooms overlook Active Pass and have private balconies or terraces. En suite bathrooms feature heated floors, air-jetted Jacuzzis or soaker tubs, separate showers—and 24-karat gold fixtures. Expansion plans are well underway, which will almost double the inn's capacity. The Atrevida! restaurant is an island favorite (see "Where to Dine," below) and the Madrona del Mar Spa, with its zen garden, has made this a popular destination getaway for urbanites from Victoria and Vancouver. Be sure to try its exclusive hemp-inspired spa treatments, which give a whole new dimension to the infamous BC bud. Rates are consistent year-round. In winter, however, they include several extra-value items, such as certificates to the spa. *Tip:* The inn is located only 2 blocks from the ferry terminal, so save yourself some dollars and travel to the island as a foot passenger.

134 Madrona Dr., Galiano Island, BC V0N 1P0. ℂ **877/530-3939** or 250/539-3388. Fax 250/539-3338. www.galianoinn.com. 10 units. Year-round C$249–C$299. Rates include breakfast. Extra person C$25. MC, V. **Amenities:** Restaurant; lounge; spa; hot tub; activities desk; room service; laundry service; wine shop; Wi-Fi. *In room:* TV/DVD, coffeemaker, hair dryer, iron, massage.

Rocky Ridge B&B Although it's only a 13km (8-mile) drive from the ferry, half of that is on an unpaved road that traverses a spectacular cliffside location overlooking Trincomali Channel. It's worth the effort—this modern, wood-beamed B&B is one of the more upscale and relaxing places to stay on the island. All rooms boast comfortable queen-size beds and plenty of personal amenities, from chocolates to binoculars. Two of its three rooms are oceanfront with wraparound windows; the larger Yellow Room has a full en suite and sitting area, while the Blue Room has a small en suite and shares the shower with the back-of-house twin-bedded African Room. You can get a game in on the pool table in the upper lounge; enjoy the library, fireplace, and expansive views on the main level; or watch a favorite movie in a small theatre/TV room. Breakfast is substantial and tasty.

55-90 Serenity Lane, Galiano Island, BC V0N 1P0. ℂ **250/539-3387.** www.cedarplace.com/rockyridge. 3 units. Year-round C$100–C$110. C$10 extra for 1-night stay. No credit cards. Pets not accepted. Children not accepted. **Amenities:** 2 lounges; hot tub; sauna; Wi-Fi. *In room:* Hair dryer, no phone.

Whaler Bay Lodge Lying at the end of a dirt road—be sure to follow directions or you'll miss the place—picturesque Whaler Bay is the backdrop to this secluded getaway. There's no doubt that it's a home-turned-B&B and, with only three rooms, staying here feels like being a house guest. Fortunately, you have complete freedom to enjoy the living room, outdoor pool, gazebo garden, and private beach access. Two rooms are lavish suites, but the third, while comfortable, is a bit of an afterthought, and the rate is negotiable. The owner is a jazz buff and sometimes hosts informal concerts, which puts the grand piano to work, and if you're lucky you can sample his impressive 900-bottle wine collection. Other amenities include a private 9.7m (32-ft.) dock and the free use of kayaks, canoes, and rowboats. Watch for eagles from the dock, since the bay is a known nesting spot.

725 Cain Rd., Galiano Island, BC V0N 1P0. ℂ **877/539-3199** or 250/539-2249. Fax. 250/539-2257. www. whalerbaylodge.com. 3 units. Year-round C$175–C$195. MC, V. **Amenities:** Pool; Wi-Fi. *In room:* TV/DVD, hair dryer, iron.

Finds **Have Meals Will Travel**

The Max and Moritz truck at Sturdies Bay ferry terminal (☏ **250/539-5888**) serves up an excellent combination of Indonesian noodles, German bratwurst, North American burgers, and Italian gelati. Try it to believe it.

Woodstone Country Inn ★★★   This inn is set amid towering fir trees, overlooking an expanse of meadow and cultivated gardens. In summer, both meadow and garden overflow with flowers, and birds are everywhere. Inside, the inn is graciously decorated with quality antiques, folk art, and exotic sculptures, all garnered during the owner's travels around the world. Guest rooms are named for meadow flowers, and are exceptionally spacious and bright, with bathrooms that positively sparkle. Pampering touches include luxury Lord & Mayfair toiletries. All main-floor guest rooms have private patios. The inn's restaurant is one of the finest in the Gulf Islands (see "Where to Dine," below).

743 Georgeson Bay Rd., RR#1, Galiano Island, BC V0N 1P0. ☏ **888/339-2022** or 250/539-2022. Fax 250/539-5198. www.woodstoneinn.com. 13 units. May–Sept C$159–C$209; Oct–Apr C$139–C$199. 2-night minimum. Rates include breakfast and afternoon tea. AE, MC, V. Closed Dec–Jan. Children not accepted. **Amenities:** Restaurant; lounge. *In room:* Hair dryer, no phone.

WHERE TO DINE

Atrevida! ★ PACIFIC NORTHWEST   Galiano Island's only oceanfront restaurant is a treat. Watch the ferries ply through Active Pass as you enjoy rock crab croquette with cilantro chipotle tamarind, grilled beef tenderloin with green peppercorns, crème fraiche, and lobster sweet-pea risotto or sandalwood-smoked salmon with brown butter. The vegetarian Moroccan tajine is rich and aromatic, served in the traditional pottery tajine with eggplant, zucchini, and red peppers, butternut squash, couscous, garbanzo beans, carrot, grape tomatoes, almonds, and spices of every description. It's a very exotic, flavorful experience. The wine list focuses on special orders from British Columbia, some of which you can purchase from the wine store. If you've a ferry wait, park your car in the lineup and head over to the outdoor patio to chill out over a cold drink.

In the Galiano Inn, 134 Madrona Dr. ☏ **250/539-3388.** Reservations required. Main courses C$18–C$29. MC, V. Daily 5:30–9:30pm.

Hummingbird Pub PUB FARE   Serving hearty pub grub (burgers, fish and chips, steaks, and pasta) at reasonable prices, the Hummingbird is *the* local watering hole, and tempts with ales on tap from Vancouver Island Brewery on Salt Spring Island and wines from Saturna Island. The classic West Coast cedar-and-beam architecture creates a warm atmosphere for playing pool and darts, and although there's no water view, the decor and perennial garden more than make up for it. From mid-May to October, this resourceful pub runs its own shuttle bus to the ferry at Sturdies Bay, and from the Montague Park Marina. The pub could be of particular interest to boaters seeking some liquid libations on dry land.

47 Sturdies Bay Rd. ☏ **250/539-5472.** Main courses C$7–C$17. MC, V. Sun–Thurs 11am–midnight; Fri–Sat 11am–1am.

La Berengerie ★ FRENCH   Shrouded by evergreen clematis, this tiny log cabin is a jewel in the forest. Floral linen tablecloths, soft classical music, and watercolor paintings by local artists set a romantic tone. The food rarely disappoints. Described as French-Algerian, the cuisine uses herbs to bring Middle Eastern flavor to classics such as duck à l'orange, coq au vin, and red snapper with gingered tomato sauce. La Berengerie also does an excellent bouillabaisse. The seafood gratinee is delicious—creamy and light, with a host of delicate flavors. A four-course menu features a choice of appetizers, entrees, and desserts. The homemade breads and comfort desserts are delicious. In July and August, the vegetarian sundeck opens up, as does a garden patio. The drawback is that it closes in winter.

Montague Harbour Rd. ℂ **250/539-5392.** http://galiano.gulfislands.com/laberengerie. Reservations recommended on weekends. Main courses C$15-C$22; 4-course prix-fixe dinner C$31. MC, V. July–Aug daily 5–9pm; Apr–June and Sept–Oct Fri–Sun only, call ahead for hours. Closed Nov–Mar.

Wisteria Restaurant ★★ FRENCH/INTERNATIONAL   This enchanting restaurant is one of the best on the Gulf Islands and certainly the place of choice to celebrate something special. Service is impeccable, and the cuisine is a blend of classic French and vivid international flavors such as in the yellow fin tuna with sweet peppers, artichokes, olives, and roasted garlic aioli, and the seared duck breast prepared with sweet-and-sour braised pearl onions and an orange demi-glace sauce. Each day's menu offers a choice of three entrees (which determines what you'll pay) and also includes homemade bread, soup, and salad. Desserts are decadent—the warm bread pudding with rum sauce is exceptional, and the wine list is an interesting mix of Okanagan, Californian, and French vintages. There are no additional a la carte items.

At the Woodstone Country Inn, 743 Georgeson Bay Rd. ℂ **250/539-2022.** Reservations required. 4-course dinner C$24–C$33. AE, DC, MC, V. Feb–Nov nightly from 5pm. Closed Dec–Jan.

5 MAYNE ISLAND

Mayne has always been a transfer point between islands. This began in the 1860s, when prospectors rested up in Miners Bay before crossing the Georgia Strait on their way to the gold mines in the Fraser Valley and the Cariboo. Back then, this rowdy social and drinking hub was known as "Little Hell," but as gold fever faded, so did Mayne's importance. Today, stopovers are much tamer. The 900 permanent residents like it this way, as it's enabled the island to retain much of its charm and heritage.

Because most of Mayne Island is privately owned, there are few public trails, so walkers and cyclists take to the network of hilly roads, traveling past 19th-century buildings, farms, beaches, and home studios. Avid cyclists could complete Mayne's 25km (16-mile) circuit in a day. There are numerous sheltered bays, including **Village Bay, Miners Bay,** and **Horton Bay,** all with docking facilities and accommodations that run the gamut from bare bones to luxurious.

ESSENTIALS
Getting There
BC Ferries sails to **Village Bay,** on the northwest side of the island. Pleasure boaters dock at **Horton Bay,** at the southwest corner of the island. Floatplanes arrive at the docks at **Miners Bay**.

Visitor Information
Mayne Island Community Chamber of Commerce (ℂ **250/539-5034**) doesn't have a bricks-and-mortar headquarters but does maintain a resource site at www.mayneisland chamber.ca. Useful maps and event information are usually posted on bulletin boards in

(Tips) **The Cob Wave**

Mayne Island is cob-house central in the Gulf Islands, in large part because an enterprising islander helped put earth houses back on the map. Using only unprocessed, natural products such as sand, clay, straw, and recycled materials, these are the ultimate in eco-friendly, earthquake-resilient dwellings that are surprisingly modern in design and functionality. Cob is a mixture of sand, clay, and straw that is applied wet and molded into curved walls, arches, and creative niches. Workshops in building earth houses, as well as tours of existing homes, are available year-round. Contact ℂ **250/386-7790** or www.cobworks.com for details.

the windows of the gas station (which doubles as a video-movie rental place), and the grocery store. This is where you can also purchase a copy of *The Mayneliner* (C$2.50), a monthly publication of gossip, happenings, and island issues.

Getting Around

ALOHA taxi company (ℂ **250/539-3132** or 250/539-0181) offers pick-up and drop-off service to the ferry, as well as island tours. The Dodge Caravan seats six and can carry bikes, pets, oversize luggage, and camping or fishing gear.

EXPLORING MAYNE ISLAND

Miners Bay is the hub of Mayne, housing a surprisingly well-stocked supermarket, a small library, and a bakery-cafe. The liquor store, which is actually only a counter with a separate till, is part of a store that has sold goods and groceries since World War I. On summer Saturdays, a small farmers' market is held outside the **Agricultural Hall,** which on other days doubles as a theater, bingo hall, and exhibition center. The fairly new community center, the venue for ongoing programs such as yoga, choir, and drop-in Tai Chi, added tennis courts to its mix in 2008. The **Mayne Island Museum** is in a former one-room jail dating from 1896, and displays all manner of local artifacts from the early 1900s. Located on Fernhill Road, just up from the Springwater, it usually opens on July and August weekends, as well as holiday weekends, from 10am to 3pm. Admission is by donation; C$2 is suggested. Kayak and canoe rentals are available at **Blue Vista Resort** (see "Where to Stay," below). Rates range from C$38 per person for a 2-hour rental to C$68 per person for a 24-hour rental of a fiberglass kayak, with an option to extend the rental. Guided tours include a 5-hour paddle to Saturna's winery for a tasting (C$95), and the company also offers bike rentals at C$18 for a half-day or C$25 for a full-day.

The road from Miners Bay to **Georgina Point** and the **Active Pass Lighthouse** is the most picturesque on Mayne Island. En route, you'll pass **St. Mary Magdalene Anglican Church,** built in 1898, on a hill amid a grove of red arbutus trees. The steeple of the church overlooking Active Pass has been a landmark for sailors for more than a century. Many of the headstones in the mossy graveyard are silent testament to Mayne Island's pioneers, whose names are also reflected in the names of the coves and streets of the island. Established in 1885, the lighthouse marks the entrance to Active Pass and, now automated, is open daily from 9am to 3pm, with free admission. This is a great spot from which to see seals, seabirds, and the occasional whale.

THE GULF ISLANDS

9

MAYNE ISLAND

Because most of Mayne Island is privately owned, there are few public parks in which to hike. **Mount Parke Park**, (www.crd.bc.ca/parks/mountparke) however, is an exception. Although many islanders have "back routes" to the top of Mount Parke itself, officially there's only one public hiking trail up, and it's a fairly strenuous 30- to 40-minute uphill hike. (Cyclists must leave their bikes at the trail-head rack.) At 255m (837 ft.), the end of the trail is the highest point on Mayne, and if you can forgive the obligatory antennae towers, you'll be rewarded with wonderful views and maybe an air show of soaring eagles and turkey vultures. Six beaches on the island are open to the public, but since a distinct lack of signs to access points makes them easy to miss, keep your eyes peeled for road markers that lead down to the shoreline—and avoid tromping on private land. Two of the best beaches for picnics are at **Georgina Point** and at **Dinner Bay,** so-called because it once teemed with fish and shellfish. "When the tide goes out," the old prospector's slogan goes, "the table is laid for breakfast." A **Japanese Garden** is a part of Dinner Bay and commemorates the Japanese who settled and worked on the island between 1900 and 1942. Admission is free. **Bennett Bay,** now a part of the Gulf Islands National Park Reserve, has an undisturbed waterfront that is home to herons, kingfishers, and unusual pink seashells. When the tide goes out far enough (which doesn't seem to happen often), the pebbly beach eventually gives way to fine sand. **Oyster Bay, Piggott Bay,** and **Campbell Bay** are good for swimming. The latter has eye-catching rock formations that served as models for the artificial rocks around the killer whale pool in the Vancouver Aquarium.

WHERE TO STAY

Blue Vista Resort (Value)   Blue Vista's freshly updated one- and two-bedroom cabins are good value and ideal for family vacations. Comfortable, but not fancy, each of the blue-painted, wood-framed units comes with a fully equipped kitchen, private bathroom, fireplace, deck, and barbecue. The resort's open, park-like setting encourages children to play with newfound friends. Bikes are available for rental. If you're staying over a weekend, be sure to catch the resort's Saturday Sundaes, for which they provide all the fixings for personalized and delicious ice-cream treats. Each session becomes a sundae-creating contest among guests. Blue Vista are *the* experts when it comes to kayaking (see "Exploring Mayne Island," above).

563 Arbutus Dr., Mayne Island, BC V0N 2J0. (© **877/535-2424** or 250/539-2463. Fax 250/539-2463. www. bluevistaresort.com. 8 units. June–Sept C$99–C$145; Oct–May C$79–$125. Kayaking packages and weekly rates available. MC, V. Pets accepted w/prior approval (C$10). **Amenities:** Bike and kayak rentals; free ferry pickup/dropoff; washers and dryers; Wi-Fi. *In room:* TV, kitchen, no phone.

(Fun Facts)   **Respites from Bully Birds**

The nest boxes you'll see mounted on pilings in the water in Bennett Bay, beside the Mayne Inn's dock and in front of the Springwater Lodge, are all part of a stewardship and recovery program for the purple martin. Muscled out of their traditional nesting areas by house sparrows and starlings, the Western Purple Martin is at risk in British Columbia. Placing these boxes over water minimizes competition from the "bully birds" and is working. In 2006, Mayne Island welcomed their first nesting Purple Martin pairs.

Mayne Island Eco Camping   Of the two campsites on Mayne, this is by far the superior, with waterfront sites, outdoor hot and cold showers amid the trees, outhouses, a communal fire pit, and even a hot tub. Many kayakers choose to paddle right up to the beach—a pretty but pebbly cove near Miners Bay—or take advantage of the free pickup and delivery service to and from other islands.

359 Maple Dr., Mayne Island, BC V0N 2J0. (C) **250/539-2667.** Fax: 250/539-3187. www.mayneisle.com/camp. May–Sept C$12; Oct–Apr C$10. Children 13 years and under half price. **Amenities:** Hot tub; kayak rentals.

Oceanwood Country Inn ★   This waterfront English country inn is as upscale as you can get on Mayne. It's a gated property, so the deer haven't ravaged the gardens of tulips, irises, and other tasty morsels, as they have most Mayne gardens. Every guest suite is decorated in a floral or bird theme, with names like Kingfisher, Daffodil, and Rose. Most are romantic, with deep-soaker bathtubs and private balconies. Many have fireplaces. The Wisteria Suite even has a sunken living room and private outdoor soaking tub—perfect for a moonlit soak *àdeux*. The Geranium is particularly large, and also has a private outdoor soaking tub—on a rooftop deck, no less. The living room in the main lodge features a crackling fireplace, full bookshelves, board games, and good listening music. Enjoying dinner at Oceanwood's gourmet restaurant is a highlight of most people's stays (see "Where to Dine," below). *Note:* At time of printing, new owners had just taken over the helm, and although it's "business as usual," we suggest you call ahead to avoid disappointment.

630 Dinner Bay Rd., Mayne Island, BC V0N 2J0. (C) **250/539-5074.** Fax 250/539-3002. www.oceanwood.com. 12 units. Mid-June to mid-Sept C$179–C$349; mid-Mar to mid-June and mid-Sept to Oct C$139–C$299. 2-night stay required if staying over Sat. Rates include breakfast and afternoon tea. MC, V. Closed Nov to mid-Mar. Children not accepted. **Amenities:** Restaurant; lounge; Jacuzzi; sauna; complimentary bikes; library. *In room:* Hair dryer, no phone.

Sage Cottage   The two oceanfront bedrooms are sumptuous, decorated in neutral earth tones of sand and sage, and with all the trimmings of luxurious bathrobes, toiletries, duvets, and a satellite TV and DVD player with a growing title list to choose from. A shared deck overlooks a picturesque beach and boat launch. Rates include a gourmet breakfast that includes Brie-stuffed French toast or an herb-flavored egg soufflé. Scones and jams are homemade, and usually made in such abundance that guests depart with a doggy-bag of snacks for the road. Custom-made picnic lunches can be ordered, too, for a nominal additional charge. If you would like to eat dinner in, this can also be arranged. The cost is a reasonable C$25 and includes a full three-course meal such as a mixed green salad, BBQ pork tenderloin, and a lemon cheesecake pie.

782 Steward Dr., Mayne Island, BC V0N 2J0. (C) **250/539-2859.** www.sageonmayne.com. Mid-Nov to Apr C$90–$120; May to mid-June and Oct to mid-Nov C$120–C$130; mid-June to Sept C$120–C$145. V only. **Amenities:** Deck; Wi-Fi; Internet and phone access. *In room:* TV/DVD, no phone.

WHERE TO DINE

Oceanwood Country Inn ★★ PACIFIC NORTHWEST   Opening onto a terrace overlooking the water, Oceanwood's restaurant has a romantic, Mediterranean ambience in which it dishes up extravagant daily creations. Set, four-course menus change nightly, but are posted a week in advance on notice boards throughout the island so that diners can plan a visit according to their taste buds. Cuisine highlights fresh local ingredients, as imaginative to read as they are to experience. Try the Oceanwood day lilies stuffed with smoked salmon mousse, fennel snap bread, and nasturtium flower oil; or the smoked sablefish and beet terrine with stinging nettle juice; or the roast venison strip loin with spaetzle and mushroom-balsamic vinaigrette. It's these sorts of culinary creations that have earned Oceanwood multiple gold medals at the Vancouver Food & Restaurant Show. The wine list, too, is an award-winner for its focus on West Coast labels, especially those from British Columbia. This is the only place on the island where you'll want to doff your Reeboks for something a little smarter (though clean jeans are fine). Note, however, that the Inn has just changed hands, so double check with the locals before making your reservation.

In the Oceanwood Country Inn, 630 Dinner Bay Rd. ✆ **250/539-5074.** Reservations required. 4-course prix-fixe dinner C$55–C$65. MC, V. Daily 6–9:30pm.

Spring Water Lodge PUB FARE/PACIFIC NORTHWEST Built in the 1890s, this pub and restaurant is the heart of the Mayne Island community. In summer, people crowd the flower-brightened outdoor decks to watch the boats thread through Active Pass. In winter, the pub overflows with boisterous gossip. Live bands are often featured on Saturday nights. On the whole, food is good, though sometimes the restaurant specials are overly ambitious and don't live up to their promise. The fish and chips are great, and the onion rings are the best. Despite service that's rather offhand, it's a great place to kick back and grab a meal. Unfortunately, this good review doesn't extend to the guest rooms. Despite what you might hear, they are nothing to write home about, and the beach cabins are even less appealing.

400 Fernhill Rd. ✆ **250/539-5521.** Reservations accepted. Pub main courses C$8.50; restaurant main courses C$19. MC, V. Mid-May to mid-Sept daily 9am–9pm; mid-Sept to mid-May Mon–Thurs 11am–8:30pm and Fri–Sun 9am–8:30pm. Pub may be open later.

Wild Fennel Food & Wine Located in the middle of the island at Fernhill Centre, the funky ambiance here, let alone the terrific food, will brighten your day. The wine list features mostly local ciders, microbrewed beer, and BC wines; try Bad Dog Blonde, a private-label house wine that's become a bestseller in large part because of its whimsical label. The menu changes weekly according to food availability and freshness, but the crab cakes are amazing, and hope that when you visit one of the shellfish soups—or the plum-glazed Pacific salmon with house-made udon noodles and sashi broth and water chestnuts—will be available. Although there's a strong seafood focus here, meat eaters will find lamb, pork tenderloin, or steak, alongside comfort foods such as macaroni 'n' cheese, sweet 'n' sour apple pie, and portions geared for children. Grab a spot on the small but popular deck and garden.

574 Fernhill Rd. ✆ **250/539-5987.** Reservations accepted. Lunch C$9; dinner C$15. MC, V. Apr–Sept daily 7am–8:30pm.

---

6 SATURNA ISLAND

Time seems to have bypassed Saturna Island, making remote tranquility the island's star attraction. Home to approximately 325 permanent residents, Saturna is still fairly primitive. There are no banks, no pharmacies or drug stores; the library's located in the church basement, and the general store doubles as a tiny coffee shop. In fact, Jose Maria Narvaez would probably still recognize the forests and shorelines of the island named after his ship, Santa Saturnina, even though his last visit was in 1791. The Gulf Islands National Park Reserve protects some 44% of Saturna's 49 sq. km (19 sq. miles), making the island great for hiking, boating, and communing with nature. Of all the Gulf Islands, Saturna is the most ecologically vigilant. It also boasts one of British Columbia's largest estate wineries, Saturna Island Vineyards, which alone is worth the ferry trip.

Visitors may quickly note the island's drawbridge mentality, but Saturna people aren't unfriendly—they just prefer to keep their own company.

Laced with trails through mixed forest and marshland, the island is ideal for hikers, who usually head for **Winter Cove Marine Park,** a sanctuary to eagles, shorebirds, kingfishers, seals, and otters; or up to the summit of Mount Warburton. Kayakers will prefer **Thomson Park,** or **Cabbage Island Marine Park,** near **Tumbo Island,** and **Veruna Bay** and **Russell Reef** are the hot spots for family swimming. What commerce there is happens around the community center at **Lyall Harbour,** where the ferry docks. Here you'll find a grocery store, pub, gas station, kayak rentals, and a gallery, as well as a couple of B&Bs. *Note:* There are no public campgrounds.

ESSENTIALS
Getting There
BC Ferries sails to **Lyall Harbour.** Most trips involve a transfer at Mayne Island. Boaters dock at **Winter Cove Marine Park,** north of Lyall Harbour. Seaplanes can dock at Lyall Harbour.

Visitor Information
Head to the **Saturna Island General Store,** 101 Narvaez Bay Rd., Saturna Island, BC V0N 2Y0 (✆ **250/539-2936;** www.saturnatourism.com). Wi-Fi hot spots are sporadic; your best bets are the **Recreation & Cultural Center** (104 Harris Rd.); and the library at **St. Christopher's Church,** 140 East Point Rd. (✆ **250/539-5312**). The latter offers terminals but is only open 11am to 3pm, Wednesdays and Saturdays. The **Saturna Point Lighthouse Pub** at the Ferry Dock is home to the island's only ATM.

Ⓕinds Saturna Island Vineyards

The location is idyllic, and offers visitors more than just a taste of wine. Nestled among the Pacific Ocean, a soaring granite cliff face, and picturesque Campbell farm, these south-facing vineyards are a pleasure to explore. The first wines from the 1998 harvest were released to critical acclaim, and just keep getting better, garnering a silver medal in 2008 for the Vintner's Select Chardonnay in the All Canadian Wine Championships, and a gold for their Pinot Noir. Look, also, for good Pinot Gris, Merlots, and Gewürztraminers for less than C$20 per bottle in the wine shop, as well as other merchandise. The small terraced bistro is big on taste: recommended items include the halibut ceviche with its jalapeno miso-citrus dressing, the West Coast bouillabaisse, and the charcuterie plate of local cheeses, house-made pickles, and cured meats. The vineyards are at 8 Quarry Rd. (✆ **877/918-3388** or 250/539-5139; www.saturnavineyards.com). They are open daily May through October from 11am to 4:30pm, and through the winter by appointment. Tours and tastings are free. Take East Point Road from Lyall Harbour, and then Harris Road for 2.5km (1¹/₂ miles).

> **(Fun Facts)   Island Legend: Warburton Pike**
>
> Mount Warburton Pike is named for the legendary English "gentleman adventurer," the biggest property owner on Saturna at the turn of the 20th century. A member of the British gentry and an Oxford graduate, Pike was temperamentally better suited to life in the great outdoors and much preferred to sleep under a large maple tree in the yard than in his pretty, well-furnished bungalow. During his life, Pike was a big-game hunter, a Wyoming cowboy, an Arctic and Icelandic explorer, a businessman and community benefactor, a mining and railroad promoter, a Yukon gold prospector, a sheep rancher, and author of two books on the North. Among many stories about this elusive adventurer is the one tale about how Pike used the ocean as his washtub. He just tied his clothes to a long rope and trailed them behind his sailboat *Fleetwing* while he stretched out and relaxed on the gunwale.

Getting Around

At time of printing, the island had no pickup or touring service, although your B&B may step in to fill this need on an as-required basis. Bring your own bike (there are no rentals) or come to kayak. **Saturna Sea Kayaking** (✆ **250/539-5553**) is located in the village and can fit you out with single and double fiberglass kayaks from C$30 to C$65 for 3 hours. Multiple-day rates are available. **Island Discovery Tours** (✆ **250/539-3211** or 604/377-5385) offers 2¹/₂ to 5 hour tours and hikes of the neighboring islands with the added bonus of circumnavigating Saturna. Rates range from C$85 to C$160 per adult; C$65 to C$120 per child under 12 years of age. Group size is limited to eight passengers; departure points include Lyall Harbour, Saturna Island, as well as Hope Bay on Pender Island and Horton Bay on Mayne Island.

EXPLORING SATURNA ISLAND

East Point Regional Park ★★, on the island's southeastern tip, is a naturalist's delight. It starts with the ocean views from the sculptured sandstone headlands and just gets better. Strong tides curl around the point to create back eddies where salmon and small fish congregate; rocks, honeycombed by wind and waves, form tidal pools filled with starfish, limpets, spider crabs, and more; and waving kelp beds attract cormorants, oystercatchers, eagles, seals, and even whales. Take the very short trail down to the **East Point Lighthouse,** built in 1888, and you'll be standing at the easternmost edge of the Gulf Islands, looking over to **Patos Island Lighthouse,** on the U.S. side of the border. Together, the lighthouses guide large vessels through the channel's surging waters. Some of the area is on private land; be careful not to trespass off the trails. A longer trail (300m/984 ft.) leaves the parking lot and heads north to a viewpoint of Tumbo Channel and the Strait of Georgia.

If you've time, make the 4.5km (2³/₄-mile) drive or hike up to the 497m (1,631-ft.) summit of **Warburton Pike.** If you can disregard the unbecoming sprawl of TV towers, the sweeping vistas from the top are nothing short of fantastic. The way up is via a winding gravel road that's narrow and sometimes slippery in wet weather, but the beautiful Douglas fir forest more than makes up for the occasional rough patch of road. Look out for feral goats, wild descendants of domestic goats imported here in the early 1900s, along the paths at the edge of the bluff.

Breezy Bay B&B ★ (Kids)   This charming 1890s heritage house, Saturna's oldest home, lies at the heart of a 20-hectare (49-acre) farm approximately 2km (1 mile) from the ferry dock. You enter beneath a canopy of century-old Lombardy poplars that gives way to gardens filled with trees: walnut, maple, scented linden, and hawthorne. Inside, you'll find architectural details such as Victorian wainscoting and period wood paneling. The guest library is full of assorted titles, from nature books to historical novels, while the spacious piano lounge is comfortable without being pretentious. The four guest rooms are small, simply furnished, but inviting; they share two bathrooms. On the first floor, an outside veranda runs the length of the house and overlooks the orchard, water-fowl pond, and pastures of sheep and llama. The beach at the end of the garden is ideal for swimming and launching kayaks. The kids will love it.

131 Payne Rd., Saturna Island, BC V0N 2Y0. ℰ **250/539-5957** or 250/539-3339. www.saturnacan.net/breezy. 4 units. May–Sept C$85–C$95. Rates include full breakfast. No credit cards. Closed Oct–Apr. **Amenities:** Lounge; library. *In room:* No phone.

Lyall Harbour B&B ★   Three points are in its favor: The home epitomizes the West Coast, with a ton of windows and views; it's within walking distance of the ferry terminal, a big incentive to leave your gas-guzzling car behind; and it's one of the only B&Bs that's open year-round. All three guest rooms have queen-size beds and high quality (i.e., 425-thread-count) linens, full en suites, views and private decks, and while there's no air-conditioning per se, overhead vents and a return-air system keep the inside temperature comfortable even on the hottest of days. The house is filled with original art by owner-artist Donna Digance; her adjoining studio welcomes visitors. Her husband, Len, is a potter with his own on-site studio and also just happens to be a professional chef who turns breakfast into a gourmet affair. The West Coast Smoked Salmon Benny is the house specialty.

121 East Point Rd., Saturna Island, BC V0N 2Y0. ℰ **877/473-9343** or 250/539-5577. www.lyallharbour.com. 3 units. Year-round C$105–C$135. Extra person C$30. 2-night minimum stay in peak season. Rates include full breakfast. MC, V. Children not accepted. **Amenities:** 2 lounges; Wi-Fi. *In room:* No phone.

Saturna Lodge & Restaurant   Set amid the rustic, rural charms of the island, a stone's throw from the Saturna Island Vineyards, new owners have turned this casual country inn into an unexpected delight. Guest rooms are named after wine grapes, and are comfortably appointed with duvet-covered queen-size beds and private en suites (twin beds in the Ambrosia Suite). This and the Napa Suite share a bathroom and can be joined for family accommodation. All have views of Plumber Sound (though some more than others) and the Riesling Suite has a private deck. TV-hungry urbanites can cozy up in front of the fireplace in the downstairs lounge, or pick a DVD/VHS title from the lodge's small library. In shoulder season, the lodge discounts its nightly rate by C$20 per night. The other surprise is the quality of its small restaurant, Dejavu Seafood & Steak-house, where dinner focuses on local fare such as Saturna Island lamb, organic produce, and local seafood. The mussels, steamed in orange coconut lemongrass broth, are a perfect choice with a chilled chardonnay on the outdoor deck overlooking the cove.

130 Payne Rd. (P.O. Box 54), Saturna Island, BC V0N 2Y0. ℰ **866/539-2254** or 250/539-2254. Fax 250/539-3091. www.saturna.ca. 6 units. Mid-Mar to mid-Nov C$125–$170. Discounts for longer stays. Extra person C$30. Rates include full breakfast. MC, V. Closed mid-Nov to mid-Mar. Pets not accepted. **Amenities:** Restaurant; lounge; Jacuzzi; complimentary bikes; free shuttle to and from vineyard, float planes, and ferries; library. *In room:* TV/DVD on request, no phone.

The San Juan Islands

Beckoning just off the coast of Vancouver Island, south of the Gulf Islands, the San Juan Islands are a mostly blue-sky oasis in a region better known for its clouds. Like their island neighbors, they provide mariners with spectacular waters, hundreds of small, protected coves, and a landscape where stands of coastal trees give way to grassy meadows and gardens. It's a landscape that earned the number-four spot in *Travel & Leisure's* list of "Top 5 Islands in North America." The ferry trip between the San Juan Islands and Sidney, on Vancouver Island, is a delightful 1¹/₂-hour mini-cruise and provides the opportunity to create a really diverse islands adventure. From Sidney, you can choose to explore Vancouver Island, or take a ferry to the Gulf Islands, creating an itinerary that can stretch from a few days to a few weeks. The alternative trip is via the Washington State Ferries out of Anacortes; the crossing time is about an hour.

For years the San Juans' pastoral tranquility was a favorite getaway for Washingtonians, but this is now taking its toll. Today, land deals for would-be homeowners are long gone. There are more than 30 different real-estate dealers on the San Juans—that's one for every 40 residents; and assessed property values are almost three times the state average. Although development is controlled somewhat by the San Juan Preservation Trust, monumental homes are appearing in what was once humble rock and farmland.

In the 1800s, because of their proximity to British Columbia (San Juan Island lies only 26km/16 miles from Sidney), many British settlers moved to the islands alongside their American counterparts. Remnants of those pioneering years are seen throughout the islands, and many landmarks are listed in the National Register of Historic Places. On San Juan Island, in particular, you'll find the Anglo-American rivalry especially well documented in the American and English camps.

The three largest islands, San Juan, Orcas, and Lopez, are home to about 12,000 people. For much of the year, the residents' easygoing lifestyle is quite solitary, but when summer arrives, the population triples, with the arrival of eco-adventurers and vacationers. **Note:** If you're traveling with children, be aware that family fun is derived mainly from beachcombing, kayaking, and hiking, with the larger resorts providing children's programs and supervised swimming. (Consult the individual hotel reviews to see whether an establishment offers these programs.) Also note that despite the annual influx of visitors, accommodations on the San Juans are limited, and prearranged accommodations are highly recommended. Touring all three islands can be done in 3 or 4 days, but chances are that you'll acclimatize to "island time," slow down, and wish you had set aside a day or two longer. But leave your jet skis at home. When locals complained that the incessant buzzing of city folk zipping around their waterfront was disrupting the serenity and marine habitat of the islands, San Juan County promptly outlawed the noisy watercraft. The only wild time you'll find on the San Juan Islands is pretty much what nature provides.

GETTING THERE

BY PLANE **Kenmore Air Seaplanes** (✆ **800/543-9595** or 425/486-1257; www.kenmoreair.com) provides daily flights from **Seattle** to the three major San Juan Islands May through September. One-way fares are US$150 for adults, US$109 for children 3 to 11, free for children 2 and under. Cheaper fares are sometimes available depending on traffic flow, so if you're flexible, the savings can be up to US$40. Kenmore Air also offers daily departures from Seattle to Victoria. Fares are US$149 one-way and US$269 round-trip for adults, US$109 one-way and US$219 round-trip for children 3 to 11, free for children 2 and under. Check out discounted Internet specials. **San Juan Airlines** (✆ **800/874-4434** or 360/293-4691; www.sanjuanairlines.com) has daily land plane flights from **Anacortes** and **Bellingham** at US$68 per person and offers charters that start from US$80 per person. Locally owned **Island Air** (✆ **888/378-2376** or 360/378-2376; www.sanjuan-islandair.com) offers on-demand and scenic flights at US$165 per hour—you can see the entire San Juan archipelago and Vancouver Island in that time. **Rose Air** (✆ **503/675-ROSE** [7673]) also offers similar flights, but operates more like a private inter-island taxi service; hitching a ride aboard the three-passenger plane costs US$220 per hour. Small public airstrips on San Juan, Orcas, and Lopez islands accommodate these flights and private plane arrivals.

BY FERRY **Washington State Ferries,** Column Dock/Pier 52, Seattle (✆ **888/808-7977** or 206/464-6400; www.wsdot.wa.gov/ferries), offers multiple daily sailings between **Anacortes** and the San Juan Islands, and limited service from **Sidney,** on Vancouver Island. From Anacortes, loading is on a first-come, first-served basis. It's a good idea to get in line about 30 minutes in advance of the scheduled sailing. If you bring a vehicle, allow for at least an hour's wait—up to 3 hours at peak travel times on summer and holiday weekends. Also, be sure to fill your tank in Anacortes. Gas stations on the islands charge at least 30% more for gas than on the mainland. Some food service and a picnic area are available near the terminal. Check out **www.ferrycam.net** to see live images of the ferry lanes.

One-way passenger fares during the high season, from May to mid-October, are US$13 for adults, US$11 for children 6 to 18 years, US$7 for seniors, US$36 to US$51 for a driver and standard-size vehicle. Inter-island travel is US$19 for a driver and standard-size vehicle; passengers and bicycles are free.

Twice a day in summer (once a day in winter), the ferry continues to Sidney, 26km (16 miles) north of Victoria, and returns. Summer vehicle reservations are recommended

---

 Makes Cents

Ferry foot-passengers are charged only in the westbound direction; eastbound travel within the San Juan Islands or from the San Juan Islands to Anacortes is free (the only exception to this is for travelers leaving from Sidney, BC). If you're planning to visit all the San Juan Islands, save money by heading straight to Friday Harbor on San Juan Island, the most westerly of the islands, and work your way back through the others at no additional charge.

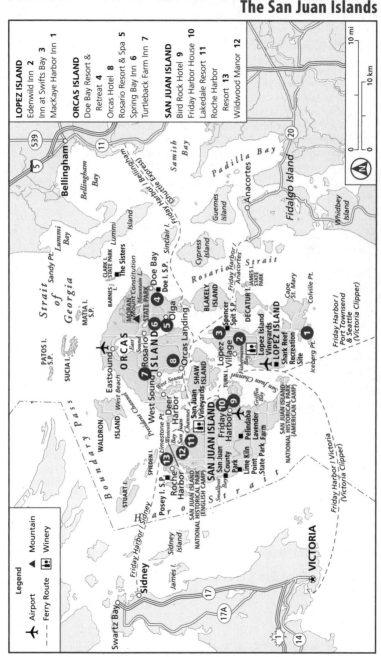

LOPEZ ISLAND
Edenwild Inn **2**
Inn at Swifts Bay **3**
MacKaye Harbor Inn **1**

ORCAS ISLAND
Doe Bay Resort &
Retreat **4**
Orcas Hotel **8**
Rosario Resort & Spa **5**
Spring Bay Inn **6**
Turtleback Farm Inn **7**

SAN JUAN ISLAND
Bird Rock Hotel **9**
Friday Harbor House **10**
Lakedale Resort **11**
Roche Harbor
Resort **13**
Wildwood Manor **12**

Legend
✈ Airport
▲ Mountain
□ Winery
--- Ferry Route

THE SAN JUAN ISLANDS

10

ESSENTIALS

(Fun Facts) San Juan Trivia

- There are no traffic lights anywhere in the islands. People don't even honk.
- San Juan County has more miles of marine shoreline (657km/408 miles) than any other county.
- The marine highway that follows the historic canoe route of the Coast Salish peoples, from Anacortes to the San Juans, as well as several county roads, is Washington State's newest legislated Scenic Byway.
- There are no rivers in the islands, but several waterfalls on Orcas Island.
- There are 83 National Wildlife Refuge sites in the San Juans. A number are clustered on the southern coast of Lopez Island, and near Spieden and Waldron islands.

to and from Canada, and must be made by 5:30pm the day prior to travel, at least 24 hours in advance. One-way passenger fares from May 1 to mid-October are US$16 for adults, US$8 for seniors, US$13 for children 6 to 18 years, US$54 for a driver and standard-size vehicle. From mid-October to April 30, fares remain the same for adults, seniors, and children, but reduce to US$43 for driver and standard-size vehicle. Crossing time is 3 hours. From the San Juan Islands to Sidney, one-way fares are US$6 for adults, US$3 for seniors, US$5 for children, US$28 for a standard-size vehicle and driver. Fares are lower October 2 through May 2.

Victoria Clipper (✆ **800/888-2535** or 206/448-5000; www.victoriaclipper.com) is a popular way to reach the San Juan Islands from either **Seattle or Victoria.** This passenger-only catamaran departs from Seattle's **Pier 69** daily. Fares from Seattle to Friday Harbor, on San Juan Island, are US$75 each way for adults, and US$38 each way for children 1 to 11. Advance purchase discounts and an add-on whale-watching feature are also offered. Reservations originating in Victoria should call ✆ **250/382-8100.** A sister company runs daily passenger-only sailings between Port Angeles and Friday Harbor aboard the **Victoria Express** (✆ **360/452-8088** from US or 250/361-9144 from Canada; www.victoriaexpress.com). The cost is US$40 each way; bikes and kayaks are free. **Puget Sound Express** (✆ **360/385-5288**) offers passenger-only service between **Port Townsend,** northwest of Seattle, and Friday Harbor. The captain takes the 3-hour scenic route. Round-trip fare is about US$79 per person. All of the above operate May through September. The **San Juan Island, Island Express** (✆ **877/473-9777** or 360/299-2875) runs a year-round passenger taxi from downtown Anacortes to the three major San Juan Islands, and many of the smaller ones, too, that are so popular for kayakers. Fares are based on the number of passengers sharing a common destination and generally range from US$38 to US$95 per person. Bicycles are US$6 and kayaks are US$15 extra.

VISITOR INFORMATION

The **San Juan Islands Visitor Information Service,** 640 Mullis St., Building A, Suite 210, Friday Harbor, San Juan Island, WA 98250 (✆ **888/468-3701** or 360/378-6822; www.visitsanjuans.com), offers a range of maps and information throughout the islands. For live images of the San Juan Islands, check out **www.islandcam.com.** San Juan, Lopez, and Orcas islands also operate visitor services through their local chambers of commerce (see "Essentials," in separate sections devoted to each island).

Compared to sleepier Orcas and Lopez islands, San Juan Island is "downtown central." Home to about 7,000 people, most of whom prefer this island's quicker pace, and covering over 142 sq. km (55 sq. miles), San Juan is a popular holiday destination, offering visitors the most in terms of urban amenities, relaxing hideaways, and wilderness hikes. For those who like to fill their days with different types of activities, San Juan is your best bet. It is also the most practical destination in the San Juan Islands if you're traveling without a car, since restaurants, shops, and museums are within walking distance of the ferry landing. Car and moped rentals are available all the same. The island even has a small winery, the **San Juan Vineyards** (3136 Roche Harbor Rd.; © **360/378-9463;** www.sanjuanvineyards.com), housed in a century-old schoolhouse near **Roche Harbor.**

San Juan Island has historic appeal, too. Its colorful past stems from a boundary dispute between the U.S. and Great Britain when, from 1860 to 1872, both countries occupied the island. In one of the stranger pieces of history, the killing of a British homesteader's pig by an American settler nearly sent the two countries to the battlefield. Ill will quickly escalated, but fortunately cooler heads prevailed, so that what is now referred to as the Pig War of 1859 only resulted in one casualty: the pig. The San Juan Islands were eventually declared American territory.

The history of this little-known war is chronicled through the interpretive centers in **San Juan Island National Historical Park,** divided into **English Camp** and **American Camp** (see "Exploring the Area," below). The Pig War was the last time that Great Britain and the U.S. opposed each other in war. General George Pickett, of the famed "Pickett's Charge" at the Civil War's Battle of Gettysburg, was commander of U.S. forces during the Pig War.

ESSENTIALS
Getting There
Washington State Ferries arrive at **Friday Harbor** on the island's eastern coast. See "Getting There," above, for information about fares and schedules.

Visitor Information
The **San Juan Island Chamber of Commerce,** 135 Spring St. (P.O. Box 98), Friday Harbor, WA 98250 (© **360/378-5240;** www. sanjuanisland.org), will be happy to tell you what you need to know about the island.

Getting Around
There are two island taxi services, **Bob's Taxi & Tours** (© **360/378-6777**) and **San Juan Taxi** (© **360/378-3550**). In summer months, **San Juan Transit** (© **800/887-8387** or 360/378-8887) provides bus transportation. Rental cars are available year-round from **M&W Auto,** 725 Spring St., Friday Harbor (© **800/323-6037** or 360/378-2886; www. sanjuanauto.com). Rates for a mid-size car are US$60 per day mid-May through September, US$10 less per day October through mid-May. Touring the island via bicycle, scooter, or moped is great fun. Rent bikes at **Island Bicycles,** 380 Argyle Ave., Friday Harbor (© **360/378-4941;** www.islandbicycles.com). Rates for mountain and hybrid bikes are US$36 per day. Hourly and multiple-day rates are available. Burley "tail wagon" bike trailers are also available for small dogs. Rent mopeds and "Scootcars", an inventive composite of a car and scooter, at **Susie's Mopeds** (© **800/532-0087** or 360/378-5244;

125 Nichols St., www.susiesmopeds.com), located 2 blocks up from the ferry landing at Friday Harbor. Moped rentals are US$25 per hour; Scootcars are US$65 per hour. Per-day rates are available.

EXPLORING THE AREA
Friday Harbor

The busy fishing village of **Friday Harbor** was first populated by a feisty bunch of scala-wags in the mid-1800s, and only gained respectability when it became the county seat in 1873. Today it encompasses 259 hectares (640 acres), which, as the bustling business center of the San Juan Islands, the National Trust for Historic Preservation added to its 2008 list of Dozen Distinctive Destinations. Its harbor teems with commercial fishing boats and pleasure craft. From the docks of the Friday Harbor marina, **Trophy Charters** (✆ **360/378-2110;** www.fishthesanjuans.com) runs salmon fishing trips, starting from US$98 per person. **Western Prince Cruises** (✆ **800/757-6722** or 360/378-5315; www.orcawhalewatch.com) offers nature and **whale-watching** expeditions from US$69 for adults, US$49 for children 12 and under. The 46-foot vessel accommodates up to 30 passengers; and with plenty of indoor and outdoor seating, inclement weather is no deterrent. Tours are 3 to 4 hours. **Maya's Whale Watch Charters** (✆ **360/378-7996;** www.mayaswhalewatch.biz) take out smaller groups (six passengers); 3-hour tours are US$75 adults and US$65 children 12 and younger. Guides are exceptionally wildlife-savvy, having written several wildlife books. They are also accomplished photographers who will give you tips beyond just point and shoot. **San Juan Kayak Expeditions** (✆ **360/378-4436;** www.sanjuankayak.com) has been in business near to 30 years, and will set you up for 3- and 4-day kayaking trips around the islands from US$450 to US$550 per person. They are the only folks to offer kayak-sailing, a combination of sail, paddle, and a following wind that has you traveling up to three times the speed of just paddling. They also rent standard double kayaks for US$80 per day.

San Juan Historical Museum   Housed in an 1890s wood-frame farmhouse, the museum includes a crowded collection of antiques, old photos, and American Indian artifacts, plus intriguing old farm equipment that makes you wonder how on earth they did what they purport to have done. Unless you're really into maritime "stuff," save your visit for a rainy day, though the other buildings—a carriage house, a pioneer cottage, and what was once declared the "worst county jail in the state of Washington"—are fun to wander around. On Friday nights July through August, the museum stages musical evenings on the lawn—bring a blanket and a picnic.

405 Price St., Friday Harbor. ✆ **360/378-3949.** www.sjmuseum.org. Admission US$1.20 for adults, US65¢ for children 6 to 18. May–Sept Thurs–Sat 10am–4pm, Sun 1–4pm; Mar–Apr and Oct Sat 10am–4pm; by appointment Nov–Feb.

The Whale Museum   Although the maritime displays (other than the whale skele-ton) are on the ho-hum side, a visit does give you a good insight into whale behavior: Learn the difference among breaching, spy hopping, and tail lobbing, as well as the many vocalization patterns; listen to their songs on the Whale Phone Booth. If whale-watching is on your agenda, check out the photo collection with the names and identification markings of some of the 90 or so resident orcas in the area. The museum has an orca adoption program to help fund ongoing research, and operates a **24-hour hotline** (✆ **800/562-8832**) to report whale sightings and marine mammal strandings.

62 1st St. North, Friday Harbor. ✆ **360/378-4710.** www.whalemuseum.org. Admission US$6 adults, US$5 seniors, US$3 children 5 to 18. May–Sept daily 10am–5pm. Hours variable Oct–Apr. Call to confirm.

(Fun Facts)   **Saving the Whales**

Orcas roam between 97 and 129km (60–80 miles) per day in Puget Sound and the Salish Sea, following a feeding route through the islands and up the west coast of Vancouver Island to northerly feeding grounds. For 30 years, San Juan Islands' Ken Balcomb, an ex-marine biologist, has observed, photographed, and catalogued the three pods that make up the southern resident killer whales. His work proved that high-powered sonar is harmful to the hearing of cetaceans (thus halting the device from being used in local waters), and helped convince the federal government in 2005 to declare the southern resident killer whales endangered, in part because of the dwindling King salmon runs throughout the Pacific Northwest on which they are so dependent.

American Camp ★

When British and American settlers were tilling the soil of San Juan Island, soldiers on both sides attempted to stake a national claim to these fertile lands. Sovereignty was eventually settled and, although not entirely accurate, today Americans refer to that time as the British occupation. However you view it, the American Camp, 10km (6¼ miles) south of Friday Harbor, serves as a historic reminder of those early days. The windswept grassy peninsula is a wonderful place to spend a sunny summer afternoon. On any other day, though, the winds make it barren and rather inhospitable, though some might say deliciously lonely. Two buildings remain, an abandoned officers' quarters and a laundresses' quarters, along with a cemetery and a defensive fortification built by Henry M. Roberts, of *Roberts Rules of Order* fame. A white picket fence circles the grounds, which include a Hudson's Bay Company farm on Grandma's Cove at the southern border of the park, along the water.

American Camp is really all about the great outdoors and limited facilities—you'll find a pit toilet along the way but little else. The approach road, Cattle Point Road, can get pretty busy with cyclists heading for the southernmost tip of the island, and trails throughout the park are popular for hikers, though none of them seem to get overcrowded. An on-site **Visitor Centre** (𝄘 360/378-2902) is open year-round daily 8:30am to 4:30pm. Admission is free.

Hiking Highlights

There are various routes to gain beach access, the easiest and most direct being from the respective parking lots and a 5- to 10-minute walk. These include **South Beach,** the longest public beach on San Juan Island, and a great place to see shorebirds and whales. The beach is mainly gravel, so shoes or sandals are a must. It's a short walk to reach the secluded **Fourth of July Beach** where, appropriately, eagles nest nearby. Getting to **Picnic Cattle Point,** arguably the prettiest beach on the island, is a precarious scramble down a rocky ledge, but again, only minutes from the parking lot. **Grandma's Cove** is a downhill stroll for half a kilometer (⅓ mile) to a picturesque beach. Use caution in descending the bluff, the gravelly soil gets very dry in summer and it's easy to lose your footing.

Prairie Walks are primitive tracks that crisscross the prairie and trace the bluff from Grandmas's Cove. It feels wild, and on a clear day, you can see views of Mount Baker, the Olympic and Cascade ranges, Vancouver Island, and even Mount Rainier, 209km (130 miles) up Admiralty Inlet. Mind your step; watch for rabbit warrens. A more protected walk is the 2.4km (1.5-mile) **Jakle's Lagoon Trail,** which travels along the old roadbed beneath a canopy of Douglas fir, cedar, and hemlock trees.

Hardy hikers usually opt for the upward trail to reach **Mount Finlayson**—90m (295 ft.) from where you can see the Coastal Mountains—as well as the Olympic and Cascade ranges on the horizon and seascape below. *Tip:* From the parking lot, follow the trail along the ridge; you have a dense evergreen forest to your left and a prairie of golden grass down to the beach on your right. From the summit, choose the well-worn path on the east side of the bluff and you descend into a cool, thick forest and a network of trails that twist and turn along the shore of Griffin Bay and pass two saltwater lagoons. You can enjoy the best of both worlds—different as night and day—as the two trails connect in a 4km (2.5-mile) loop. Birders come to the camp to catch a glimpse of the only nesting Eurasian skylarks in the U.S.

English Camp ★★

In sharp contrast to American Camp, English Camp is located in an area of protected waters, with maple trees spreading out overhead. About 16km (10 miles) from Friday Harbor, the site includes a restored hospital, a commissary, an impressive formal garden, and small white **barracks,** which are open to the public mid-May through Labor Day. The blockhouse, built right on the beach, served to protect the marines from marauding Natives, not Americans, and was later used as a guard house for miscreant troopers. You'll find interpretive displays on a hillside terrace overlooking the camp, close to where the officers' quarters were built. A small cemetery holds the graves of six British Marines who died accidentally during the occupation from 1860 to 1872 (there were no war-related casualties, other than the pig), and a trail leads through second-growth forests up to **Mount Young,** a fairly easy 198m (650-ft.) ascent. A **Visitor Centre** (✆ **360/378-2902**) operates June through August daily from 8:30am to 4:30pm. It is housed in what was once the officer's mess hall, and is staffed by rangers in period costume. At opening and closing times, these rangers create a fair to-do about raising the British flag, although it's lower than the American flag just up the hill. For information at any time of year for English and American Camps, contact the **Park Headquarters,** 125 Spring St., Friday Harbor (✆ **360/378-2240**). Admission is free.

Hiking Highlights

Hiking here is not as rigorous as in American Camp. The easiest trail is **The Bell Point Trail,** a 1.5km-long (0.9-mile), fairly level walk to Bell Point—it's a 3.2km (2-mile) loop—for a view of Westcott Bay. If you like to harvest shellfish, check with the park ranger at the visitor center for locations, daily limits, and red tide warnings, when the growth in algae is so prolific that they render shellfish unsafe to eat. Red tides usually occur from May to August. Conversely, the **Young Hill Trail** climbs 198m (650 ft.) to the top of Young Hill for a panoramic view of the island's northwest corner. Novice walkers should take care to pace themselves, as most of the gain is in the last half-kilometer (¹/₃ mile). **Royal Marine Cemetery** is located about 46m (151 ft.) off the Young Hill Trail, about a third of the way up. Five Royal Marines are interred here, and a memorial stone is in place for two other marines.

Roche Harbor ★★

Roche Harbor is a heritage destination resort about 14km (8²/₃ miles) away from Friday Harbor, San Juan's commercial center. A favorite getaway of the late John Wayne, Roche Harbor is a mix of historic buildings, modern conveniences, and marine-related activities.

The Westcott Bay Reserve (www.wbay.org) is an 8-hectare (20-acre) nature interpretive park filled with a rotating exhibit of more than 100 modern sculptures in
bronze, stone, wood, metal, glass, and ceramics. The art is on loan to the park,
and many can also be purchased from the artists.

Listed on the National Register of Historic Places, Roche Harbor was once the home of
lime and cement tycoon John S. McMillin. In its heyday during the 1890s, the town had
the largest limeworks west of the Mississippi, operating kilns that each burned 10 cords of
wood every 6 hours—just to keep functioning. The remains of several kilns are still visible.
Much of the lime sweetened the huge salt marsh that was filled in and became the tulip
fields of the Skagit Valley.

The renovated **Hotel de Haro** still maintains much of its historic character, and a
number of the heritage cottages used by workers in the lime kiln business have been
converted to overnight lodgings (see "Where to Stay", below).

The resort has some walks to enjoy: through pretty Victorian gardens beside the hotel,
along the docks, and on some heritage trails that take you through the old lime quarries;
past historic sites such as the woodyard, the site of the original company cottages; and
onto the hillside, where you can take in views of the Spieden Channel and small San Juan
Islands. Some of the paths are paved with the same bricks that lined the original lime
kilns. Pick up a trail map (US$1) at the hotel. The one walk you don't want to miss is to
the **Mausoleum,** a bizarre McMillin family memorial that's about 20 minutes from the
harbor. The structure itself is covered with Masonic symbols: an open, Grecian-style
columned complex surrounds six inscribed chairs, each containing the ashes of a family
member, set before a round table of limestone. Rumors abound as to why the seventh
chair and column have been removed. Some say it was part of Masonic ritual, others
believe a family member was disinherited. Or was it because the seventh member considered life to be everlasting?

Although open year-round, the resort is at its best in summer, not only for the land-
scaping but for the activities. Sea kayaking and whale-watching expeditions are available
through the **Marine Adventure Centre,** and a naturalist guide hangs around to answer
any questions about the local wildlife and terrain. The resort also becomes a showcase of
local talent. By day, the resort's pathways and docks fill up with artists' booths displaying
watercolors, oil paintings, photography, jewelry, knitted products, alpaca yarns, handmade handbags, and pottery. You can even get your portrait painted. By night, **Island
Stage Left,** a local outdoor theater company, takes to the boards with productions such
as *The Tempest* and *The Merchant of Venice.* It can get a bit chilly by final curtain, so dress
warmly, and bring bug spray and a blanket to sit on. Performances are free.

Lime Kiln Point State Park ★

Head due west from Friday Harbor, through the center of the island, and you'll wind up at
Lime Kiln State Park. Named for an early lime-kiln operation on site (remnants of its old
structures are still evident), this is the only park in the world dedicated to whale-watching.
Researchers use the **Lime Kiln Lighthouse,** built in 1914 and listed on the National Register of Historic Places, to watch for whales and to determine whether passing boats are

affecting their behavior. Other whale-watching enthusiasts crowd the bluff, or set up camp around picnic benches scattered along the beach. Your chances of sighting success are especially good in late August and early September, when major salmon runs head for the Fraser River spawning grounds. En route, they pass through **Haro Strait** in front of the park, along the west side of San Juan Island, attracting whales, which feed on them. You might spot orca, minke, and pilot whales, or their smaller cousins, harbor and Dall's porpoises. Bring your binoculars and cameras with telephoto lenses. There are 12 picnic sites and decent washroom facilities, so it's a good family destination, especially since the trails are short (from less than 0.8km/^{1}/$_2$ mile to the longest at 2.5km/1.6 miles) and easy to navigate. The park is open year-round daily from 8am to dusk. It operates a recorded information line at ✆ **360/378-2044.**

Pelindaba Lavender Farm

More than 10,000 lavender plants grow in scenic rows on slopes leading to the forest's edge and make for a fragrant stroll on a hot summer's day. Just be sure to close the gate behind you. Designated "certified organic," the plants are transformed into essential oils, processed on site in a custom-built distillery, along with handcrafted perfumes, soaps, pet grooming products, candles, truffles, and other foodstuffs. True to its name, which is the Zulu word for "gathering place," Pelindaba operates a cafe/lavender store in Friday Harbor where it serves a first-class lavender lemonade and lavender cheesecake. They have also opened an outlet in Seattle.

33 Hawthorne Lane. ✆ **866/819-1911** or 360/378-4248. www.pelindabalavender.com. Free admission. May–Sept daily 10am–5pm. Closed Oct–Apr.

WHERE TO STAY

Bird Rock Hotel   This historic inn (ca. 1891) is forever reinventing itself, and a recent half-million-dollar makeover has transformed it into a sassy little boutique hotel that manages to maintain the gracious atmosphere of yesteryear while still appealing to the Gen-X crowd. Guest rooms are decorated in rich colors against light walls, with a blend of modern and period furnishings, some plusher than others. Every room is a different size and shape, as might be expected in an old building, but that's part of its quirky charm. Four of the rooms share two bathrooms; the other 11 have private en suites. All bathrooms have heated floors. The Marrowstone Suite has a private outdoor Jacuzzi, and the Bainbridge Suite can sleep seven and even has three flatscreen TVs. The San Juan Suite is a favorite. It's near the top of the house and offers a kitchen, a private deck, and a bird's-eye view of the harbor. The inn is associated with **Elements Hotel & Spa** (✆ **800/ 793-4756** or 360/378-4000), an upgraded 72-room motel down the road (think polished hardwood floors versus shag carpet), and guests here have access to the motel's heated indoor swimming pool, hot tub, and sauna. A separate cottage houses the three-room Lavendera Day Spa. *Note:* The inn is right downtown, 2 blocks from the ferry landing and from a couple of boisterous bars; noise can sometimes be a problem if you're normally early-to-bed.

35 1st St. (P.O. Box 2023), Friday Harbor, WA 98250. ✆ **800/352-2632** or 360/378-5848. Fax 360/378-2881. www.birdrockhotel.com. 15 units. June–Sept US$217–US$287 superior, US$167–US$187 standard, US$117–US$147 simple; Oct–May rooms are US$30–US$40 less. Rates include continental breakfast. Extra person US$20. Children 3 and under stay free in parent's room. MC, V. **Amenities:** Lounge; complimentary bikes; room service. *In room:* TV, iPod docking station, Wi-Fi, coffeemaker, no phone.

Friday Harbor House ★   This elegant hotel on the bluff above the harbor offers the finest modern accommodations on San Juan Island, and the best views of the harbor to boot. The inn is a welcome relief from all the Victorian-style B&Bs found elsewhere on

the San Juan Islands. The interior is distinctly West Coast, with lots of windows, wood, slate tiles, and plush carpets. And this goes for the rooms, too. A standout feature is a double-person (but noisy) Jacuzzi strategically situated so that you can see through into the bedroom, enjoying the views beyond. It's also within sight of the fireplace, so you can enjoy its warmth. All rooms have queen-size beds save for three, which each feature a king. The continental breakfast includes home-baked scones and muffins. If you're on the early morning ferry, park your car in the lineup and return to enjoy these goodies; and be sure to ask for a treat box "for the road." Harbor View Restaurant has also earned a reputation for a creative fine-dining restaurant (see "Where to Dine," below).

130 West St., Friday Harbor, WA 98250. ✆ **360/378-8455.** Fax 360/378-8453. www.fridayharborhouse. com. 23 units. Mid-May to Sept US$250–US$325 queen, US$360 suite; Oct to mid-May US$150–US$200 queen, US$265 suite. 2-night minimum stay required in summer and on weekends. Rates include continental breakfast. Extra person US$35. Children 17 and under stay free in parent's room. AE, MC, V. **Amenities:** Restaurant. *In room:* TV/VCR/DVD, fridge, coffeemaker, hair dryer, iron, fireplace.

Lakedale Resort at Three Lakes Surrounded by three fresh springwater lakes, on 33 hectares (82 acres), this resort is a rarity inasmuch as it has successfully combined a myriad of accommodations to offer something for everyone, including a waterfront lodge, cabins, romantic glamping (glamorous camping) canvasses, and tent and RV sites. Lodge rooms have double French doors that open onto a private deck, with fireplaces and comfortable furnishings. The self-contained two-bedroom (and one three-bedroom) cabins are tucked away in the woods, complete with large decks and full kitchens. From May through September, the glamping canvasses are the most exotic; although they have no electricity or running water, they're only a short walk to the showers. Besides, these 21-sq.-m (225-sq.-ft) structures have wood floors, proper beds, warm duvets, linens, and a cordless lantern just in case the moon and stars aren't lighting the way. Rates include a continental breakfast that's served in the Longhouse Tent. The regular tent sites are nicely laid out, too, with easy access to fishing in the well-stocked lakes, swimming areas, and paddle-boat and canoe rentals.

4313 Roche Harbor Rd., Friday Harbor, WA 98250. ✆ **360/378-2350.** Fax 360/378-0944. www.lakedale. com. 10 lodge rooms, 18 cabins, 86 campsites, 4 RV sites. May–Sept US$249 lodge, US$339–US$489 cabin, US$139 glamping, US$57 RV (power/water), US$32–US$42 tent site; Oct–Apr US$179 lodge, US$249– US$439 cabin. No glamping/camping in winter. Children and pets not accepted in lodge. **Amenities:** Lounge; swimming; fishing; canoeing; trails; Wi-Fi. *In room:* TV/DVD, full kitchen (some), coffeemaker, hair dryer, iron, fireplace.

Roche Harbor Resort ★★ (Kids) A village unto itself, Roche Harbor offers many different kinds of lodging, as well as a marina large enough for 377 vessels, for seafaring guests. First, there is the century-old Hotel de Haro, where lace-trimmed beds, antiques, and roaring fireplaces transport you back to an earlier time. Originally a log bunkhouse, the hotel evolved into the distinctive three-story structure you see today, sophisticated enough to entertain company brass and dignitaries, including President Theodore Roosevelt (look for his signature in the guestbook). Suites have killer views, welcoming big beds, and large, claw-foot soaking bathtubs. Some single guest rooms share a bathroom. The one on the second floor contains the bathtub that John Wayne used to soak in. If you enjoy old and historic, the Haro delivers—slanted floors, crooked windows, and all. However, in addition to the hotel, there are nine former workers' cottages that have been converted into two-bedroom units close to the swimming pool, as well as one- to three-room condominiums and carriage houses. Cottages, carriage houses, condos, and the ultra-deluxe spa suites all have contemporary furnishings, full kitchen facilities, and of course, great views. Dining options are numerous, and include McMillin's Restaurant, housed in the former home of John S. McMillin, Roche Harbor Lime & Cement company president. The menu is expensive enough that you would expect the prime rib to be outstanding or presented with designer panache. It's good, but for better value for the money, opt for the less formal Madrona Grill downstairs. *Note:* Either restaurant is a great place to view the nightly closing taps ceremony when half a dozen resort staff march up the main dock, music blaring over the loud speakers, to lower the flags.

4950 Reuben Tarte Memorial Dr., Roche Harbor, WA 98250. (℃) **800/451-8910** or 360/378-2155. Fax 360/378-6809. www.rocheharbor.com. 72 units, some w/kitchens. Mid-May to Sept US$120–$142 shared bathroom, US$161–US$209 private bathroom, US$235–US$425 condominium and carriage house, US$335–US$395 spa suites, US$320–US$339 cottage; Oct to mid-May US$70–US$86 shared bathroom, US$86–US$100 private bathroom, US$143–US$395 condominium and carriage house, US$100–US$295 spa suites, US$130–US$190 cottage. Children 18 and under stay free in parent's room. AE, MC, V. **Amenities:** 3 restaurants; lounge; large outdoor heated pool; 2 tennis courts; playground; activities desk. *In room:* TV/VCR, DVD (some), fridge (some), coffeemaker, hair dryer, fireplace (some).

Wildwood Manor B&B ★   New owners have added so many comfort touches to this manor inn that it ranks right up there with the best. A winding drive leads you through a canopy of evergreens to a picture-book country manor. The surrounding woods offer easy trails on which to wander, and the views include rolling hills down to the San Juan Channel. Common areas include a large living room with comfortable, oversize lounge chairs, floor-to-ceiling bookshelves lined with books and movie titles, hand-painted murals, hardwood floors, a large Georgian fireplace, and a refreshment station that includes candies, gourmet coffee, and home-baked cookies. As soon as your feet hit the stairs, they sink into high-grade, plush carpeting that's also in every guest room. Beds have down duvets and high-quality linens, and furnishings include antiques alongside flatscreen plasma TVs. Bathrooms are stocked with everything from Q-tips to robes. Be prepared for a stellar breakfast—menu items change to guest preferences and may include items such as vanilla bean panna cotta with fresh strawberries or wild rice and goat cheese frittata. The warm and genuine hospitality extends beyond inn guests; there's a deer-feeding station near the front drive, frequented by entire families of deer for some good Kodak moments.

5335 Roche Harbor Rd., Friday Harbor, WA 98250. (℃) **877/298-1144** or 360/378-3447. Fax 360/378-6095. www.wildwoodmanor.com. 4 units. May–Sept US$205–US$275; Oct–Apr US$155–US$205. **Amenities:** Lounge; refreshment bar; library; trails. *In room:* TV/DVD, Wi-Fi, hair dryer, no phone.

WHERE TO DINE

Coho Restaurant (Finds) PACIFIC NORTHWEST   With only eight tables, the place fills up quickly, and this is a popular venue for intimate tête-à-têtes as well as group celebrations. The owner-chefs actually run two B&Bs, Harrison House Suites and Tucker House Inn, each set in a historic building nearby, and this restaurant, also housed in a craftsman house, expands their horizons beyond breakfast. Both are big in the Slow Food movement, so dinner plates are packed with local fare. Try the roasted beet and goat cheese salads, Westcott Bay oysters, and homemade pasta de giorno tossed in a fresh tomato basil sauce. The hazelnut-encrusted lavender chicken is exceptionally flavorful, as are the homemade ice creams and sorbets. Even the art on the walls is by local artists. Book a table between 5 and 6pm if you want to try the chef's three-course tasting menu (US$35).

120 Nichols St., Friday Harbor. ℰ **360/378-6330.** www.cohorestaurant.com. Reservations recommended.
Main courses US$24–US$36. AE, MC, V. Apr–Sept daily from 5pm; Oct–May Thu–Mon from 5pm.

Duck Soup Inn (Finds) PACIFIC NORTHWEST   Set in the woods overlooking a
pond, the restaurant is housed in a former woodworking shed. Cozy booths and small
tables create an intimate atmosphere, especially with the fieldstone fireplace, walls decorated with local art, and hurricane-lamp sconces. The seasonal menu changes daily
around the best island produce, meat, and poultry; the surrounding garden, a stunning
sight in its own right, provides most of the herbs, fruits, and edible flowers. The menu
usually offers only four appetizers, two or three entrees, and a handful of decadent desserts. But don't be put off by the lack of selection: This is a case where less is definitely
more. And even if you're a meat-and-potatoes diehard, chances are you'll find something
unexpectedly delicious. It's the innovative breads and creative combinations that set this
restaurant apart. For example, there might be pineapple prawns with rice noodles and
coconut sauce spiced with Thai basil and hot chiles, or tempura squash blossoms stuffed
with goat cheese and thyme and served with tangy apricot orange jam.

50 Duck Soup Lane, Friday Harbor. ℰ **360/378-4878.** www.ducksoupinn.com. Reservations required.
Main courses US$25–US$36. AE, MC, V. Apr–Oct Tues–Sun daily from 5pm. Closed Nov–Mar.

Harbor View Restaurant   With views looking down on Friday Harbor, this smart-
casual restaurant is a popular spot for locals to celebrate special occasions. The menu
changes weekly to take advantage of what's fresh and new on the island, though you can
always expect flavorful homemade soups, imaginative salads with all sorts of edible herbs
and flowers, and a catch-of-the-day special such as seared halibut with lemon basmati rice
and acorn bisque. The rack of lamb served with island-made goat-cheese pesto and the
flatiron steak with bourbon tarragon jus are two great choices if meat's your thing; both
are served with mainstay garlic mashed potatoes. Pastas are always creative—try the
pumpkin and goat cheese ravioli with walnut cream sauce. Desserts are different every
night except for the signature homemade ice creams. One scoop of each flavor is the only
way to go. Because hotel guests have preferred seating, reservations are highly recommended. Ask about their special 4- to 6-course Wine Dinners, held periodically to
showcase new dishes and local wines.

130 West St., Friday Harbor. ℰ **360/378-8455.** www.fridayharborhouse.com. Reservations recommended.
Main courses US$20–US$35. AE, MC, V. May–Sept daily 5:30–10pm; Oct–Apr Thurs-Mon 5–10pm.

Steps Wine Bar & Cafe ★ PACIFIC NORTHWEST   Small, with burgundy walls
that give it a jazzy atmosphere, this is the kind of eatery you'd expect to find in Seattle;
its presence reflects the slow gentrification of Friday Harbor. The wine list offers more
that 60 wines by the glass, as well as an extensive specialty selection. Meals are tapas-style
starters, small plates, or large plates depending on how hungry you are. Many ingredients
are from San Juan Island, as well as neighboring Waldron and Lopez islands, to create
items such as beer-battered oysters, chipotle grilled beef skewers with pinto bean fritters
and cilantro crema, seared Ahi tuna with blackberry-cucumber salsa, and a crab-stuffed
chicken breast that melts in your mouth. Desserts, too, won't disappoint, especially the
flourless dark chocolate cake with caramel sauce and toasted peanuts. Because it has the
largest wine-by-the-glass list on the island, you can easily experiment with your own
pairings.

The Alley, 140A First St., Friday Harbor Center. ℰ **360/370-5959.** www.stepswinebarandcafe.com. Main
courses US$12–US$20. MC, V. Wed–Mon from 5pm. Closed Tues.

THE SAN JUAN ISLANDS

10

SAN JUAN ISLAND

Named for the viceroy of Mexico in 1792, and not, in fact, for the orca whales common to its waters, Orcas Island is the largest (148 sq. km/57 sq. miles), hilliest, and most beautiful of the San Juan Islands. Half the fun of exploring this island is traveling its roads, which, in addition to going up and down, twist and turn among hedgerows, fields, and orchards. Around any bend might lie a jewel of a bay or an unexpected hamlet filled with quaint cottages and wildflower gardens. You can climb to the top of **Mount Constitution,** in **Moran State Park,** where the panorama stretches from the Lions, over Vancouver, to Mount Rainier, south of Seattle, or stroll down lanes that give way to picturesque havens such as **Deer Harbor** and **Orcas Landing.** Early settlers logged, fished, and farmed, but today most of the island's 4,500 population are artisans, entrepreneurs, retirees, and eco-adventurers. In **Eastsound,** the heart of "commercial" activity on Orcas, you'll find horseback and kayaking excursions, in addition to galleries, restaurants, and some shops. The **Rosario Resort,** an elegant mansion that regularly graces the pages of travel magazines, is probably the island's most prominent landmark. Hiring 200 staff, it is the largest private employer on the islands (see "Where to Stay & Dine," below).

ESSENTIALS
Getting There
Washington State Ferries dock at **Orcas Landing,** at the central southern peninsula of the island. See "Getting There," at the beginning of the chapter, for information about fares and schedules.

Visitor Information
Stop in at **Orcas Island Chamber of Commerce,** Moran State Park, Olga Rd. (P.O. Box 252), Eastsound, WA 98245 (© **360/376-2273;** www.orcasisland.org), which operates from June to Labor Day (first Mon in Sept) daily from 8:30am to 4:30pm.

Getting Around
Once there, **Orcas Taxi** (© **360/376-TAXI** [8294]) provides pickup and dropoff service throughout the island, year-round. From May to September, **Orcas Moped & Car Rental,** which has an association with M&W Auto on San Juan, (© **360/376-5266**) offers a limited number of rental cars for about US$60 a day. **Orcas Mopeds** (© **360/376-5266**), near the ferry landing, rents mopeds for US$25 per hour or US$65 per day, Scootcars for US$40 per hour and US$110 per day. Bike rentals are available from **Dolphin Bay Bicycles** (© **360/376-4157**), at the ferry landing, as well as from **Wildlife Cycles,** 350 North Beach Rd., Eastsound (© **360/376-4708;** www.wildlifecycles.com). Mountain bike and hybrid bike rentals are US$30 to US$40 per day. If time is of the essence, why not opt for a vintage biplane tour with **Magic Air Tours** (© **800/376-1929** or 360/376-2733; www.magicair.com) and get the lay of the land from the air? Trips are US$299 for two people, US$249 single.

EXPLORING THE AREA
Eastsound Village
From the ferry dock, head due north 23km (14 miles) to **Eastsound Village,** at the center of the island. This is the commercial hub of Orcas Island, and it's both lovely to look at and a delight to stroll through. Catering to backpackers and the well-to-do alike,

Eastsound sports galleries, potters, and a charming village green that hosts a number of special events. Check out the **Saturday morning market,** or watch a craftsperson whittle all manner of furniture and kitchen utensils with a foot-powered lathe at a pioneer display.

Eastsound is also where you'll want to base any **outdoor activities.** You may want to go horseback riding with Tennessee Walking Horses, known for their comfortable gait, at **Walking Horse Country Farm,** 180 Westbeach Rd. (© **360/376-5306**). Each session costs US$60, and includes a demonstration, some instruction, and an hour's trail ride along the farm's many bridal trails. Private rides are US$100. **Once in a Blue Moon Farm,** 412 Eastman Rd. (© **360/376-7035;** www.onceinabluemoonfarm.com), is a 1915 farmhouse that a former owner, a wealthy oil heiress, converted into a 465-sq.-m (5,000-sq.-ft.) villa. Mediterranean influence aside, the farm is a delight to visit; tours include petting llamas (guardians of the farm's sheep and chickens), gathering eggs, enjoying the lovely gardens, and picking fruit in the orchards and strawberry fields.

For guided kayak tours, head for **Shearwater Adventures,** 138 North Beach Rd. (© **360/ 376-4699;** www.shearwaterkayaks.com), which operates launch points from Deer Harbor, Rosario, and Doe Bay. Three-hour trips cost US$60 for adults; full-day trips cost US$125 per person. The sunset tour (US$80) is highly recommended. For a historical twist to kayaking, take a look at what **Osprey Tours** (© **360/376-3677**) has to offer. These folks use handcrafted Aleutian-style kayaks, and every kayaker is given an Aleutian whale-hunter's hat. Shaped like conical visors that resemble bird beaks, these hats served to disguise hunters, while their shape amplified the sounds of whales moving through the water. Osprey Tours specializes in private tours, and will accommodate families. Call for reservations and to arrange a venue based on your itinerary; one of their launch sites is right beside the ferry landing. Half-day trips cost US$70 per adult; full-day trips cost US$150; overnight trips start at US$250. Children's rates are negotiable.

The Orcas Island Historical Museum, 181 North Beach Rd. (© **360/376-4849;** www.orcasmuseum.org), makes for a brief diversion, mainly for a look at the building itself. It comprises six one-room log cabins constructed by homesteaders in the 1880s. Between 1951 and 1963, cabins were disassembled and transported to Eastsound Village, where they were painstakingly reconstructed and connected to create the museum you see today. Admission is US$3 for adults, US$2 for seniors and students. Children 12 and under are free. The museum is open June through September daily from 11am to 4pm, until 7pm on Friday.

Moran State Park

A favorite destination for visitor and islander alike, Moran State Park's 1,864 hectares (4,606 acres) offer a number of outdoor recreational activities, including camping, picnicking, canoeing and kayaking, hiking, horseback riding, and more. Over 48km (30 miles) of hiking trails, most built by the Civilian Conservation Corps (CCC), cover everything from easy nature loops like the 4.3km (2.7-mile) walk around Cascade Lake to challenging out-of-the-way hikes such as the 7.6km (4.7-mile) Mount Pickett Trail that ascends 338m (1,109 ft.) through part of the largest tract of unlogged, old-growth forest in the Puget Sound Trough. Pick up a trail map from the Park Office at Cascade Lake. Unlike quieter Mountain Lake (that's where to put in for a quiet paddle, and where fishing enthusiasts angle for trout), Cascade Lake gets a little like Grand Central Station in summer with canoe and paddleboat renters, picnickers, swimmers, day hikers setting off from the lakeside's many trail heads, and overnight campers. It's the only place in the

Finds **Get Potted**

In operation for more than 60 years, **Orcas Island Pottery,** 338 Old Pottery Rd, Eastsound (✆ **360/376-2813;** www.orcasislandpottery.com), is one of the oldest potteries in the region and represents the work of almost two dozen potters. Look for a weathered log cabin festooned with colorful oversize pottery plates, and jewel-tone glazed vases in the garden. Inside is a working studio with artists throwing pots on the wheel, hand-building and glazing. **Crow Valley Pottery & Gallery,** 2274 Orcas Rd., Eastsound (✆ **360/376-4260;** www.crowvalley.com), is also housed in a log cabin, built around 1866, and showcases the works of more than 70 artists and craftspeople. Located in a renovated strawberry-packing plant, **Olga Artworks,** 11 Point Moran Rd., Olga (✆ **360/376-4408;** www.orcas artworks.com), is just east of Moran State Park, and features the work of more than 60 local artists displayed in a fashion almost as creative as the pieces themselves: on shelves made of railroad ties, benches of driftwood, and tree-stump pedestals. **Café Olga** (✆ **360/376-5098**) is also located here, legendary for its crab quesadillas, lemon shaker pie tart (made with the entire lemon), and homemade cinnamon rolls, which tend to sell out pretty quickly.

park where you'll find bathhouses, kitchen shelters, and a sani-station. Call ✆ **888/ CAMPOUT** [226-7688] or 888/226-7655 for campsite reservations or visit www.parks. wa.gov. The park's landmark, **Mount Constitution,** is the highest point in the islands. Rising 734m (2,408 ft.) above sea level, the summit is reached by a steep, paved road, where you'll discover a 16m (52-ft.) stone tower patterned after a 12th-century fortress. You can drive to the top; if you take your bike, you'll find the hard ride up rewarded with an exhilarating ride back down. Because the gradient is so steep, the road is generally closed from mid-November to mid-April, as it can get slick and dangerous. Information on trails, campsites, and activities in the park is available from **Washington State Parks,** 7150 Clearwater Lane, Olympia, WA 98504 (✆ **360/902-8844**). You can also go online to www.orcasisle.com/moran.

Deer Harbor

Lying at the end of a winding country lane, Deer Harbor has some of the best marine views in all of the San Juans, as well as a marina with showers and a laundry, boat charters, gift shops, and a new waterfront park. **Deer Harbor Charters** (✆ **800/544-5758** or 360/376-5989; www.deerharborcharters.com) offer year-round 4-hour marine wildlife tours with a professional naturalist at US$69 per adult and US$44 per child under 14 years of age, while **Deer Harbor Marina** (✆ **360/376-3037;** www.boattravel.com/ deerharbor) can arrange for kayak, small boat, and bicycle rentals. The Resort at Deer Harbor (✆ **888/376-4480**), which lies just above the marina, is a complex of deluxe timeshare cottages, so the only place left to stay in the area is the **Deer Harbor Inn** (✆ **877/377-4110** or 360/376-4110). It offers both lodge and private cottage accommodations, unpretentious but comfortable (country quilts on the beds and paper cups in the bathroom versus down duvets and glasses), and only peek-a-boo harbor views, sometimes across the parking lot. The Inn does run a casual restaurant in the original 1915 building, serving mostly comfort foods and seafood, family-style with salad and soup.

Very Expensive

Rosario Resort & Spa ★★★   This turn-of-the-20th-century mansion, originally the private residence of shipping magnate Robert Moran, is worth the look even if you don't have the money to stay. Listed on the National Register of Historic Places, the building has been beautifully restored, and as befits a ship building, is still as solid and elegant as an ocean liner of the period. Walls are 30 centimeters (12 in.) thick and paneled with mahogany. Windows are inch-thick plate glass. And the mansion boasts 557 sq. m (5,995 sq. ft.) of teak parquet floors that took craftsmen more than 2 years to lay. The music room features a Tiffany chandelier and a working 1,972-pipe Aeolian organ, which, when installed in 1913, was the largest organ in a private home in the United States. Don't miss the free hour-long concerts held nightly—they're entertaining, and reminiscent of when Moran used to play the complicated organ for his guests—only the real secret is, he never knew how to play. In winter, concerts are performed on Saturday evening only. The mansion is one of 10 buildings that make up the Rosario Resort & Spa, which is spread out over 3 hectares (7¹/₂ acres), and surrounded by several more acres of countryside. Guest rooms vary from standard accommodations either scattered along the waterfront in motel-style buildings or near the mansion, to one- and two-bedroom suites, with kitchens and private balconies, perched on the hillside. All are spacious (especially those on the hill), with bright, modern decor in neutral tones accented with floral-print accessories and down duvets, and they offer terrific views of Cascade Bay. Hillside rooms also have fireplaces and sunken Jacuzzi tubs. The **Avanyu Spa** offers everything from early morning yoga and cardio workouts to aromatherapy wraps, massage, and other personalized body treatments. There are three restaurants, suitable to all tastes and budgets. **The Mansion Dining Room** is the must-reserve, dress-up restaurant. The menu features popular steak and salmon dishes as well as organic island-grown produce, although its real pièce de résistance is its all-you-can-eat buffet. The wine list has many selections from local northwest wineries. In summer, a poolside bar and grill is also open. Rates drop for weekday stays year-round, and winter rates are more than 50% less than those charged in summer.

1 Rosario Way, Eastsound, WA 98245. ℂ **800/562-8820** or 360/376-2222. Fax 360/376-2289. www.rosario resort.com. 122 units, some w/fireplaces and Jacuzzis. July to mid-Sept US$199–US$299 standard, US$407–US$797 suite; mid-Sept to June US$89–US$149 standard, US$119–US$399 suite. Extra person US$20. Children 17 and under stay free in parent's room. AE, DC, DISC, MC, V. No pets. **Amenities:** 3 restaurants; lounge; small heated indoor pool; large heated outdoor pool; health club; spa; sauna; concierge; activities desk; car-rental desk; library; museum; Wi-Fi. *In room:* TV, coffeemaker, hair dryer.

Spring Bay Inn ★ (**Finds**)   It's a long drive on a dirt road to get here, but your efforts are amply rewarded. Situated on 23 hectares (57 acres) of woods, the Spring Bay Inn does what it can to showcase its setting, mainly through 270 custom windows that peek through the trees to stunning water views from every room. The angular Great Room has hardwood floors, an impressive fieldstone fireplace, and a vaulted ceiling; and the four guest rooms upstairs have wood-burning fireplaces, feather mattresses, down comforters, high ceilings, private bathrooms, and fresh flowers. The fifth guest room, the Ranger's Suite, downstairs, has 27 windows and its own outdoor Jacuzzi. In the morning, coffee, muffins, and fresh fruit are delivered to your door—a little sustenance for the 2-hour guided kayak tour to follow, included with the room rate. Brunch is served on your return. The innkeepers are an engaging pair of retired state park rangers, who go out of their way to share their knowledge and make beginner kayakers feel like pros.

464 Spring Bay Trail (P.O. Box 97), Olga, WA 98279. *℡* **360/376-5531.** Fax 360/376-2193. www.springbay inn.com. 5 units. Year-round US$240–US$280. Rate includes continental breakfast, brunch, and kayaking trip. AE, DISC, MC, V. **Amenities:** Lounge; Jacuzzi. *In room:* Fridge, hair dryer, no phone.

Moderate

Cascade Harbor Inn   Situated among madrona trees, across the bay from Rosario Resort, this is a more affordable alternative (compare rates). Studio, one- and two-bedroom suites have a motel feel, with fully equipped kitchen including a fridge, microwave, and coffeemaker, making them a good choice for families and those indulging in longer island stays. The studio Murphy beds are surprisingly comfortable, as are the sofa pullouts for additional guests. Every room has a great marine view and private balcony overlooking Cascade Bay. Summer rates include continental breakfast.

1800 Rosario Rd., Eastsound, WA 98245. *℡* **800/201-2120** or 360/376-6350. Fax 360/376-6354. www. cascadeharborinn.com. 44 units. June to Labor Day US$129–$399; Sept–May US$65–US$199. US$25 extra person. AE, DISC, MC, V. Free parking. **Amenities:** Breakfast lounge; Wi-Fi. *In room:* Fridge, coffeemaker, microwave, hair dryer.

Doe Bay Resort & Retreat Center   Spread over 12 hectares (30 acres) of waterfront property, this resort is a throwback to the 1970s, offering a congenial, New Age atmosphere, and an impressive organic garden. There's a wide range of accommodations: rustic cabins (one-, two-, and three-bedroom configurations, some with no running water; others with fully equipped kitchen), yurts (canvas and wood structures) with skylights, treehouses (kids and romantics love them), greenhouse cabins, geodesic domes, tents, limited RV sites, and a hostel. There are shared central bathrooms and a community kitchen. The fully equipped, self-contained "retreat house" accommodates ten. A wonderful, clothing-optional, three-tiered sauna and a creekside mineral springs Jacuzzi perch on a covered deck. Bring an oversize towel or two, and a flashlight. Sea kayak tours and bike rentals are available. The Cafe Doe Bay is decorated with lava lamps, and it dishes up good vegetarian and seafood selections, although you might have to wait a bit because service can be casual. The cafe is housed in a former general store and post office (built in 1908 and listed in the National Register of Historic Places). It's open daily in summer for breakfast, brunch, and dinner, with restricted hours in winter. Call to confirm. It's also one of the few Wi-Fi hot spots at the resort.

107 Doe Bay Rd. (P.O. Box 437), Olga, WA 98279. *℡* **360/376-2291.** Fax 360/376-5809. www.doebay.com. 64 units. June–Sept US$35–US$50 tent and hostel; US$85–US$260 cabin, dome, and yurt; US$450 retreat house. Minimum 2-night stay. Rates 20% lower Oct–May. MC, V. Pets accepted June–Sept (US$20). **Amenities:** Restaurant; Jacuzzi; sauna; limited watersports rentals; bike rentals; massage; yoga classes; library-lounge; Wi-Fi. *In room:* No phone.

Orcas Hotel ★   Built in 1904 as a boarding house, this restored Victorian home is on the National Register of Historic Places and overlooks the ferry terminal. Guest rooms aren't deluxe, but they're clean and comfortable, decorated with faux country quilts, earth tones, and period furniture that provides a simple, old-world appeal. Some share bathrooms; others have private toilets but shared showers. The newer guest rooms have private balconies and Jacuzzis. In the summer, there's a tiny attic room—a great find for the budget conscious. For those who really want to get away from it all, there's also a small, self-contained cottage that sleeps six. Rates include a continental breakfast in the Orcas Café, which also has a grandstand veranda to wait out the ferry with a beer or a sandwich later on in the day. Octavia's Bistro adjoins the hotel and serves a good selection of seafood, steaks, and pasta.

(Finds) Shaw Island

Shaw Island is the most remote of the accessible San Juan Islands, and makes for a terrific bike trip; most roads are paved. If you visit, however, take care to be as self-sufficient as possible, bringing along enough food, water, and other supplies to last. Home to less than 200 permanent residents, most of Shaw Island's 20 sq. km (7.7 sq. miles) are undeveloped. With the exception of a **wildlife refuge** and a tiny country park offering limited picnicking and camping facilities, the island is completely privately owned. Its store, **Shaw General Store,** on Blind Bay Rd. (© **360/468-2288**), is, by law, the only commercial business allowed, which is why it acts as ferry terminal, grocery store, gas station, and post office. Although the store sells a number of tourist trinkets, it also boasts a surprising selection of gourmet items, such as mustards, herbs, and vinegars produced on the island. For many years, a cloistered order of nuns ran the ferry dock operations, so if you spy a soul crossing her chest as the ferry departs, don't be alarmed; the blessing of each sailing is a tradition that continues today. Nearby, **The Little Red Schoolhouse** (listed on the National Register of Historic Places) is one of the few one-room schools still in use. Across the road, a tiny log cabin houses the **Shaw Island Museum**—a display of mostly old photographs and island artifacts. Whether you go by bike or car, there are enough sailings to and from Shaw to make a day trip possible. You'll need to check sailing times carefully, though, since arrivals and departures are a mix of eastbound and westbound destinations.

P.O. Box 155 (Orcas ferry landing), Orcas, WA 98280. © **888/672-2792** or 360/376-4300. Fax 360/376-4399. www.orcashotel.com. 12 units, 1 cottage. May–Oct and year-round holiday weekends US$89–US$94 standard, US$121–US$208 with Jacuzzi; Nov–Apr US$94 standard, US$142 with Jacuzzi; year-round US$125 cottage. Extra person US$15. AE, MC, V. **Amenities:** Restaurant; pub; lounge; Wi-Fi. *In room:* TV/DVD on request, hair dryer, no phone.

Turtleback Farm Inn ★★ Set away from the water, the pastoral setting of Turtleback Farm is refreshingly bucolic, with its lush meadows, duck ponds, and forests. Originally constructed in the late 1800s, the farmhouse has been completely redone and yet still retains a heritage feel, with lots of wood paneling, antiques, comfortable lounge chairs, and a living room that boasts a Rumford fireplace. Bedrooms tend to be on the small side but exude so much charm that you'll want to nest. Linens include woolen comforters and down pillows. Most en suites have claw-foot tubs. Orchard House, separate from the farm, resembles an upscale barn from the outside. Set in the apple orchard, it has four spacious rooms with king-size beds, completed with gas fireplaces and private decks from which you can watch the farm's handful of sheep and cows, including some Scottish Highlanders, set the pace for the day. Wi-Fi is available as a must-have concession "for a farm on an island in the middle of nowhere."

1981 Crow Valley Rd., Eastsound, WA 98245. © **800/376-4914** or 360/376-4914. Fax 360/376-5329. www.turtlebackinn.com. 11 units. US$150–US$260; lower rates Nov–May. Extra person US$35. MC, V. Children must be 8 and over to stay in Farmhouse. 2-night minimum in Orchard House. Pets not accepted. Nonsmoking. **Amenities:** Lounge; coffeemaker; iron; Wi-Fi. *In room:* No phone.

THE SAN JUAN ISLANDS

10

ORCAS ISLAND

Laced with country lanes, picturesque farms, and orchards, Lopez Island is just about as bucolic and pastoral as it gets. Cows and sheep are a common sight, as are bright fields of daffodils, tulips, lilies, and delphiniums. Home to approximately 2,100 people, and covering 76 sq. km (29 sq. miles), Lopez has a rich agricultural heritage. Once known as the "Guernsey Island" for its exports of cream, eggs, and poultry, the land now supports more than 50 working farms. In summer, cyclists flock to the gently rolling hills, and birdwatchers take to the expanses of protected tidal flats to watch a myriad of shorebirds: horned grebes, double crested cormorants, yellow legs, peeps, ospreys, and peregrine falcons.

Spencer Spit State Park is a 56-hectare (138-acre) marine and camping park, named for the lagoon-enclosing sand spit on which it lies. Clamming, crabbing, and saltwater fishing are among the park's most popular activities. It's also a sun-drenched picnic area with 37 sought-after standard camping sites at US$17 to US$23 per night March through October. Call ✆ **888-CAMPOUT** [226-7688] for reservations or visit www.parks.wa.gov. **Lopez Farm and Cottages** (✆ **800/440-3556**) is a private, alternate camping spot for tents only and is the only site on the island with showers. **Shark Reef Recreation Area** is a favorite spot from which to watch harbor seals, sea lions, and bald eagles diving for dinner. Or you can head for **Agate Beach,** one of the few beaches open to the public, and one of the most romantic places to watch the sun go down. The southernmost point, Iceberg Point, is another easy trail to the bluffs that edge the shore.

Come winter, Lopez Island seems to go into virtual hibernation, save for a fairly recent phenomenon: When one of the original Microsoft team built his compound here a few years back, techies followed, and vacation mega-houses have been popping up all along the waterfront ever since. Real estate prices are soaring. Lopez village has developed a new gentrified air, and now has street names and sidewalks. Lopez is, however, still the friendliest of the San Juan Islands. Waving to passing cars and cyclists is a time-honored local tradition.

ESSENTIALS
Getting There
The ferry arrives at the northerly tip of the island. See "Getting There," at the beginning of the chapter, for information about fares and schedules.

Visitor Information
The **Lopez Island Chamber of Commerce,** P.O. Box 102, Lopez, WA 98261 (✆ **360/468-4664;** www.lopezisland.com), distributes literature and maps in shops and galleries throughout the island.

Getting Around
Folks on foot could be out of luck. Taxi service is an on-off affair (at time of printing, there was none available, although there's talk about starting some sort of bus service). Call the Chamber of Commerce (above) to get the latest scoop. One of the best bike routes around the island is a 48km (30-mile) circuit that can be done in a day and is suitable for the whole family. If you don't have your own wheel power, here are some rental options: **Lopez Bicycle Works & Kayaks,** 2847 Fisherman's Bay Rd. (✆ **360/468-2847;** www.lopezkayaks.com), offers mountain bikes, tandems, and children's bikes, as well as repairs and sales.

Lopez Village is the business center of the island, and has a scattering of cafes, shops, a charming farmers' market (held Wed and Sat), and, of course, real estate offices. The **Library,** 2225 Fisherman Bay Rd. (© **360/468-2265**), housed in a bright red and white 19th-century schoolhouse, is the *only* place to get the Sunday *New York Times, Los Angeles Times,* and *Wall Street Journal.* Copies are donated, which might mean you're reading 2-day-old news. Well, call it being on island time. Nonresidents pay a refundable US$10 fee to check out books while on the island. This is also where you can find computer and Internet access.

When you're browsing through Lopez Village, be sure to drop in to the **Soda Fountain & Pharmacy** (© **360/468-4511**), where you'll find an old-fashioned ice-cream parlor with a slew of fountain treats: killer banana splits, hand-dipped malts, and suck-'til-your-brain-hurts thick-and-creamy milk shakes. The place is a bit scruffy, but the lunch counter is gossip central for Lopez locals, just in case you're interested in the low-down on island life. For picnic supplies of rustic breads, pizzas, and sweet treats, visit **Holly B's Bakery** (© **360/469-2133**), open April through November. The **Lopez Historical Museum,** 28 Washburn Place (© **360/468-2049**), houses artifacts such as a foot-powered cow-milking machine, and a 1903 Orient buckboard—the first car driven on the island. The museum puts out an island tour map of historic landmarks, which, believe it or not, has 34 destinations! You have to be a history nut to really appreciate this, though. Museum operating hours are sporadic, particularly in winter, although you can usually count on Friday through Sunday from 10am to 3pm. It's a fun 20-minute visit while you're wandering around the village. Admission is US$1.50 for adults, US$1 for children 18 and under.

Touring island farms is another fun excursion, especially if you're into market produce, herbs, or hand-woven blankets. Call the **Lopez Community Land Trust** (© **360/468-3723**) for information. If you're a wine lover, or are even just learning to love it, pay a visit to **Lopez Island Vineyards,** 724 Fisherman Bay Rd. (© **360/468-3644;** www.lopezislandvineyards.com). This small, family-owned winery is the oldest in San Juan County, producing organically grown grapes and some pretty drinkable wines. Until recently, if you bought any wines with labels stating an origin of Friday Harbor or Orcas Island, they were tourist gimmicks. The wine was actually made in the Yakima Valley. These folks, however, have matured their early-ripening vines from the mid-1980s, so they now produce grapes that create more flavor. In addition to a Cabernet and Merlot, there's a medium-dry white apple-pear wine, as well as a full-bodied blackberry dessert wine, all of which are made on the premises. The vineyard is open for tastings from April 15 to December 15, Friday and Saturday, from noon to 5pm. It's also open in July and August on Wednesday and Thursday.

WHERE TO STAY

Edenwild Country Inn ★ This is the Victorian centerpiece of Lopez Village, complete with picturesque flower garden and large wraparound porch. Although the inn is not located on the water, many guest rooms have views of the San Juan Channel. Pleasant antique furnishings decorate the recently refurbished rooms, and there are quality bathroom amenities and delicious Bavarian chocolates at your bedside. Three guest rooms also have large wood-burning fireplaces. All have private bathrooms, some of which feature deep-soaker claw-foot bathtubs. Room no. 2 is the most comfortable, notable for its size and cozy sitting area, the family heirlooms (ca. 1920), and vistas of Fisherman's

(Moments) **A Wonderful Walk**

Iceberg Point, at Lopez's southernmost coast, beyond Agate Beach, is located minutes away from MacKaye Harbor, and leads to some of island's most spectacular (and sometimes windy) coastline. But you need to pay attention to find it, and to make sure you're not an unwelcome visitor on private land. Park your car at the Agate Beach parking area and walk south to where the pavement ends. Go through the private gate onto the gravel road, past a large tree line on the right. When you come to a beach house on your left, turn right at the telephone on your right, down a well-driven driveway and through the metal gate. Continue down the grassy road, and stay left at the fork—or you'll be trespassing. This shaded trail passes huckleberry and blackberry bushes, and soon the forest opens up to Iceberg Point State Park. It's about a 20-minute walk, and you'll want to spend at least an hour exploring the bluffs, more if you have a picnic.

Bay. In answer to the island's lack of cable TV, there are books everywhere—you can actually take them home thanks to Lopez's phenomenal recycling program. The European-style breakfast is generous, with plenty of cold cuts, cheeses, bread varieties, eggs, and fresh fruit.

132 Lopez Rd. (PO Box 271), Lopez Island, WA 98261. (✆) **800/606-0662** or 360/468-3238. Fax 360/468-4080. www.edenwildinn.com. 8 units. May–Sept US$170–US$195. Rates 20% lower Oct–Apr. Rates include full breakfast. Extra person US$25. AE, MC, V. Pets not accepted. Children under 12 not accepted. **Amenities:** Lounge; Wi-Fi. *In room:* Coffeemaker, hair dryer, iron, no phone.

Inn at Swifts Bay ★★ Set among tall cedars above Swifts Bay, this elegant Tudor inn, formerly a summer home, offers luxury in a casual atmosphere. The entrance is a bit forbidding—the trees make everything seem so dark—but once inside, you'll notice California-style furnishings happily mixed with antique reproductions, and details such as goose-down comforters, fresh flowers, crocheted antimacassars, and needlepoint pillows. The overall appeal, though, might lean to guests age 50-plus. Shared areas are warm and inviting; the lounge contains a fireplace, a piano, decanters of sherry and port, many books, and a movie library of over 350 films. The two-person sauna and tiny exercise studio are unexpected finds, with just enough equipment to work up a sweat: a universal gym, treadmill, stationary bike, and some weights. Three of the comfortable guest rooms have fireplaces, fridges, and private bathrooms; the remaining two guest rooms share a bathroom. The breakfasts are feasts: crab cakes are the reputed favorite, although the hazelnut waffles with fresh Lopez Island berries and the dill crepes filled with smoked salmon and herbed eggs can't be far behind.

856 Port Stanley Rd., Lopez Island, WA 98261. (✆) **800/903-9536** or 360/468-3636. Fax 360/468-3637. www.swiftsbay.com. 5 units. Year-round US$110–US$125 shared bathroom; US$175–US$210 private bathroom. Rates include full breakfast. AE, DISC, MC, V. **Amenities:** Lounge; exercise room; Jacuzzi; sauna, high-speed Internet. *In room:* No phone.

MacKaye Harbor Inn Originally built in 1904, and dramatically rebuilt 20 years later when it was the first island homestead to have electricity, the upgraded farmhouse still retains much of its homey style. Rooms are large, ceilings are high, picture windows overlook the bay, and there's a long porch. Decor and furnishings are unpretentious but comfortable, and an enclosed garden gazebo is a private sanctuary where guests can read, meditate, or enjoy watching the hummingbirds at the feeder. Rates include truffles and port in the evening, and a large continental breakfast with very wholesome muffins, hard-boiled eggs, fresh fruit, and granola. Guests have free use of 21-speed mountain bikes and can rent kayaks for US$25 per day, or US$35 for their entire stay. There are also two self-contained cottages on the property, suitable for families.

949 MacKaye Harbor, Lopez Island, WA 98261. ℭ **888/314-6140.** Fax 360/468-2253. www.mackaye harborinn.com. 5 units, 4 with en suite bath. US$155–US$215. Rates are less in early spring. Retreat packages available. Rates include breakfast. MC, V. Closed mid-Oct to late Apr. **Amenities:** Lounge; kayak rentals; free use of mountain bikes; Wi-Fi. *In room:* Hair dryer, no phone.

WHERE TO DINE

The Bay Cafe ★★ (Finds) PACIFIC NORTHWEST Located at the entrance to Fisherman's Bay, this bright, spacious restaurant is a delight. Colorful and contemporary art adorns the walls, while row upon row of windows give way to terrific sunsets and waterside views. The views are only outdone by the food: the ever-changing selection of seafood tapas is imaginative (the shrimp cakes with a citrus-sesame soy sauce are to die for), and the entrees cover all the bases, with dishes to please carnivores, herbivores, and everything in between. The Thai curry is exceptionally good, as is almond-crusted Alaskan halibut with gingered boysenberries and the pork tenderloin char grilled with roasted corn relish and lime chipotle cream. Homemade soup and salad are included with your meal, which makes the menu a particularly good value. There's a patio in summer. In winter, call ahead.

9 Old Post Rd, Lopez Village. ℭ **360/468-3700.** www.bay-cafe.com. Reservations required July–Aug. Main courses US$17–US$25. AE, DISC, MC, V. May–Aug daily 5:30–10pm; Sept–Apr Wed–Sun 5:30–10pm (variable).

Love Dog Café (Finds) ECLECTIC Its name is derived from a 13th-century poem by philosopher Rumi: "There are love dogs in this world no-one knows the names of, give your life to be one." The chef-owner-storyteller is (self-)named White Bear for her white hair and somewhat stocky appearance. And the food is some of the best Italian fare in the San Juan Islands There are always half a dozen different pasta specials (pray that you're there for the pesto capellini) usually served family-style, as well as a couple of fresh-fish features. In the morning, the cafe serves some of the best breakfasts too, and true to its eclectic nature is able to transform from an eatery serving burgers, quiche, and good salads by day, to quite a romantic spot at night, especially if you hit an evening with live jazz. Service can be on the slow side, but it's worth the wait. All the basics and baked goods are made from scratch, and the desserts are delicious, especially the pot au chocolate or bread pudding with whiskey sauce.

1 Village Center, Lopez Island. ℭ **360/468-2150.** Main courses US$12 dinner. MC, V. Daily 8am–8pm (variable in winter).

Appendix: Fast Facts, Toll-Free Numbers & Websites

1 FAST FACTS: VANCOUVER ISLAND, THE GULF ISLANDS & SAN JUAN ISLANDS

AREA CODES Numbers are made up of the 3-digit area code and the 7-digit local number. On Vancouver Island and the Gulf Islands, this prefix is 250. For the San Juan Islands, the area code is 360.

AUTOMOBILE ORGANIZATIONS Motor clubs will supply maps, suggested routes, guidebooks, accident and bail-bond insurance, and emergency road service. The **American Automobile Association (AAA)** is the major auto club in the United States. If you belong to a motor club in your home country, inquire about AAA reciprocity before you leave. You may be able to join AAA even if you're not a member of a reciprocal club; to inquire, call AAA (© **800/222-4357**; www.aaa.com). AAA is actually an organization of regional motor clubs, so look under "AAA Automobile Club" in the White Pages of the telephone directory. AAA has a nationwide emergency road service telephone number (© **800/AAA-HELP** [222-4357]). In British Columbia, the reciprocal organization is the BCAA (© **604-293-2222**).

BUSINESS HOURS In Victoria and other major urban centers, banks are open Monday through Thursday from 10am to 3pm, Friday from 10am to 6pm, and sometimes on Saturday mornings. Stores typically open Monday through Saturday

from 10am to 6pm. Stores in Victoria are also open Sundays in summer. Although business hours on the San Juan Islands and Gulf Islands tend to follow this pattern, you may come across unexpected closures of individual stores, especially early in the week when tourist traffic is slower.

CAR RENTALS See "Toll-Free Numbers & Websites," p. 271.

DENTISTS Most Gulf Islanders commute to Victoria for dental services. However, **Pender Island Dental Clinic** (5715 Canal Rd.; © **250/629-6815**) offers family and emergency dental care. San Juan Islanders find major services in Anacortes and Seattle. **Tooth Ferry Dental Office** is located in Friday Harbor (385 Court St.; © **360/378-5300**).

DOCTORS On most of the islands, doctors operate out of medical clinics (see also "Hospitals" below). These include **Galiano Island Health Centre,** 908 Burrill Rd. (© **250/539-3230**); **Pender Island Medical Clinic,** 5715 Canal Rd. (© **250/629-3323**); **Mayne Island Health Centre,** 526 Felix Jack Rd. (© **250/539-2312**); **Orcas Island Family Health Center,** 1286 Mt. Baker Rd. (© **360/376-7778**), and **Inter-Island Medical Center,** 550 Spring St., Friday Harbor (© **360/378-2141**).

DRINKING LAWS In British Columbia, the minimum drinking age is 19. Liquor is sold only in government-run liquor stores, although in the larger communities such as Victoria and Nanaimo, you may find beer and wine sold from independent, government-licensed specialty shops. In the Gulf Islands, liquor is sold over a specific counter in one of the local stores. In Washington State, the legal age for purchase and consumption of alcoholic beverages is 21; proof of age is required and often requested at bars, nightclubs, and restaurants, so it's always a good idea to bring ID when you go out. Spirits, wine, and beer are available for purchase in most grocery stores and at outlets adjoining bars. Closing time is usually earlier than you would find in big cities, at around 11pm to midnight.

Do not carry open containers of alcohol in your car or any public area that isn't zoned for alcohol consumption. The police can fine you on the spot. And nothing will ruin your trip faster than getting a citation for DUI ("driving under the influence"), so don't even think about driving while intoxicated.

DRIVING RULES See "Getting There and Getting Around," p. 35.

ELECTRICITY Like Canada, the United States uses 110–120 volts AC (60 cycles), compared to 220–240 volts AC (50 cycles) in most of Europe, Australia, and New Zealand. Downward converters that change 220–240 volts to 110–120 volts are difficult to find in the United States, so bring one with you.

EMBASSIES & CONSULATES The U.S. Embassy is in Ottawa at 490 Sussex Dr., (*©* 613/688-5335); it has a consulate office in Vancouver, at 1095 West Pender St., (*©* 604/685-4311).

The embassy of **Australia** is at 1601 Massachusetts Ave. NW, Washington, DC 20036 (*©* **202/797-3000;** www.austemb. org). The nearest consulates are in Los Angeles and San Francisco.

In Canada, the **Australian Consulate** is at Suite 710, 50 O'Connor Street, Ottawa, Ontario, K1P 6L2 (*©* **613/236-0841**), with the nearest location located in Vancouver at Suite 2050, 1075 West Georgia St., (*©* **604/684-1177**).

The embassy of **Canada** is at 501 Pennsylvania Ave. NW, Washington, DC 20001 (*©* **202/682-1740;** www.canadian embassy.org). The nearest Canadian consulate is in Seattle: 1501 4th Ave., (*©* **206/443-1777**).

The embassy of **New Zealand** is at 37 Observatory Circle NW, Washington, DC 20008 (*©* **202/328-4800;** www.nz embassy.com). The nearest New Zealand consulate is in Seattle: 10649 North Beach Rd. (*©* **360/766-8002**).

In Canada, the **New Zealand High Commission** is at Metropolitan House (Suite 727), 99 Bank Street, Ottawa, K1P 6G3 (*©* **613/238-5991**). A consulate office is in Vancouver: Suite 1200-888 Dunsmuir St., (*©* **604/684-7388**).

The embassy of the **United Kingdom** is at 3100 Massachusetts Ave. NW, Washington, DC 20008 (*©* **202/588-7800;** www.britainusa.com). Although there is a trade office in Seattle, the nearest consulate general is in San Francisco: Suite 850, 1 Sansome St., (*©* **415/617-1300**).

The **British High Commission** in Canada is at 80 Elgin St., Ottawa, Ontario K1P 5K7 (*©* **613/237-1530**). The nearest office is in Vancouver: Suite 800, 1111 Melville St., (*©* **604/683-4421**).

EMERGENCIES Dial *©* **911** for fire, police, or ambulance, in either the U.S. or Canada. This is a toll-free call. (No coins are required at public telephones). In British Columbia, the Royal Canadian Mounted Police (RCMP) administer a **Tourist Alert** program by posting emergency notices at visitor information centers, at provincial park sites, and on BC ferries.

If you encounter serious problems, contact **Traveler's Aid International** (*©* **202/546-1127;** www.travelersaid.org) to help direct you to a local branch. This nation-wide, nonprofit, social-service organization geared to helping travelers in difficult straits offers services that might include reuniting families separated while traveling, providing food and/or shelter to people stranded without cash, or even giving emotional counseling. If you're in trouble, seek them out.

GASOLINE (PETROL) At press time, the cost of gasoline (also known as gas, but never petrol), is abnormally high and in many cities and towns, it's not unusual to see per-unit prices fluctuate by the day. Prices can also vary from one gas station to another within the same block, and gas is certainly more expensive in the rural areas, particularly on the relatively isolated San Juan and Gulf islands. Taxes are already included in the printed price. One U.S. gallon equals 3.8 liters or .85 imperial gallons. Canadian gas is sold by the liter and by law must be paid for in advance of purchase. Fill-up locations are known as gas or service stations.

HOLIDAYS Banks, government offices, post offices, and many stores, restaurants, and museums are closed on the following legal national holidays.

In Washington In the United States, there are 10 public holidays: New Year's Day (January 1); Martin Luther King Jr. Day (third Mon in Jan); President's Day/Washington's Birthday (third Mon in Feb); Memorial Day (last Mon in May); Independence Day (July 4); Labor Day (first Mon in Sept); Columbus Day (second Mon in Oct); Veteran's Day (Nov 11); Thanksgiving (fourth Thurs in Nov); Christmas Day (Dec 25).

In British Columbia Although banks, offices, and government agencies close for holiday periods, tour operators and main shops remain open in the major cities, such as Victoria, to take advantage of holiday travelers. There are nine official public holidays: New Year's Day (Jan 1); Good Friday; Victoria Day (the Mon on or preceding May 24); Canada Day (July 1); BC Day (first Mon in Aug); Labor Day (first Mon in Sept); Thanksgiving (second Mon in Oct); Remembrance Day (Nov 11); Christmas Day (Dec 25).

HOSPITALS Most major cities and towns, such as **Victoria, Nanaimo,** and **Campbell River,** have hospitals. These include Royal Jubilee Hospital, 1900 Fort St., Victoria (✆ **250/370-8000**) and Lady Minto Hospital, 135 Crofton Rd., Salt Spring Island (✆ **250/538-4800**). On the Gulf and San Juan islands, however, there are only medical clinics; for life-threatening situations, airlift services are used. (See "Doctors" and "Dentists" above.)

INSURANCE **Travel Insurance** The cost of travel insurance varies widely, depending on the cost and length of your trip, your age and health, and the type of trip you're taking, but expect to pay between 5% and 8% of the vacation itself. You can get estimates from various providers through **InsureMyTrip.com.** Enter your trip cost and dates, your age, and other information, for prices from more than a dozen companies.

Trip-Cancellation Insurance Trip-cancellation insurance will help retrieve your money if you have to back out of a trip or depart early, or if your travel supplier goes bankrupt. Permissible reasons for trip cancellation can range from sickness to natural disasters to the State Department declaring a destination unsafe for travel. Your credit card coverage may include coverage for lost luggage, canceled tickets, and medical expenses, so review card policies before purchasing separate travel insurance.

For more information, contact one of the following recommended insurers: **Access America** (✆ **866/807-3982;** www.accessamerica.com); **Travel Guard International** (✆ **800/826-4919;** www.travelguard.com); **Travel Insured International** (✆ **800/243-3174;** www.travelinsured.

com); and **Travelex Insurance Services**
(𝄞 **888/457-4602;** www.travelex-insurance.
com).

Medical Insurance Most health insurance policies cover you if you get sick away from home—but check, particularly if you're insured by an HMO. If you require additional medical insurance, try **MEDEX Assistance** (𝄞 **410/453-6300;** www.medexassist.com) or **Travel Assistance International** (𝄞 **800/821-2828;** www.travelassistance.com). Canada's national health insurance system will not cover non-Canadians; Canadian doctors and hospitals can bill U.S. health insurers or European health systems, so bring appropriate documentation or insurance cards.

Lost-Luggage Insurance On international flights (including U.S. portions of international trips), baggage coverage is limited to approximately C$9.07 per .5kg (1 lb.), up to approximately C$635 per checked bag. If you plan to check items more valuable than what's covered by the standard liability, see if your homeowner's policy covers your valuables, get baggage insurance as part of your comprehensive travel-insurance package, or buy Travel Guard's "BagTrak" product.

If your luggage is lost, immediately file a lost-luggage claim at the airport, detailing the luggage contents. Most airlines require that you report delayed, damaged, or lost baggage within 4 hours of arrival. The airlines are required to deliver luggage, once found, directly to your house or destination free of charge.

Car Insurance Car insurance is compulsory in British Columbia. Basic coverage consists of "no-fault" accident and C$200,000 worth of third-party legal liability coverage. If you're driving your own vehicle, check with your insurance agent to make sure your policy meets this requirement. If you are renting, your rental agreement will outline these insurance options.

INTERNET ACCESS Although you will find wireless access and Internet cafes in Victoria, public Internet access becomes increasingly scarce away from the city center, particularly on the Gulf Islands and San Juan Islands. Please see specific chapters and Staying Connected (p. 49).

LEGAL AID If you are "pulled over" for a minor infraction (such as speeding), never attempt to pay the fine directly to a police officer; this could be construed as attempted bribery, a much more serious crime. Pay fines by mail, or directly into the hands of the clerk of the court. If accused of a more serious offense, say and do nothing before consulting a lawyer. Here the burden is on the province or state to prove a person's guilt beyond a reasonable doubt, and everyone has the right to remain silent, whether he or she is suspected of a crime or actually arrested. Once arrested, a person can make one telephone call to a party of his or her choice. International visitors should call their embassy or consulate.

LOST & FOUND Be sure to tell all of your credit card companies the minute you discover your wallet has been lost or stolen and file a report at the nearest police precinct. Your credit card company or insurer may require a police report number or record of the loss. Most credit card companies have an emergency toll-free number to call if your card is lost or stolen; they may be able to wire you a cash advance immediately or deliver an emergency credit card in a day or two. Visa's emergency number is 𝄞 **800/847-2911** or 410/581-9994. American Express cardholders and traveler's check holders should call 𝄞 **800/221-7282.** MasterCard holders should call 𝄞 **800/307-7309** or 636/722-7111. For other credit cards, call the toll-free number directory at 𝄞 **800/555-1212.**

If you need emergency cash over the weekend when all banks and American Express offices are closed, you can have money wired to you via **Western Union** (© 800/325-6000; www.westernunion. com).

MAIL At press time, domestic U.S. postage rates were US27¢ for a postcard and US42¢ for a letter. For international mail, a first-class letter of up to 1 ounce costs US94¢ (US72¢ to Canada and Mexico); a first-class postcard costs the same as a letter. For more information go to **www. usps.com** and click on "Calculate Postage."

If you aren't sure what your address will be in either the United States or Canada, mail can be sent to you, in your name, c/o General Delivery at the main post office of the city or region where you expect to be. (Call © **800/275-8777** for information on the nearest U.S. post office or for a Canadian location, visit www.canadapost. ca.) The addressee must pick up mail in person and must produce proof of identity (driver's license, passport, etc.). Most post offices will hold your mail for up to 1 month, and are open Monday to Friday from 8am to 6pm, and Saturday from 9am to 3pm.

Always include zip codes when mailing items in the U.S. If you don't know your zip code, visit www.usps.com/zip4.

Within Canada, the postal rates are C54¢ for standard letters and postcards, C98¢ to the U.S., and C$1.65 overseas. For more information, including postal codes, go to www.canadapost.ca.

MAPS Tourism agencies both for the islands and townships are excellent resources for driving maps. See "Getting There" and "Getting Around" sections in the respective chapters.

MEASUREMENTS See the chart on the inside front cover of this book for details on converting metric measurements to nonmetric equivalents.

NEWSPAPERS & MAGAZINES For regional and world news, Gulf Islanders have access to Victoria's major newspaper, *The Victoria Times-Colonist* and to the *Vancouver Sun. The Gulf Islands Driftwood* is a small community newspaper published every Wednesday. Local papers on the San Juans include *The Journal* (San Juan Island), *The Sounder* (Orcas Island), and on Lopez, the *Islands Weekly,* all owned by the same publisher but each reporting on their specific island news.

PASSPORTS The websites listed below provide downloadable passport applications as well as the current fees for processing applications. For an up-to-date, country-by-country listing of passport requirements around the world, go to the "International Travel" tab of the U.S. State Department site at **http://travel.state.gov.** Allow plenty of time before your trip to apply for a passport; processing normally takes 4 to 6 weeks (3 weeks for expedited service) but can take longer during busy periods (especially spring). And keep in mind that if you need a passport in a hurry, you'll pay a higher processing fee.

For Residents of Canada Passport applications are available at travel agencies throughout Canada or from the central **Passport Office,** Department of Foreign Affairs and International Trade, Alberta, ON K1A 0G3 (© 800/567-6868; www. ppt.gc.ca). *Note:* Canadian children who travel must have their own passport. However, if you hold a valid Canadian passport issued before December 11, 2001, that bears the name of your child, the passport remains valid for you and your child until it expires.

For Residents of Australia You can pick up an application from your local post office or any branch of Passports Australia, but you must schedule an interview at the passport office to present your application materials. Call the **Australian Passport Information Service** at © 131-232, or visit the government website at www. passports.gov.au.

For Residents of New Zealand You can pick up a passport application at any New Zealand Passports Office or download it from their website. Contact the

Passports Office at © 0800/225-050 in New Zealand or 04/474-8100, or log on to www.passports.govt.nz.

For Residents of the United Kingdom To pick up an application for a standard 10-year passport (5-year passport for children under 16), visit your nearest passport office, major post office, or travel agency; or contact the **United Kingdom Passport Service** at © 0870/521-0410 or search its website at www.ukpa.gov.uk.

POLICE (See "Emergencies")

SMOKING British Columbia by-laws prohibit smoking in a public place, including restaurants, offices, shopping malls, and even transit shelters. There is also a 3m (9-ft.) smoke-free zone around most public and workplace doorways, opening windows, and air intakes. Although this is adhered to in the larger cities, individual pubs and bars in the island communities sometimes turn a blind eye to the legislation. Ask before you light up publicly anywhere in the province. No smoking is also the "norm" in most public places in Washington State.

TAXES British Columbia charges both a provincial sales tax (PST) of 6% and the federal goods and services tax (GST) of 5%, meaning you will pay an additional 11% on most purchases. In San Juan County, the retail sales tax is 7.7%, with an additional 2% on lodging.

TELEPHONES In both Canada and the U.S., many convenience groceries and packaging services sell **prepaid calling cards** in denominations up to $50; for international visitors these can be the least expensive way to call home. Many public pay phones at airports now accept American Express, MasterCard, and Visa credit cards. **Local calls** made from pay phones in most locales cost either 25¢ or 35¢ (no pennies, please). Most long-distance and international calls can be dialed directly from any phone. **For calls within the United States and to Canada,** dial 1, followed by

the area code and the seven-digit number. **For other international calls,** dial 011 followed by the country code, city code, and the number you are calling.

Calls to area codes **800, 888, 877,** and **866** are toll-free. However, calls to area codes **700** and **900** (chat lines, bulletin boards, "dating" services, and so on) can be very expensive—usually a charge of 95¢ to $3 or more per minute, and they sometimes have minimum charges that can run as high as $15 or more.

For **reversed-charge or collect calls,** and for person-to-person calls, dial the number 0, then the area code and number; an operator will come on the line, and you should specify whether you are calling collect, person-to-person, or both. If your operator-assisted call is international, ask for the overseas operator.

For **local directory assistance** ("information"), dial 411; for long-distance information, dial 1, then the appropriate area code and 555-1212.

Note: Other than in the major centers, cellphone signals may vary in strength in different areas of all these islands, ranging from nonexistent to mediocre.

TELEGRAPH, TELEX & FAX Telegraph and telex services are provided primarily by **Western Union** (© 800/325-6000; www. westernunion.com). You can telegraph (wire) money, or have it telegraphed to you, very quickly over the Western Union system, but this service can cost as much as 15% to 20% of the amount sent.

Most hotels have **fax machines** available for guest use (be sure to ask about the charge to use it). Many hotel rooms in the major centers are wired for guests' fax machines. A less expensive way to send and receive faxes may be at stores such as **Kinkos** and the **UPS Store.**

TIME British Columbia and Washington State are in the Pacific Time Zone, 3 hours behind Eastern Standard Time. **Daylight saving time** is in effect from 1am on the second Sunday in March to

1am on the first Sunday in November. Daylight saving time moves the clock 1 hour ahead of standard time.

TIPPING Tips are a very important part of certain workers' income, and gratuities are the standard way of showing appreciation for services provided. (Tipping is certainly not compulsory if the service is poor!) Tipping etiquette is the same in Canada and the United States. In hotels, tip **bellhops** at least $1 per bag ($2–$3 if you have a lot of luggage) and tip the **chamber staff** $1 to $2 per day (more if you've left a disaster area for him or her to clean up). Tip the **doorman** or **concierge** only if he or she has provided you with some specific service (for example, calling a cab for you or obtaining difficult-to-get theater tickets). Tip the **valet-parking attendant** $1 every time you get your car.

In restaurants, bars, and nightclubs, tip **service staff** 15% to 20% of the check, tip **bartenders** 10% to 15%, tip **checkroom attendants** $1 per garment, and tip **valet-parking attendants** $1 per vehicle.

As for other service personnel, tip **cab drivers** 15% of the fare; tip **skycaps** at airports at least $1 per bag ($2–$3 if you have a lot of luggage); and tip **hairdressers** and **barbers** 15% to 20%.

TOILETS You won't find public toilets or "restrooms" on the streets, but they can be found in hotel lobbies, bars, restaurants, museums, department stores, railway and bus stations, and service stations. Not all the islands have all these facilities; on the San Juans, for example, you're more likely to find an outhouse or two, strategically placed at a trail head or public beach.

USEFUL PHONE NUMBERS U.S. Dept. of State Travel Advisory: ✆ **202/647-5225** (manned 24 hrs.). U.S. Passport Agency: ✆ **202/647-0518.** Canada Passport Office: ✆ **800/567-6868.** U.S. Centers for Disease Control International Traveler's Hotline: ✆ **404/332-4559.** Public Health Agency of Canada (British Columbia branch): ✆ **604/666-2083.**

VISAS For information about U.S. Visas, go to **http://travel.state.gov** and click on "Visas." Or go to one of the following websites:

Australian citizens can obtain up-to-date visa information from the **U.S. Embassy Canberra,** Moonah Place, Yarralumla, ACT 2600 (✆ **02/6214-5600**) or by checking the U.S. Diplomatic Mission's website at **http://usembassy-australia.state.gov/consular**.

British subjects can obtain up-to-date visa information by calling the **U.S. Embassy Visa Information Line** (✆ **0891/200-290**) or by visiting the "Visas to the U.S." section of the American Embassy London's website at **www.usembassy.org.uk**.

Citizens of **New Zealand** can obtain up-to-date visa information by contacting the **U.S. Embassy New Zealand,** 29 Fitzherbert Terrace, Thorndon, Wellington (✆ **644/472-2068**), or get the information directly from the website at **http://wellington.usembassy.gov**.

Like Canada, Australia and New Zealand are members of the British Commonwealth, and therefore need no special visas to travel between their respective countries, only a valid passport.

WATER Canada boasts some of the world's most pristine water, resources which the U.S. is vying for on the political front. Population growth and industry is certainly threatening this quality, and on the Gulf Islands in particular it has become a precious commodity (see chapter 9). West Coasters tend to carry a water bottle where ever they go; and these days it's likely to be a recyclable, eco-friendly container.

WEATHER The nature of the Pacific Northwest, with its mountainous coastline, means that weather can change quickly. Call ✆ **604/664-9010** for regional weather updates; ✆ **604/666-3655** for local marine forecasts.

MAJOR U.S. AIRLINES

(*flies internationally as well)

Alaska Airlines/Horizon Air
✆ 800/252/7522
www.alaskaair.com

American Airlines*
✆ 800/433-7300 (in U.S. or Canada)
✆ 020/7365-0777 (in U.K.)
www.aa.com

Continental Airlines*
✆ 800/523-3273 (in U.S. or Canada)
✆ 084/5607-6760 (in U.K.)
www.continental.com

Delta Air Lines*
✆ 800/221-1212 (in U.S. or Canada)
✆ 084/5600-0950 (in U.K.)
www.delta.com

JetBlue Airways
✆ 800/538-2583 (in U.S.)
✆ 080/1365-2525 (in U.K. or Canada)
www.jetblue.com

Northwest Airlines
✆ 800/225-2525 (in U.S.)
✆ 870/0507-4074 (in U.K.)
www.flynaa.com

United Airlines*
✆ 800/864-8331 (in U.S. or Canada)
✆ 084/5844-4777 in U.K.
www.united.com

U.S. Airways*
✆ 800/428-4322 (in U.S. or Canada)
✆ 084/5600-3300 (in U.K.)
www.usairways.com

Virgin America*
✆ 877/359-8474
www.virginamerica.com

MAJOR INTERNATIONAL AIRLINES

Aeroméxico
✆ 800/237-6639 (in U.S.)
✆ 020/7801-6234 (in U.K., information only)
www.aeromexico.com

Air France
✆ 800/237-2747 (in U.S.)
✆ 800/375-8723 (in U.S. or Canada)
✆ 087/0142-4343 (in U.K.)
www.airfrance.com

Air New Zealand
✆ 800/262-1234 (in U.S.)
✆ 800/663-5494 (in Canada)
✆ 0800/028-4149 (in U.K.)
www.airnewzealand.com

British Airways
✆ 800/247-9297 (in U.S. or Canada)
✆ 087/0850-9850 (in U.K.)
www.british-airways.com

Cathay Pacific
✆ 800/233-2742 (in U.S.)
✆ 800/268-6868 or 604/606-8888 (in Canada)
www.cathaypacific.com

China Airlines
✆ 800/227-5118 (in U.S.)
✆ 022/715-1212 (in Taiwan)
www.china-airlines.com

Hawaiian Airlines
✆ 800/367-5320 (in U.S. or Canada)
www.hawaiianair.com

Japan Airlines
✆ 012/025-5931 (international)
www.jal.co.jp

Korean Air
✆ 800/438-5000 (in U.S. or Canada)
✆ 0800/413-000 (in U.K.)
www.koreanair.com

Lufthansa
☎ 800/399-5838 (in U.S.)
☎ 800/563-5954 (in Canada)
☎ 087/0837-7747 (in U.K.)
www.lufthansa.com

BUDGET AIRLINES

Aer Lingus
☎ 800/474-7424 (in U.S. or Canada)
☎ 087/0876-5000 (in U.K.)
www.aerlingus.com

AirTran Airways
☎ 800/247-8726
www.airtran.com

AirTransat
☎ 866/847-1112
www.airtransat.ca

CAR RENTAL AGENCIES

Advantage
☎ 800/777-5500 (in U.S.)
☎ 021/0344-4712 (outside of U.S.)
www.advantagerentacar.com

Avis
☎ 800/331-1212 (in U.S. or Canada)
www.avis.com

Budget
☎ 800/527-0700 (in U.S.)
☎ 800/268-8900 (in Canada)
www.budget.com

Dollar
☎ 800/800-4000 (in U.S.)
☎ 800/848-8268 (in Canada)
www.dollar.com

Enterprise
☎ 800/261-7331 (in U.S.)
☎ 514/355-4028 (in Canada)
www.enterprise.com

Quantas Airways
☎ 800/227-4500 (in U.S.)
☎ 084/5774-7767 (in U.K. or Canada)
☎ 13 13 13 (in Australia)
www.quantas.com

Frontier Airlines
☎ 800/432-1359
www.frontierairlines.com

Southwest Airlines
☎ 800/435-9792 (in U.S., U.K., or
   Canada)
www.southwest.com

WestJet
☎ 800/538-5696 (in U.S. or Canada)
www.westjet.com

Hertz
☎ 800/645-3131
☎ 800/654-3001 (for international
   reservations)
www.hertz.com

National
☎ 800/CAR-RENT [227-7368]
www.nationalcar.com

Rent-A-Wreck
☎ 800/944-7501
☎ 800/327-0116
www.rentawreck.com

Thrifty
☎ 800/THRIFTY [847-4389]
☎ 918/669-2168 (international)
www.thrifty.com

MAJOR HOTEL & MOTEL CHAINS

Best Western International
☎ 800/780-7234 (in U.S. or Canada)
www.bestwestern.com

Clarion Hotels
☎ 800/CLARION [252-7466] or
   877/424-6423 (in U.S. and Canada)
www.choicehotels.com

Comfort Inns
☎ 800/424-6423 (in Canada)
☎ 877/424-6423 (in U.S.)
www.comfortinn.com

Courtyard by Marriott
☎ 888/236-2427 (in U.S.)
www.marriott.com/courtyard

Crowne Plaza Hotels
☎ 877/227-6963 (in U.S. and Canada)
www.crowneplaza.com

Days Inn
☎ 800/329-7466 (in U.S.)
www.daysinn.com

Embassy Suites
☎ 800/EMBASSY [362-2779]
www.embassysuites1.hilton.com

Fairfield Inn by Marriott
☎ 800/228-2800 (in U.S. or Canada)
☎ 0800/221-222 (in U.K.)
www.marriott.com/farfieldinn

Four Seasons
☎ 800/819-5053 (in U.S. or Canada)
www.fourseasons.com

Hilton Hotels
☎ 800/HILTONS [445-8667] (in U.S.
   or Canada)
www.hilton.com

Holiday Inn
☎ 800/315-2621 (in U.S. or Canada)
www.holidayinn.com

Howard Johnson
☎ 800/446-4656 (in U.S. or Canada)
www.hojo.com

Hyatt
☎ 888/591-1234 (in U.S. or Canada)
www.hyatt.com

InterContinental Hotels & Resorts
☎ 800/424-6835 (in U.S. or Canada)
www.ichotelsgroup.com

Marriott
☎ 877/236-2427 (in U.S. or Canada)
www.marriott.com

Motel 6
☎ 800/4MOTEL6 [466-8356]
www.motel6.com

Quality
☎ 877/424-6423 (in U.S. or Canada)
www.QualityInn.ChoiceHotels.com

Radisson Hotels & Resorts
☎ 888/201-1718 (in U.S. or Canada)
www.radisson.com

Ramada Worldwide
☎ 888/2-RAMADA [272-6232] (in U.S.
   or Canada)
www.ramada.com

Renaissance
☎ 888/236-2427
www.renaissance.com

Residence Inn by Marriott
☎ 800/331-3131
www.marriott.com/residenceinn

Sheraton Hotels & Resorts
☎ 800/325-3535 (in U.S.)
☎ 800/543-4300 (in Canada)
www.starwoodhotels.com/sheraton

Super 8 Motels
☎ 800/800-8000
www.super8.com

Travelodge
☎ 800/578-7878
www.travelodge.com

Westin Hotels & Resorts
☎ 800/937-8461 (in U.S. or Canada)
www.starwoodhotels.com/westin

Wyndham Hotels & Resorts
☎ 877/999-3223 (in U.S. or Canada)
www.wyndham.com

INDEX

See also Accommodations index, below.